Virtualizing SQL Server with VMware®

Doing IT Right

VMware Press is the official publisher of VMware books and training materials, which provide guidance on the critical topics facing today's technology professionals and students. Enterprises, as well as small- and medium-sized organizations, adopt virtualization as a more agile way of scaling IT to meet business needs. VMware Press provides proven, technically accurate information that will help them meet their goals for customizing, building, and maintaining their virtual environment.

With books, certification and study guides, video training, and learning tools produced by world-class architects and IT experts, VMware Press helps IT professionals master a diverse range of topics on virtualization and cloud computing and is the official source of reference materials for preparing for the VMware Certified Professional Examination.

VMware Press is also pleased to have localization partners that can publish its products into more than forty-two languages, including, but not limited to, Chinese (Simplified), Chinese (Traditional), French, German, Greek, Hindi, Japanese, Korean, Polish, Russian, and Spanish.

For more information about VMware Press, please visit vmwarepress.com.

vmware® PRESS

VMWARE PRESS

Official **Cert Guide**
VCAP5-DCA
VMware® Certified Advanced
Professional 5 - Data Center
Administration

STEVE BACA
JOHN DAVIS

VMWARE PRESS

Essential Virtual SAN
Administrator's Guide to
VMware VSAN

Cormac Hogan
Duncan Epping

VMWARE PRESS

**Networking for
VMware®
Administrators**

Chris Wahl
Steve Pantol

VMWARE PRESS

Official **Cert Guide**
VCP5-DCV
VMware® Certified
Professional 5 - Data Center
Virtualization

BILL FERGUSON

vmwarepress.com

Complete list of products • User Group Info • Articles • Newsletters

VMware® Press is a publishing alliance between Pearson and VMware, and is the official publisher of VMware books and training materials that provide guidance for the critical topics facing today's technology professionals and students.

With books, eBooks, certification study guides, video training, and learning tools produced by world-class architects and IT experts, VMware Press helps IT professionals master a diverse range of topics on virtualization and cloud computing, and is the official source of reference materials for preparing for the VMware certification exams.

Make sure to connect with us!
vmwarepress.com

vmware® | **PEARSON**
IT CERTIFICATION | **Safari**
Books Online

PEARSON

Virtualizing SQL Server with VMware®

Doing IT Right

Michael Corey
Jeff Szastak
Michael Webster

vmware® PRESS

Upper Saddle River, NJ • Boston • Indianapolis • San Francisco
New York • Toronto • Montreal • London • Munich • Paris • Madrid
Capetown • Sydney • Tokyo • Singapore • Mexico City

Virtualizing SQL Server with VMware®

ISBN-13: 978-0-321-92775-0

ISBN-10: 0-321-92775-3

Library of Congress Control Number: 2014941961

Printed in the United States of America

First Printing August 2014

Warning and Disclaimer

Special Sales

For information about buying this title in bulk quantities, or for special sales opportunities (which may include electronic versions; custom cover designs; and content particular to your business, training goals, marketing focus, or branding interests), please contact our corporate sales department at corpsales@pearsoned.com or (800) 382-3419.

For government sales inquiries, please contact governmentsales@pearsoned.com.

For questions about sales outside the U.S., please contact international@pearsoned.com.

ASSOCIATE PUBLISHER
David Dusthimer

ACQUISITIONS EDITOR
Joan Murray

VMWARE PRESS PROGRAM MANAGER
David Nelson

DEVELOPMENT EDITOR
Eleanor C. Bru

MANAGING EDITOR
Sandra Schroeder

PROJECT EDITOR
Mandie Frank

COPY EDITOR
Bart Reed

PROOFREADER
Sarah Kearns

INDEXER
Erika Millen

EDITORIAL ASSISTANT
Vanessa Evans

DESIGNER
Chuti Prasertsith

COMPOSITOR
Tricia Bronkella

This book is dedicated to my wife of 28 years, Juliann, who has supported me in every way possible, and my three children, John, Annmarie, and Michael.
-Michael Corey

This book is dedicated to my wife, Heather, and my three children, Wyatt, Oliver, and Stella.
-Jeff Szastak

This book is dedicated to my wife, Susanne, and my four sons, Sebastian, Bradley, Benjamin, and Alexander, for their ongoing support. I also dedicate this book to the VMware community.
-Michael Webster

Contents

Foreword

About 10 years ago, I started a new job. The company I started working for had a couple hundred physical servers at the time. When several new internal software development projects started, we needed to expand quickly and added dozens of new physical servers. Pretty soon we started hitting all the traditional datacenter problems, such as lack of floor space, high power consumption, and cooling constraints. We had to solve our problems, and during our search for a solution we were introduced to a new product called VMware ESX and Virtual Center. It didn't take long for us to see the potential and to start virtualizing a large portion of our estate.

During this exercise, we started receiving a lot of positive feedback on the performance of the virtualized servers. On top of that, our application owners loved the fact that we could deploy a new virtual machine in hours instead of waiting weeks for new hardware to arrive. I am not even talking about all the side benefits, such as VMotion (or vMotion, as we call it today) and VMware High Availability, which provided a whole new level of availability and enabled us to do maintenance without any downtime for our users.

After the typical honeymoon period, the question arose: What about our database servers? Could this provide the same benefits in terms of agility and availability while maintaining the same performance? After we virtualized the first database server, we quickly realized that just using VMware Converter and moving from physical to virtual was not sufficient, at least not for the databases we planned to virtualize.

To be honest, we did not know much about the database we were virtualizing. We didn't fully understand the CPU and memory requirements, nor did we understand the storage requirements. We knew something about the resource consumption, but how do you make a design that caters to those requirements? Perhaps even more importantly, where do you get the rest of the information needed to ensure success?

Looking back, I wish we'd had guidance in any shape or form that could have helped along our journey—guidance that would provide tips about how to gather requirements, how to design an environment based on these requirements, how to create a performance baseline, and what to look for when hitting performance bottlenecks.

That is why I am pleased Jeff Szastak, Michael Corey, and Michael Webster took the time to document the valuable lessons they have learned in the past few years about virtualizing tier 1 databases and released it through VMware Press in the form of this book you are about to read. Having gone through the exercise myself, and having made all the mistakes mentioned in the book, I think I am well qualified to urge you to soak in all this valuable knowledge to ensure success!

Duncan Epping

Principal Architect, VMware

Yellow-Bricks.com

Preface

As we traveled the globe presenting on how to virtualize the most demanding business-critical applications, such as SQL Server, Oracle, Microsoft Exchange, and SAP, it became very clear that there was a very real and unmet need from the attendees to learn how to virtualize these most demanding applications correctly.

This further hit home when we presented at the VMworld conferences in San Francisco and Barcelona. At each event, we were assigned a very large room that held over 1,800 people; within 48 hours of attendees being able to reserve a seat in the room, it was filled to capacity. We were then assigned a second large room that again filled up within 24 hours.

Recognizing that the information we had among the three of us could help save countless others grief, we decided to collaborate on this very practical book.

Target Audience

Our goal was to create in one book—a comprehensive resource that a solution architect, system administrator, storage administrator, or database administrator could use to guide them through the necessary steps to successfully virtualize a database. Many of the lessons learned in this book apply to any business-critical application being virtualized from SAP, E-Business Suite, Microsoft Exchange, or Oracle, with the specific focus of this book on Microsoft SQL Server. Although you don't have to be a database administrator to understand the contents of this book, it does help if you are technical and have a basic understanding of vSphere.

Approach Taken

Everything you need to succeed in virtualizing SQL Server can be found within the pages of this book. By design, we created the book to be used in one of two ways. If you are looking for a comprehensive roadmap to virtualize your mission-critical databases, then follow along in the book, chapter by chapter. If you are trying to deal with a particular resource that is constraining the performance of your database, then jump to Chapters 5 through 8.

At a high level, the book is organized as follows:

- Chapters 1 and 2 explain what virtualization is and the business case for it. If you are a database administrator or new to virtualization, you will find these chapters very helpful; they set the stage for why virtualizing your databases is "doing IT right."

- Chapters 3 through 9 are the roadmap you can follow to successfully virtualize the most demanding of mission-critical databases. Each chapter focuses on a particular resource the database utilizes and how to optimize that resource to get the best possible performance for your database when it is virtualized. We purposely organized this section into distinct subject areas so that you can jump directly to a particular chapter of interest when you need to brush up. We expect that you will periodically return to Chapters 5 through 8 as you are fine-tuning the virtualized infrastructure for your mission-critical databases.

- The last two chapters walk you through how to baseline the existing SQL Server database so that you adequately determine the resource load it will put onto the virtualized infrastructure. In these chapters, we also provide detailed instructions on how to configure a stress test.

Here are the three major sections of the book with the associated chapters:

What Virtualization Is and Why You Should Do It

In this section, the reader will learn about the benefits of virtualization and why the world is moving towards 100% virtualization. The reader will learn the benefits of breaking the bond between hardware and software, and the benefits this brings to the datacenter and why virtualization is a better way to do IT.

Chapter 1: Virtualization: The New World Order?

Chapter 2: The Business Case for Virtualizing a Database

Optimizing Resources in a Virtualized Infrastructure

In Chapters 3-9, the reader will gain knowledge on how to properly architect and implement virtualized SQL Server. The reader will start off learning how to put together a SQL Server virtualization initiative, and then dive into an in-depth discussion on how to architect SQL Server on a vSphere platform. This section includes deep dives on storage, memory, networking, and high availability.

Chapter 3: Architecting for Performance: The Right Hypervisor

Chapter 4: Virtualizing SQL Server: Doing IT Right

Chapter 5: Architecting for Performance: Design

Chapter 6: Architecting for Performance: Storage

Chapter 7: Architecting for Performance: Memory

Chapter 8: Architecting for Performance: Network

Chapter 9: Architecting for Availability: Choosing the Right Solution

How to Baseline and Stress Test

The final two chapters walk the reader through the importance of setting up a baseline for their virtualized SQL Server implementation. Chapter 10 speaks to the why and the how of baselining, which is critical to successfully virtualizing SQL Server. In the final chapter, the reader will put all the knowledge presented in the previous chapters together and will be walked through a beginning-to-end configuration of SQL Server 2012 with AlwaysOn Availability Groups running on Windows Server 2012 on a vSphere 5.5 infrastructure.

Chapter 10: How to Baseline Your Physical SQL Server System

Chapter 11: Configuring a Performance Test—From Beginning to End

A database is one of the most resource-intensive applications you will ever virtualize, and it is our sincere intention that with this book as your guide, you now have a roadmap that will help you avoid the common mistakes people make—and more importantly, you will learn how to get optimal performance from your virtualized database.

We want to thank you for buying our book, and we hope after you read it that you feel we have achieved our goal of providing you with a comprehensive resource on how to do IT right. Feel free to reach out to us with any questions, suggestions, or feedback you have.

Michael Corey (@Michael_Corey) Michael.corey@ntirety.com

Jeff Szastak (@Szastak)

Michael Webster (@vcdxnz001)

About the Authors

 **Michael Corey** (@Michael_Corey) is the President of Ntirety, a division of Hosting. Michael is an experienced entrepreneur and a recognized expert on relational databases, remote database administration, and data warehousing. Microsoft named Michael a SQL Server MVP, VMware named him a vExpert, and Oracle named him an Oracle Ace. Michael has presented at technical and business conferences from Brazil to Australia. Michael is a past president of the Independent Oracle Users Group; he helped found the Professional Association of SQL Server, is a current board member of the IOUG Cloud SIG, and is actively involved in numerous professional associations and industry user groups. Michael currently sits on the executive committee for the Massachusetts Robert H. Goddard Council for Science, Technology, Engineering, and Mathematics.

 **Jeff Szastak** (@Szastak) is currently a Staff Systems Engineer for VMware. Jeff has been with VMware for over six years, holding various roles with VMware during his tenure. These roles have included being a TAM, Systems Engineer Specialist for Business-Critical Applications, Enterprise Healthcare Systems Engineer, and a CTO Ambassador. Jeff is a recognized expert for virtualizing databases and other high I/O applications on the vSphere platform. Jeff is a regular speaker at VMworld, VMware Partner Exchange, VMware User Groups, and has spoken at several SQL PASS events. Jeff holds a Master of Information Assurance degree as well as the distinguished CISSP certification. Jeff has over 13 "lucky" years in IT and is passionate about helping others find a better way to do IT.

 **Michael Webster** (@vcdxnz001) is based in Auckland, New Zealand. He is a VMware Certified Design Expert (VCDX #66), author of long-whiteclouds.com (a top-15 virtualization blog), and a Top 10 VMworld Session Speaker for 2013. In addition, he is a Senior Solutions and Performance Engineer for Nutanix, vExpert, MCSE, and NPP. Michael specializes in solution architecture and performance engineering for Unix-to-VMware migrations as well as virtualizing business-critical applications such as SQL, Oracle, SAP, Exchange, Enterprise Java Systems, and monster VMs in software-defined data centers. Michael has more than 20 years experience in the IT industry and 10 years experience deploying VMware solutions in large-scale environments around the globe. He is regularly a presenter at VMware VMworld, VMware vForums, VMware User Groups, and other industry events. In addition to this book, Michael was technical reviewer of *VCDX Boot Camp* and *Virtualizing and Tuning Large-Scale Java Platforms*, both published by VMware Press.

About the Technical Reviewer

Mark Achtemichuk (VCDX #50) is currently a Senior Technical Marketing Architect, specializing in Performance, within the SDDC Marketing group at VMware. Certified as VCDX #50, Mark has a strong background in data center infrastructures and cloud architectures, experience implementing enterprise application environments, and a passion for solving problems. He has driven virtualization adoption and project success by methodically bridging business with technology. His current challenge is ensuring that performance is no longer a barrier, perceived or real, to virtualizing an organization's most critical applications on its journey to the software-defined data center.

Acknowledgments

We would like to thank the entire team at VMware Press for their support throughout this project and for helping us get this project across the line—especially Joan Murray for her constant support and encouragement. We would like to thank our editorial team. Thank you Ellie Bru and Mandie Frank for your attention to detail to make sure we put out a great book, and last but not least, we would especially like to thank our technical reviewer, Mark Achtemichuk (VCDX #50).

Michael Corey

Anyone who has ever written a book knows first hand what a tremendous undertaking it is and how stressful it can be on your family. It is for that reason I thank my wife of 28 years, Juliann. Over those many years, she has been incredible. I want to thank my children, Annmarie, Michael, and especially John, who this particular book was hardest on. John will know why if he reads this.

Jeff and Michael, my co-authors, are two of the smartest technologists I have ever had the opportunity to collaborate with. Thank you for making this book happen despite the many long hours it took you away from your families. Mark Achtemichuk, our technical reviewer, rocks! He helped take this book to a whole new level. To my friends at VMware—Don Sullivan, Kannan Mani, and Sudhir Balasubramanian—thank you for taking all my late-night emails and phone calls to discuss the inner workings of vSphere. To the publishing team at Pearson, what can I say? Thank you Joan Murray for believing and making this book possible.

Special thanks go to my Ntirety family—Jim Haas, Terrie White, and Andy Galbraith are all three incredible SQL Server technologists. And special thanks to people like David Klee and Thomas LaRock and to the entire SQL Server community. Every time I attend a SQLSaturday event, I always think how lucky I am to be party of such a special community of technologist who care a lot and are always willing to help.

Jeff Szastak

I would like to thank my loving wife, Heather, for her love, support, and patience during the writing of this book. I want to thank my children, Wyatt, Oliver, and Stella, for it is from you I draw inspiration. A huge thank-you to Hans Drolshagen for the use of his lab during the writing of this book! And thanks to my mentor, Scott Hill, who pushed me, challenged me, and believed in me. Thanks for giving a guy who couldn't even set a DHCP address a job in IT, Scott.

Finally, I would like to thank the VMware community. Look how far we have come. I remember the first time I saw a VMware presentation as a customer and thought, "If this software works half as well as that presentation says it does, this stuff will change the world." And it has, because of you, the VMware community.

Michael Webster

I'd like to thank my wife, Susanne, and my four boys, Sebastian, Bradley, Benjamin, and Alexander, for providing constant love and support throughout this project and for putting up with all the long hours on weeknights and weekends that it required to complete this project. I would also like to acknowledge my co-authors, Michael and Jeff, for inviting me to write this book with them. I am extremely thankful for this opportunity, and it has been a fantastic collaborative process. Finally, I'd like to thank and acknowledge VMware for providing the constant inspiration for many blog articles and books and for creating a strong and vibrant community. Also, thanks go out to my sounding boards throughout this project: Kasim Hansia, VMware Strategic Architect and SAP expert, Cameron Gardiner, Microsoft Senior Program Manager Azure and SQL, and Josh Odgers (VCDX #90), Nutanix Senior Solutions and Performance Architect. Your ideas and support have added immeasurable value to this book and the IT community as a whole.

We Want to Hear from You!

As the reader of this book, *you* are our most important critic and commentator. We value your opinion and want to know what we're doing right, what we could do better, what areas you'd like to see us publish in, and any other words of wisdom you're willing to pass our way.

We welcome your comments. You can email or write us directly to let us know what you did or didn't like about this book—as well as what we can do to make our books better.

Please note that we cannot help you with technical problems related to the topic of this book.

When you write, please be sure to include this book's title and author as well as your name, email address, and phone number. We will carefully review your comments and share them with the author and editors who worked on the book.

Email: VMwarePress@vmware.com

Mail: VMware Press
      ATTN: Reader Feedback
      800 East 96th Street
      Indianapolis, IN 46240 USA

Reader Services

Visit our website at www.informit.com/title/9780321927750 and register this book for convenient access to any updates, downloads, or errata that might be available for this book.

Chapter 1

Virtualization: The New World Order?

"It is not the strongest of the species that survives nor the most intelligent but the one most responsive to change."

—Charles Darwin

This chapter is about a new computing paradigm where your SQL Server databases are virtualized. In this chapter, we discuss what it means to break the tether of the database from the physical server. We use real-world examples to demonstrate how a virtualized database will better enable you to respond to the needs of your business, day in and day out.

Virtualization: The New World Order

Imagine this: It's Friday afternoon, a beautiful spring day, and you are driving down the highway talking on your cell phone. Hands free, of course—we know you would never consider doing it any other way. As you are talking on the cell phone, do you think about what cell tower you are using? Do you even give it a second thought? The short answer is "no," as long as your cell phone keeps working, that is all you care about.

Why do we as database professionals care what physical server we are using as long as our SQL Server database gets all the resources it needs, when it needs those resources. Isn't that what really matters?

Now imagine that each cell tower represents a physical server. Imagine the cell tower you are currently on is overloaded. Instead of getting the dreaded message "All lines are busy right now, please try your call later," in a virtualized infrastructure, your phone call would be re-routed to a cell tower that had capacity so the call goes through uninterrupted. In this new way of computing, your database will find the next "best available" cell tower to move to, so that you are able to place your call. In this new way of computing, you would be better able to provide service-level guarantees not possible before database virtualization. In a virtualized infrastructure, you have resource mobility. You can use technologies such as vMotion within VMware to move your database to another server while it is in use. Just as your cell phone moves cell tower to cell tower, so can your database move server to server when more or fewer resources are needed.

Now imagine that a cell tower you are using suddenly becomes unavailable. Perhaps lighting has struck it. In this example, your cell phone would reassign itself to another cell tower to ensure you would still be able to make more phone calls. Worse case, your phone might roam to another carriers infrastructure. In a virtualized infrastructure, your database would restart itself on another server and continue processing its workload. A byproduct of database virtualization is high workload resiliency.

When you break the bond between the physical server and your database, a whole new computing paradigm opens up to you—*a world where your SQL server database has access to any computing resource, any physical server, at any time.* Just as your cell phone can travel from cell tower to cell tower as needed, your database can now travel from physical server to physical server as needed, thus allowing you to leverage resources in a way that was previously not possible. No longer do you have one physical server sitting idle while another has more work than it can comfortably handle without impacting database response times.

In this new paradigm, database availability becomes expected. The same as when you get up in the middle of the night and turn on the light switch, it just works. What has to happen to ensure the electricity is always available is handled by the utility company. You don't think about how your electricity is generated or where it ever comes from. The power company deals with the fact that your power comes from multiple locations, and they deal with what it takes to make it always available. You just plug in your appliance to the electrical outlet, and it works. When your SQL Server database is virtualized, the infrastructure just works. As the DBA, your primary concern is no longer the physical server your database is sitting on—just as when you hit the light switch, you are not concerned with which physical electrical generation plant is creating your electricity. It's a new computing paradigm that requires a new way of thinking about the database, the resources, and the infrastructure the database is relying on. A virtualized infrastructure is highly resilient. When outages happen, the virtualized infrastructure is able to take care of things. Just as you no longer think about where your electricity comes from, you will no longer worry about where your computing power comes from.

Virtualization Turns Servers into Pools of Resources

Virtualization enables you to turn all the x86 physical servers in your data center into a pool of resources the business can use as needed. Resources such as a database can move freely among the servers in the pool (or cluster) as needed. What's more, you can offload applications from one server to another as people are using them to free up resources, or you can move an application such as a database onto a different server in the pool as people are using it to give your database access to additional needed resources.

No longer do you have a physical server dedicated to a particular purpose that cannot be easily reprovisioned. In the virtual world, that pool of resources is available to be used as the business sees fit. No longer is one physical server sitting at 90% CPU utilization, with your users on the phone complaining how slow things are, while the other three physical servers in the cluster are sitting at 10% CPU utilization, and you have no easy way to reallocate resource to meet the business current demands

Without virtualization, it is inefficient and very costly to have physical servers dedicated to a particular purpose that cannot easily be reprovisioned as the business needs them.

As Charles Darwin stated, "It is not the strongest of the species that survives nor the most intelligent, but the one most responsive to change." Our ability to help our business adapt to change quickly is critical to ensuring your company stays competitive.

Living in the New World Order as a SQL Server DBA

It's Cyber Monday, the busiest online shopping day of the year. As you think about last year, you remember how much of a nightmare it was. Users were calling the support lines unable to process orders; it was taking minutes to transverse the online catalogue instead of seconds. Customers were leaving your site to go elsewhere to shop because of the slow response times. There was just so little you could do as all the performance problems tumbled down upon you like an avalanche, bringing your database to its knees—which in turn was bringing your business to its knees.

However, this year you are ready—you have a new secret weapon. You convinced your company to virtualize your production database. You took the risk to adopt a new computing paradigm, breaking your database from the chains of the physical server.

Hot-Add CPU

Everything has been going great. Now the real test is about to happen. At midnight, the shopping begins. Your marketing department has come up with some great deals, and people are coming to the site in volumes that far exceeded last year.

You notice the database is fully utilizing the four vCPUs (virtual CPUs) you allocated and could even use more. Think of a virtual CPU as a physical CPU. Even though the physical host has 16 physical CPUs, you could choose to assign a particular virtual machine one or more of them.

You want to avoid what happened last year and decide to give the database another vCPU. You right-click and allocate another vCPU to the virtual machine housing the database. As you can see in Figure 1.1, you will notice a slight degradation in performance as the database virtual machine adds the additional vCPU, but then performance takes off again as the database is fully able to utilize the additional CPU to process transactions.

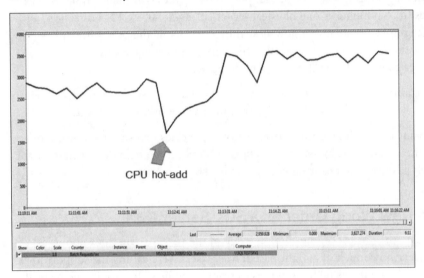

Figure 1.1   CPU hot-add.

A crisis is avoided, and unlike last year customers are not leaving your site due to slow response times to shop elsewhere. Another hour goes by. You are watching database performance, still anxious to avoid a repeat of last year. You then realize the database is starting to become memory constrained, and it's starting to impact performance.

Hot-Add Memory

You go into the management console and you add more memory to the virtual machine housing the database. As you can see in Figure 1.2, the SQL Server database is now able to utilize the additional memory allocated to the virtual machine it is housed in. The arrow represents where the memory was added, and you can see how SQL Server is able to process substantially more transactions with the additional memory available to the database. Another problem is averted. You hold the avalanche of performance problems at bay once again.

VM memory increased from 8 GB to 16 GB

SQL max server memory increased from 6 GB to 14 GB

SQL Server made use of the additional memory in subsequent executions

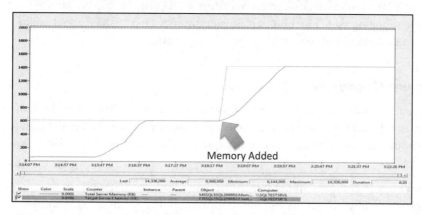

Figure 1.2 Hot-add additional memory.

The World Before Database Virtualization

You think to yourself what the world used to be like for you. You would size the physical server housing the database to accommodate the workload you expected at the time, and at some point in the future, you would buy as much excess capacity as you were able to justify to management, knowing full well that this excess capacity in the server would go unused. However, as a DBA, you would have peace of mind. The company, on the other hand, would have spent a lot of money without receiving real value for it in return.

In this scenario, you would have undersized the server, and Cyber Monday would have come upon you and you would be completely out of luck. You would not have any options. But you are desperate—there must be some way you can get the server more memory.

Wait, you realize you have two identical servers in your environment. One housing the database, and one housing the other applications. You could take both systems down and then borrow memory from one server to put in the server with the database. While you are swapping the memory around, the database would be down, but you decide to do it anyway. You take the systems down. You swap out the memory. You put the additional memory in the database server. You reboot the system and then start up the database so that it can see the additional memory and take advantage of it.

Now think of what would have happened to the customers on your site while you were doing all this. They would be a click away from the competition. Fortunately, in the virtual world, you have the ability to allocate memory as needed.

In this example, the database is in a virtual container that is sized for the normal needs of the database 11 months out of the year. Cyber Monday happens only once a year, and with virtualization you now have ability to give the database the additional resources it needs, on the fly, thus ensuring your company's retail website can meet the special demands of this very profitable shopping day. The best part is, everything we have talked about could have been automated utilizing the tools within the VMware suite.

A Typical Power Company

A nor'easter is about to come barreling down (in Boston, we say "nor'easta"). For those of you who have never experienced one, this is a snowstorm where the snow is wet and heavy and comes at you sideways. Incidentally, as I am writing this chapter, Hurricane Sandy is happening.

So you are a typical power company in the Northeast, and a bad storm has hit. In the middle of the storm, one of your servers running critical support systems fails. Murphy's Law has struck, and at the worst possible time, the system has crashed. The DBA is called in. The restoration process starts, as you lose precious hours.

Wait, you wake up—this is just a bad dream. You live in the virtual world, and VMware detects the server has gone down. The database virtual machine is restarted on another physical server in the cluster. Within a few minutes, you are back up and running.

Calls start flooding into your call center at a pace unheard of as tens of thousands of users are losing power. In the virtual world, you are able to cycle down unneeded virtual machines that are running noncritical applications to free up precious cycles needed to help support the business-critical applications such as your database during this critical time.

Virtualization makes your business agile in ways that were not possible before. The examples in this chapter show you practical ways in which you can use virtualization to make your business better respond to the challenges it will have to face now and in the future. We have not begun to demonstrate the full power of virtualization, but as you can see, this new paradigm of computing—this new world order—offers some major advantages over the traditional computing paradigm our database have lived in up until now.

Summary

In this chapter, we introduced you to a new world where all your SQL Server databases are virtualized—a world where your database is not physically tethered to a physical server, just as your cell phone is not tethered to a particular cell tower. In this new world order, your database can move from physical server to physical server as resource demand fluctuates. If a cell phone is dropped or broken, you are out of luck, but with virtualization you can protect your database from all kinds of failures. Using the example of Cyber Monday, we showed how you could dynamically allocate additional vCPU or memory, as it was most needed, to a SQL Server database running a retail website. This new world order is a world where your SQL Server database has access to any computing resource, on any physical server, at any time.

Chapter 2

The Business Case for Virtualizing a Database

In this chapter, we review the business case for why you should virtualize your business, with specifics around the benefits of virtualizing a business-critical application such as a Microsoft SQL Server 2012 database. Topics covered include the following:

- Server/database consolidation

- Database as a Service (DBaaS)

- IT efficiency (the golden template)

- Service-level agreements (SLAs on steroids)

- Is your database to big to virtualize?

These topics will be discussed in the context of virtualizing a business-critical application, which is different from a non-business-critical application. Specifically, what are common drivers for virtualizing a database and what are not.

Challenge to Reduce Expenses

Businesses in today's world are constantly searching for ways to save money, so it should not be a surprise to anyone given the strong return on investment (ROI) virtualization offers that we have seen this giant groundswell of adoption across industries. Virtualization also offers the unique opportunity to save money while not negatively impacting service levels. Yes, with virtualization, it is possible for you to have your cake and eat it too.

When I think back on the many seminars and presentations I have attended, it's quite normal to see vendors touting the following:

- A 50%–60% reduction in CAPEX (capital expense)

- A 30% reduction in OPEX (operating expense)

- An 80% reduction in energy costs

- A 60%–80% utilization rate

From my experience, these numbers ring true. A virtualized platform offers a really powerful return on investment over a traditional physical infrastructure.

For years the industry talked about right-sizing or downsizing applications, but it never really seemed to take off until one day someone calculated the ROI. They figured out you could buy new equipment, rewrite your application, and get a return on your investment within five years. Next thing I knew, everyone in the world was doing it, and I spent quite a few years of my career working on right-sizing and downsizing applications. As soon as your CEO or CFO understands the ROI, there will be real pressure from senior management for your organization to adopt virtualization as the platform of choice.

Notice I used the word "platform." Virtualization is a more robust platform on which your business can operate, providing a number of advantages over a traditional physical infra-structure.

Another advantage of virtualization is shrinking the data center footprint, and as a consequence the carbon footprint (that is, "going green"). VMware customers have seen as much as an 80% decrease in energy costs through virtualization.

The Database Administrator (DBA) and Saving Money

Whenever I am in a room of DBAs, I ask, "How many of you are evaluated on or have a bonus tied to saving the company money?" Only one person has ever answered yes to this question. Surprisingly, this ability to save money is not a motivator for DBAs to want to start down the path of virtualizing their databases.

I think it ironic that the DBA is not in sync with the rest of the corporation, who are constantly reminded to find ways to save money. Yet, as you can see in Figure 2.1, once a company starts down the path of a virtualized infrastructure, it tends to increasingly virtu-alize over time. So if not to save money, why does a DBA increase the rate of virtualization once started?

The short answer to this question is that the quality of life for the DBA improves when the databases are virtualized. What's more, the quality of service improves for the stakeholders who rely on these databases to do their jobs. As you read further in this book, you will learn about capabilities, such as vMotion, that enable you to move a database while in use to another physical server so that you do not have to work off hours to patch the physical server, and the stakeholders do not have to experience database downtime as this happens.

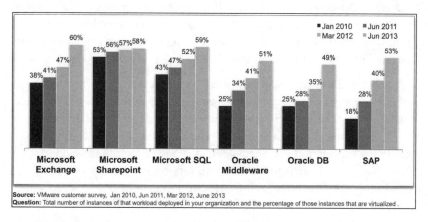

Figure 2.1   Percentage of workload instances that are virtualized.

Service Level Agreements (SLA) and the DBA

Let's face it: As DBAs, we are all about meeting and exceeding the service-level commitments we made to the organization, no matter how unreasonable they are. It's one of the major reasons we do the critical updates off hours when everyone else is sleeping, or during a holiday when everyone else is celebrating. Given the expectation of the Internet being available and accessible 24 hours a day, seven days a week, finding time to take a system down is no easy task. Here is a dialogue I had recently with a client that illustrates this point very nicely—and is a common occurrence.

The company in question specialized in medical equipment monitoring—ensuring that the medical equipment is running continuously and properly. As you can imagine, it is vital for this company to be able to perform its job without interruption; lives literally depend on it. The company was having severe performance problems on one of its most critical SQL Server databases, which was at the heart of this monitoring system. To help alleviate the performance problems, we put basic procedures in place, such as index reorganizations, to keep the SQL Server database running optimally.

As we were troubleshooting the physical environment, database configuration, and application, one of the key things we identified was that the BIOS setting on the physical hardware needed to be changed. The physical server as it was configured prevented the SQL Server database from accessing more than 50% of the available CPU. This was causing severe performance problems. Each time we approached the client to find a time to reboot the physical server so the new BIOS settings could take effect, we got "not now" as the answer. The client understood that this new BIOS setting would enable SQL Server to access 100% of the available CPU, thus alleviating the performance problems. No matter how many times we asked the client, there was never a good time to take the system down for a few minutes. This reply happens all too often.

I finally met with the client and we had a heart-to-heart conversation. I explained to them that based on how their system was configured, they would always experience performance problems with the database until this BIOS adjustment was made. The client was then willing to work with us for a time to take the server down. Yet, this situation points to a bigger issue concerning the expectations of "management" concerning the availability of the database and the physical infrastructure's ability to support the business requirements for the system. In this case, the physical infrastructure was *not* capable of supporting 24/7 access with little or no downtime. I call this the "No-Win SLA." This is when management has an expectation of zero downtime, yet the combination of the database, application, and physical infrastructure was not architected to meet this expectation.

The bottom line: Given the critical nature of the medical devices it monitors and subsequent database requirements, the company never should have been using a single instance of the SQL Server database sitting on a lone physical server. There was no inherent high availability capabilities built in to this infrastructure. There were too many single points of failure present in the current infrastructure. It was just a matter of time before the database went down and stayed down for a long time.

A virtualized infrastructure by its very nature provides a very redundant, highly available platform to run a database on, thus allowing the DBA to meet very robust service levels. In this example, the company would have been better able to meet the implied SLA of little or no downtime had the database been virtualized. When it was determined the BIOS setting on the physical server would have to be changed, the company could have simply used vMotion, a feature of VMware, to move the SQL Server database onto another server, without shutting it down, and then move it back onto the original server once the BIOS change had been made.

Avoiding the Good Intention BIOS Setting

You might be curious what the BIOS setting was that so negatively affected the performance of the SQL server database mentioned previously—and, more importantly, whether you have it set incorrectly within your own environment.

One of the first things experience has taught me to check is the power management settings for any server a database may be placed on. The default BIOS setting for a lot of servers is a "green" friendly setting. The intention of this setting is for the server to save energy when it becomes inactive and then for the server to restore itself as quickly as possible back to a fully operational mode when activity is again detected. That was the idea in theory; in practice, many times the server does not ramp up the CPU quickly and in some cases never allows the CPU to reach its maximum speed.

Another BIOS setting to be aware of is called "dozing." Dozing slows down the CPU only, to about half its speed. The good news is it does save energy; the bad news is it slows down the CPU to half its speed. The proper setting for any server hosting a database is "High Performance" or an equivalent setting, even though this most likely means higher energy consumption.

Here are some other settings in the BIOS you should look for:

- Enable Turbo Mode in the BIOS if your processors support it.
- Enable hyper-threading in the BIOS for processors that support it.
- Enable all hardware-assisted virtualization features in the BIOS.

TIP

Check the BIOS power management settings on all servers that may host a database to ensure they are enabled for performance versus power savings. You may use more energy but your database performance will improve.

As you can see, you have a lot to consider when configuring a virtualized environment to optimally support a database.

DBAs' Top Reasons to Virtualize a Production Database

What DBAs like most about virtualization is the many service-level agreement enhancements it makes possible. One customer I met with made an interesting observation. They had gone down the path of virtualizing everything but their production databases. They then noticed six months later the development and test databases had more uptime than the production databases that the company ran its business on. This was also noticed by the other stakeholders in the organization. Let's use Figure 2.2 as a high-level guide to the many reasons why, as a DBA, you would virtualize your production databases.

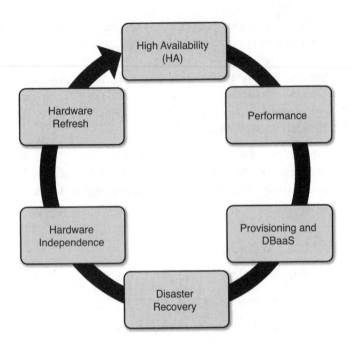

Figure 2.2   Reasons to virtualize a production database.

High Availability and Database Virtualization

Numerous industry reports document the fact that a typical production database will double in size every three years. As you can see in Figure 2.3, the Petabyte Challenge: 2011 IOUG Growth Survey shows how databases keep getting bigger and more complex. The IOUG Research Wire study was produced by Unisphere Research, a Division of Information Today. This survey is available at no charge from Database Trends & Applications (www.dbta.com).

As these databases get bigger and more complex, the ability to recover also becomes more complex. With virtualization, you have redundancy up and down the entire infrastructure stack. By maintaining a high level of redundancy, you can avoid a situation where you would have to perform a database recovery in the first place.

Figure 2.4 illustrates the many levels of redundancy you have when your database is virtualized. For example, if a network interface card (NIC) or even a port were to fail, the VMware hypervisor would detect the failure and reroute traffic to another available port. If a host bus adapter (HBA) path were to fail, the VMware hypervisor would detect the failure and reroute the request to the storage system another way. Best part, all this is built in to the hypervisor and is transparent to the database and applications.

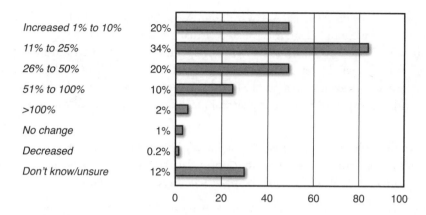

Increased 1% to 10%	20%
11% to 25%	34%
26% to 50%	20%
51% to 100%	10%
>100%	2%
No change	1%
Decreased	0.2%
Don't know/unsure	12%

Figure 2.3 The Petabyte Challenge: 2011 IOUG Database Growth Survey. "The Petabyte Challenge: 2011 IOUG Database Growth Survey" was produced by Unisphere Research, and sponsored by Oracle. Figure provided courtesy of Unisphere Research, a Division of Information Today, Inc. and the Independent Oracle Users Group (IOUG).

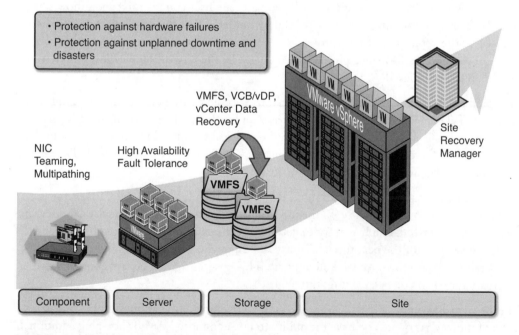

Figure 2.4 Virtualization protections at every level.

"The Petabyte Challenge: 2011 IOUG Database Growth Survey" was produced by Unisphere Research, and sponsored by Oracle. Figure provided courtesy of Unisphere Research, a Division of Information Today, Inc. and the Independent Oracle Users Group (IOUG).

At the server level, you have options such as VMware High Availability (HA). With VMware HA, if your server were to fail, all the affected virtual machines would be restarted onto another available server with capacity. If an operating system failed within a virtual machine, VMware HA would detect the failure and restart the VM. VMware Fault Tolerance takes the level of protection up a notch. In the event of a server failure, VMware Fault Tolerance provides transparent failover at a virtual machine level with no disruption of service.

Moving all the way to the right side of Figure 2.4, you have VMware Site Recovery Manager (SRM). This maps virtual machines to the appropriate resources on a failover site. In the event of a site failure, all VMs would be restarted at the failover site.

With these tools as a DBA, you now have more options than ever before to improve the availability of the database and are now able to take high availability to a new level.

Performance and Database Virtualization

How many times have you received a call from an irate user complaining about how slow the database is performing? As DBAs, we know firsthand that this problem is most likely caused by the application. In my professional experience in the physical world, well over 80% of database performance problems are caused by the way the application was architected, built, or indexed.

It would be great if I could inform you that those problems are going to go away, but they will not. Taking a poorly performing database/application and just virtualizing it won't change anything. What performs poorly in the physical world will perform slowing in the virtualized world, unless something has changed. Virtualization is not a silver bullet that will solve all that ails you.

With the new capability to hot-add more RAM or to hot-plug additional CPUs, you as a DBA need to behave differently. In the physical world, you always size the database server with future growth in mind. You try to get the server configured with enough CPU and RAM to last you for the next three to four years. In effect, you are hoarding resources for a rainy day (as DBAs, we have all done it). This ensures there is always enough spare capacity for when you needed it up the road.

In the virtual world, you live in a shared-resource realm where that physical host contains one or more VMs on it. You have the ability to hot-add more RAM or hot-plug additional

CPUs, as needed. You have the added capacity to move VMs onto other hosts that are underutilized or just to more effectively load balance the workload between the physical hosts.

The VM can even contain a SQL Server database that's in use. You are able to move the database to a different physical host that's being underutilized as the users are accessing the database, without ever shutting it down. In this shared world, it's important that you only ask for the resources you need. If you need more, you will be able to get more resource quickly or reallocate how virtual machines are being used to free resources where they are needed most.

In this new paradigm, the DBA has the ability to shut off resources that are not currently needed. In this world of shared resources, you not only can get more resources when needed, you have options that were never available before in terms of how resources are used and allocated.

In this highly redundant shared-resource world, as a DBA you will get more sleep and work fewer weekends. Think about it: The more redundant your setup is, the less your database will fail, and the fewer times you will have to perform an unexpected database recovery. This all translates into more sleep for you as a DBA.

Provisioning/DBaaS and Database Virtualization

It seems these days everything is a service, so why not databases? To begin this discussion, let's put aside all our preconceived notions concerning the difficulties of deploying databases programmatically. Let's talk about the benefits of what this type of offering would enable for you as a DBA and for the business you serve.

Let's start with a simple question: How long does it take from the time a database request is initiated until the database is released to the requestor? The workflow might resemble something like Figure 2.5.

Now each organization will have its own modifications to this workflow; however, for purposes of this discussion, let's take the workflow shown in Figure 2.5 and add the time to complete for each step. In Figure 2.6, I have added timeframes based on multiple customers' feedback.

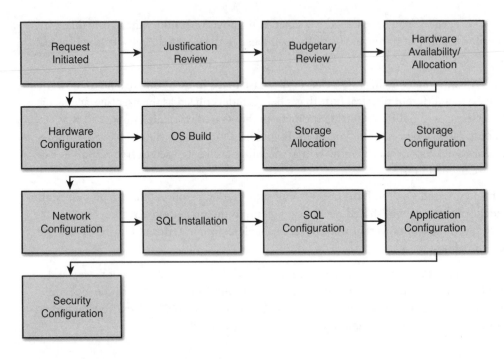

Figure 2.5   SQL Server database-provisioning process example.

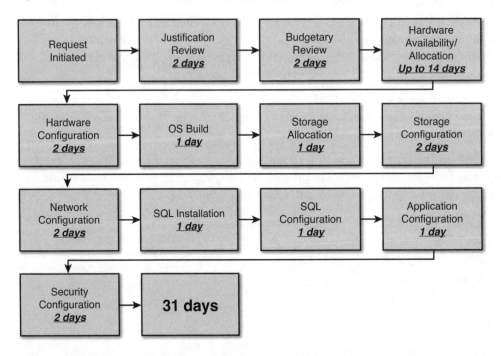

Figure 2.6   SQL Server database-provisioning process example with timeframes.

Now, the flowchart with timeframes added might look slightly different in your organization; however, it should give you a general idea concerning the time it takes to deploy a database into an infrastructure. If we were to move up a level in this discussion, we could ask how this affects our business's ability to generate revenue. If it takes a month just to provision the database for a project, how are we helping time-to-market for new corporate initiatives?

What if we could automate our workflow, through abstraction and predefined policies, to reduce this process to half the amount of time, or even a quarter of the amount of time, so that we can quickly respond to the business's needs?

As a DBA, you now can create the "golden template." That template can be a combination of different interrelated VMs. For example, if one VM contains the application layer and another VM contains the database layer, the two VMs are tightly interconnected. You could create a single template that contains both and also include all the security rules associated with them. You can very quickly create consistent and complete copies of this complex production database environment, thus taking this process from weeks to hours.

Database Tiering

One of the strategies we see in more mature installations is the practice of database tiering, where a predetermined class or grouping of resources is put together. Then, based on the criteria selected by the requestor, the database can be placed in one of those predetermined groups or tiers. For example, you might establish three basic levels to choose from:

- Basic tier
  - Low utilization
  - Suitable for test/development and QA databases
  - One vCPU × 1GB RAM
- Medium tier
  - Medium utilization
  - Burst workloads
  - Suitable for Tier 2 and 3 production
  - Highly elastic resource reservations with overcommit
  - Two vCPU × 4GB RAM

- Premium tier

  - High-performance workloads

  - Suitable for highly visible applications

  - Suitable for production databases

  - Dedicated resource reservations (fully predetermined)

  - Four vCPU × 16GB RAM

By setting up tiers of service, you can quickly place a VM in an environment that is put into an infrastructure class of service that's able to effectively support the workload associated with it. As you deploy your database onto virtualized platforms, give some thought to this concept of different levels of service and performance.

A Virtualized Environment Is a Shared Environment

In a virtualized environment, it's a shared environment. It's important that you sit down with the different players and stakeholders to determine what the required specification is for each tier.

This shared environment means you no longer have to do it all. You have others who can help you get the job done. With their help, you will be able to offer complete environments that can meet the security requirements, application requirements, and performance requirements, all in a template that is quick and easy to deploy in an automated manner. No longer as a DBA do you have to stop what you are doing and manually build out these requested environments. The best part is, this could be an associated set of VMs. For example, in an environment with an application server layer, middle layer, and database backend, the template could include three VMs, with all the associated security and inter-connects. With virtualization, that golden template we have all strived for as DBAs is now possible. Yes, Database as a Service is possible.

Hardware Refresh and Database Virtualization

When we virtualize, we are no longer operating in a world where one physical server equals one application. We no longer live in a world where we have to understand all the nuances of a particular suite of hardware. Before virtualization, the operating environment would look something like Figure 2.7.

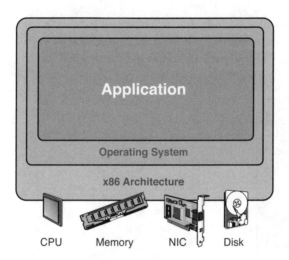

Figure 2.7 Before virtualization.

In the traditional (nonvirtualized) world, we would have a single operating system loaded onto a single physical server. Also, the SQL Server database would be on a physical server that is not a shared resource. The server would exist for one purpose—to support the Microsoft databases running on the server; it was never meant to be a shared resource.

In this physical server, the software and hardware would be tightly coupled. An upgrade of the server or any of its components has to be handled carefully because it could affect how particular applications loaded on the server work. In the case of a complex application such as a SQL Server database, this process of upgrading could take weeks of planning. As we go through the process of testing the database and applications against the new hardware configuration, we could spend weeks just to determine the proper patches needed so that everything works correctly post-upgrade.

The Virtual World

According to a VMware white paper titled "Virtualization Overview," the term virtualization "broadly describes the separation of a resource or request from the underlying physical delivery of the service." By creating this abstraction or decoupling from the underlying physical hardware, a whole computing paradigm has emerged—a world where a proposed change in the physical hardware in which your Microsoft SQL Server database resides does not instantly send waves of anxiety to the DBA.

As you can see represented in Figure 2.8, resources such as CPU, memory, network, and disk are made available through the VMware virtualization layer (hypervisor). By separating the physical resource request from the underlying hardware, you have truly turned hardware into a commodity. Need more hardware? Purchase it, install the hypervisor onto it, and move the VMs over to start using it. Does it matter if the original server and the new one are from different manufacturers? No, it does not.

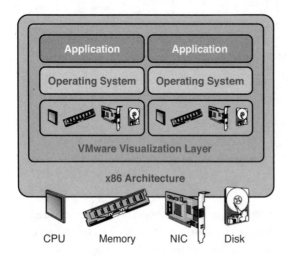

Figure 2.8   After virtualization.

In this new paradigm, hardware is truly a commodity. It's common practice every few years to update your hardware as the newer hardware become available or your older hardware becomes obsolete. No longer does this process require weeks of planning. As Nike says, "Just do it." No longer as a DBA do you have to sit down with your user community to work out an outage window for when the database can come down to support the hardware upgrade.

In this new paradigm, you are living in a shared environment. It's important that you understand what you need for resources. Chapter 10, "How to Baseline Your Physical SQL Server System," is one of the most important chapters of this book—if not the most important. Understanding what your SQL Server needs for resources and sizing the virtual machine that houses it accordingly will avoid a lot of problems. The opposite is also true: Oversizing or over-allocating your VMs will introduce a lot inefficiencies and potential problems into your shared environment.

Is Your Database Too Big to Virtualize?

A common objection I hear from DBAs when they are first asked to consider virtualizing a database is that their database is too big and complex to be virtualized. Consider this example of a very large and complex database that was virtualized. It had the following characteristics:

- 8TB in size
- 8.8 billion rows of data
- 52 million transactions per day
- 79,000 IOPS
- 40,000 named users
- 4,000 peak concurrent users
- Complex ERP system

After this database was virtualized, all transaction types got better. According to the DBA, they saw more than a 50% reduction in time for online transactions. When done correctly, it's possible to virtualize very large and complex databases.

Summary

In this chapter, we discussed the business case for virtualization, including ROI. Companies operating in a one-server-to-one-application environment has led to a number of costly inefficiencies in how businesses operate. Companies that adopt virtualization typically see significant cost savings and increased utilization.

This has created a very powerful financial reason to adopt virtualization. Combined with the many capabilities of a virtualized infrastructure, this provides a DBA with many options. The inherent capabilities surrounding redundancy up and down the entire infrastructure stack that comes with a virtualized platform will improve the availability of the databases, enabling you to exceed the documented and undocumented service levels you have with your customers.

We also discussed how virtualization has created an abstracted layer from the physical environment; once you break your databases away from the shackles of the physical server hardware, hardware becomes a commodity you can easily leverage. We stressed the importance of understanding the resource requirements of your database in a shared environment, and how important it is to size the VM that houses the database appropriately. A proper baseline of your database is key to understanding resource requirements and will help you avoid a lot of problems up the road.

Chapter 3

Architecting for Performance: The Right Hypervisor

In this chapter, we discuss what a hypervisor is and the different types of virtualization hypervisors on the market. We also discuss why some hypervisors run applications true to the native or physical stack whereas other hypervisors do not.

This is especially important to understand given that a SQL Server database is one of the most complex applications you may ever virtualize. When a hypervisor does not run true to the physical stack, it is possible to encounter bugs that would not exist in the physical world, thus introducing an additional level of complexity and risk that you need to be aware of.

We look at the different generations of VMware vSphere hypervisor in this chapter. Just as there are many versions of the SQL Server database, there are many versions of the vSphere hypervisor. You would not run your most demanding SQL server workloads on SQL Server 2000, just as you would not run your most demanding virtualized workloads on VMware Infrastructure 3.0. It's important that you are running on a version of vSphere that was built to support the complex resource needs and demands of a SQL Server database. Finally, we discuss some additional things to consider when virtualizing your SQL Server database.

What Is a Hypervisor?

To help you better understand what a hypervisor is and the role it plays, let's look at a portion of a typical infrastructure before and after it has been virtualized. Figure 3.1 illustrates a small slice of a much larger infrastructure. Imagine you have three physical servers. Each server is running a different operating system. One server or physical host is running a flavor of Linux, another server is running a version of the Windows Server 2008 operating system, and the final server is running a version of the Windows Server 2012 operating system. For the purposes of this example, it is not important what version of the particular operating system the different physical machines are running.

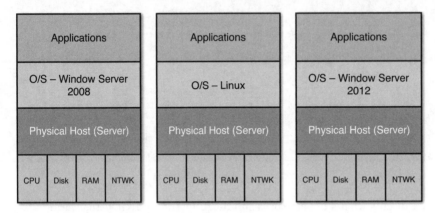

Figure 3.1   Three physical hosts before virtualization.

Each of these individual operating systems is responsible for providing physical resources such as CPU, memory, disk, and network to the different applications sitting on it.

For example, sitting on the Windows Server 2008 operating system could be a series of applications that include a SQL Server database and a number of other applications. The Windows operating system would provide each of those applications access to the physical resources CPU, memory, and disk.

This would also hold true for the other servers in Figure 3.1. There would be a series of applications running on those servers, including databases and various other applications, and each OS would provide access to its resources. Figure 3.1 is a high-level illustration of this before the environment is virtualized.

Hypervisor Is Like an Operating System

Think of a hypervisor in the same way as you think of an operating system. It sits on top of the physical hardware, and just like the operating systems in Figure 3.1, it provides access to resources such as CPU, memory, disk, and network. However, there are two major differences between a hypervisor and an operating system:

- A hypervisor's customer is the guest operating system running on the virtual machines (VMs), not an application such as SQL Server or Microsoft Exchange running on the guest operating system. Another way of saying this is that operating systems provide services to many different programs and applications running on them. The hypervisor provides services to the many different operating systems running on the different virtual machines it contains.

- A hypervisor shares physical resources such as CPU, memory, disk, and network among the many virtual machines through the guest operating systems. This is a level of complexity an OS does not have. The operating system only deals with the applications running on top of it. It does not have to deal with the complex needs of another operating system.

DEFINITION

Guest operating system—The operating system that runs on a virtual machine.

Figure 3.2 illustrates the same environment when it is virtualized. Sitting on the physical host is the hypervisor. The hypervisor's job is to provide physical resources such as CPU, memory, and disk to its customers. Its customers are the many guest OSs running on the virtual machines.

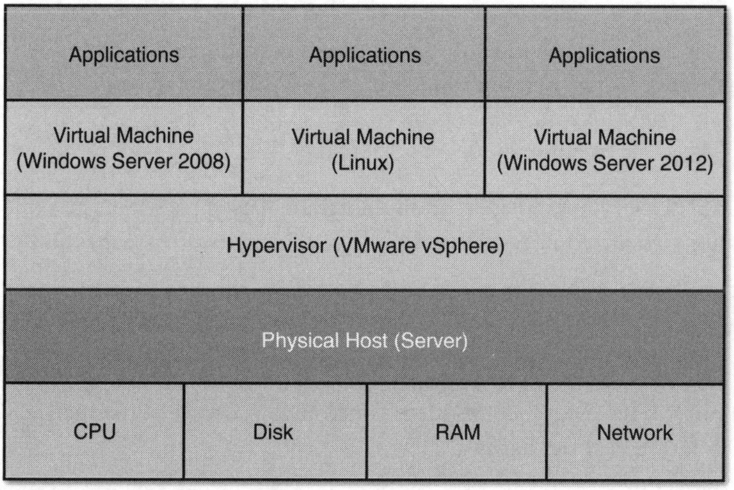

Figure 3.2   Three physical hosts after virtualization.

A virtualized infrastructure uses a many-to-one relationship: There are many applications running on a server or physical host. A natural byproduct of working this way is the use of resources such as CPU, memory, and disk much more efficiently. No longer will you live in a world of 8%–12% average utilization that is caused by having every system sit on a different physical server.

What Is a Virtual Machine?

Think of a virtual machine (VM) as a software-based partition of a computer. It is not emulation at all because it passes through the CPU instructions directly to the processors. An emulator would not be able to take advantage of the embedded virtualization assist instructions, which manufacturers such as Intel and AMD have been building into their processors for over 10 years, that help accelerate the performance of vSphere.

When you first create a VM, you must load an operating system on it, just like you would with a physical server. Without the operating system being loaded on the virtual machine, it is of little or no use. The same applies to your physical server. Without an operating system loaded onto it, the physical server is of little or no use.

It's important to understand that when programs are loaded onto the virtual machine, they then execute in the same way they would on a nonvirtualized infrastructure. The guest operating system provides access to resources such as CPU, memory, and disk in the same way an operating systems does in a nonvirtualized infrastructure. The difference is that the hypervisor is providing those resources to the guest operating system, not the physical server itself.

> **NOTE**
>
> A virtual machine is a software-based partition of a computer. It contains an operating system. The many applications running on the VM, such as a SQL Server database, execute the same way they would on a physical server.

Applications such as your SQL Server databases run in a software-based partition the same way they would run in a nonvirtualized infrastructure. The core tenants of virtualization include the following:

- **Partitioning**—The ability to run multiple operating systems on one physical machine. Also, the ability to divide resources between different virtual machines.

- **Isolation**—The ability to have advance resource controls to preserve performance. Fault and security isolation is at the hardware level.

- **Encapsulation**—The ability to move and copy virtual machines as easily as moving and copying files. The entire state of a virtual machine can be saved to a file.

- **Hardware independence**—The ability to provision or migrate any virtual machine to any similar or different physical server.

As a DBA, these are important points to keep in mind as you manage the database.

Paravirtualization

Some other vendors decided to implement paravirtualization. To quote Wikipedia, "paravirtualization is a virtualization technique that presents a software interface to virtual machines that is similar, but not identical to that of the underlying hardware." The key words here are "but not identical."

The definition goes on further to say, "The intent of the modified interface is to reduce the portion of the guest's execution time spent performing operations which are substantially more difficult to run in a virtual environment compared to a non-virtualized environment. The paravirtualization provides specially defined 'hooks' to allow the guest(s) and host to request and acknowledge these tasks, which would otherwise be executed in the virtual domain (where execution performance is worse)."

The goal of paravirtualization was to get lower virtualization overhead. In order to accomplish this goal, vendors enable the guest operating system to skip the virtual layer for certain types of operations. In order to enable this functionality, the vendors have to alter the guest operating system so it is able to skip the virtualization layer.

For example, Red Hat Linux running on a physical host will be a different version of Red Hat Linux running on a hypervisor that uses paravirtualization. Every time the hypervisor is updated, it requires modifying the operating system. This opens up the possibility for a database to behave *differently* when it is virtualized.

In the context of this conversation, we have been talking about CPU instructions. The authors of this book agree with the VMware approach to virtualization: Altering the guest operating system is not acceptable. There are too many inherent risks associated with running a database on an altered OS.

When it comes to device drivers, making them aware they are virtualized can be a real advantage. The classic example of this is the VMXNET3 driver for the network. In the section titled "Paravirtual SCSI Driver (PVSCSI) and VMXNET3," we discuss these types of drivers in more detail.

The Different Hypervisor Types

Earlier in this chapter, we talked about what a virtual machine is, how it is a software-based partition of a computer, and that this partitioning happens through the hypervisor. We also discussed how there are different types of hypervisors. For the purposes of this book, we will be talking about different types of hypervisors that offer full virtualization. Full virtualization is a complete abstraction of the underlying hardware. Anything that would run on the physical machine would also be able to be run on the virtual machine in the same manner. The bottom line: The operating system doesn't have to change.

Two approaches were taken when building a hypervisor, commonly known as a Type-1 hypervisor and a Type-2 hypervisor. To help you understand the difference between hypervisor types, refer to Figure 3.3.

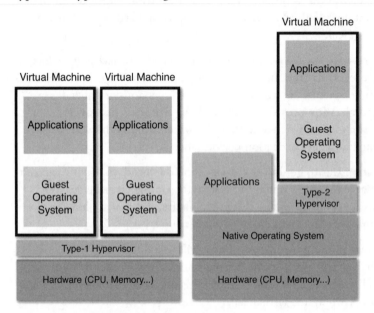

Figure 3.3   Type-1 and Type-2 hypervisors.

Type-1 Hypervisor

A Type-1 hypervisor sits on the bare metal or physical hardware. Think of "bare metal" as a computer without any operating system.

Starting at the bottom in Figure 3.3, on the left side you have the physical hardware, or bare metal. Sitting on top of that is the Type 1 hypervisor. VMware vSphere ESXi is an example of a Type-1 hypervisor. Moving further up on the left side of the Type-1 hypervisor are the many different self-contained virtual machines with the guest operating systems. In the example, we show two virtual machines, but there would typically be many. An important point to make is that until the hypervisor is started, none of the virtual machines are able to run.

Type-2 Hypervisor

A Type-2 hypervisor runs directly on another operating system. This means until the underlying operating system has booted, you would not be able to use the Type-2 hypervisor. That is an easy way to distinguish the type of hypervisor you are running. Once again, refer to Figure 3.3, only on the right side this time.

Starting at the bottom-right side, the physical hardware is illustrated. Moving up from there sitting on top of the physical hardware is the operating system (for example, Linux). Note that this is the native operating system, not a guest operating system. On top of the native operating system, you could have both applications running on the native operating system itself and a Type-2 hypervisor also running. Then running on the Type-2 hypervisor could be one or more virtual machines and their various guest operating systems.

Drawbacks to the Type-2 Hypervisor

If the operating system sitting on the hardware crashes, it will bring everything down on the box, including the Type-2 hypervisor. If a hacker breaches the operating systems on which the Type-2 hypervisor is running, then everything is at risk. This makes the Type-2 hypervisor only as secure as the underlying operating system on which it is running. If critical security patches are released for that operating system that have nothing to do with virtualization, you are now required to patch those boxes and work these patches in with your patching of the guest operating systems. In our opinion, serious virtualization requires a Type-1 hypervisor at a minimum.

Paravirtual SCSI Driver (PVSCSI) and VMXNET3

PVSCSI is a great driver to use for all your I/O-intensive virtual machines. we can't think of a more I/O-intensive VM than a SQL Server database. Based on our experience, you will see a 10%–12% improvement in I/O throughput. You will also experience up to a 30% reduction in CPU usage.

This driver is best suited for all your I/O-intensive workloads, especially a SAN environment. It is not well suited for direct attached storage. In order to use this driver, you will have to have the VMware tools installed on the VM.

Bottom line: You will have much lower latency to the underlying storage layer and much lower CPU consumption. This is a win-win situation. This is very useful with an I/O-intensive application such as a SQL Server database on a virtualized infrastructure. Chapter 6, "Architecting for Performance: Storage," will go into great detail about the underlying storage layer.

VMXNET3 is the third-generation paravirtualized NIC designed for network performance. Think of VMXNET3 as a network adapter that is optimized for network performance in a virtualized infrastructure. The key point is that the OS does not get altered in any way in order for VMXNET3 to be able to enhance network performance.

Installation Guidelines for a Virtualized Database

A common question that's asked is, "When installing my virtualized SQL Server database, what installation guidelines should I follow?" The answer is quite simple: the same installation guidelines you have always followed. The same as you would on a physical environment. A virtualized database running on vSphere behaves exactly like a nonvirtualized database, and you should not treat it any differently from when you install the database on a physical infrastructure.

To illustrate the point that you should treat a virtualized database installation in the same way you would a physical implementation, let's look at some common things you would normally take into consideration during an installation and see if they change in any way.

1. Make sure the physical hardware and software configuration is sufficient to support the version of SQL Server you are about to install.

   In a virtualized infrastructure, this still holds true. You would want to make sure the virtual machine is sized appropriately. Does it have enough RAM to support the database version you are about to install? Is the operating system version and patch level appropriate? Is there enough disk space? Do you have at least the minimum X86 or X64 processor speed required?

2. It is important to make sure the Disk layout and IOPS requirement as configured are adequate to meet the demands the database will place upon the storage layer.

   Taking into consideration the storage layer available to you, will the IOPS capability of the disk meet the requirements of the database? What is the optimal way to lay out the database with storage infrastructure available to you? When laying out the database, where should TempDB be placed? Where should the transaction logs be placed? Where should the Data and Index segments be placed? These considerations are the same for both the physical implementation of the database and the virtual implementation of the database.

3. Does the account where the database is installed from have the appropriate Permissions assigned to it to support the database installation?

   When you install a SQL Server database, it's important to make sure the account you are installing from has the appropriate permissions. Anyone who has ever had to deal with a permissions problem knows firsthand how important this is. This is just as important an issue for when a database is virtualized.

As you can see, these and many more considerations are the same when installing any SQL Server database. If you take the same care you would to install a database on a physical infrastructure, all will go well. The important thing is to make sure the environment, both the physical host and virtual machine, is sized to give the database the resources it needs when it needs them.

> **TIP**
>
> When installing your database on a virtualized infrastructure, follow the same installation guidelines you would on a physical infrastructure.

It's About Me, No One Else But Me

From your perspective as a DBA, when you set up a database in the physical world, it's typically about "me," just "me," and no one else but "me." It's your database server, and everyone else on it is either an invited guest or an unwanted visitor. As we have been discussing, this is the world of a one-to-one relationship. Your production database sits on a server whose only purpose is to support the production SQL Server database that supports the business. When it sits idle, those resources go to waste. If you need more resources, you are limited to what the physical server the database sits on was purchased with.

As a DBA, you tune up the database to take full advantage of all resources available to it. For example, Max Server Memory would be configured to take advantage of the entire RAM on the box, except what is needed for the operating systems. You are only setting a small amount of RAM aside because it is good for me. Max Server Memory is talked about in great detail in Chapter 7, "Architecting for Performance: Memory." In fact, when databases get moved onto storage arrays, as DBAs, we don't take too well to that at first. This means it's not just about "me." You have to deal with a storage array administrator who may not have the best interests of the database as their top priority. The storage administrator needs to ensure performance for all the systems connected to the array, not just the database servers.

Let's face it: As DBAs, we don't play well in the sandbox with others. We have grown up in a world where we don't have to share and we are not historically good about it. We have grown up in a world where we have to solve problems by ourselves all the time. When you virtualize your database, it's important to note that the world changes. There are others in the sandbox with you. You have to learn how to share and rely on others if you are to succeed. Good communication and understanding of your requirements among the different teams is critical in this new world.

Virtualized Database: It's About Us, All of Us

In the case of a virtualized environment, it is a shared environment. This means you have to consider that others need access to the CPU, memory, and disk resources, which is why we talked about virtualization being a one-to-many relationship, where the "many" represent the different hosts running a single physical host/server.

As DBAs, this means we need to behave a little differently if we want to be successful when we virtualize the database. As DBAs, we understand that everything has tradeoffs. When we give the database more CPU, it typically minimizes I/O. In fact, as database administrators we are constantly being asked to look at the infrastructure and make decisions on how the database and programs running on the database consume resources to help the overall throughput within the database improve. We now need to make those tradeoffs within the overall shared environment. If we behave a little differently with this virtualized infrastructure, there are lots of advantages over a physical infrastructure that we can leverage. Even though the resources are shared, it also means we can get more resources when it's critical.

DBA Behavior in the Virtual World

Let's discuss how the DBA's behavior needs to change and look at a real-life example of how things are different when your database is virtualized. Every few years, it's time to buy a new server on which to run your production database. This happens for a variety of reasons. The most common is the equipment you are running on is getting too old or the database needs to be on a server with more resources. Bottom line: The database has outgrown the capacity of the machine, and no matter what you do as a DBA, it can't keep up.

Management asks you to determine the requirements for the new server on which to house the database. This is where the games begin. It's pretty simple to look at the transaction load of the database, extrapolate out some basic growth, and determine a configuration that will get the job done for four years. As DBAs, that's what we do. But then we do one more thing: On top of figuring out what we need, we figure out how much more we think we can get management to purchase. We become like squirrels getting ready for the winter. We want to gather as many nuts as we can (think of nuts as CPU, memory, and disk resources) and have them hidden away just in case we need them. As DBAs, we do this for self-preservation.

The world we have lived in up until this point has been about what we purchase is what we will have available to us, and we have to make sure it's enough. The problem is that this behavior, which has worked so well for us over the years, will get us into a lot of trouble very quickly in a virtualized environment.

The worst thing we can do is oversize those virtual machines that house our databases. In this shared resource environment, by oversizing the VMs the database sits on, you are hoarding resources from the other VMs that won't be able to get those resources when they need them. When VMs cannot get the resources they need, performance is negatively impacted. It's important that we work with the vSphere administrator, storage administrator, and network administrator to communicate how much of the resources we really need and not hoard them. It's also just as important that the team supporting the virtualized environment provides you the resources you need.

IMPORTANT

A virtualized database is housed on a shared environment. It's important as DBAs that we don't hoard resources such as CPU, memory, and disk. Its important we communicate clearly what the VM that houses the database needs. It's also important for the vSphere administrator, storage administrator, and network administrators to work with you to meet your requirements.

This means working closing with the storage administrator, network administrators, and vSphere administrators. As our coauthor Michael Corey likes to say, "I flunked Mind Reading. If you don't tell me what you need, I won't know."

Shared Environment Means Access to More If You Need It

By embracing this new way of thinking, you can start to harvest the advantages of virtualization. As the DBA, let's say you know that there is special processing that happens every year that is critical to the business. This year-end processing has historically brought database performance to a slow crawl. In this shared environment, you now have more resources to work with. You as part of a team have choices you can make. You could give the virtual machine that houses the database access to more resources; you could also take resources away from other VMs, freeing them up for the database. What is important to realize is that a virtualized database can be given resources quickly and easily. In fact, you could also just move the database while it's being used onto another physical host that has more resources available. No longer do you have to hoard or squirrel away resources.

Check It Before You Wreck It

I want to talk about the "check it before you wreck it" rule. As a DBA, you embrace this new way of doing business. You determine how many IOPS the new database you are about to build needs. In this new world of shared responsibilities, we would encourage you to work with the storage administrator to determine together the IOPS requirements of the database. The more you start approaching the support of the infrastructure as a team, the better off you will be down the road.

For the purposes of this example, it is assumed you determined the IOPS requirements for the database and then communicated all the requirements to the team. You are handed back a virtual machine to put the new database on. Before you go install the database, do a simple IOPS test. Make sure the VM was configured with what you asked for. You can use simple tools such as SQLIO and IOMETER to check it. Before you go and install the database, as Jeff would say, "Check it before you wreck it."

If it's not as you specified, revisit the request with the team so that it can be reconfigured. Use this as a learning experience and stress with the team the importance of providing you a VM capable of meeting the demands the database requires.

The database is too resource intensive a VM not to be configured appropriately. Experience has taught us that early on, many virtual environments were built for capacity, not performance. That the vSphere administrators have been able to overcommits a lot of resources like CPU and memory in the vSphere environment and all has performed well. Now a database comes along—one of the most resource-intensive programs you will ever virtualize. This same environment where over commitment of resources like CPU and memory has performed well will very quickly see performance degrade to unacceptable levels.

It is important that the team has embraced this new way of thinking, where you ask for what you really need to ensure resources are not being hoarded so they are available more needy virtual machines. That they take to heart that ,more can be had in terms of resources, if needed, down the road quickly and easily.

Why Full Virtualization Matters

Just as there are different hypervisor types, there are also different ways of virtualizing. VMware made a decision to not cut any corners and do a full virtualization implementation of the hypervisor. VMware built a Type-1 hypervisor that means your database will behave exactly as a database would behave on a physical implementation.

Another way of saying this is, the guest operating system does not know it's being virtualized and requires no modification in order to run in a virtualized environment. It also means that the many applications (such as a SQL Server database) running on the guest operating system also do not know they are virtualized and require no modification to run. In addition, the guest operating system and applications running on the guest operating system will run the way they always have, with no surprises, provided you allot them the resources they need. This in our opinion is a powerful differentiator.

Okay, so for those vSphere admins reading this, you are right, the VMXNET3 network driver and the PVSCSI driver are "paravirtualized," which means these drivers know they are running on a virtualized stack, but the point is the operating system is unaware it is residing on a hypervisor (more on that later).

Living a DBA's Worst Nightmare

We had a customer running a SQL Server database on a Type-2 hypervisor that utilized paravirtulization. The customer had backups being done on this SQL Server database, as you would expect.

We asked the customer if we could perform fire drills on all the production database backups to validate them. We consider testing backups a best practice that should be done at least once a year, at minimum, and quarterly if possible; you don't want an entire year to go by and find out your backups for the last eight months are no good. By testing, we mean performing an actual restoration to ensure that when you really need it, it will work. The client made a business decision not to test the backups of this key production SQL Server database.

TIP

Test each database backup by doing an actual database restoration at least every quarter.

The customer had a mission-critical third-party application they ran their business on that required updating. The application and the database ran on a virtual machine. An upgrade plan was put in place. As part of this upgrade, we had to take the most current backup and restore the database onto a new virtual machine, and then proceed with an upgrade of the application.

When we attempted to restore the database on the new virtual machine, it would not work. We double-checked the backup logs to see if there was a problem with the original SQL Server backup. Every indication we had was there were no issues. We then decided to do another full backup of the production SQL Server database and apply that to the new virtual machine. No matter what we did, we could not restore the database. We could not find a problem anywhere with the backups that were being performed.

This was a production SQL Server database where the backups were being taken with no errors, yet would not work on the restore. As a database administrator, this is a serious problem—and a DBA's worst nightmare. We immediately opened up critical tickets with Microsoft, the vendor that provided the hypervisor, and the third-party application vendor. When we got the answer, we nearly lost it. This was a known problem when a SQL Server database was being virtualized on this vendor's hypervisor. The virtualization vendor did not have any workarounds and acted like this was not a big deal.

From a DBA's perspective, this was a huge problem. By altering the operating stack, they had created a situation that could have put the company out of business. Because the database was running on a Type-2 hypervisor, the database was running differently than it would have on physical equipment. The combination of the alterations to the operating system and the lack of full virtualization created this very dangerous situation.

When you virtualize a database, make sure it's on VMware vSphere, which has been proven by hundreds of thousands of customers successfully running mission-critical systems. vSphere is a full-virtualization implementation and *does not alter the operating stack in any way*. This means the virtualized database will perform *exactly* as its counterpart on physical hardware, and you won't ever have to worry about your database backup not being valid like our customer experienced in this example.

Do not confuse a paravirtual hypervisor with paravirtual drivers. Paravirtual drivers are built to optimize performance in a virtual environment. In our experience, you should take full advantage of these drivers where it makes sense. A great example of a driver you should consider for your SQL Server database is the Paravirtual SCSI driver.

Physical World Is a One-to-One Relationship

In the physical world, there is a one-to-one relationship between applications and hardware. The reason we say "one-to-one relationship" is that it is very typical to have a separate server to host each key application. For example, a server to host Microsoft Exchange and another physical server for your production SQL Server database would be common. As you can see, there is typically one physical server for each major application. There is also a lot of unused capacity/resource when there is one server dedicated for each major application.

One-to-One Relationship and Unused Capacity

How often is each one of those dedicated physical servers busy seven days a week, 24 hours a day? It has been the authors' experience that across an organization, it is not very likely the servers are fully utilized seven days a week, 24 hours a day. This is further compounded by the mindset of always having spare capacity just in case. Here is a personal example of that mindset in play.

Years ago, I worked for a very prestigious hospital. My database was on a very large server. At times we would be doing intensive processing within the database and start to pin the CPU in the 90%–100% range. When I say "pin," just to be clear I mean the CPU utilization would stay above 90% for long periods of time. The system administrator (SA) would come running into my office to figure out what was going on. He did not like to see the CPU get above 60%. I, on the other hand, like the idea that if I buy a computer, I am taking full advantage of its capabilities. The SA's way of thinking was commonplace in my experience. Other SAs might have higher thresholds, but they still like to see very ample spare capacity. I wonder if management realized they were buying computers at that hospital that had almost twice the computer capacity they really needed. Could that money have been put to better use elsewhere in the organization? That mindset is one of the many reasons we tend to have dedicated servers for each major application.

In the SA's defense, if he needed more resources, they were not easy to come by. Unlike a virtualized platform, where adding another CPU is a click away, at that hospital another CPU was not a simple click away. If it was not sitting there idle, it could not be added easily. My grandfather used to have a saying: "When they keep telling you about the good old days, don't believe them. I lived them. They were not that good. People died from lots of things we can prevent today, we did not have air-conditioning, and a car beat a horse and buggy any day." Well, times have changed, and so has technology. We can choose to live in the past or embrace the now.

By having dedicated servers for each application, we ensure those applications have the resources they need (CPU, memory, and disk) when they need them. It also means that a lot of very expensive hardware is sitting idle. According to the VMware literature, 8%-12% average utilization is typical. We cannot speak to that number directly. What we can speak to is that when we undertake one of the many database-consolidation engagements we do each year, our experience has taught us that 60% database-consolidation ratios would be a very conservative number. Our clients typically experience better than 60% database consolidation ratios. This means we are able to place all their current databases in half the footprint they consume today. There is a lot of wasted spare capacity out there, which tells me if we were to look across a large organization, then 12% overall utilization would not be that far off, especially if you take weekends into consideration. I cannot think of a bigger workhorse than a server managing a database—and look at all the wasted capacity out there. Therefore, the 12% number rings true.

Having a one-to-one relationship between applications and hardware is a very expensive proposition, yet this was the world before virtualization.

This was driven in part by the inability of the operating system's resource management capabilities to prevent different applications from impacting each other. This was further complicated by incompatible DLLs and libraries between different applications running on the same operating system. This was a world we lived in because we did not have options in the past. It's a world a lot of companies still live in. It is a very expensive world to live in. Cost and business agility are some of the many drivers why companies are virtualizing more and more of their infrastructure.

One to Many: The Virtualized World

In the new computing paradigm of virtualization, it is a one-to-many relationship, where a single physical server will now have many applications residing on it, improving overall utilization rates but still offering the same level of service.

If you refer back to Figure 3.1, you'll see that it illustrates the one-to-one world before virtualization. Before virtualization, you would have three separate physical servers handling all the work. If those servers were only busy 50% the time, which is being generous, then the other half of the time the available resources such as CPU and memory went to waste. The other physical servers have no way of taking advantage of that spare capacity no matter how badly they need it.

In Figure 3.2, on the other hand, we illustrate a virtualized infrastructure where every one of those physical servers is now represented by different virtual machines on a single host. When there is spare capacity, the other VMs are able to take advantage of those resources if they are in need. Another advantage of virtualization is that those three physical servers could be the right size on a physical host containing the capacity of two servers. Because at 50% utilization, the overall footprint was, at most, half utilized. By right-sizing, an organization should be able to save money in licensing and physical equipment costs. When you add onto this the additional capabilities a virtualized infrastructure offers an organization, there is a very powerful business case to be made.

The Right Hypervisor

SQL Server has been around for quite a while, but in 2005 Microsoft was finally able to compete with Oracle. I became a real fan starting with SQL Server 2005. To me, it was when Microsoft finally had a database that could give Oracle a run for its money. This was when an average company could put its database workload on SQL Server and it would meet or exceed all their needs. The product has only gotten better over the years. On a personal note, we are really excited over SQL Server 2014 and its in-memory capabilities.

When you go to virtualize your mission-critical SQL Server database, it's important to use a version of vSphere that was built with a database in mind; this means starting with

VMware vSphere 4 or higher, which was built to handle the demands of a SQL Server database and business-critical applications. Figure 3.4 outlines the difference in capabilities through the generations of VMware product. Just as SQL Server 2000 was a great database and you could do a lot of great things with it, so were the earlier versions of ESXi. Today, the most demanding of databases can be virtualized without fear.

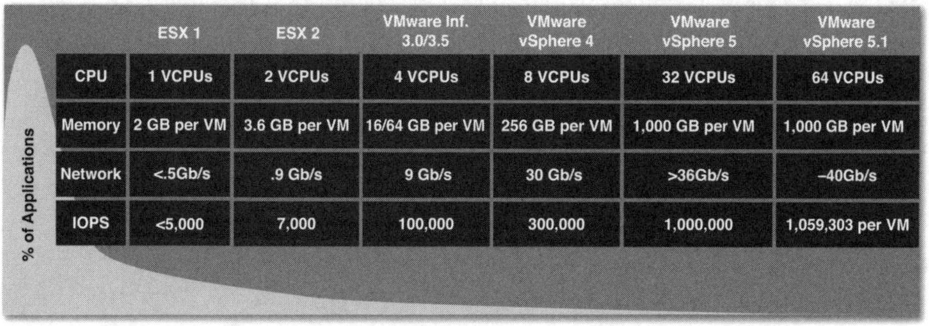

	ESX 1	ESX 2	VMware Inf. 3.0/3.5	VMware vSphere 4	VMware vSphere 5	VMware vSphere 5.1
CPU	1 VCPUs	2 VCPUs	4 VCPUs	8 VCPUs	32 VCPUs	64 VCPUs
Memory	2 GB per VM	3.6 GB per VM	16/64 GB per VM	256 GB per VM	1,000 GB per VM	1,000 GB per VM
Network	<.5Gb/s	.9 Gb/s	9 Gb/s	30 Gb/s	>36Gb/s	~40Gb/s
IOPS	<5,000	7,000	100,000	300,000	1,000,000	1,059,303 per VM

% of Applications

Figure 3.4 Overview of vSphere ESXi capabilities.

When you consider that the average application requires only one or two CPUs, less than 4GB RAM, and less than 5,000 IOPS, and contrast that with the ability of the latest release of vSphere and its ability to use over a million IOPS as well as 1,000GB of RAM and 64 CPUs, then even the largest, most mission-critical SQL Server databases can be virtualized as long as it's done correctly. The limitation has not been the hypervisor for a very long time; instead, it's the underlying hardware.

Summary

In this chapter, we focused on the hypervisor and the underlying virtual machines. We discussed the computing paradigm before virtualization, one we described as a one-to-one relationship where we would purchase one physical server for each critical application.

The new computing paradigm of virtualization is a one-to-many relationship, where a single physical server will now have many applications residing on it, thus improving overall utilization rates but still offering the same level of service. In the virtual world, your SQL Server database will be in a shared resource, which means it's important to work with the storage administrator and vSphere administrator to accurately communicate your requirements. It's also important to size the virtual machine that houses your database properly; hoarding or oversizing resource in a shared environment hurts everyone.

We discussed the different type of hypervisors, and the difference between full virtualization and paravirtualization. We stress the fact that vSphere ESXi uses full virtualization and does not alter the operating stack in any way, which means your database will operate in the same way it does on physical hardware. We also discussed a common paravirtual driver that I/O-intensive workloads such as a SQL Server database will benefit from.

We ended with an illustration that highlights the major difference with the many different versions of VMware ESXi. We stressed that the latest versions were built specifically to handle the demands of a complex workload such as Microsoft SQL Server. No other hypervisor on the market today has the proven track record of VMware, nor the ability to scale up; it is ready for the most demanding SQL Server databases today.

Chapter 4

Virtualizing SQL Server: Doing IT Right

This chapter focuses on the things you need to know and do as you start down the path of database virtualization. The advice given in this chapter takes a very conservative approach, with the end goal of helping you avoid the common traps and pitfalls encountered when you first virtualize a production SQL Server database. Topics covered include the following:

- Documentation

- The implementation plan

- The importance of obtaining a baseline

- Additional considerations

- A bird's-eye view of the implementation process

Doing IT Right

Our experience has taught us that the best place to start down the path of database virtualization is to read the documentation. The first thing many DBAs do when a new version of the database comes out is to install it and start using it. (In a nonproduction environment, of course—no DBA is going to deploy a new version of the database, including a database patch, without first testing it.)

The problem is that those same DBAs don't always circle back and do a complete read of the documentation from front to back. This is further compounded by the fact that vSphere is easy to install and use right out of the box—it lulls you into thinking you do not need to read the documentation. A strong word of caution is in need here: What has worked up until now in your virtualization infrastructure will not necessarily work when you put the demands of a production database onto that environment!

TIP

Read all the documentation from all the vendors. That includes VMware, Microsoft, the network vendor, and especially the storage array vendor—in particular, their SQL Server Best Practice Guides.

A virtualized database is sitting on a shared environment, even if it is only shared with other SQL database systems. Therefore, it is very important that you take the time to read all the different vendors' documentation. We place special emphasis in this book on reading the storage array documentation. Our experience has taught us that over 80% of the problems with virtualization implementations occur at the storage layer. Here are some examples:

- The storage layer is not configured properly.
- The storage layer is not sized properly.
- The storage layer is not used properly.

Our friends at VMware Support provide facts and figures that show the actual number is much higher than 80%, which further supports our real-world experience. Now that you know this fact, do not let this problem happen to you. Break out your storage array vendor documentation and do a little light reading at the breakfast table.

Beyond reading the vendors' documentation and this book, there is a whole world of additional resources out there for you, ranging from industry user groups and technology conference to websites and blogs. We have identified some of the more relevant sources of additional information in Appendix A, "Additional Resources."

The Implementation Plan

Experience has taught us the best way to start down the path of database virtualization is to have a plan. The development of the plan forces you to connect the many dots needed to successfully virtualize your production SQL Server databases. When you are virtualizing a database, it is a whole new infrastructure on which you will be running your business. There are a number of things you need to consider:

- Service-level agreements

- Recover point objectives

- Recovery time objectives

- Maximum time to recover

- Maximum tolerable downtime

- Baselining the current workload

- Baselining the existing vSphere implementation

- Estimating growth rates

- I/O requirements (I/O per sec, throughput, latency)

- Storage options (disk type/speed, RAID, flash cache)

- Software versions (vSphere, Windows, SQL Server)

- Licensing (may determine architecture)

- Workload types (OLTP, Batch, DSS, and so on)

- The accounts needed for installation and service accounts

- How you will migrate the database

- Backup and recovery options

This list is not meant to be a substitute for a real implementation plan. Instead, it is intended to get you thinking about the many things you have to consider if you want to successfully virtualize your SQL Server database. Let's talk about a few of the items in this list in more detail.

Service-Level Agreements (SLAs), RPOs, and RTOs

Take the time to sit down with your stakeholders and understand what they need from the database in terms of performance, recoverability, and uptime. Take the time to understand what the business requirements are around recovery point objectives (RPOs) and recovery time objectives (RTOs) concerning the database.

Table 4.1 is a useful chart you can use to translate the different levels of availability and what they really mean in terms of database downtime for the year, month, or week. Work with the stakeholders who rely on the database to determine just how long the business can tolerate the database being down, and then map that back to an infrastructure that is able to meet or exceed those requirements.

Table 4.1 Availability Chart

Availability Percentage	Downtime Year	Downtime Month*	Downtime Week
"Two Nines" (99%)	3.65 days	7.2 hours	1.69 hours
"There Nines" (99.9%)	8.76 hours	43.2 minutes	10.1 minutes
"Four Nines" (99.99%)	52.56 minutes	4.32 minutes	1.01 minutes
"Five Nines" (99.999%)	5.26 minutes	25.9 seconds	6.06 seconds

* Using a thirty-day month

A common mistake people make during this process is not taking into consideration the maximum tolerable database downtime for a single incident. What would be the impact if all of your acceptable annual downtime occurred in a single event? As you can see in Table 4.1, **it is possible for the database to be down for three days in a row and still have 99% availability**, but if that event happened at the wrong time of year, it could be a disaster for the business.

Our experience has taught us that many times the ways organizations are doing things today are based on the constraints that existed in the past. A virtualized infrastructure offers you options that did not exist before, and by leveraging this technology, you should be able to change the way you are currently doing things that will meet the requirements of the business, improve overall availability of the infrastructure for the database, and at the same time save money.

It also important that you set proper expectations with your stakeholders concerning what service levels you can provide. If you have not had the conversation about realistic service-level agreements that are achievable, then use this opportunity to sit down with your stakeholders and set the correct expectations.

Baselining the Existing vSphere Infrastructure

It's important to understand the capabilities of your existing vSphere implementation and what its expansion capacity is for additional workloads. It's so important that Chapter 10, "How to Baseline Your Physical SQL Server System," focuses on how to baseline your existing infrastructure to accurately determine what the current demand is in terms of memory, disk, CPU, and network.

Will the existing spare capacity of the vSphere environment be able to service the needs of a resource-intensive application such as a SQL Server database? You will hear this many times as you read this book. A common mistake people make is introducing a production database onto an existing vSphere environment that was built for capacity, not for performance, and then wonder why the database is not performing well. A database is about acceptable performance first and foremost. Therefore, before you move the database onto that existing infrastructure, make sure it's ready to get the job done.

vSphere Environment: Things to Consider

There are a number of things you should consider as you baseline your existing vSphere environment. All the information shown in Table 4.2 can be gathered using ESXTOP. This table is a subset of Table 10.4 in Chapter 10. The thresholds shown in Table 4.2 are specific to when a vSphere environment contains a mission-critical SQL server database.

The CPU metric %RDY is the percentage of time the virtual machine was ready but could not get scheduled to run on a physical CPU. Normally a value of less than 10% is acceptable, but our experience has taught us that a critical production SQL Server database is more sensitive to a lack of CPU being available, so we have lowered the recommended threshold to less than 5%. Databases that don't have enough CPU will cause increased response times for the end users.

Table 4.2 vSphere Environment SQL Server–Specific Considerations

Resource	Metric	Host/VM	Description	Threshold
CPU	%RDY	VM	CPU time spent in ready state.	<5% / VCPU
	%MLMTD	VM	The percentage of time the vCPU was ready to run but deliberately wasn't scheduled because that would violate the "CPU limit" settings. If larger than 0, the world is being throttled due to the limit on CPU.	0
Memory	MCTLSZ (MB)	Both	Amount of memory reclaimed from the resource pool by way of ballooning.	0
DISK	READs/s, Writes/s	Both	Reads and writes issued in the collection interval.	Dependent on DB Type (OLTP, Batch, DSS)

Resource	Metric	Host/ VM	Description	Threshold
	DAVG/cmd	Both	Average latency (ms) of the device (LUN).	Target for Logfiles (<2–5ms)
				Target: <10ms for ESX hosts running DBs

The CPU metric %MLMTD has been added to the list. This is the percentage of time the vCPU was ready to run but deliberately wasn't scheduled because that would violate the "CPU limit" settings. It is *not* recommended that you set CPU limits. It's important that you are aware of this metric and what it means so that you can avoid the negative impact on database performance.

The memory metric MCTLSZ is the amount of memory reclaimed from the virtual machine due to ballooning. A virtual machine in a vSphere environment that houses production SQL Server databases should never be ballooning. This is a sign of the vSphere environment experiencing memory shortages, which in turn could seriously affect that virtual machine's database performance.

The disk metric READs/s, Writes/s you should expect to see is dependent on the type of SQL Server database that is being housed on the environment. A batch environment should come back with a write-intensive profile, whereas a DSS environment should present itself as very I/O-intensive profile.

The last metric shown is DAVG/cmd. Normally for a database environment, we like to see a target of less than 10ms. In the case of SQL Server log files, our experience has taught us to strive for less than 5ms. When database log files back up, it can cause an entire domino effect on the database, thus quickly degrading overall database performance. By their very nature, database log files are heavy on sequential write activity. We like to recommend that log files be put on RAID-10 if available, or even flash drives if possible. Slow log files can mean a very slow database.

Baselining the Current Database Workload

Capturing a proper baseline is one of the most important steps you will ever take to ensure the virtualization of a production database is successful. It is very important to understand the amount of CPU, memory, disk, and network your database will need when virtualized. In Chapter 10, we go into great detail on how to perform a proper baseline.

When you baseline a production SQL Server database, it is very important that you sample that database for a *complete* business cycle. Otherwise, there is a good chance you will miss a critical workload that happens each cycle you need to account for.

Another common mistake people make is that they choose a sample set of the database that is not taken frequently enough. The default for some of the baseline tools used out there is one hour. A lot can happen within your SQL Server database in a short period of time. The smaller the sample set taken of a SQL Server database, the more accurate the baseline you will be able to build. Experience has taught us to sample CPU, memory, and disk in your SQL Server database in 15 seconds intervals or less. Experience has also taught us that you should take T-SQL samples every minute.

TIP

When you baseline a SQL Server database, make sure your sample interval is frequent. CPU, memory, and disk should be sampled in 15-second intervals or less. A lot can happen in a database in a short amount of time.

SQL Server Baseline: Things to Consider

A proper baseline of the SQL Server database is one of the most important steps you need to take to ensure the virtualization of the SQL Server database is successful. In Table 4.3, which is a subset of Table 10.2, we are noting specific targets for a SQL Server database versus an overall healthy vSphere environment, as shown in Chapter 10. The two metrics we have specific recommendations for are the Buffer Cache Hit Ratio and the Cache Hit Ratio, due to their importance on overall database performance.

The Buffer Cache is your SQL Server data cache. Before any data can be manipulated by the database, it must first reside in the buffer cache, even if it is just to be read by a simple SQL statement. This metric tells you the percentage of time a page containing the data the database needed is already sitting inside the cache. Our experience has taught us a healthy database maintains greater than a 97% hit ratio on average. When a database is first started, you would expect the ratio to be low due to the cache being cold, but over the normal course of a business cycle, this ratio should attain an average greater than 97%.

Table 4.3 SQL Server Perfmon Counters

Resource	Metric	Physical Host/VM	Description	Target
SQLServer: Buffer Manager	Buffer Cache Hit Ratio	Both	Percentage of time that the pages requested are already in cache.	>97%
	Cache Hit Ratio	Both	Percentage of time that the procedure plan pages are already in cache (for example, procedure cache hits). That is how frequently a compiled procedure is found in the procedure cache (thus avoiding the need to recompile).	Busy DB >95%, Med > 80%, Slow >70%

The Cache Hit Ratio is the database's program cache. This Cache Hit Ratio tells us how often a compiled procedure is sitting in the cache, ready for the database to execute, versus how often the procedure needs to be recompiled first. Our experience has taught us that over a business cycle, a healthy database should see a hit ration on this cache of greater than 70%. The busier the database, the higher this hit ratio should be.

A lot of great information can be harnessed from within the database concerning how it is performing and how much it needs in terms of resources. The more you know about how many resources the database needs to consume to perform its job and make sure the virtualized infrastructure can provide those resources in the amount the database needs them, when it needs them, the better your virtualized database will perform. Experience has taught us that when an effort to virtualize a database fails, it has nothing to do with the capabilities of vSphere; instead, it has to do with how the database was being implemented on the virtualized infrastructure.

Bird's-Eye View: Virtualization Implementation

Let's now take a step back and look at the overall virtualization implementation plan and then review how a database virtualization implementation plan is different. In the following outline, we show a fairly representative high-level plan for an organization taking its first steps toward virtualization:

- Phase 1: Requirements Gathering (Business and IT)
    - SLAs, RPOs, RTOs
    - Business requirements

- Phase 2: Discovery
    - Inventory the current systems
    - Baseline the current nondatabase workloads
    - Compute requirements, memory, disk, and network
    - Assess the current physical infrastructure
- Phase 3: Architecture and Design
    - License considerations
    - Rightsizing considerations
    - System configuration
- Phase 4: Validation and Testing
    - Load-test the new environment
    - Validate failover/HA
- Phase 5: Migration and Deployment
    - Physical-to-virtual conversions
    - Deployment plan
- Phase 6: Monitoring and Management
    - Resource monitoring and alerting
    - Troubleshooting and support plan
    - Backup plan

As you review this plan, notice how it has all the basic elements you would expect. Experience has taught us that when you are virtualizing databases, the plan is distinctly different from when you are taking your first steps toward virtualization. Let's now look at why a plan to virtualize a database is different.

How a Database Virtualization Implementation Is Different

In the following outline, we have an implementation plan that has been modified to fit the steps you need to follow to successfully virtualize your databases. In Phase 1, you are gathering the business and information technology requirements.

It is import to remember during this phase to fully understand the capabilities of a virtualized infrastructure and look for ways to leverage those capabilities to better meet the business requirements around high availability, service-level agreements, and database recoverability. Do not just replicate the way you do things today on a virtualized infrastructure; instead, make sure you fully leverage the capabilities of the virtualized infrastructure.

Work with your stakeholders to understand what is an acceptable database outage window for the migration to the virtualized infrastructure.

Keep in mind during requirements gathering that you will be doing a database migration as part of the implementation. For this migration, it is important that you determine when the database can be down and for how long. The requirements you gather for this one-time migration will help you determine an appropriate strategy for migrating the database.

- Phase 1: Requirements Gathering (Business and IT)
    - SLAs, RPOs, RTOs
    - Business requirements
    - *Determine acceptable database outage for migration*
- Phase 2: Discovery
    - *Baseline the current vSphere environment*
    - *Baseline the current database workloads*
    - Compute requirements, memory, disk, and network
    - Assess the current physical infrastructure
- *Phase 2.1: Database Consolidations*
    - *License considerations*
- *Phase 3: Infrastructure Adjustments*
    - System configuration
    - *Load balance environment*
- Phase 4: Validation and Testing
    - Load-test the environment
    - Validate failover/HA options
- Phase 5: Migration and Deployment
    - Physical-to-virtual conversions
    - Deployment plan

- *Database migration plan*
  - *Backup/restores*
  - *Log shipping*
  - *Database backups*
- Phase 6: Monitoring and Management
  - Resource monitoring and alerting

Phase 2: Discovery

Phase 2 is the discovery stage of the process. This is unlike the discovery phase shown in the previous plan, which is focused on obtaining a proper inventory of the current system and an assessment of the current physical infrastructure to ensure you understand the full scope of what you will be virtualizing and then establishing a baseline of the current workloads so you can establish the requirements of CPU, memory, disk, and network.

The discovery stage for virtualizing a database is focused on establishing a baseline of the existing vSphere environment and comparing it to the baseline of the existing database workload to understand where the *environment is deficient*. At this point in time, you already have an existing vSphere infrastructure onto which you will be introducing the database workload. You need to understand what will happen when you introduce the demands of a production database onto that infrastructure. Identifying those deficiencies in the existing environment and making the necessary adjustments to support the production database are important at this stage.

Phase 2.1: Database Consolidations

This is an excellent point in the process to give some serious consideration to going through a database consolidation exercise. A lot of the information you need for the database consolidation you are already gathering in the discovery phase. Based on our experience with SQL Server database consolidation efforts, we typically see greater than 50% consolidation ratios. Not only does this lower the database management footprint of the environment, it can have an impact on licensing.

Phase 3: Infrastructure Adjustments

At this point, you have analyzed the vSphere baseline and compared it to the database baseline and fully understand where the existing infrastructure is deficient. You need to make the necessary adjustments to that infrastructure so it is able to meet the resource needs of the database.

This could be as simple as adding more memory to a host, adding additional hosts to a cluster, moving virtual machines off a host to free up resources for a database, or adding a high-performance storage array to the existing environment. What is important is that once you understand where the existing infrastructure is deficient, you make the needed adjustments so when you virtualize the database your efforts will be successful.

Phase 4: Validation and Testing

It is always important you take the time to test the infrastructure and validate that it will be able to meet the demands of the database once it is placed onto that infrastructure. One of the scenarios you need to take the time to test is what happens when the physical host that houses your production database fails. You want to make sure that the infrastructure, as configured, will still be able to meet the business requirements for availability with adequate performance during this scenario.

Phase 5: Migration and Deployment

As you prepare for the migration of the database over to the virtualized environment, you have a number of ways to accomplish this. During the requirements-gathering phase, you will have determined the acceptable amount of downtime for each of the database instances you are about to virtualize. For those production databases where you have an adequate downtime window, it is common to see a backup/restore used.

For those database instances where downtime needs to be minimized, experience has taught us that the go-to method with low impact is log shipping. You pre-create the database instance on the virtualized infrastructure, move over the instance-level objects (such as database mail settings and profiles, instance-level logins, agent jobs, maintenance plans, SSIS packages, and server-level triggers), and then use log shipping to move over the data to the new database instance.

The plans for how the virtualized database will be backed up should also be reviewed. The most important step is to perform an actual restoration from this backup to ensure it works and that the DBA team is confident in the database-restoration process.

Phase 6: Monitoring and Management

You will read over and over in this book how a virtualized infrastructure is a shared infrastructure. This means changes in how you monitor and manage the environment once the production databases go live on it. It's important that the DBA communicates what they need from the team responsible for the shared environment and recognizes moving forward that they need to work with the team for the common good of all.

Summary

The focus of this chapter is summarized in its title: "Virtualizing SQL Server: Doing IT Right." That fact that you are virtualizing already means you are well on the path to doing information technology right. It's important to start off right by reading the documentation. I know this sounds old school, but sometimes old school is the right way to do things. Make it a point to read all the vendor documentation, including VMware, Microsoft, the network vendor, and the storage array vendor. We strongly encouraged you to pay special attention to the storage array vendor documentation. Our experience and VMware Support data both support the fact that the storage layer is the source of many issues that can be avoided if one takes the time to understand the storage capabilities and deploy it correctly.

We stressed the importance of a proper baseline of both the existing vSphere infrastructure and the current database infrastructure. You use these two baselines to determine where the existing infrastructure needs to be adjusted to be able to meet the demands of a production SQL Server database when it is added to the environment. We ended the chapter by walking through how a database virtualization implementation plan is different from when you first start virtualizing your infrastructure.

Chapter 5

Architecting for Performance: Design

A database can be one of the most resource-intensive systems in an environment. When I think about architecting a virtualized database for performance, I think about it in the same terms as I think about good nutrition. A healthy body requires the right intake and foundation of foods, more commonly known as the basic food groups. A properly performing virtualized database requires the right balance of memory, disk, CPU, and network resources, as shown in Figure 5.1. Without enough of any single one of these essential resources, you will never have a properly performing system. How you balance these resources is the key to getting optimal performance from your virtualized database.

If any of these resources in the IT food group is not properly sized, the overall performance of the database can be negatively impacted. One of the primary concerns DBAs have about virtualizing a database how the database will perform once it goes virtual.

In this chapter, we provide architectural considerations for running SQL Server on vSphere. The following topics are covered:

- Building a team
- Workload characterization
- Deployment considerations
- Physical hardware
- The four core resources, both virtual and physical

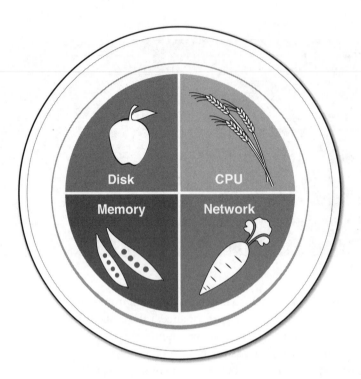

Figure 5.1   The IT food group.

Communication

Before we get into the technical aspects of architecting SQL Server, let's talk about what is likely the single most import aspect of virtualizing SQL Server. As you will see, this is a chapter of "one words," and the "one word" we have found most critical to successfully running databases in a virtual environment is *communication*. For example, when a virtualization administrator mentions vMotion, DRS, or VAAI, does the DBA know what that means? What about the term "cluster"? Whose cluster are we talking about? For DBAs, the term means one thing and for vSphere administrators it means something different.

TIP

Effective communication starts with everyone using the same language, so cross-train each other. Once everyone is speaking the same language, then when terms are thrown around, everyone understands what is being discussed. Reduce the ambiguity.

What does communication have to do with architecture? You can have the biggest servers, fastest storage, best-tuned network, but if effective communication does not exist between the teams responsible for running SQL Server, then expectations are improperly set. At some point, when the system either breaks (hey, this is IT after all) or performance does not meet "expectations," the blame game will begin. In addition, despite how good someone is at his or her job, nobody can know everything. You need to be able to rely on your coworkers who have deep knowledge and years of experience in their related fields.

If the necessary individuals are brought on board and made part of the process from the beginning, they are more likely to buy into the success of the project. They buy into it because they are part of the process. Because they are part of the process, they will want to succeed. Or, if that psycho mumbo jumbo does not work, they will buy into the project because their name is associated with it and self-preservation will kick in. They will assist because they want to keep their job.

> **NOTE**
>
> We have been on many database virtualization initiatives over the years. We have seen plenty of DBAs start the process kicking and screaming, hugging their physical servers not wanting to let them go. However, when management states the direction is to virtualize SQL and they are part of a successful project, it is fun to watch their attitudes change. (We *might* need to get out more often.)

Mutual Understanding

For the VMware administrators out there, please take off your shoes and hand them to the DBAs. DBAs, please take off your shoes and hand them to the VMware admins. Now, let's walk a bit in each other's shoes. Based on our combined years of experience working with VMware administrators and DBAs (and, yes, this is a generalization), we have found it is not always the fear of virtualization that prevents database virtualization; instead, it is the unknown, a lack of knowledge by both sides of each other's world that stalls this initiative. In addition, most vSphere administrators do not understand what it takes to manage and maintain a production database that holds more than application configuration information.

When we look at virtualization through the eyes of a DBA, their view can be summed up in one word: *shared*. DBAs have spent hours designing, sizing, and optimizing a database for a dedicated environment, and now the virtualization team is asking them to move it from their dedicated environment to a shared environment. The fact that their SQL virtual machine will be sharing the resources of the physical host with other guest operating systems causes grave concerns and raises anxiety to unprecedented levels.

So how do we lower these anxiety levels and address these concerns? In a word, *education*. Education of both the DBA and the vSphere administrator is a necessity. The DBAs need to be educated as to the benefits of virtualization, how virtualization works, and the best practices, management, and troubleshooting of a virtualized database environment. Once DBAs better understand the virtual environment, they are able to communicate with their coworkers in an effective manner.

We have spoken with many DBAs, and many of them understand that virtualization is a train that is coming and that they are staring down the tracks at its headlamp. They want to get on board and begin the process of virtualizing their databases, but they just don't know how or where to get started. They do not know what they do not know. Lack of knowledge creates fear, and it is this fear that causes angst and opposition in meetings. It is through education that we are able to reduce this angst and make progress on providing the best infrastructure on which to run a database.

For the VMware administrators, it is all about taking a breath and understanding that although the virtualization journey has been successful so far (let's face it, you are talking about putting databases onto vSphere, so you are doing something right), the way you approach the virtualization of databases is going to need to change. It needs to change because the way you virtualize nondatabase workloads is different from how you virtualize database workloads. When looking to virtualize large, complex, mission-critical workloads, vSphere administrators need to slow down and work with the individuals on other teams who have deep expertise in their respective knowledge domain to create a trusted platform for these applications. Remember, this is a journey, not something that is going to happen overnight. Also, you only get one shot to get this right. You must take the time to understand the database and DBA requirements in order to ensure success.

FROM THE TRENCHES

When hosting these educational sessions, make sure you have representation from all responsible parties. Make sure the DBAs, vSphere admins, SAN admins, security admins, and network admins are all present. This ensures everyone is hearing the same message and is able to use the same dialect.

The Responsibility Domain

We often meet with individuals who design for the highest availability possible for items that fall into their responsibility domain. We have met DBAs who design highly available clustered databases running on an enterprise flash disk with 10GB Ethernet; however, the applications connecting to the databases are not cluster aware, or better yet, they simply hold configuration information for another application. When we peel back the layers, we find the metric reported to the business is database uptime, not application end-to-end availability. As one customer told us, we cluster to protect against administrative error. The business is unaware that a particular node may be down for a month; we just show them that the database was up and able to accept requests, which is why we have 99.999% uptime.

Is that what the business has asked for? Does the business know the true cost of that uptime?

When it comes to the virtualization side of the house, any issue in the stack must be a virtualization issue, right? VMware, we are the new network (depending on how long you have been in IT will determine whether you find that funny). Virtualization administrators do not have the ability to say, "vSphere was up, and the ESXi host was up and ready to run workloads."

For the combined team, when designing a virtual SQL Server infrastructure, start with the business objectives in mind first. You can design a highly performing database that chews up and spits out IOPS, has 99.9999% availability, is spanned across multiple sites with incredible RTO, RPO for business continuity and disaster recovery; however, if these do not meet the availability requirements the business is looking for, then the design is invalid.

Center of Excellence

If you don't have time to do it right, when will you have time to do it over?
—John Wooden

We started this section with a quote from a coach. Virtualization of business-critical workloads requires a team effort, and it requires individuals on that team to work together for the good of their organization. What's needed to be successful when virtualizing SQL Server—and what we have seen lead to successful virtualization projects with our customers—is the building of a Center of Excellence (CoE) team. Now, we all need another reason to have a meeting because we do not have enough of them throughout the day. Sarcasm aside, we deem this a critical piece of successful SQL (and other mission-critical workloads) deployments.

The structure of a CoE is straightforward. The CoE team consists of one or two individuals from a respective technology to represent their team during a CoE meeting. For example, the following teams would have representation during this meeting: virtualization, DBA, networking, storage, security, and procurement, as depicted in Figure 5.2.

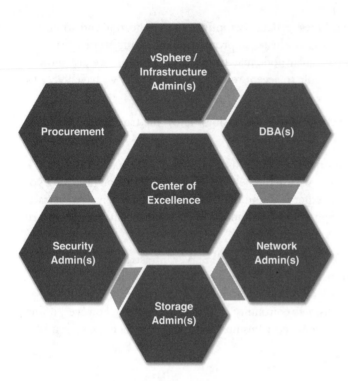

Figure 5.2   Example of a Center of Excellence team structure.

The meeting structure serves multiple purposes. One purpose is to ensure proper communication of information between teams. The CoE should be looked at as a means for teams to discuss upcoming technologies, patches, updates, upgrades, and so on that may affect the infrastructure. This is key because virtualization has a symbiotic relationship with multiple aspects of the IT landscape.

For example, say the storage team is looking to upgrade the firmware on their controllers. By communicating this change during a CoE meeting, the respective teams affected (vSphere administrators and infrastructure administrators) are responsible for checking their systems for compatibility prior to the upgrade. The last thing someone wants is an upgrade to occur and it generate problems with the infrastructure, especially if we are talking mission-critical workloads.

TIP

Always double-check the hardware compatibility list between versions of vSphere. Ensure that the hardware you are using is on the compatibility list. Also, double-check firmware versions for HBA drivers with your hardware vendors.

Another purpose of the CoE is for it to be leveraged during a database-migration project. Where we have seen this work successfully is when a migration plan has been put in place and the CoE is used to work through the migration plan. For example, as the DBAs complete their analysis of a database and determine its requirements for the virtual world, they bring these requirements to a CoE meeting. The network administrators will verify the network is configured correctly (that is, that the necessary VLANs are presented to the ESXi hosts). The vSphere administrators will determine if CPU and RAM capacity is sufficient. The SAN team will review the IOPS and capacity requirements to determine if they are able to satisfy the database requirements. If at any point a team raises its hand and says, "Stop, we can't move forward because we do not have the *<insert requirement here>* available to meet the database's requirement," the migration is put on hold until the issue is resolved. The CoE provides the means for anticipating and dealing with problems that can delay progress on your projects.

Yes, this does sound simple, even basic, but so many times these simple, basic steps are bypassed in order to get projects completed. And in the end, they end up costing more than just the time—often one's reputation takes a hit. Remember, you get one shot to virtualize these workloads, so slow down, get it right, and become an asset to your organization, not an expense.

Deployment Design

Now that we have a team in place and everyone is speaking the same language, let's start looking at the technical aspects of virtualizing SQL Server. We will begin this section with gaining an understanding of the current environment and then discuss deployment options. Most of the customers we meet with have existing databases on physical servers that they want to migrate into their VMware environment.

We are going to start with a simple exercise—understanding the SQL Server workload types. We will then move on to deployment considerations. We are talking about deployment considerations in this chapter because if we standardize our deployment process so that we have a consistent, repeatable process, then we can better predict the impact of additional SQL workloads on the existing infrastructure. This makes capacity planning easier. Consistent and repeatable deployments make management and monitoring of systems easier. When something goes wrong, having a consistent, repeatable deployment makes troubleshooting easier.

SQL Workload Characterization

When architecting for performance, it's important you first understand the different SQL Server workload types you may encounter in your environment and the characteristics associated with them. There are four types of SQL workloads:

- OLTP (Online Transaction Processing)
- OLAP (Online Analytical Processing)
- Batch/ETL (Extract Transform Load)
- DSS (Decision Support System)

OLTP workloads tend to have large amounts to small queries, sustained CPU utilization during working hours (8 a.m. to 5 p.m., for example), and are sensitive to the contention that occurs during peak resource utilization. Common examples of an OLTP database include the backend database for an online retailer as well as ERP systems such as SAP or CRM (Customer Relationship Management) systems. In addition, these workloads often experience very large amounts of very small network packets and queries and can therefore be sensitive to network latency. These systems must perform because any performance impact to these systems can directly affect a company's bottom line.

OLAP workloads are read heavy and typically contain complex queries that span a limited number of columns but a larger number of rows. These queries tend to touch a large data set.

Batch/ETL workload types tend to be write intensive, run during off-peak hours, tolerate contention better than OLTP workloads, and sometimes are network intensive. Batch workloads are often run at the end of the business day to generate reports about transactions that occurred throughout the business day. Batch/ETL workloads are broken down into three distinct phases:

- **Extract**—When multiple sources are contacted and data is obtained from these sources. This is the first phase.
- **Transform**—When an action (or actions) is taken upon the obtained data to prepare it for loading into a target system. This is the second phase.
- **Load**—When the data is loaded into the target system (which is often a data warehouse). This is the third phase.

DSS workloads are characterized by a few queries that are longer running, resource intensive (CPU, memory, I/O), and often exhibit these characteristics during month, quarter, or year-end. DSS queries favor read over write, so it is important for the system to be able to provide that data in the quickest manner possible. An example of a query run in a DSS system is "Show me all the customers over the past ten years who ever bought our 'Baseball Package' but did not buy it this year."

Putting It Together (or Not)

It is imperative architects understand the workload types they are going to virtualize before the virtualization project begins, which is why we are talking about this in the architecture section. vSphere provides functionality that helps automate the process of resource allocation to ensure databases get the resources they need, when they need them, and in the amounts needed. An example would be vSphere DRS. From a performance perspective, individuals will segment out, if possible, the OLTP, batch, and DSS workload types. The reason for this is multifaceted.

One reason, which is not often considered, is that OLTP and DSS can (and often do) run simultaneously during production hours, whereas batch workloads run during off-production hours. Another reason is OLTP transactions are shorter in duration but higher in frequency, with a mixed read/write ratio. OLTP architectures focus on delivering the highest possible IOPS and throughput to avoid disrupting business-critical operations.

DSS systems are optimized to fewer but longer running queries that are read intensive. Architects will design these systems to retrieve and present data as fast as possible to the end user's application.

With OLTP and DSS running concurrently and executing different query types and different read/write ratios, architects will segment these systems. The last thing an architect wants is for a long-running DSS query to affect their revenue-generating customer-facing application.

When comparing OLTP workloads against batch workloads, we notice their activity levels occur during different part of the business day. Put another way, OLTP runs during production hours whereas batch workloads run during off-hours. Because of this, we are able to leverage the power of virtualization and place both of these workload types onto the same physical host. This is industry specific. For some industries, we find the previous statement to be accurate, but for others this is not the case. Therefore, you need to understand the workload types and patterns associated with those workload types.

Figure 5.3 displays an OLTP-only database server running production workloads during production hours, considered to be from 7 a.m. to 6 p.m. (18:00). The average workload utilization throughout the entire day for this server is 21.9%, with 36.8% during production hours and peak utilization of 53% occurring at 10 a.m. During non-peak hours, average utilization is 7.1%, which lasts for approximately 12 hours. Translation: 50% of the day the system is working, and 50% of the day the system is not working.

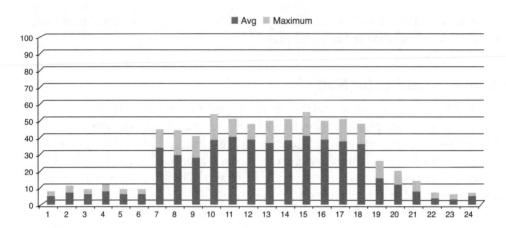

Figure 5.3   CPU utilization for an OLTP-type system.

Figure 5.4 graphs data from a system that is running batch databases. The database enters the work cycle at 1 a.m. and exits at 4 a.m. The average workload utilization for this server is 17.4%, with 75% during active hours, peaking at 95% utilization at 3 a.m. During non-peak hours, average utilization is 5.9%, which lasts for approximately 20 hours.

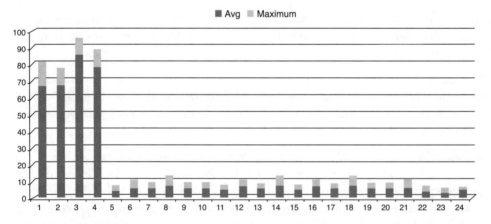

Figure 5.4   CPU utilization on a batch workload system.

When these workload types are combined on the same physical host, in separate virtual machines, there is an increase in system utilization throughout the day, without contention for the physical CPU, as depicted in Figure 5.5. Average physical CPU utilization increases to 33.3%, up from 21.9% (OLTP) and 17.4% (batch), and the server is only inactive for eight hours versus 12 hours for OLTP and 20 hours for the batch server.

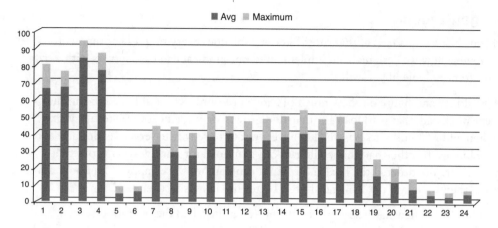

Figure 5.5 OLTP and batch workloads combined.

The benefits of this integration are better physical server utilization, improved consolidation ratios, less physical equipment to patch, service, and maintain, less power, less cooling, less cabling, cost savings due to a reduction in licensing—and the list goes on.

Let's be realistic. Today, the business is pressuring IT to perform better, deploy systems faster, all while cutting budgets year over year. If you are able to put an initiative in place where you show tangible increases in efficiency that lead to OPEX optimizations and reduction in cost, then the conversation changes and the way IT is viewed by the business also changes. Whether you want to admit it or not, you are competing against cloud providers out there who claim they can do it better, faster, and cheaper than internal IT can.

SOAPBOX

When you are virtualizing SQL Server and Tier 1 workloads in general, the emphasis on virtualization ratios must be deemphasized. Although virtualization of SQL can yield cost savings, consolidation, and other great benefits, this is not the primary reason for virtualizing SQL. If management is basing virtualization success by consolidation ratios, it is time to adjust expectations because virtualizing brings more to the table than just consolidation and cost savings. It can help improve service levels overall.

As part of a virtualization architecture design, it is important to consider workload type and factor this into the design. Use the features present within the VMware vSphere platform, such as Distributed Resource Scheduler (DRS), Affinity, and Anti-Affinity rules, to either keep virtual machines together on the same host, such as batch and OLTP databases, or to keep virtual machines apart, such as OLTP and DSS databases.

Reorganization

Did your heart skip a beat at that title? I know mine does every time I hear that word. Let's review how we designed and implemented our physical database servers with a trip down Memory Lane, if you will.

We would try and figure out how much of a given resource we would need to run the current workload, that workload's anticipated growth over the next three to five years, and then add X% buffer to be safe. Then we went to our favorite server vendor and asked for the biggest box they had that could run our workload for our five-year projected requirement. We ordered the box, and when it came in, we were happy… for about a week because then we found out a bigger, faster, better model was just released!

We unboxed our new hardware, racked it, stacked it, installed the operating system, installed SQL, and then we were off and running—and, boy, weren't we happy. It was the best of times… for about a week. Because, sure enough, a project popped up and, wouldn't you know it, the project required a database and there was nowhere to put it. Therefore, the database ended up on the database server you just racked and stacked.

Over time, these database servers become populated with "projects," DBAs shift to a mentality of "if it fits, put it on." This is known as "consolidation." So many times when we speak to DBAs about the benefits of virtualization, they reply in kind with, "We already consolidate our databases to get the maximum performance out of our servers." True, they are running those boxes to the limit, but are they running them as efficiently and as effectively as possible? Perhaps the single biggest downside we have seen with this configuration is security.

Let's dive into what we are talking about concerning security. What we find in the majority of our conversations with customers is that as these database servers are filling up, the speed at which the business is requesting database creation does not allow for proper segmentation. So what ends up happening is that internal, production databases are now run among third-party databases, test databases, development databases, and so on.

There are a couple challenges here. With SQL Server patching, the lowest common denominator is the instance level. So what happens when a third party does not support the latest SQL Server patch that your information security team is asking you to install to prevent a serious security risk? Do you patch the server to prevent the risk and satisfy the information security team, or do you run in an unsupported configuration for this third-party application? What if this is a customer-facing, revenue-generating application?

Another item to consider and discuss is compliance. We have had many DBAs tell us they are being asked by Audit and Compliance whether their database server will meet their particular industry's regulatory guidance. For a lot of customers, the answer is no.

What do we do about all of this? Reorganization. Because we are going down the path of virtualizing our physical SQL Server environment, why not take the opportunity to reorganize our database servers into compliant stacks. Identify and group databases according to their operational level (production, QA, test, development), internal development, third party, adherence to industry regulation (HIPPA, SOX, and so on), and whether they play well with others. This last grouping of databases includes recipients of bad up-level code, those that have unique performance requirements, those that require special maintenance windows outside the other database, those that host applications from a third party that does not always support the latest patches, and so on. The design goals here are to group databases that will optimize security, stability, and performance, thus leading to decreased operational overhead and producing a less complex environment to manage with a smaller group of standard configurations.

> **TIP**
>
> Grouping databases according to function, operational level, compliance requirement, and other factors can lead to improved operations, increased security, and a more stable SQL Server environment.

As we have discussed in this section, the typical deployment we see in the physical world within our customer base is a large physical server loaded with as much RAM as the server can possibly hold. The SQL Server is configured with multiple instances and many databases sitting behind each instance. What we see after customers begin their journey down SQL Server virtualization is smaller virtual machines ("smaller" being relative), with SQL Server being configured with only one instance. However, we do have customers who carry over the same model of SQL Server running multiple instances and supporting many databases.

It is important to remember the entire system when designing your architecture. Do not forget about features within the vSphere platform, such as DRS, vMotion, Storage DRS, Storage I/O Control, and Network I/O Control, just to cite a few, and how some of these features work more efficiently with smaller virtual machines than larger virtual machines. We are not saying these features do not work or work well with larger systems. Instead, what we are trying to convey is that you need to make your design agile, flexible, and highly available while delivering the necessary performance requirements. There are more places for smaller virtual machines to fit and schedule than there are for very large virtual machines.

The reason customers end up with a design featuring relatively smaller virtual machines running only one instance and many databases behind it is to take advantage of the scale-out performance and operational benefits of cloud computing. Customers find it easier to scale out than to scale up. Yes, this means there may be more operating systems to manage, but with the amount of automation that exists today, this is becoming less and less of a concern—especially when one of the objectives of virtualizing mission-critical databases is reducing operational risk and improving SLAs.

Tiered Database Offering

Traditionally administrators have been accommodating (albeit reactive) to requests for physical SQL Servers. Let us know if this sounds familiar: A request comes in for a database server and it takes a team of individuals to satisfy the request. Usually someone (and by "someone" we mean multiple people) undergoes requirements gathering, scopes and designs the architecture, procures the hardware (server, storage, network ports, and so on), deploys the physical server, installs the operating system, and finally turns the system over to the individual who requested it. That sound about right? How long does this process take? Weeks or months?

As we move toward a more "on-demand" world, where our internal customers are looking to outside sources (that is, cloud infrastructure providers) to acquire resources because "it takes internal IT too long to provision my system," we need to become more agile, more responsive, and more dynamic in order to meet these demands. The first step in this journey is virtualization—surprise! But to virtualize is simply not enough. Self-service and automation are two key ingredients that must be implemented.

Your internal customers must have the ability to access a self-service portal that allows them to "build" a database server of their choosing. Controls must be placed around this, because you cannot have end users running around provisioning servers left and right with no controls or governance in place. It is important that this portal be configurable to meet the needs of your business. It needs to be flexible and agile, and it cannot be tied (dependent) in any way to the physical infrastructure. Enter VMware vCloud Automation Center, because a key design principle of this product is infrastructure independence, meaning there is a layer of abstraction, not dependence, between the automation tool and the things it automates.

VMware vCloud Automation Center allows you to provide a directory-integrated portal for end user self-service that provides single- and multiple-tier systems that are customizable (CPU, RAM, disk), provides simple and complex approval processes, and offers lifecycle management of the system (whether physical, virtual, or residing in a supported cloud vendor's infrastructure). In addition to vCloud Automation Center, we suggest the use of VMware App Director. App Director provides application release management. Between these two products, you can have an end user sign on to vCenter Automation Center, request a multitier application (web server, application server, and database server) with their desired amount of RAM, vCPU, and disk, and have the operating system and appropriate applications such as SQL Server deployed into the guest system. You can even populate tables within the SQL Server database!

Although we highly recommend implementing a solution that automates the creation and management of a server, we understand that organizations may be at different stages along their journey. Other options are available to help with the automation of SQL Server deployments. One of those options is to leverage SQL Server SysPrep. With SQL Server SysPrep, you can deploy a standalone installation of SQL Server to an end point and finish the configuration of SQL Server at a later time. An option here is to create a VMware template with both Windows and SQL Server SysPrep so that when a database is requested, the machine is turned over to the requestor, with the operating system and most of the SQL Server installation completed.

> **NOTE**
>
> SQL Server SysPrep is limited to standalone instances of SQL Server and is supported with SQL Server 2008 R2 and later. To learn more, including limitations, go to http://msdn.microsoft.com/en-us/library/ee210754.aspx. For information on deploying SQL Server 2012 via SysPrep, go to http://msdn.microsoft.com/en-us/library/ee210664.aspx.

It is important to combine automation with choice. What we mean by "choice" may be different from what has been in place previously in your infrastructure. As stated earlier in this section, if we were to audit the database servers in your infrastructure, would any two of them be the same? Maybe, but more likely than not there is a wide variance between deployed servers. What we suggest is working with the business to predetermine SQL Server baselines. We typically start with four baselines in customer deployments— small, medium, large, and custom—with "custom" requiring a variance document being submitted to obtain the appropriate approvals. Here's a list of the items that make up the baselines:

- Windows operating system(s)
- SQL Server version(s)
- SQL Server edition(s)
- Virtual CPU(s)
- Amount of RAM
- Disk configuration options
- Networking options
- Virtual SCSI adapter (number/type)

- High availability options

- Backup options

- Business continuity and disaster recovery options

Some of the items listed will be dynamic within all tiers, meaning at any tier of the stack a user can choose between two different operating system choices currently supported by the organization. Other options will be toggled on or off within a tier. The reason for the toggle is that a database does not have to be large to be mission critical to your organization. Table 5.1 provides an example of what a tiered model in your organization might look like. It is important to remember that this is a starting point and that the information in the table may look different in your organization. The memory in the table is based on the recommendation of 6–8GB per vCPU. On the lower vCPU limit, we use the 6GB calculation, and for the top vCPU limit, we use the 8GB calculation.

Table 5.1   Sample Tiered Database Offering

Database Tier	SQL Server Version	SQL Server Edition	Virtual CPUs	RAM	Disks	vSCSI Adapters
Platinum	2008R2 or 2012	Enterprise, Standard	8–12	48–96GB	1 OS/Binary 1-3 Data 1-3 Log 1 TempDb	2–4
Gold	2008R2 or 20012	Enterprise, Standard	4–7	24–56GB	1 OS/Binary 1 Data 1 Log	2
Silver	2008R2 or 2012	Standard	1–3	6–18GB	1 OS/Binary 1 Data/Log	2
Custom	2008R2 or 2012	Datacenter, Enterprise, or Standard	1 max supported	50% to 75% of physical host size	Custom layout	2–4

Remember, Table 5.1 is meant to be used as a starting point for your organization. Work with the appropriate individuals within your organization to determine the correct options and variables to place into your tiered database offering. In addition, if a database is deployed in a specific tier and needs more than what was assigned, then the self-service portal should allow the user to request additional resources and have this request adhere to existing approval and change-control procedures.

By moving to a tiered database offering, commonly known as Database as a Service (DaaS), you will achieve several benefits—the first being improved time to delivery. Remember, you are being measured against a cloud provider that can deploy systems in minutes. By working to achieve standards and shifting the decision making to the individual requesting the system, you have accomplished two things. Now the end user feels empowered to make the appropriate decision based on their requirements. The second is a byproduct of the first: how many man-hours have been returned to the business because we no longer have a team of individuals determining what is the "right" server to provide the individual requesting the server.

But wait, there's more! Service providers charge their customers based on the options they choose when building their systems. Putting a solution such as VMware vCenter Automation Center in place lays the foundation to begin showing the application owner and the business what it costs to run these systems and, if IT decides to, to begin charging for the services delivered. Think about it: If someone is paying for the number of CPUs and RAM they are consuming, are they not more likely to appropriately size their systems? You can use the term "business transparency" to replace "charge back."

Procurement now shifts from managing individual requests as they come into the infrastructure and all the individual components of that infrastructure (server, storage, network, and so on) to the platform level. Procurement now becomes about ensuring enough resources to satisfy the platform. Having a centralized system managing the life cycle of your infrastructure components provides greater insight into consumption of services, which in turn gives better transparency and visibility into hardware utilization and the need for additional resources.

TIP

To drive down operational complexities and increase the ability to deliver requests to the business, consider a tiered database offering and personalized delivery of these services. Use this service to provide transparency concerning the cost of running these services.

Physical Hardware

Now we are going to discuss the importance of selecting the right hardware for running your database workloads. Buy the biggest, fastest, baddest servers and storage and you will be alright. There, that about does it, right? If it were only that simple. However, this is how a lot of physical servers that are running database workloads today are purchased. One of the main reasons for this is the limitations of the physical world. We have to plan for how large this database (or databases) will be three to five years out—and how often are we right? How often do we end up placing databases on these servers because there is room and not because this is where we intended them to reside when we originally designed the system. Say it with me, "consolidation."

One of the first places to start when considering physical server hardware to run your SQL virtual machines is to take an inventory of the makes and models of hardware present in the data center today and combine this with the future direction of the organization. For example, is the organization moving away from rack mount servers toward blade servers? Then try to determine whether the direction in which the organization is moving will impose any constraints to your design. An example may be that a Tier 1 database requires more RAM than is currently available in the blade make and model that your organization procures.

CPU

Next, it is important to understand the proper amount of physical CPU power that will be necessary to run the databases you are looking to virtualize. Remember, a virtual environment pools and abstracts resources; therefore, we must adjust our vernacular to reflect this change. For DBAs, it is important to change from "how many CPUs the database requires" to "what the aggregate clock cycle is the database requires." Let's look at this in more detail.

Historically, from a CPU perspective, in the physical world DBAs look to procure as many CPUs as possible in their systems because they are planning for three to five years out and they want to get these resources upfront and not have to fight for them later. When SQL Server is virtualized and the right versions of the Windows operating system and SQL Server are running, virtual machines can have the memory size and virtual CPU count increased while the systems are running. If the required versions of Windows for an operating system or SQL Server are not available, the option still remains; however, it may become a downtime operation. If AlwaysOn is used and automated failover is available, you can update the configuration of the standby node, let it catch up and then fail over, and then update the primary node, let it sync back up, and then fail back—all with almost no disruption. The same could be said of a Failover Cluster Instance environment: You only have as much downtime as it takes for two failovers to occur.

Another point to understand in a virtual environment is how resources from virtual machines are allocated time against physical components of the server. For vSphere, this is handled by the Scheduler. The CPU Scheduler's main goal is to "assign execution contexts to processors in a way that meets system objectives such as responsiveness, throughput, and utilization" (https://www.vmware.com/files/pdf/techpaper/VMware-vSphere-CPU-Sched-Perf.pdf). Therefore, scheduling is when the hypervisor needs to identify and execute the CPU instructions of a given virtual machine. The more virtual machines that exist on a physical server, the more complex this operation becomes. Complexity becomes further increased as virtual machines vary in virtual CPU configurations because the hypervisor needs to schedule all the virtual CPUs to execute in a timely order.

The design goal is to run your SQL Server virtual machines with enough virtual CPUs to satisfy peak requirements, and not a single virtual CPU more. By adding unnecessary virtual CPUs to the virtual machines, you make the hypervisor's job of scheduling more complex, and this may cause unnecessary delays in the scheduling of your virtual machines, thus introducing unnecessary performance issues.

> **TIP**
>
> It is important to understand how the current version of vSphere handles scheduling of virtual CPUs. To learn more, read this whitepaper: https://www.vmware.com/files/pdf/techpaper/VMware-vSphere-CPU-Sched-Perf.pdf.

For those who are looking to migrate physical databases into vSphere, a good starting point is VMware Capacity Planner. Run VMware Capacity Planner against the target servers to get an understanding of the current CPU workload. It is important to understand the sample intervals for which VMware Capacity Planner has been configured and whether this meets the cyclical nature of the databases under analysis. The last thing you want is your analytical tool to miss a workload spike inside the database because it did not fall within the sample interval. Several analytical tools are available to perform this analysis, so be sure to choose the right one. We recommend reviewing the baselining discussion in Chapter 10, "How to Baseline Your Physical SQL Server System."

> **NOTE**
>
> Use the right tool that will capture the peaks and valleys of the target database server's resource utilization. In addition, understand what level the tool operates at: the entire server, SQL Server instance, or individual database. If you miss peaks, you risk under-sizing your virtual machines and the physical hardware required to run them successfully.

From a design perspective, a typical starting point is 2 vCPUs:1 physical core . As you increase the number of vCPUs in your virtual machines, this starting point will require adjustment due to the requirements necessary to schedule this virtual machine's vCPUs. The previously stated numbers are to be treated as dynamic and not as definitive guidance or used as a benchmark for density. This is a starting point that should be adjusted up or down based on workload, processor type, processor speed, and other factors. Remember, our guidance is to always start conservative with Tier 1 workloads such as SQL Server. It is always easier to add additional work to a physical server than it is to ask management for a new physical server because you underestimated the requirements.

Memory

When it comes to sizing databases running on virtual machines and physical servers, we will again start with understanding what the current environment supports and can tolerate as well as the future stated direction. It should come as no surprise that in the majority of our engagements, we find customers run out of physical RAM before they run out of physical CPU resources on their vSphere hosts running database workloads. The exception to this, we have found, is when customers insert flash into the physical servers. From a design and architectural perspective, you need to understand if there is a desire and need to implement flash storage inside the physical server. If this is the case, work with VMware and the flash storage vendor to understand how the implementation affects the overall memory sizing of the physical hosts and potentially the consolidation ratio to ensure maximum benefit for your investment.

Balancing the cost of memory versus the number of virtual machines a physical host can run is an art. As we have stated several times throughout this book, when we begin to virtualize database workloads, consolidation ratios are the least important, and they should not be the primary goal. Again, a good starting point for this is to leverage VMware Capacity Planner against your physical database servers to get a high-level understanding of the RAM requirements for a system.

Earlier in this chapter, we discussed reorganization. If this is a strategy you are looking to implement for your database virtualization initiative, it is critical to use a tool that can provide per-database statistics. Not all tools are created equal and will report at different levels of the server. What we mean by this is that some tools work at the system level, some work at the SQL instance level, and others work at the individual database level. Make sure the tool you select for this project can provide the granularity needed for your initiative.

Virtualization Overhead

In addition to understanding what the current environment will require, it is important to understand the virtualization overhead of running virtual machines and to account for this in your sizing and management of the physical ESXi hosts. Table 5.2 is from the vSphere 5.5 Resource Management Guide and provides a sample overview of the memory overhead associated with running a virtual machine. It is important to note that changing either the number of virtual CPUs or amount of RAM assigned to a virtual machine changes the amount required by ESXi to run the host.

Table 5.2 Sample Overhead Memory on Virtual Machines

Memory (MB)	1 VCPU	2 VCPU	4 VCPU	8 VCPU
256	20.29	24.28	32.23	48.16
1024	25.90	29.91	37.86	53.82
4,096	48.64	52.72	60.67	76.78
16,384	139.62	143.98	151.93	168.60

It is important to understand the virtual machine overhead and to manage this appropriately as you scale your systems. Not managed appropriately, the physical host can run out of physical memory, thus affecting virtual machine performance. Ensuring SQL Server has the appropriate amount of memory available is crucial to SQL performing well in any environment.

We will get into more detail concerning the memory-reclamation techniques that vSphere leverages in Chapter 7, "Architecting for Performance: Memory." However, we do want to mention them here, along with our recommendations. Here is a list of the techniques employed by the vSphere hypervisor:

- Transparent page sharing

- Memory ballooning

- Memory compression

- Swapping

Our recommendation is to leave these settings enabled. This comes from the fact that in a properly designed production environment, the environment should be architected to avoid memory contention. In addition, should an event arise that causes memory exhaustion of the physical host, if some of the recommendations are disabled, you are forcing vSphere to default to the action of last resort, swapping, which has the heaviest impact on performance. Based on the details covered in Chapter 7, it is our opinion that when we compare the overhead associated with functions such as transparent page sharing, memory ballooning, and memory compression, there is greater benefit to leaving these features enabled compared to the performance benefits associated with disabling them.

Swapping, Paging? What's the Difference?

Regarding the swap file location, it is important that you understand the two areas within a virtualized SQL Server implementation that need attention. The first is the Windows page file. This is created and managed by the operating system. Windows, if it deems necessary, can move pages from memory to local disk. The second level is at the ESXi host level. vSphere will reclaim memory when the host is under memory contention. A properly architected implementation will ensure that the operating system has been configured to avoid paging and that the VMs have been configured and are running on ESXi hosts that are properly sized to avoid swapping.

vSphere provides the ability to locate the ESXi host swap file location on SSDs inside the ESXi host. This is called "host-local swap." Although this is an option, it should be viewed as a failsafe option used as a stopgap measure until the memory exhaustion issue can be resolved. If you are implementing host-local swap, keep in mind vMotion times will take longer because the swap file must also be migrated across the network from the source host to the destination host. This also means you have expensive SSDs in each host that are not being optimally utilized given that memory contention should be very unlikely in a properly designed environment.

We have seen some customers design their ESXi host swap files on shared storage and present this to all their ESXi hosts (for example, implementations using replication technologies and not wanting to replicate the virtual machine swap file). A word of caution around this design: If the LUN containing the vswp files fails, then all virtual machines configured to use this LUN have just had their vswp files ripped out from under them, and this could potentially lead to guest operating system failure. If you are considering relocation of your vswp files (for which there are valid reasons), run them on a reduced number of LUNs or a particular LUN per host. We do not think it is a good economic use of SSDs to have swap files on them; plus, if your VMs have large RAM allocations, you could find a situation where a VM can't power on because of insufficient local SSD space for the swap file if there isn't a big enough reservation. Once you're swapping, it's already too late. A LUN expands the failure zone to all virtual machines having vswp files residing on that LUN. Consider two LUNs, at a minimum, because this reduces complexity while reducing risk.

> **NOTE**
>
> To change the default location of the virtual machine swap file, see this VMware KB article: http://kb.vmware.com/kb/1004082. Keep in mind your failure zones and operational impact when making this change.

Large Pages

By default, VMware vSphere enables large pages. Mem.AllocGuest.LargePage is set to 1 out of the box, which means it is enabled. By default, ESXi will back all memory requests with large pages. These large pages are broken down to 4KB in size to support transparent page sharing (TPS). This is done to maximize the use of the precious translation lookaside buffer (TLB) space and to increase performance.

Microsoft SQL does support the use of large pages, and beginning with SQL Server 2012 this is enabled by default when the account running sqlservr.exe has been given the Lock Pages in Memory permission. Versions prior to SQL Server 2012 require the Lock Pages in Memory right as well as Trace Flag 834 to be enabled. More information on how to configure these settings can be found in Chapter 7. Note that large pages are allocated at boot time by SQL Server, so a restart of the virtual machine is required after configuration of these settings.

> **NOTE**
>
> Make sure to set the Lock Pages in Memory privilege (SQL 2012) and also turn on large pages for SQL (version prior to SQL 2012). See this Microsoft KB article for more information: http://support.microsoft.com/kb/920093.

> **TIP**
>
> When large page support has been properly configured, SQL Server will attempt to allocate contiguous pages in memory at boot time. This can cause longer boot times for the SQL Server virtual machine. Refer to this blog post for more information: http://blogs.msdn.com/b/psssql/archive/2009/06/05/sql-server-and-large-pages-explained.aspx.

NUMA

NUMA stands for non-uniform memory architecture. When looking at your server, you will notice sockets, cores, and memory residing on these servers. Memory is associated with the sockets and core. Cores will preferably access memory local to them versus memory located on another "stack." This is all about data locality: The better the locality, the better the performance. The goal here is to have the cores access memory local to them versus having to travel to another socket and core stack to access memory. This is known as "remote memory access" or "cross-socket communication" and has performance implications because the request has to travel across the front-side bus of the motherboard to access the remote memory region and then back to the originating core to return the information. Figure 5.6 details out a NUMA configuration. NUMA cross-talk occurs when the CPU on a NUMA node must traverse interconnects to access memory on another NUMA node.

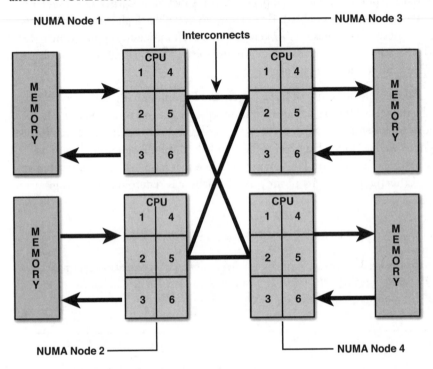

Figure 5.6   Sample NUMA architecture.

NUMA is configured in the BIOS of your physical servers. Always read your server vendor's documentation, but typically NUMA is enabled by disabling node interleaving in the BIOS. Having NUMA enabled is usually the default setting.

VMware has supported NUMA since ESX 2.5. This means that if your physical hardware both supports and is configured for NUMA, the hypervisor will work to maximize performance of the system. There are features in the vSphere platform that we will discuss in the paragraphs that follow because they will come into play when architecting SQL Server databases to run on a vSphere host.

The first feature is Wide NUMA. Wide NUMA was introduced in vSphere 4.1. Using the image in Figure 5.6, we have a four-socket, six-core system with hyper-threading enabled. If a virtual machine was created that had six vCPUs, this virtual machine would be assigned to run on one of the four available NUMA nodes. This designation is called the virtual machine's home NUMA node. Now, a 12 vCPU virtual machine is created. As part of determining placement, hyper-threading is ignored, so that means this virtual machine will span two and only two NUMA nodes in our physical server. The way this works is the maximum number of physical cores in a socket will become the minimum number of vCPUs assigned for that virtual machine. For the 12-vCPU virtual machine running on a four-socket, six-core box with hyper-threading enabled, the NUMA Scheduler will assign a home NUMA node (node 1, 2, 3, or 4) and then manage six of the 12 vCPUs on this NUMA node. The remaining six will be assigned another home node on another NUMA node. Figure 5.7 provides a visual example of this. Notice how NUMA node 3 has been designated as home node 1, and six vCPUs are assigned to this NUMA node. Then, NUMA node 1 was selected as home node 2 to run the remaining six vCPUs.

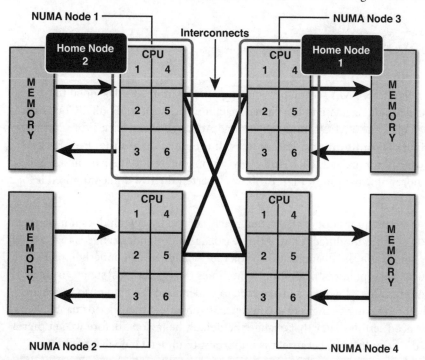

Figure 5.7   Placement of a 12-vCPU virtual machine by NUMA Scheduler.

You will notice the NUMA Scheduler did not use more NUMA nodes than necessary to accomplish this allocation. The reason for this is data locality. Also, remember that hyper-threading is ignored during the factoring of NUMA node assignment, and the number of cores is used. However, if the memory of a NUMA node is insufficient, then memory from a remote NUMA node will be accessed. Often, people forget to include the memory size of a NUMA node when designing their systems. It is important to note with Wide NUMA managing a Wide VM that the memory is interleaved across the two NUMA nodes. How did VMware address this? They introduced the second feature, vNUMA

VMware introduced vNUMA in vSphere 5.0. vNUMA requires virtual hardware version 8.0 (or higher). vNUMA exposes the underlying physical servers' NUMA architecture to the guest virtual machine. With most major operating systems being NUMA aware, exposing NUMA to the guest operating system allows for better memory locality. vNUMA is automatically enabled for guest virtual machines with nine or more vCPUs. Why the reason for nine? Well, vSphere 4.1 had support for up to eight vCPUs, and vSphere 5.0 introduced support for 32 vCPUs. Therefore, to avoid any legacy issues with upgrades, this feature was enabled, by default, for virtual machines with nine or more vCPUs.

> **NOTE**
> vNUMA is disabled when CPU Hot Plug is enabled.

To change the default vNUMA setting of requiring nine or more vCPUs, open the vSphere Web Client and navigate to the virtual machine you want to modify. Click **Edit Properties**, then click the **VM Options** tab, expand **Advanced**, and click **Edit Configuration** to the right of **Configuration Parameters**. If the **numa.vcpu.maxPerVirtualNode** parameter is not present, click **Add Row** and manually add the parameter. See Figure 5.8 for more information. In Figure 5.8, we inserted the row and configured it for eight cores.

vNUMA is set upon the first boot of the virtual machine, and by default does not change unless the vCPU count is modified. One of the reasons this does not change is that not all operating systems (or even all applications) tolerate a change to an underlying physical NUMA infrastructure topology. In addition, sometimes the operating system can adjust, but the application cannot. Therefore, make sure to understand the applications you are working with before making changes that could negatively affect their performance. We will discuss advanced settings later that change the default behaviors. Before we get there, we will discuss the defaults first, because it is important to understand what vSphere is doing under the covers and to use this information to determine whether a change is necessary.

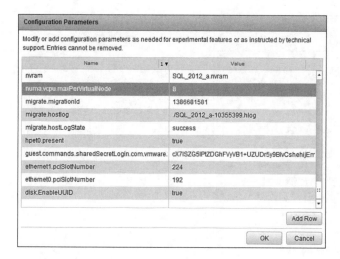

Figure 5.8 Advanced setting numa.vcpu.maxPerVirtualNode.

The method by which the vNUMA topology is set is as follows: Upon the first boot of a vNUMA-enabled virtual machine, a check is made to see if the Cores per Socket (virtual socket) setting has been changed from the default value of 1. If the default value of 1 is present, then the underlying physical server's NUMA architecture is used. If the default value of Cores per Socket has been modified, this determines the virtual machine's NUMA architecture. See Figure 5.9 for a screenshot of where this setting is located.

If you are going to change the default Cores per Socket setting, change it to an integer multiple or integer divisor of the physical server's NUMA architecture. For example, if you have a four-socket, six-core server, the Cores per Socket setting should be 2, 3, or 6. Do not factor hyper-threading into your calculation. When you are running a vSphere cluster that has mixed physical NUMA configurations and you elect to modify the default Cores per Socket setting, select a setting that aligns with the smallest NUMA node size across all physical hosts in that vSphere cluster.

It is our recommendation that the default setting of 1 for Cores per Socket be used. The reason for this recommendation is due to simplification, maintenance, and long-term management. This parameter is set upon first boot for the virtual machine and does not change if the virtual machine is vMotioned or cold-migrated to a physical server with a different underlying NUMA architecture. This can result is a negative performance impact on the virtual machine. The only time this setting is updated, by default, is when the vCPU count is modified.

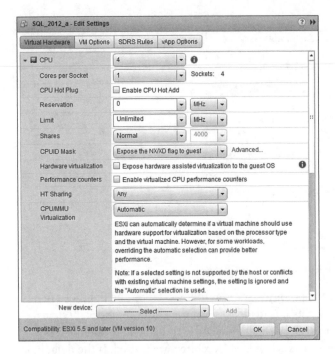

Figure 5.9   The Cores per Socket setting.

REAL WORLD

Let's be honest for a minute. Let's say that 21 months (I like odd numbers) after modifying this setting on a SQL Server virtual machine, you introduce new hardware into your vSphere cluster with a different underlying NUMA architecture, and you vMotion the SQL virtual machine to the new hardware. Are you going to remember to change the setting? When the DBA team calls and says that despite you moving the SQL virtual machine to newer, bigger, faster hardware, performance is worse, are you going to remember that the Cores per Socket setting may be causing this performance dip? If you need to adjust the parameter, adjust it. Just make sure you have well-defined operational controls in place to manage this as your environment grows.

If possible, when selecting physical servers for use in your clusters, attempt to adhere to the same underlying NUMA architecture. We know, this is easier said than done. Initially when a cluster is built, this is more realistic; however, as time is introduced into the cluster and servers need to be added for capacity or replaced for life cycle, this makes adhering to the same NUMA architecture more difficult.

One final note on NUMA. We are often asked, "How do I figure out my server's NUMA node size?" The best way is to work with your server provider and have them detail out sockets, cores, and memory that make up a NUMA node. This is important to ask, because the size of a NUMA node is not always the number of cores on a chip; take, for example, the AMD Piledriver processor, which as two six-core processors on a single socket. AMD Bulldozer has two eight-core processors on a single physical socket, also making it two NUMA nodes.

Hyper-Threading Technology

Hyper-Threading Technology (HTT) was invented by Intel and introduced in the Xeon processors in 2002. At a high level, HTT has two logical processors residing on the same physical core, and these two logical resources share the same resources on the core. The advantage of this is if the operating system is able to leverage HTT, the operating system can more efficiently schedule operations against the logical processors. When one logical core is not being used, the other processor is able to leverage the underlying resources, and vice versa.

> **NOTE**
>
> IBM had simultaneous multithreading as early as the 1960s: http://en.wikipedia.org/wiki/Simultaneous_multithreading.

In a vSphere environment, this provides the Scheduler more logical CPUs to schedule against, thus increasing throughput. This allows for concurrent execution of instructions from two different threads to run on the same core. This is not a doubling of throughput, and the amount increase varies depending on the processor, workload, and sometimes which way the wind is blowing.

HTT is enabled in the BIOS of the physical server, so double-check with your server manufacturer on validating if this feature is turned on for your hardware. HTT is enabled by default on ESXi. The VMkernel, which is responsible for the scheduling, will do its best to schedule a multi-vCPU virtual machine on two or more different cores. The VMkernel will attempt to spread this as wide as possible, unless you have changed the preferHT advanced setting, while adhering to things like NUMA, to get the best possible performance. If this is not possible, the VMkernel will schedule the multi-vCPU virtual machine against logical processors on the same core. vSphere will attempt to schedule against cores first, and once those are in use it will move on to using the logical portion of the core. In addition, the CPU Scheduler will track how much time is spent by a world (an execution context that is scheduled against a processor) scheduled against a full core versus a partial core. Because time spent in a partial core does not equate to equivalent performance of time spent in a full core, the CPU Scheduler will track this time and, if necessary, move a world from executing against a partial core to executing against a full core.

> **NOTE**
>
> A virtual machine is a collection of "worlds." A world exists for each vCPU, MKS (mouse, keyboard, screen), and the virtual machine monitor (VMM). These worlds are executed against a CPU (physical or logical) via the CPU Scheduler.

There have been two changes in vSphere 5.0 that allow for fairer balancing of worlds against full and partial cores. The first is a contention check. The CPU Scheduler tracks how much time is lost due to contention on behalf of HTT. Because time lost can even out over time, meaning laggards can catch up, as longs as the fairness threshold that would cause the CPU Scheduler to migrate the world from a partial core to a full core is not exceeded, the world will continue to be scheduled against the logical processor.

The second change in vSphere 5.0 is that the CPU Scheduler will take into account when both logical processors are busy on a core; in previous versions of vSphere this was not the case. The amount of time a world spends executing is tracked as CPU Time, and the tracking of this is called "charging." The amount of time charged for a world in CPU Time is affected by execution against a partial core. As of vSphere 5.0, the amount of time charged when both logical CPUs are busy is greater, which leads to the ability of a vCPU that has fallen behind to catch up to its other vCPU partners in a more timely fashion.

> **NOTE**
>
> To learn more about the CPU Scheduler and optimizations, we recommend reading "The CPU Scheduler in VMware vSphere 5.1" (https://www.vmware.com/files/pdf/techpaper/VMware-vSphere-CPU-Sched-Perf.pdf) and "The vSphere 5.5 Resource Management Guide" (https://www.vmware.com/files/pdf/techpaper/VMware-vSphere-CPU-Sched-Perf.pdf).

So, what does all this mean for virtualizing SQL Server? It is important that the DBAs and the vSphere administrators both understand whether HTT is enabled and in use. In addition, it is important that performance be monitored on the system. Remember, the Windows OS has no idea it is being virtualized, so when it sees it has been assigned 32 cores, it thinks these are full cores, although under the covers these vCPU worlds may be executing against a logical core. HTT is good; it allows you to get more useful work done and more performance out of SQL. Our recommendation is to use HTT. Just remember to account for HTT when it comes to performance and sizing of the SQL Server virtual machines on your ESXi hosts.

Memory Overcommitment

Next up on the memory train is a discussion of memory overcommitment. Earlier in this chapter, we discussed vSphere's memory-reclamation techniques and our recommendation to leave them enabled. When running SQL Servers on vSphere, it is our recommendation to allow the SQL Servers time to bake, or run in production, on the vSphere hosts. The baking time we recommend is at least one business cycle. This will allow you to capture, via your monitoring tool, the performance peaks of the SQL Server. There are some databases that sit dormant for 2.9 months a quarter, but when they ramp up for that last week of the quarter, there better not be anything in their way or else! This also where a tool like vCenter Operations Manager comes in handy because it can track performance of the database over extended periods of time. Basically, make sure vCenter is reporting state usage less than what is present on the physical host.

Reservations

To reserve or not to reserve, that is the question. From a DBA perspective, the concept of a shared environment can be, well, not appealing. DBAs are coming from an environment in which they knew exactly how much of the physical server's RAM they had (for those wondering, the answer is "all of it") and they are moving into a world where the physical server's RAM is now shared—and don't even think about those newfangled memory-reclamation features. From the vSphere administrator's perspective, it is about optimization of the underlying resources—getting as much out of the physical asset as possible.

Before we get too far down this road, our advice to you is to remember there is no such thing as a free lunch. Remember, there are tradeoffs whenever you enable or disable a feature, turn this dial up, or turn that dial down. So how does one resolve this conundrum? Enter reservations. Reservations provide vSphere the ability to reserve, or dedicate, a set amount of a resource to a virtual machine and only that virtual machine. Even when the physical host enters an overcommitted state for vRAM, a reservation guarantees physical RAM will be available for the virtual machine with the reservation. Reservations are set on a per-virtual machine basis. Therefore, if you build a SQL Server virtual machine with 32GB of virtual RAM on top of a host with 256GB of physical RAM, you can reserve and dedicate 32GB of RAM on the physical host to this SQL Server virtual machine. The benefit of this is that no other virtual machine can use this physical RAM. The downside is that no other virtual machine can use this RAM.

From the DBA's perspective, this is great, just like the physical world! No sharing of the underlying RAM and no need to worry about those "other" virtual machines using physical RAM that his SQL Server may require. From the vSphere administrator's perspective, there are a lot of things that change under the covers now that a reservation has been configured.

One of the items that changes that must be taken into account is how reservations are accounted for with vSphere's Admission Control Policy for vSphere HA. Admission Control is a feature within vSphere that is designed to ensure resources (CPU and memory) are available at a vSphere Cluster level during a failure event, such as losing a physical host. We will go into more detail on how Admission Control works in Chapter 9, "Architecting for Availability: Choosing the Right Solution." Just know this is affected by reservations and the Admission Control Policy selected. Read Chapter 9 to get further information on Admission Control, because this feature needs consideration when you are planning a SQL Server installation.

Another item affected is the vswp file size. The vswp file is one of the files that makes up a virtual machine. By default, it is located in the VM folder containing the other virtual machine files. The purpose of the vswp file is to accommodate memory overhead from a virtual machine. In times of contention, the hypervisor can swap out memory from physical RAM into the vswp file. By default, this file is set to the size of the virtual RAM assigned to your virtual machine. Therefore, if you create a 32GB SQL Server virtual machine, you have a 32GB vswp file on your storage. If you set a reservation, the size of this file is affected by the reservation size. This means the amount reserved is subtracted from the amount allocated, and the difference is the size of the vspw file. Therefore, if you set a reservation for the full 32GB, you still have the vswp file, but it is 0.0KB in size. Table 5.3 shows a virtual machine with no reservation set, with a partial reservation, and with the Reserve All Guest Memory (All Locked) setting checked, respectively.

> **NOTE**
>
> The size of the vswp file is determined at boot time of the virtual machine. Changing this setting while the virtual machine is powered on will not change the size of the vswp file. The virtual machine must be powered off and powered back on for the changes to update.

Table 5.3 VSWP File Size Based on Memory Reservation

Virtual Machine		
8GB RAM 0MB reservation	SQL_2012_a-10355399.vswp	8,388,608.00 KB File
8GB RAM 4,096MB reserved	SQL_2012_a-10355399.vswp	4,194,304.00 KB File
8GB RAM Reserve All Guest Memory enabled	SQL_2012_a-10355399.vswp	0.00 KB File

From a design perspective, with regard to reservations, it is important to balance performance, availability, and cost. Reenter our tiered database discussion. We typically recommend for production Tier 1 databases that customers start off with reservations to ensure protection of these resources, along with the proper vSphere HA configuration for the cluster running these workloads. This is a broad-brush statement, so remember the "spirit" of this statement when designing and then adapt your design as appropriate for the target environment.

Depending on how you define Tier 2, Tier 3, and quality assurance, the recommendation is to not use reservations but to monitor your vSphere environment for signs of memory contention—mainly ensuring the balloon driver (vmmemctl) is not active. We recommend the use of a tool such as vCOPs that can provide longer-term trending and reporting analysis of the data.

Test/development is where we do not see customers using memory reservation for any SQL Server virtual machines and allowing the hypervisor and the built-in memory-reclamation features handle memory.

Remember, the previously provided guidance to those just starting off with SQL Server virtualization. These shops are usually defined by skilled vSphere administrators who have done a great job virtualizing applications and skilled DBAs who are good at running SQL. What we don't have is a shop with vSphere administrators skilled at running SQL on vSphere and DBAs skilled at running on the vSphere platform. This is a way to ease into the journey and build a foundation before undertaking more advance actions.

Once the environment is running for several business cycles and consumers are satisfied with the performance of the systems, we begin the discussion of modification of the initial implementation. We recommend that analysis be performed on the systems to determine if further actions, such as removing reservations in the Tier 1 environment, should take place. Yes, we do have customers who run large Tier 1 databases in production without reservations. These are vSphere admins who have built a trust and understanding with the DBA team to provide the resources necessary to the SQL Servers and DBAs who are upfront and honest about the resources necessary to run these systems.

SQL Server: Min/Max

As we peer into the SQL Server virtual machine, there are some memory-specific settings we will mention here, but these are covered in much more granular detail in Chapter 7. Why is memory configuration important? Simple, to minimize the number of reads and writes that need to go to physical media. It may seem obvious, but we will mention it now: Accessing data from memory is faster than accessing data from disk.

The first item to consider is the use of the Sql Server Min Server Memory / Max Server Memory setting to create a memory buffer pool for SQL Server. The Min setting establishes the lower boundary and the Max setting establishes the upper boundary. The default setting for Min Server Memory is 0. The default setting for Max Server Memory is 2,147,483,647MB. If you do not change these settings, SQL Server will dynamically manage memory requirements based on the availability of system resources. Based on the availability of resources, SQL Server will release or acquire memory dynamically.

From our travels, we've found that most DBAs prefer to configure these settings themselves. When setting these parameters, keep in mind the following: The SQL Server buffer pool will begin to acquire memory and keep this memory up until the Min Server Memory value is reached. Administrators will use this setting to configure a minimum amount of memory to allocate to an instance of SQL. The SQL Server buffer pool will not release memory below the value configured for Min Server Memory. Above Min Server Memory, SQL Server will acquire memory up to the value specified in Max Server Memory.

Ensure you know what you are doing before configuring these parameters. Configuring the Max Server Memory setting too low could prevent SQL Server from starting. The initial guidance we give is to leave Min Server Memory at the default 0, unless you are experienced with configuring this setting. In addition to understand the setting, understand the memory requirements of non-SQL applications running in the virtual machine. These applications may require memory, but be sure to allocate the appropriate amount for the application.. Chapter 7 goes into details and recommendations for configuring the Max Server Memory setting.

> **TIP**
>
> If the value configured for Max Server Memory prevents the SQL Server from starting, start SQL Server with the -f option to start an instance of SQL with a minimum configuration. See this TechNet article for more information: http://technet.microsoft.com/en-us/library/ms190737.aspx.

> **NOTE**
>
> When using Max Server Memory and vSphere Hot Plug Memory, be sure to increase the Max Server Memory configured value any time memory is adjusted to ensure SQL Server takes advantage of the additional memory provided.

So what if you are running more than one instance on the SQL Server virtual machine? There are two options you have, and doing nothing isn't one of them. The first option is to use Max Server Memory and create a maximum setting for each SQL Server instance on the SQL Server. The configured value to should provide enough memory so that it is proportional to the workload expected of that instance. The sum of the individually configured Max Server Memory settings should not exceed the total assigned to the virtual machine.

The second option is to use the Min Server Memory setting. Use this setting to create a minimum amount of memory to provide each instance. Ensure the configured value is proportionate to the workload expected by the individual instances. The sum of the individually configured Min Server Memory settings should be 1–2GB less than the RAM allocated to the virtual machine.

Our recommendation is to leverage the first option—that is, configure the Max Server Memory setting. Table 5.4 provides the pros and cons of the individual settings.

Table 5.4 Configuration Pros and Cons for Multiple Instances of SQL Server

Technical Factor	Pro	Con
Max Server Memory	When a new process or instance starts, memory is available immediately to fulfill the request.	If instances are not running, the running instances cannot access the available RAM.
Min Server Memory	Running instances can leverage memory previously used by instances that are no longer running.	When a new process or instance starts, running instances need to release memory.

SQL Server: Lock Pages in Memory

The Lock Pages in Memory setting will help SQL Server protect memory that has been allocated into the SQL Server buffer pool. This setting will let SQL Server page memory the SQL Server buffer pool less aggressively and keep as much in the buffer pool as possible. This setting is enabled by default on SQL Server 2012 for both 32-bit and 64-bit Standard versions and higher when the account given rights to run sqlservr.exe has been given the Windows Lock Pages in Memory right. Figure 5.10 shows the configuration of this setting with a service account we used when configuring SQL Server (svcSQL2012).

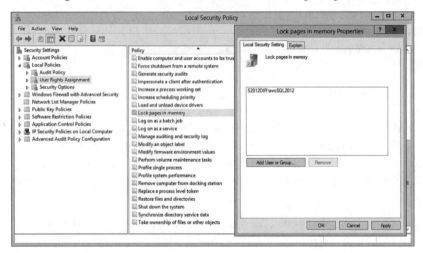

Figure 5.10   Configuring the Lock Pages in Memory setting.

We recommend configuring this setting for your Tier 1 databases that are running in production. When using this setting, you should configure reservations at the virtual machine level (previous section) to prevent the vSphere balloon driver from encroaching on the SQL Server's memory footprint. The reason for this suggestion is if memory is locked by SQL Server and the vSphere balloon driver kicks in, there can be a negative impact to the performance of your SQL Server virtual machine.

For Tier 2, Tier 3, quality assurance, test, and development systems, we suggest a review of this setting prior to implementation. If consolidation and memory optimization are the desired goals for one or more of the aforementioned tiers, then do not implement the Lock Pages in Memory setting, because this will have a negative impact on the performance of the SQL Server if the vSphere balloon driver (vmmemctl) kicks in and attempts to reclaim memory from these virtual machines. As discussed in the "Large Pages" section in this chapter, when large pages are configured for SQL Server, the default behavior at boot time is to find contiguous pages in memory and claim these, thus affecting the overall memory footprint for SQL Server.

Storage

How you configure and present storage to the SQL Server virtual machines will have a profound impact on their performance. Chapter 6, "Architecting for Performance: Storage," goes into immense detail around storage configuration, so we will only discuss the highlights in this chapter.

First, remember that the rules used to size SQL Server in a physical world carry over to the virtual world—they just need to be tweaked. Too often we see customers just pick up SQL and throw it over the proverbial wall. Why is this? Well, let's take a trip down Memory Lane; let's look back at the last 10 years and compare virtualization and database implementations.

When we look at virtualization and how virtualization became mainstream, we notice that the first systems virtualized were test and development systems. These systems did not impact the business, and if they went down or had poor performance, only IT noticed. As the software matured and the hardware evolved, we saw departmental applications go onto the platform, starting with those owned by IT, and eventually moving outward to non-IT departmental applications. And here we are today, where there are few workloads that exist that cannot be virtualized due to the work by VMware, independent software vendors, and hardware vendors. However, what we didn't see keep up was the systems running vSphere, particularly the storage subsystems.

Now, hold that thought for a second while we examine the database trajectory. Some argue that data is the lifeblood of any company and that the health, performance, and availability of databases are a reflection of how much a company relies on this data. For a large number of companies, this was important, so when the DBA team said they needed more compute power, faster disks, and so on, they tended to get what they wanted. They were the recipients of some nice powerful Tier 1 equipment.

So, if we put those two items together, vSphere coming up and running on Tier 2 equipment along with database servers running on Tier 1 equipment, and someone migrates databases over to this environment without doing basic engineering and architecture work such as the number and speed of disks supporting the database, that person could be in trouble. Trust us, we see this all the time. One of the first things we do when customers say, "It ran better in the physical world than in the virtual world," is ask them for a side-by-side comparison of the supporting subsystem of each environment. We ask them to detail out disk type, disk speed, RAID, paths, directories, and so on. Although some of this may seem "obvious," we cannot tell you how many calls we get concerning SQL performance being "slow" (love those ambiguous troubleshooting calls) and we find that storage is sized incorrectly.

Obtain Storage-Specific Metrics

The first storage consideration for virtualizing SQL is to do your best to obtain the I/O and throughput requirements for the databases you are going to virtualize. Remember to account for the sum of all databases on a host/LUN, not just what one database requires. Although this data is necessary, remember you must factor in the physical hardware's limitations. In addition, I/O and throughput are two different and important items to account for in your sizing. For existing databases, this is easier because we have the ability to reference monitoring tools to gather this data from the actual system. For net new applications, well, this can be tough. Trying to get the I/O profile from an application vendor is often akin to pulling teeth.

Along with what the application will drive, you need to understand the workload pattern of the database. Is the workload OLTP, batch, or DSS? These have different I/O patterns in terms of read/write ratios and should be taken into consideration when sizing the subsystem.

Next, size for performance, not capacity. This is where tight integration and team work between the DBAs, vSphere administrators, and SAN administrators is paramount. After the workload profile has been established and sizing has been determined, it is key that all teams work together to put the proper infrastructure in place to support this workload.

Think this is "common sense"? Well, we once worked with a customer who was looking to virtualize a database that could sustain 20,000 IOPS for their VOIP recording program. We had all the best-practice sessions, reviewed all the detail, told the SAN team what was coming down the pipe, and what they were going to have to architect the SAN to handle. "No problem" they told us; they just got a big, bad, shiny array that could eat IO for breakfast and then spit it out. So we left the customer to build, install, and test the server once the SAN team ordered the disks and the SAN vendor installed them.

Fast-forward several weeks when the phone rings. The customer says, "Um, yea... our first IOMETER test yielded a whopping 1,000 IOPS. We are 19,000 short of where we need to be for this server." What!? After troubleshooting the installation, starting with the subsystem, we discovered the SAN team ordered enough disks to accommodate the amount of data the SQL team said was needed, but forgot about the IOPS requirement. After the customer reordered the right drive configuration (oops!) and put it in the array, the IOMETER test yield far beyond the 20,000 IOPS necessary to support this database.

LSI Logic SAS or PVSCSI

It is important to understand the differences at a technical level that the different virtual SCSI adapters provide. Out of the box, supported by Windows 2012, is the LSI Logic SAS virtual SCSI adapter. This adapter will install without needing to have additional drivers loaded into the operating system during the virtual machine build.

The PVSCSI adapter is a paravirtualized adapter that is aware it is sitting on the vSphere platform, and the drivers are part of the VMware Tools install. The PVSCI adapter will utilizes fewer physical host CPU resources compared to the LSI Logic SAS driver, offers a configurable queue size (covered in Chapter 6), and can deliver better throughput for demanding workloads.

Our recommendation is to use PVSCSI. We have seen some customers mix and match, using the LSI Logic SAS for the Windows OS and SQL Binaries (adapter 0) and PVSCSI for running the remaining VMDKs (databases, logs, and tempdbs).

> **NOTE**
>
> When PVSCSI was first introduced in vSphere 4.0, it was recommended for work-loads requiring 2,000 or more IOPS. This has been resolved as of vSphere 4.1, and the PVSCSI adapter can be used for all workloads. For more information, see http://kb.vmware.com/kb/1017652.

> **CAUTION**
>
> Double-check that you are running at the appropriate patch level for vSphere because there have been updates to address an issue with Windows Server 2008 and Server 2008/R2 reporting operating system errors when running SQL Server. vSphere versions prior to vSphere 5.0 update 2 should be checked. For more information, review http://kb.vmware.com/kb/2004578.

Determine Adapter Count and Disk Layout

Once the performance requirements have been gathered, the next step is to determine the virtual machine layout. How many PVSCSI adapters is this virtual machine going to use? Remember, the more paths back to the storage array, the more options you provide the operating system to send I/O out to the array. However, just because you can add four PVSCI adapters, does not mean that you should. If you have a database that is housing configuration information for an application, does it need four PVSCSI adapters and the VMDK files fanned out across all these controllers? Probably not. Balance performance requirements with management overhead. Again, this is where database tiering can assist.

VMDK versus RDM

In terms of choosing VMDK files or RDM, the guidance we provide is to choose VMDK files unless you have a specific requirement that will drive you to choosing RDMs. Choosing VMDK files and building your virtual machines with VMDK files is on par from a performance perspective with RDMs, so performance capabilities should not be taken into consideration. In addition, going with VMDKs is a way to future-proof your implementation. As VMware introduces new features, functions, and capabilities to the storage stack, your virtual machines will be able to benefit from these new features. What are the reasons to choose RDM? The main driver is the decision point to use Microsoft Windows AlwaysOn Failover Cluster Instance. VMware requires that RDMs be used as part of this configuration. The other reasons customers will choose RDMs is due to their backup methodology and tools, along with the requirement to leverage SAN monitoring tools that function at the LUN level for granular detail around performance. Our recommendation is to use VMDKs unless driven by architectural reasons.

> **NOTE**
>
> To read more about VMDK versus RDM, read this blog article: http://blogs.vmware.com/vsphere/2013/01/vsphere-5-1-vmdk-versus-rdm.html.

VMDK Provisioning Type

When provisioning a VMDK, the vSphere administrator has three options to choose from: Thin Provision, Thick Provision Lazy Zeroed, and Thick Provision Eager Zeroed. Before we get into the details around the VMDK provisioning type, we want to cover VAAI (vStorage APIs for Array Integration) because this feature can have an impact on the default behavior of the VMDK during provisioning time and implications to the storage management of the virtual machines you are managing.

VAAI, or Storage Acceleration, allows an ESXi host to integrate nicely with a compatible SAN. This integration centers around the offloading of certain functions to the storage array instead of having them being managed by the hypervisor. If you are not familiar with VAAI features and their capabilities, we highly recommend you read up on them and work with your storage team and storage vendor to understand which features are available in your storage subsystem.

With VAAI, features such as Full Copy, Atomic Test Set (ATS), and Write Same / Zero all can have an impact on the VMDK provisioning type. The one we will focus on for this section is the Write Same / Zeroing. ESXi hosts can be configured to enable the WRITE_SAME_SCSI command, which allows them to zero out a large number of disk blocks without actually sending all this information to the array. It is important to understand the impact of this setting with the array you are using. Storage arrays will handle the WRITE_ SAME_SCSI command differently, so work with your SAN team and SAN vendor to understand *how* this setting will impact the storage subsystem and ultimately the performance of your virtual machine.

> **NOTE**
>
> For more information, read the FAQ on VAAI (http://kb.vmware.com/kb/1021976) as well as the "VMware vSphere Storage APIs—Array Integration" white paper (http://www.vmware.com/files/pdf/techpaper/VMware-vSphere-Storage-API-Array-Integration.pdf).

Now, let's move on to the provisioning types of a VMDK file. The first type we will discuss is a Thin Provisioned VMDK. A Thin Provisioned VMDK is one that does not immediately consume space on the storage in which it resides; however, the operating system believes it has the full amount assigned when created. The storage consumed is equal to the amount the virtual machine is actually using. Therefore, the size of the VMDK will start small and grow over time, up to the size configured.

Thick Provisioned Lazy Zeroed disks are VMDK files that immediately consume the VMFS space assigned to the virtual machine. The item to pay attention to with this disk type is that when the hypervisor needs to write IO to the underlying storage, it will send a zero first and then the data. This is only on the first write to a block; subsequent writes to the same block do not incur this activity. This is commonly referred to as the First Write Penalty. For general-purpose virtual machines, this is not a big deal because it is washed out in the cache of the arrays. However, if you have an application such as a database that is doing a large number of writes (to a database or log file), this could have a performance impact. If your storage array supports the Write Same / Zero primitive, then the zeroing operation, depending on your array's implementation of this primitive, may have little if any impact to the performance of the VMDK.

Thick Provisioned Eager Zeroed is the third and final type of VMDK provisioning type. In this type, all VMFS spaced assigned to the VMDK is consumed. Also, zeroes are written into each block of the VMDK file. This VMDK file type will take additional time when created because it has to zero out every block. Just keep in mind what you are doing when you create this type of VMDK file—you are sending a whole bunch of zeroes to the disk subsystem. This is something you want to plan if you are creating a lot of virtual machines with Thick Provisioned Eager Zeroed disks. As we have stated, you need to understand what you are doing when you create this VMDK file type, because the last thing you need is to have an angry storage admin hunting you down because you just created 4TB worth of activity on the production array during the middle of the day.

So which type do you use? At a high level, it really does not matter which you decide to use for your standalone or AlwaysOn Availability Group SQL Servers—remember, for AlwaysOn Failover Cluster Instance (FCI), you must use RDMs. When we look into this a bit more, if Thin Provisioned VMDKs are being considered, then management of available disk space on the LUN must be managed. Trust us, you do not want to run out of room on a LUN. From a Thick Provisioned Lazy / Eager Zeroed perspective, with the Write Same / Zero VAAI primitive, the question now becomes when to take the First Write Penalty tax. With Thick Provisioned Lazy, the tax is spread out across the life of the virtual machine, and you only pay tax on the blocks accessed. With Thick Provisioned Eager Zeroed VMDKs, the zeroing tax is paid up front. Also, you are paying tax on every block in the VMDK, some of which you may never use. If your array does not support the Write Same / Zero primitive, then our recommendation is to, at minimum, use Thick Provisioned Eager Zeroed VMDK files for the database, log, and tempdb VMDKs.

Thin Provisioning: vSphere, Array, or Both?

Storage arrays also offer the Thin Provision option. A common question we get is, should one use Thin Provision at the vSphere layer or the SAN layer? Although we do not have a definitive recommendation, it is our opinion that you understand the trade-offs and implement the option that best fits your environment.

In our discussion, it is important to consider this at two levels: the virtualization layer and the hardware layer. At the virtualization layer, you have three VMDK types, as discussed in the previous section. At the SAN level, you have two options: Thick and Thin Provisioned LUNs. Thick Provisioned LUNs are ones that consume the entire amount of space assigned to them on the storage array. Thin Provisioned LUNs are ones that present a given amount of space, but only consume what is actually used by the virtual machines running on the data store assigned to those LUNs.

We will first discuss Thick Provisioned LUNs and the three VMDK file types. If we consider Thin Provisioned VMDK files on a Thick Provisioned LUN, then management of the Thin Provisioning is handled by the vSphere administrator. As the virtual machine's VMDK files grow and acquire additional space, if the LUN needs to grow, the vSphere administrator can notify the SAN administrator to grow the LUN. Next, Thick Provisioned Lazy / Eager Zeroed will acquire all its disk space during its creation. This option has the least management overhead, given that the LUN was sized properly to accommodate for overhead (vswp files, snapshot delta files, adding too many virtual machines to a data store, and so on).

Next we will consider a Thin Provisioned LUN and the three VMDK file types. Following the same order as the previous paragraph, let's consider a Thin Provisioned VMDK file on a Thin Provisioned LUN. Can this be done? Sure. What are the implications? The implications are management by both the vSphere administrator and SAN administrator to ensure adequate space is available. Of the three possible VMDK provisioning options on a Thin Provisioned LUN, this is the option that can run out of space the quickest if the administrators are not watching disk utilization. Let's move on to Thick Provisioned Lazy Zero VMDKs on Thin Provisioned LUNs: This option will only consume SAN space that is actually used by the virtual machine. This shifts the burden of management to the SAN administrators because they have to ensure there is enough space available for the virtual machines. Finally, Thick Provisioned Eager Zeroed, based on this VMDK file type's behavior, will consume all space assigned to it when it is created, thereby nullifying any potential benefit of having a Thin Provisioned LUN.

From a VAAI perspective, the primitive you want to pay particular attention to is the UNMAP primitive. If you are presenting Thin Provisioned LUNs, there is a good chance there is wasted disk space on this LUN. What do we mean by wasted disk space? Say you delete a virtual machine: The space this virtual machine consumed is not reclaimed and made available to the SAN, so it sits there, wasted. The UNMAP primitive's job is to notify the storage array of blocks no longer being used. The UNMAP primitive was introduced initially in vSphere 5.0, and vSphere 5.5 made the UNMAP command much easier to use.

TIP

The UNMAP command must be manually initiated.

NOTE

For more information on using the UNMAP command, read http://kb.vmware.com/kb/2057513.

Data Stores and VMDKs

If you are going with VMDK files, the next topic that arises is whether to dedicate one VMDK file per data store or to run multiple VMDKs per data store. The guidance we provide here is to validate with the SAN team and or SAN vendor what VAAI primitives the SAN you are working on will support and what the performance impact is of having, or not having, certain VAAI primitives in your environment. One key VAAI primitive is Atomic Test Set (ATS). This updates the way vSphere does locking to perform metadata updates. ATS replaces SCSI locking, so check to see if your array supports this primitive. In the end, as long as the data store is capable of delivering the IOPS required by the virtual machine(s) using a particular LUN, then either option is valid. One item for consideration, given that IOPS is met, is the management overhead associated with presenting a lot of LUNs in the case of one VMDK per data store. The reason this can be of concern is that vSphere 5.5 still has a configuration maximum of 256 LUNs per host.

VMDK File Size

It is important to also consider the size of the VMDK file you are creating. Although it is possible to create a VMDK file that is 62TB on vSphere 5.5, it does not mean you should, unless you have valid reasons. Our recommendation is to design the SQL Server configuration for the best possible performance. Having more VMDKs as targets will yield better performance than having one large VMDK file. In addition, SQL Server is built to have a large database split among multiple disks. It is all about scaling and going as wide as possible to achieve the best performance possible. We go into great detail on this topic in Chapter 6.

Another consideration is the service-level agreements (SLAs) you have established with the business concerning database availability. If you have a Tier 1 database that has an SLA of no more than two hours of downtime, then a very simple question to ask is, "Can I restore a 62TB file in the time frame it takes to diagnose and restore this file?" We have seen from a recovery perspective that smaller VMDK files allow for faster recovery time and less likelihood of breaching your SLAs.

Networking

When we consider networking, we start with the virtual switch type. In terms of using a standard virtual switch or a distributed virtual switch, the choice is yours. We, the authors, recommend using the distributed virtual switch. The reasons for this come down to ease of management and the additional features available with the distributed virtual switch, such as network I/O control, which is discussed in the following sections.

Virtual Network Adapter

When it comes to choosing a network adapter (or adapters), we recommend using the VMXNET 3 network adapter, which is a paravirtualized network adapter designed for performance. VMXNET 3 requires hardware version 7 and higher and is supported on a specific set of operating systems. In addition, running the VMXNET 3 network adapter requires the drivers installed as part of the VMware Tools installation. Therefore, if this network adapter is chosen, network connectivity is not made available until the required adapters are installed.

> **NOTE**
>
> To read more about the virtual network adapter options available for your virtual machines, check out http://kb.vmware.com/kb/1001805.

Managing Traffic Types

Because our SQL Servers are now sitting on a hypervisor, we must manage the different traffic types that exist, for both the virtual machine and the hypervisor. For example, SQL Server will have to manage traffic bound for the Windows OS, possible in-guest iSCSI initiator, the database application, if clustered, and replication traffic. In addition, the ESXi host traffic must also be accounted for and managed.

Starting at the physical ESXi host layer, it is recommended that ESXi traffic, such as management, storage, vMotion, be separated onto its own physical NICs and that dedicated different physical NICs handle virtual machine traffic. At the virtual machine level, consider the traffic types and how these traffic types map to physical adapters. You want to ensure proper segmentation and balance across the adapters. There are several ways in which to architect this, which we cover in more detail in Chapter 8, "Architecting for Performance: Network." But what we do want to discuss here is the capability to segment and manage traffic at the hypervisor level for both virtual machine and ESXi host traffic should contention occur.

This ability to control traffic is enabled via network I/O control, which enables distributed switch traffic to be divided into different network resource pools. These pools determine the priority of network traffic types on a given distributed switch.

> **NOTE**
>
> Network I/O control requires a virtual distributed switch.

Network I/O control is disabled by default, and requires a distributed virtual switch. Once enabled, it allows for two types of resource pools: user-defined resource pools and system-defined resource pools. These pools are managed by shares and limits applied to the physical adapters and are only activated when contention exists on the physical adapter. If there is no contention for the physical adapter's resource, then shares are not implemented (limits could be, though, depending on how they are configured). By enabling network I/O control, an administrator can ensure that a particular traffic type, such as vMotion, does not saturate the available bandwidth on a physical adapter and cause a service interruption.

To expand, when the vMotion of a virtual machine is initiated, the vMotion traffic will use as much bandwidth as it can. If SQL Server AlwaysOn Availability group replication traffic is sharing the same physical adapter, there may be issues with SQL Server replication traffic. With network I/O control enabled, vSphere will automatically identify vMotion traffic, and by creating a user-defined network resource pool for SQL Server replication traffic, you can better protect network flows.

In addition to system-defined and user-defined resource pools, an administrator also has the ability to assign a Quality of Service (QoS) tag to all outgoing packets from a particular network resource pool—whether that pool is a system-defined or user-defined resource pool. Figure 5.11 shows how to configure QoS for a system-defined resource pool (vMotion). This is an 802.1p tag, and has the configurable range of (none) or 0 to 7 (see Table 5.5 for more information on QoS tagging).

By implementing QoS, an administrator has the ability to assign the priority (impor-tance) of a particular resource pool versus its peers. It should be noted that vSphere itself does nothing with this tag; as stated earlier, this is applied to outbound traffic. However, physical switches will use these tags to prioritize traffic. Be sure to work with your network team to ensure QoS is properly implemented.

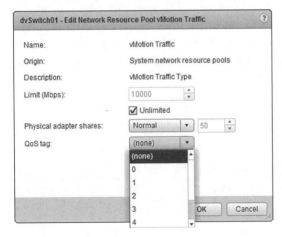

Figure 5.11   Configured QoS.

Table 5.5 displays the how the vSphere QoS tag relates to network priority and the traffic characteristics of that traffic type.

Table 5.5   vSphere QoS Configuration

QoS Priority Tag	Network Priority	Traffic Characteristics
1	0 (Lowest)	Background
None (0)	1	Best effort
2	2	Excellent effort
3	3	Critical applications
4	4	Video < 100 ms latency
5	5	Voice < 10 ms latency
6	6	Internetwork
7	7 (highest)	Network control

NOTE

To learn more about network I/O control, read the "vSphere Networking for 5.5" white paper: http://pubs.vmware.com/vsphere-55/topic/com.vmware.ICbase/PDF/vsphere-esxi-vcenter-server-55-networking-guide.pdf.

Back Up the Network

One final note on networking: vSphere allows an administrator to take a snapshot of the distributed virtual switch configuration. What? That's right. Having this snapshot allows for ease of deployment, the ability to roll back to a previous configuration, and the ability to share the configuration with your best friends. This can be done for the distributed virtual switch and/or a distributed virtual port group. By backing up your network configuration, you can restore the configuration versus having to rebuild the network configuration. We highly recommend backing up the network configuration. In addition, export and save the configuration to a location that is independent of vCenter's disk.

Summary

We covered quite a bit in this chapter. We discussed how architecting SQL Server is a team effort and how putting a Center of Excellence team in place can assist with ensuring SQL Server virtual machines are properly configured to run on ESXi hosts. We then walked through the four core resources and examined these from the physical, hypervisor, and virtual machine levels.

This chapter has provided considerations and introduced concepts that will be discussed in great detail in the following chapters. Specifically, in the next chapter, we will dive into architecting storage for a SQL Server implementation.

Architecting for Performance: Storage

All aspects of architecting your SQL Server Database for performance are important. Storage is more important than most when compared to the other members of the IT Food Group family we introduced in Chapter 5, "Architecting for Performance: Design," which consists of Disk, CPU, Memory, and Network. Our experience has shown us, and data from VMware Support validates this belief, that more than 80% of performance problems in database environments, and especially virtualized environments, are directly related to storage. Understanding the storage architecture in a virtualized environment and getting your storage architecture right will have a major impact on your database performance and the success of your SQL Server virtualization project. Bear in mind as you work through your storage architecture and this chapter that virtualization is bound by the laws of physics—it won't fix bad code or bad database queries. However, if you have bad code and bad queries, we will make them run as fast as possible.

TIP

Greater than 80% of all problems in a virtualized environment are caused by the storage in some way, shape, or form.

This chapter first covers the key aspects of storage architecture relevant to both physical and virtual environments as well as the differences you need to understand when architecting storage, specifically for virtualized SQL Server Databases. Many of the concepts we discuss will be valid for past versions of SQL Server and even the newest release, SQL Server 2014.

We provide guidance on what our experience has taught us are important database storage design principles. We present a top-down approach covering SQL Server Database and Guest OS Design, Virtual Machine Template Design, followed by VMware vSphere Hypervisor Storage Design and then down to the physical storage layers, including using server-side flash acceleration technology to increase performance and provide greater return on investment. We conclude the chapter by covering one of the biggest IT trends and its impact on SQL Server. Throughout this chapter, we give you architecture examples based on real-world projects that you can adapt for your purposes.

When designing your storage architecture for SQL Server, you need to clearly understand the requirements and have quantitative rather than subjective metrics. Our experience has taught us to make decisions based on fact and not gut feeling. You will need to benchmark and baseline your storage performance to clearly understand what is achievable from your design. Benchmarking and baselining performance are critical to your success, so we've dedicated an entire chapter (Chapter 10, "How to Baseline Your Physical SQL Server System") to those topics. In this chapter, we discuss some of the important storage system component performance aspects that will feed into your benchmarking and baselining activities.

The Five Key Principles of Database Storage Design

When architecting storage for SQL Server, it's important to understand a few important principles. These will help guide your design decisions and help you achieve acceptable performance both now and in the future. These principles are important because over the past decade, CPU performance has increased at a much faster pace than storage performance, even while capacity has exploded.

Principle 1: Your database is just an extension of your storage

"Your database is just an extension of your storage"

Figure 6.1   Quote from Michael Webster, VMworld 2012

The first principle is highlighted in Figure 6.1: that your database is just an extension of your storage. A database is designed to efficiently and quickly organize, retrieve, and process large quantities of data to and from storage. So increasing the parallelism of access to storage resources at low latency will be an important goal. Later in this chapter, we cover how to optimize the architecture of your database to maximize its storage performance and parallelism. When you understand this principle, it's easy to understand why getting your storage design and performance is so critical to the success of your SQL Server Database virtualization project.

Principle 2: Performance is more than underlying storage devices

The next key principle is that storage performance is more than just about underlying storage devices and spindles, although they are very important too. SQL Server storage performance is multidimensional and is tightly coupled with a number of different system components, such as the number of data files allocated to the database, the number of allocated vCPUs, and the amount of memory allocated to the database. This is why we like to use the term "IT Food Groups," because it is so important to feed your database the right balance of these critical resources. This interplay between resources such as CPU, Memory, and Network and their impact on storage architecture and performance will be covered in subsequent sections of this chapter.

Principle 3: Size for performance before capacity

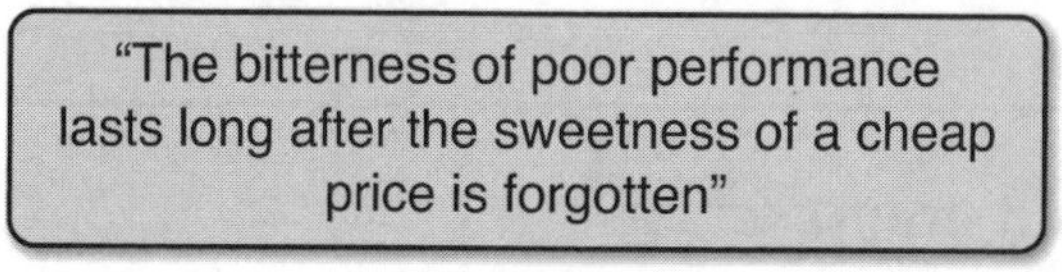

> "The bitterness of poor performance lasts long after the sweetness of a cheap price is forgotten"

Figure 6.2 Quote from Michael Webster, VMworld 2013

Figure 6.2 is loosely based on the eighteenth-century quote "The bitterness of poor quality remains long after the sweetness of low price is forgotten," by Benjamin Franklin. Both quotes are extremely relevant to SQL Server database and storage performance.

This brings us to the next key principle. In order to prevent poor performance from being a factor in your SQL Server virtualization project (refer to Figure 6.2), you should design storage for performance first (IOPS and latency), then capacity will take care of itself. Capacity is the easy part. We will show you later in this chapter how compromising on certain storage configurations on the surface can actually cost you a lot more by causing unusable capacity due to poor performance.

CAUTION

A lesson from the field: We were working with a customer, and they wanted to design and run a database on vSphere that could support sustained 20,000 IOPS. After we worked with the customer's vSphere, SAN, Network, and DBA teams, the customer decided to move forward with the project. The customer then called in a panic saying, "In our load test, we achieved 1,000 IOPS. We are 19,000 short of where we need to be." Trust me, this is a phone call you don't want to get. Playing the odds, we started with the disk subsystem. We quickly identified some issues. The main issue was the customer purchased for *capacity*, not *performance*. They had to reorder the right disk. Once the new (right) disk arrived and was configured, the customer exceeded the 20,000 IOPS requirement.

TIP

When it comes to storage devices, HDDs are cents per GB but dollars per IOP, whereas SSDs are cents per IOP and dollars per GB. SSDs should be considered cheap memory, rather than expensive disks, especially when it comes to enterprise SSDs and PCIe flash devices.

Principle 4: Virtualize, but without compromise

The next principle is that virtualizing business-critical SQL Server databases is all about reducing risk and not compromising on SLAs. Virtualize, but without compromise. There is no need to compromise on predictability of performance, quality of service, availability, manageability, or response times. Your storage architecture plays a big part in ensuring your SQL databases will perform as expected. As we said earlier, your database is just an extension of your storage. We will show you how to optimize your storage design for manageability without compromising its performance.

Believe it or not, as big of advocates as we are about virtualizing SQL Server, we have told customers in meetings that now is not the right time for this database to be virtualized. This has nothing to do with the capability of vSphere or virtualization, but more to do with the ability of the organization to properly operate critical SQL systems and virtualize them successfully, or because they are not able or willing to invest appropriately to make the project a success. If you aren't willing to take a methodical and careful approach to virtualization projects for business-critical applications, in a way that increases the chances of success, then it's not worth doing. Understand, document, and ensure requirements can be met through good design and followed by testing and validation. It is worth doing, and it is worth "Doing It Right!"

Principle 5: Keep it standardized and simple (KISS)

This brings us to the final principle. Having a standardized and simplified design will allow your environment and databases to be more manageable as the numbers scale while maintaining acceptable performance (see Principle 4). If you have a small number of standardized templates that fit the majority of your database requirements and follow a building-block approach, this is very easy to scale and easy for your database administrators to manage. We'll use the KISS principle (Keep It Standardized and Simple) throughout this chapter, even as we dive into the details. Once you've made a design decision, you should standardize on that decision across all your VM templates. Then when you build from those templates, you'll know that the settings will always be applied.

SQL Server Database and Guest OS Storage Design

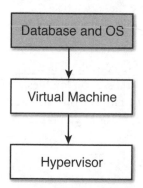

The starting point for any storage architecture for SQL Server Databases is actually with our last design principle: KISS (Keep It Standardized and Simple). But all of the principles apply. We will determine the smallest number of templates that are required to virtualize the majority (95%) of database systems, and anything that falls outside this will be handled as an exception.

Your first step is to analyze the inventory of the SQL Server Databases that will be virtualized as part of your project (refer to Chapter 4, "Virtualizing SQL Server 2012: Doing It Right"). From this inventory, you will now put each database and server into a group with similar-sized databases that have similar requirements. The storage requirements for all of these existing and new databases, based on their grouping, will be used to define the storage layouts and architecture for each of the SQL Server Databases, Guest OS, and VM template.

> **TIP**
>
> If you are virtualizing existing databases, you might consider using a tool such as VMware Capacity Planner, VMware Application Dependency Planner, Microsoft System Center, or Microsoft Assessment and Planning Toolkit to produce the inventory. VMware Capacity Planner and Application Dependency Planner are available from VMware Professional Services or your preferred VMware partner. When you're baselining a SQL Server database, a lot can happen in a minute. We recommend your sample period for CPU, Memory, and Disk be 15 seconds or less. We recommend you sample T-SQL every minute.

SQL Server Database File Layout

Database file layout provides an important component of database storage performance. If you have existing databases that will be virtualized, you or your DBAs will likely have already developed some practices around the number of database files, the size of database files, and the database file layout on the file system. If you don't have these practices already in place, here we provide you with some guidelines to start with that have proven successful.

Your SQL Server database has three primary types of files you need to consider when architecting your storage to ensure optimal performance: data files, transaction log files, and Temp DB files. Temp DB is a special system database used in certain key operations, and has a big performance impact on your overall system. The file extensions you'll see are .mdf (master data file), .ndf (for secondary data files), and .ldf for transaction log files. We will go over all of these different file types later in this chapter.

Number of Database Files

First, we need to determine the number of database files. There are two main drivers for the number of files you will specify. The first driver is the number of vCPUs allocated to the database, and the second is the total capacity required for the database now and in the future.

Two design principles come into play here: The parallelism of access to storage should be maximized by having multiple database files, and storage performance is more than just the underlying devices. In the case of data files and Temp DB files, they are related to the number of CPU cores allocated to your database. Table 6.1 provides recommendations from Microsoft and the authors in relation to file type.

> **NOTE**
>
> It is extremely unlikely you will ever reach the maximum storage capacity limits of a SQL Server 2012 database system. We will not be covering the maximums here. We recommend you refer to Microsoft (http://technet.microsoft.com/en-us/library/ms143432.aspx).

Table 6.1 Number of Data Files and Temp DB Files Per CPU

File Type	Microsoft Recommended Setting	Author Recommended Setting
Temp DB Data File	1 per CPU core	< 8 vCPU, 1 per vCPU
		> 8 vCPU, 8 total (increase number of files in increments of four at a time if required)
		Max 32
Database Data File	0.25 to 1.0 per file group, per CPU core	Min 1 per vCPU, max 32
Database Transaction Log File	1	1*
Temp DB Transaction Log File	1	1*

*If Temp DB and Transaction Log are deployed on local SSD or flash storage, especially when using AlwaysOn Availability Groups, then it is recommended to have an additional copy on SAN.

Microsoft recommends as a best practice that you should configure one Temp DB data file per CPU core and 0.25 to 1 data file (per file group) per CPU core. Based on our experience, our recommendation is slightly different.

If your database is allocated eight or fewer vCPUs as a starting point, we recommend you should configure at least one Temp DB file per vCPU. If your database is allocated more than eight vCPUs, we recommend you start with eight Temp DB files and increase by lots of four in the case of performance bottlenecks or capacity dictates.

> **TIP**
>
> Temp DB is very important because it's extensively utilized by OLTP databases during index reorg operations, sorts, and joins, as well as for OLAP, DSS, and batch operations, which often include large sorts and join activity.

We recommend in all cases you configure at least one data file (per file group) per vCPU. We recommend a maximum of 32 files for Temp DB or per file group for database files because you'll start to see diminishing performance returns with large numbers of database files over and above 16 files. Insufficient number of data files can lead to many writer processes queuing to update GAM pages. This is known as GAM page contention. The Global Allocation Map (GAM) tracks which extents have been allocated in each file. GAM contention would manifest in high PageLatch wait times. For extremely large databases into the many tens of TB, 32 files of each type should be sufficient.

Updates to GAM pages must be serialized to preserve consistency; therefore, the optimal way to scale and avoid GAM page contention is to design sufficient data files and ensure all data files are the same size and have the same amount of data. This ensures that GAM page updates are equally balanced across data files. Generally, 16 data files for tempdb and user databases is sufficient. For Very Large Database (VLDB) scenarios, up to 32 can be considered. See http://blogs.msdn.com/b/sqlserverstorageengine/archive/2009/01/04/what-is-allocation-bottleneck.aspx.

If you expect your database to grow significantly long term, we would recommend that you consider configuring more data files up front. The reason we specify at least one file per CPU is to increase the parallelism of access from CPU to data files, which will reduce any unnecessary data access bottlenecks and lower latency. This also allows for even data growth, which will reduce IO hotspots.

CAUTION

Having too few or too many Temp DB files can impact the overall performance of your database. Our guidance is conservative and aimed to meet the requirements for the majority of SQL systems. If you start to see performance problems such as higher than normal query response times or excessive database waits in *PAGELATCH_XX*, then you have contention in memory and may need to increase the number of Temp DB files further and/or implement trace flag 1118 (which we recommend), which prevents single page allocations. If you see waits in *PAGEIOLATCH_XX*, then the contention is at the IO subsystem level. Refer to http://www.sqlskills.com/blogs/paul/a-sql-server-dba-myth-a-day-1230-Temp DB-should-always-have-one-data-file-per-processor-core/ and Microsoft KB 328551 (http://support.microsoft.com/kb/328551).

NOTE

When you're determining the number of database files, a vCPU is logically analogous to a CPU core in a native physical deployment. However, in a native physical environment without virtualization, each CPU core may also have a hyper-thread. In a virtual environment, each vCPU is a single thread. There is no virtual equivalent of a hyper-thread.

Figure 6.3 shows an example of data files, Temp DB files, and transaction log files allocated to a SQL Server 2012 Database on a sample system with four vCPU and 32GB RAM.

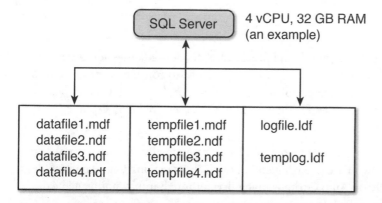

Figure 6.3   SQL Database data file allocation.

NOTE

As Figure 6.3 illustrates, there is only one transaction log file per database and per Temp DB. Log files are written to sequentially, so there is no benefit in having multiples of them, unless you exceed the maximum log file size (2TB) between backups. There is a benefit of having them on very fast and reliable storage, which will be covered later.

Size of Database Files

Let's start the discussion on data file sizes with some fundamentals that are important to understand. Data files, unlike transaction log files, are accessed in parallel and the IO pattern is more random. Temp DB files are accessed in parallel in a round-robin fashion. This is why having more database files improves the parallelism of IO access to storage. In effect, the IO is striped across the data files.

It is important to configure your database files to be equal size to start with. SQL Server will write data to the available files evenly if they are the same size, as it uses a proportional fill algorithm that favors allocations in files with more free space. If the files are the same size, then each file will have the same free space. Having equally sized files ensures even growth and more predictable performance.

TIP

Always configure SQL data files to be equal size to maximize parallelism and overall system performance. This will prevent hot spots that could occur if different files have different amounts of free space. SQL Server having equally sized data files ensures even growth and more predictable performance.

The next important point is that you should preallocate all your data files and transaction log files. This will eliminate the need for the database to constantly grow the files and resize them, which will degrade performance and put more stress on your storage platform. The files can't be accessed for the period of time they are being extended, and this will introduce avoidable latency.

It is a Microsoft best practice and our recommendation to manually and proactively manage file sizes. Because you are presizing and proactively managing your database files, you shouldn't need to rely on Auto Grow as much. Even though it may not be needed, we recommend that Auto Grow be left active as a safety net.

TIP

Auto Grow should be set to grow at the same or a multiple of the underlying storage system block size. In VMware environments, the block size on data stores will be between 1MB and 8MB. Your Database Auto Grow size should be set similarly, or at a multiple of this. Auto Grow should not be configured for unrestricted growth; it should be limited to less than the size of the underlying file system, taking into consideration the size of any other files on the file system. See VMware KB 1003565.

If you are unsure what your underlying block size is, set Auto Grow to a multiple of 1MB. To prevent Auto Grow from being active too often, consider configuring it to grow at around 10% of your initial database size rounded up to the nearest 1MB (or block size), up to a maximum of 4GB. In most cases, an Auto Grow amount of 256MB to 512MB should be sufficient. This will ensure the grow operation doesn't take too long and is aligned to the underlying storage subsystem.

CAUTION

Because Auto Grow will by default zero out all the blocks and prevent access to the files during that period, you don't want the operation to take too long. You also don't want these operations to happen too frequently. Therefore, the Auto Grow size needs to be small enough that it completes in a reasonable time but not too small as to require constant growth. The database file sizing guidelines need to be adjusted based on the performance in terms of throughput of your storage and the workload behavior of your database. If you are proactively managing the size of your database files, then Auto Grow should not be kicking in at all and this shouldn't be a concern.

TIP

By default, Auto Grow operations will expand one file at a time. This will impact the proportional fill algorithm and could result in degraded performance and storage hot spots. To avoid this behavior, you can use trace flag 1117 by specifying startup option –T1117 or by using the DBCC TRACEON command. By using this trace flag, you will ensure that each file is grown by the same amount at the same time. This trace flag is set by default when installing SAP on SQL Server 2012. Refer to SAP Note 1238993 and http://www.ciosummits.com/media/pdf/solution_spotlight/SQL%20Server%20 2012%20Technologies%20for%20SAP%20Solutions.pdf.

NOTE

To reduce the performance impact of file growth operations, Instant File Initialization can be used; this is covered in the next section.

Now that we've covered the fundamentals, we can calculate the initial size of the database files. The initial files sizes are fairly easy to determine if you're migrating an existing system—in which case, we recommend you preset your files to be the same size as the system that is being migrated, which would be the case if you are doing a standard physical-to-virtual migration. If this is a new database being virtualized, you will need to estimate the database files' initial size.

Data File Sizing

For data files, the preset size you should use is based on the estimated or actual size of your database. You should allow for reasonable estimated growth (three to six months). Once you have the total estimated size of your database, including growth, divide that by the number of files to get the size of each file. For example, if you had a database 200GB in size with four vCPUs configured, you would have four data files, assuming one file per vCPU, with a preset size of 50GB each. Each data file should always be of equal size and be extended at the same rate.

> **NOTE**
>
> As with other resource types, it is not necessary to factor in multiple years of growth to your database file sizing up front in a virtualized environment. It is quick and easy to expand the existing storage of a virtual machine online when required. By right-sizing your virtual machines and your VMware vSphere infrastructure, you will maximize your ROI.

Temp DB File Sizing

The size of your Temp DB files should be based on the high watermark usage you estimate for your queries and the overall size of your database. This can be hard to estimate without knowledge of your workload because different queries will impact your Temp DB usage in different ways. The best way to determine the appropriate size will be to monitor Temp DB usage during a proof of concept test, or benchmarking and baselining activities.

As a starting point, we recommend you consider sizing Temp DB to 1% the size of your database. Each file would then be equal to Total size of Temp DB divided by the number of files. For example, if you had a 100GB database with four vCPUs configured, you would have an initial total Temp DB size of 1GB, and each Temp DB data file would be 250MB in size. If you see significantly more Temp DB use during ongoing operations, you should adjust the preset size of your files.

NOTE

Temp DB files are cleared, resized, and reinitialized each time the database is restarted. Configuring them to be preset to the high water mark usage will ensure they are always at the optimal size.

Transaction Log File Sizing

The total size that your database transaction log file should be preset to will primarily be based on the actual or estimated high water mark of transaction storage required before the next backup or transaction log truncation. We are assuming for the purposes of this section that you care about data protection and preventing data loss of your database and are therefore using the full recovery model. Data loss is a risk when using the other available recovery models.

TIP

If you care about data protection and preventing data loss, use full recovery mode.

If you are doing daily backups, you will need to ensure that your log file is sufficiently sized to allow up to at least a day's worth of transactions. This will allow you to recover back to the point in time your database goes down by using the last backup and replaying the transaction logs. In some large database systems, you will need to back up the transaction logs much more frequently than every day.

CAUTION

If you are using Simple or Bulk Logged Recovery Model, data loss is a possibility. When using Simple Recovery Model for your database, it is not possible to perform media recovery without data loss, and features such as AlwaysOn Availability Groups, Database Mirroring, Log Shipping, and Point in Time Restores are not available. For more information on recovery models, refer to http://msdn.microsoft.com/en-us/library/ms189275.aspx.

When it comes to storage performance and sizing of your transaction log, the total size and how fast you can write transactions to it are important but are not the only considerations. You must also consider the performance of file growth, DB restart, and backup and recovery operations. With this in mind, it is critical that not only is the total size of your transaction log appropriate, but also how you grow your transaction log to that size. **The reason this is so critical is that in SQL Server, even though your transaction log may be one physical file, it's not one physical transaction log.**

Your one physical transaction log is actually made up of a number of smaller units called Virtual Log Files (VLFs). VLFs are written to sequentially, and when one VLF is filled, SQL Server will begin writing to the next. They play a critical part in the performance of database backup and recovery operations.

The number of VLFs is determined at the time a file is created or extended by the initial size allocated to the transaction log and the growth amount "chunk" each time it is increased in size. If you leave the default settings with a large database, you can quickly find yourself with tens if not hundreds of thousands of VLFs, and this will cause a negative performance impact. This is why the process of preallocating the transaction log file and growing it by the right amount is so important.

TIP

To learn more about the physical architecture of SQL Server transaction log files, refer to http://technet.microsoft.com/en-us/library/ms179355(v=sql.105).aspx.

If the VLFs are too small, your maintenance, reboots, and database recovery operations will be excruciatingly slow. If your VLFs are too big, your log backups and clearing inactive logs will be excruciatingly slow and may impact production performance. The reason for the former is that SQL Server must load the list of VLFs into memory and determine the state of each, either active or inactive, when doing a DB restart or recovery. The latter is because a VLF can't be cleared until the SQL Server moves onto the next one.

As you can see from Table 6.2, if you create or grow a transaction log file by 64MB or less at a time, you will get four VLFs each time. If you need 200GB of transaction log, and it is created or grown by this amount, you end up with 12,800 VLFs, with each VLF being 16MB. At or before this point, you'd start to notice performance problems.

Table 6.2 Number of VLFs Allocated per Chunk Size

Chunk Size	Number of VLFs
<= 64MB	4
> 64MB and <=1GB	8
> 1GB	16

Let's take a look at another example: Suppose you have a 128GB log file created as 128GB to begin with. This file will have 16 VLFs, and each VLF will be 8GB. This means that each VLF can only be cleared at more than 8GB and when completely inactive. The process of clearing the log segment will likely have a direct impact on the performance of the database.

CAUTION

The number of VLFs in your transaction log file should *not* exceed 10,000. Above this level, there will be a noticeable performance impact. In an environment with log shipping, mirroring, or AlwaysOn, the number of VLFs will have an impact on the entire related group of SQL Servers. See Microsoft KB 2653893 (http://support. microsoft.com/kb/2653893) and SAP Note 1671126 (http://service.sap.com/sap/support/ notes/1671126).

To avoid the performance problems covered previously, you should ensure your VLF size is between 256MB and 512MB. This will guarantee that even if your transaction log were to reach the maximum size of 2TB, it will not contain more than 10,000 VLFs. To achieve this, you can preset your log file to either 4GB or 8GB and grow it (either manually or with Auto Grow) by the same amount each time. If we take the example of the 128GB transaction log, you would initially create a 8GB log file and then grow it by 8GB fifteen times. This will leave you with the 128GB log file and 256 VLFs within that log file, at 512MB each. You should set your transaction log file Auto Grow size to be the same as whatever growth increment you have decided upon.

TIP

One of the quickest and easiest ways to find out how many VLFs there are in your database and to find out more about your log files is to execute the query DBCC LOGINFO. The number of rows returned is the number of VLFs.

> **NOTE**
>
> If you are creating a database to support SAP, we recommend you review the following link with regard to transaction log sizing in addition to SAP Note 1671126: http://blogs.msdn.com/b/saponsqlserver/archive/2012/02/22/too-many-virtual-log-files-vlfs-can-cause-slow-database-recovery.aspx.

> **CAUTION**
>
> There is a bug when growing log files by multiples of exactly 4GB that affects SQL Server 2012. If you attempt to grow the log by a multiple of 4GB, the first attempt will fail to extend the file by the amount specified (you might see 1MB added), but will create more VLFs. The second or subsequent attempt will succeed in growing the file by the specified amount. This bug is fixed in SQL Server 2012 SP1. As a workaround, if you are still using SQL Server 2012, you should grow in increments of 4,000MB or 8,000MB rather than 4GB or 8GB. See http://www.sqlskills.com/blogs/paul/bug-log-file-growth-broken-for-multiples-of-4gb/.

Even if your database were relatively small, we would recommend that you start with a 4GB or 8GB (4,000MB or 8,000MB) transaction log file size. You should proactively and manually manage the size of your transaction log. Proactive management will avoid Auto Grow kicking in during production periods, which will impact performance. This is especially important when considering the transaction log will be growing at 4GB or 8GB at a time and having all those blocks zeroed out. However, just as with data files and Temp DB files, you should have Auto Grow enabled as a safety net and set it to either 4GB or 8GB, depending on the growth size you have selected.

Instant File Initialization

When a database file is created or extended, SQL Server will by default zero out the newly created file space. This will cause performance to degrade if it occurs during periods of intense database write activity, which is most likely if database files are not proactively managed and Auto Grow is extending the files. There is also the length of time required to write zeros to all the new blocks during which access to the file is blocked, as mentioned previously. To greatly improve the speed and reduce performance impacts of file growth operations, you can configure SQL Server to instantly initialize the database files without zeroing them out.

To allow your database instance to leverage Instant File Initialization (IFI), you need to add the SQL Server Service account to the Perform Volume Maintenance Tasks security policy (using Group Policy Editor gpedit.msc or Local Group Policy Editor secpol.msc), as shown in Figure 6.4. We strongly recommend this setting be applied in group policy, especially when AlwaysOn Availability Groups are used or when there are multiple databases that will have this setting enabled.

Figure 6.4 Enabling the Perform Volumes Maintenance Tasks security policy.

After you have made this change, you will need to restart your SQL Server services for it to take effect. We recommend you make this setting a standard for all your SQL Server databases and include it in your base template.

> **NOTE**
>
> Instant File Initialization (IFI) is only used for data files and Temp DB files. Even when IFI is configured and active, it will not be used for transaction log files. Transaction log files will continue to zero out every block when they are created or extended. This is due to the internal structure of the transaction log file and how it is used for data protection and recovery operations. This makes it even more important for you to proactively manage your transaction log files to prevent any avoidable performance impacts.

CAUTION

Instant File Initialization is not available when you're using Transparent Data Encryption (TDE) or when trace flag 1806 is set (which disables Instant File Initialization). Although IFI has a positive impact on performance, there are security considerations. For this reason, using IFI may not be suitable for all environments. See http://technet.microsoft.com/en-us/library/ms175935(v=sql.105).aspx. Based on our experience, in most environments, the highlighted security considerations can be addressed by proper controls and good system administration practice.

SQL Server File System Layout

We have covered how you determine how many files your databases need and how big each file should be preallocated. We now need to assign these files to the appropriate locations on the file system and configure the file system within the Windows operating system to achieve the best possible performance. The file system layout may differ slightly between database instances that are standalone, that use AlwaysOn Failover Clustering, or that use AlwaysOn Availability Groups. We will discuss the possible differences and give you recommendations based on our experience to help you achieve performance that can be built in to your standardized base templates.

OS, Application Binaries, and Page File

The OS, application binaries, and page file should be separated from the data, Temp DB, and log files in a SQL Server database. These components of the system generally produce little IO, but we don't want any IO interfering with productive IO from the database. For this reason, we recommend that OS, application binaries, and the page file be on a separate drive (or drives) and IO controller from data files, log files, and Temp DB.

TIP

Separate the operating system, application binaries, and page file from core database files so they don't impact the performance of the SQL Server Database.

From a database storage performance perspective, any paging is bad and should be avoided. Details of the page file and SQL Server memory configuration will be covered in Chapter 7, "Architecting for Performance: Memory." Chapter 7 will show you how to avoid paging and optimize performance from the memory configuration of your SQL Server.

File System Layout for Data Files, Log Files, and Temp DB

When considering the design of the file system layout for data files, log files, and Temp DB, our objectives are as follows:

1. Optimize parallelism of IO (Principle 1).

2. Isolate different types of IO from each other that may otherwise cause a bottleneck or additional latency, such as OS and page file IO from database IO, or sequential log file IO from random data file IO.

3. Minimize management overheads by using the minimum number of drive letters or mount points required to achieve acceptable performance (Principle 5).

In order to achieve objectives 1 and 2, we recommend splitting out data files and Temp DB files from log files onto separate drive letters or mount points. This has the effect of killing two birds with one stone. By separating log files into their own drive or mount point, you maintain the sequential nature of their IO access pattern and can optimize this further at the hypervisor and physical storage layer later if necessary. If the log files share a drive or mount point, the access pattern of that device will instantly become random. Random IO is generally harder for storage devices to service. At the same time, you are able to increase the parallelism needed for the IO patterns of the data files and Temp DB files.

To achieve greater IO parallelism at the database and operating system layer, you need to allocate more drive letters or mount points. The reason for this is that each storage device (mount point or drive) in Windows has a certain queue depth, depending on the underlying IO controller type being used. Optimizing the total number of queues available to the database by using multiple drives or mount points allows more commands to be issued to the underlying storage devices in parallel. We will discuss the different IO controllers and queue depths in detail later.

As a starting point for standalone database instances, we recommend that you configure a drive letter or mount point per two data files and one Temp DB file. This recommendation assumes each file will not require the maximum performance capability of the storage device at the same time. The actual number of drive letters or mount points you need will be driven by your actual database workload. But by having fewer drives and mount points will simplify your design and make it easier to manage. The more users, connections, and queries, the higher the IO requirements will be, and the higher the queue depth and parallelism requirements will be, and the more drive letters and mount points you will need.

> **CAUTION**
>
> You should monitor your database for signs of contention in the underlying storage subsystem. You can do this by querying the top wait states and checking PAGEIOLATCH. If you see excessive waits, that is a sign of database IO contention, and you may need to adjust your file system layout or underlying storage that supports your virtualized databases.
>
> Refer to http://blogs.msdn.com/b/askjay/archive/2011/07/08/troubleshooting-slow-disk-i-o-in-sql-server.aspx.

The example in Figure 6.5 illustrates how you might arrange your database files for a standalone instance. If you start to see IO contention and your database is growing (or is expected to grow) very large or makes a lot of use of Temp DB, then you may wish to separate out Temp DB files onto their own drive letters or mount points. This would remove the chance of Temp DB IO activity impacting the IO activity of your other data files and allow you to put Temp DB onto a separate IO controller (point 2 of our file system layout objectives).

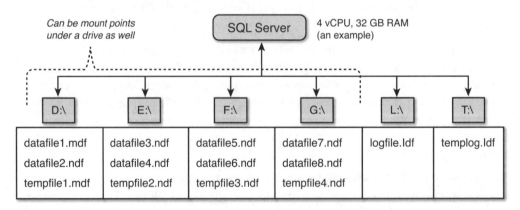

Figure 6.5   Sample SQL Server file system layout—Temp DB with data files.

Having a single Temp DB file on the same drive with two data files in general will balance the IO activity patterns and achieve acceptable performance without an excessive number of drives to manage. The reason for this layout is more likely on a standalone instance instead of with a clustered instance, which will become clear on the next page.

> **TIP**
>
> You should size each drive letter or mount point so that the preallocated database files on it consume no more than 80% of the available capacity. When you need to grow the capacity of your database, you have the option of either extending the existing drives or mount points or adding in more. These operations can be done online without any disruption to your running database. Auto Grow should be configured so that in the worst-case scenario, the maximum growth of all the files on the drive or mount point combined will never exceed the total capacity.

In the example in Figure 6.6, we have split out the Temp DB files onto separate drive letters from the data files of the production database. If you have a very large database or your database will have heavy IO demands on Temp DB, it makes sense to split it out onto its own drives and a separate IO controller.

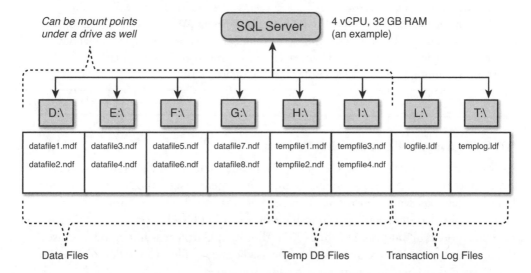

Figure 6.6   Sample SQL Server file system layout—data files separate from Temp DB.

In databases that make extremely heavy use of Temp DB, such as peaking at more than 50% of total database size, it might make sense for each Temp DB file to be on its own drive or mount point to allow each file access to more parallel IO resources. This assumes that the underlying storage infrastructure can deliver more IO in parallel, which we will cover later in this chapter.

In an AlwaysOn Failover Cluster Instance, an additional reason to separate Temp DB onto different drives or mount points from other data files is that it can be hosted locally to the cluster node, rather than on the shared storage. **This makes a lot of sense given that the Temp DB data doesn't survive instance restarts.** This allows you to optimize the performance of Temp DB without impacting the data files and log files that are shared between cluster nodes. If you have extreme Temp DB IO requirements, you could consider locating it on local flash storage, but consider that this would prevent the guest restarting in a VMware HA event. In this case, the cluster node would be unavailable if the local flash storage failed, which would trigger a failover to another node. This is a new feature available with SQL Server 2012 AlwaysOn that wasn't previously available (see http://technet.microsoft.com/en-us/sqlserver/gg508768.aspx). More details about AlwaysOn Availability Groups and Failover Cluster Instances are provided in Chapter 9, "Architecting for Availability: Choosing the Right Solutions."

TIP

In the case where you are splitting Temp DB files out onto separate drives from the other data files, it makes sense to also assign them to a separate IO controller. This will optimize the path of the IOs from the database through Windows and down to the underlying storage. We have used this as the foundation of our AlwaysOn Availability Group example configuration in Chapter 11, "Configuring a Performance Test – From Beginning to End," which is depicted in Figure 11.10.

NTFS File System Allocation Unit Size

Now that we have covered the SQL Server database layout on the file system, we need to cover another important aspect of the database file system design: the NTFS Allocation Unit Size (also known as Cluster Size). When you format a drive or mount point in Windows, you have the option of choosing a different NTFS Allocation Unit Size from the default (4KB in most cases). The NTFS Allocation Unit Size is important because it's the smallest amount of disk space that can be used to hold a file. If a file doesn't use the entire Allocation Unit, additional space will be consumed.

Having a small (default) Allocation Unit Size means there are many more times the number of blocks at the file system level that need to be managed by the operating system. For file systems that hold thousands or millions of small files, this is fine because there is a lot of space savings by having a smaller Allocation Unit in this scenario. But for a SQL Server database that consists of very few, very large files, having a much larger Allocation Unit is much more efficient from a file system, operating system management, and performance perspective.

> **TIP**
>
> For a SQL Server database that consists of very few, very large files, having a much larger Allocation Unit is much more efficient from a file system, operating system management, and performance perspective.

For the OS and Application Binary drive, keeping the default of 4KB Allocation Unit is recommended. There is no benefit in changing from the default. If your page file is on a separate drive from the OS, you should use a 64KB Allocation Unit size. For all SQL Server database drives and mount points (data files, log files, and Temp DB files), we recommend you use 64KB as your Allocation Unit Size setting (see Figure 6.7).

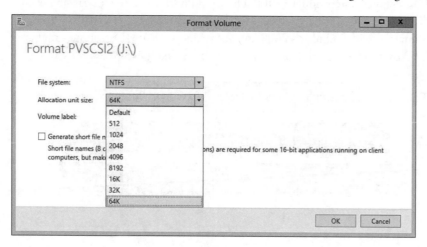

Figure 6.7 NTFS Allocation Unit Size.

> **TIP**
>
> The Default NTFS Allocation Unit size is 4KB for all volumes up to 16TB in size. Volumes greater than 16TB in size will have larger default Allocation Units. Regardless of your volume size and the default NTFS Allocation Unit size, we recommend you use 64KB. For most environments, it's unlikely you will be using more than 16TB for each volume.
>
> See http://support.microsoft.com/kb/140365 for further details of the NTFS Allocation Unit sizes for different-sized volumes.

Partition Alignment

Each storage device reads and writes data at different underlying block sizes. A block on a storage device is the least amount of data that is read from or written to with each storage option. If your file system partition is not aligned to the underlying blocks on the storage device, you get a situation called Split IO in which multiple storage operations are required to service a single operation from your application and operating system. Split IOs reduce the available storage performance for productive IO operations, and this gets even worse when RAID is involved, due to the penalty of certain operations, which we'll cover later in this chapter.

Figure 6.8 shows what would be considered a worst-case scenario, where the file system partition and the VMware vSphere VMFS partition are misaligned. In this case, for every three backend IOs, you get one productive IO. This could have the effect of causing each IO operation 3X latency, which is like getting 30% performance from your 100% storage investment. Fortunately, with Windows 2008 and above and with VMFS volumes that are created through VMware vCenter, this problem is much less likely.

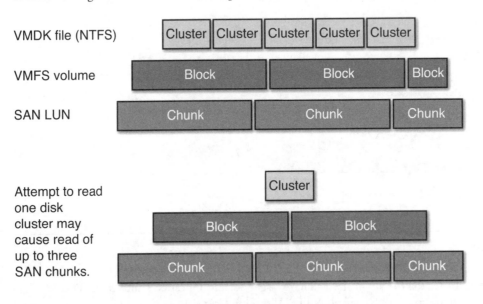

Figure 6.8   File system and storage that is not correctly aligned.

Starting with Windows 2008, all partitions are aligned to the 1MB boundary. This means in almost all cases, they will be aligned correctly. The same is true with VMFS5 partitions created through VMware vCenter. They will align to the 1MB boundary. However, if you have an environment that has been upgraded over time, you may still have volumes that are not correctly aligned. The easiest way to check is to monitor for Split IOs in both ESXTOP or in Windows Performance Monitor.

Figure 6.9 shows reading of one frontend block will require only one backend IO operation, thus providing lower latency and higher IO performance.

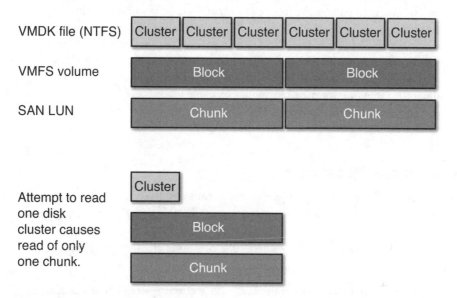

Figure 6.9   File system and storage that is aligned.

SQL Server Buffer Pool Impact on Storage Performance

The Buffer Pool is a critical region of memory used in SQL Server, and it has a large impact on storage performance. The important thing to note from a storage performance perspective is that a larger Buffer Pool produces less read IO on your storage and lower transaction latency at your database. The Buffer Pool is a big read cache for your database. If you size it incorrectly or if the Buffer Pool is paged out by the operating system, you will start to experience performance degradations and a large amount of additional read IO hitting your storage. How the Buffer Pool is covered in detail in Chapter 7, including how to avoid Windows paging out the Buffer Pool when virtualizing business critical databases.

> **TIP**
>
> There is a direct tradeoff between allocating more memory to the SQL Server Database and its Buffer Pool to reduce read IO and allocating less memory and having more read IO. For your design, you need to consider which resource will be more of a constraint and a cost. In some situations, more memory for your database and for your vSphere hosts could be cheaper than purchasing more performance via your storage systems. However, server-side flash, which could be thought of as cheap memory rather than expensive storage, combined with smart software is impacting the economics of this equitation. We will discuss in more detail later in this chapter how using flash storage local to the server can allow you to consolidate more databases per host with less memory per database without degrading performance to an unacceptable level.

Updating Database Statistics

The SQL Server Query Plan Optimizer uses statistics compiled from tables to try and estimate the lowest cost execution path for a given query. By default, statistics are updated automatically at defined thresholds (refer to http://msdn.microsoft.com/en-us/library/dd535534%28v=sql.100%29.aspx), such as when 20% of a table changes since statistics were last gathered.

The Query Optimizer's cost-based algorithm takes into account system resources such as CPU and IO to calculate the most efficient query, and overall table size and distribution of data. For example, it is better to join a three-row table to a million-row table, than to join a million-row table to a three-row table.

The cost to performance if the statistics are outdated and the impact on your storage can be high. Outdated statistics cause suboptimal query execution paths that can result in many more full table scans and therefore higher IO than would otherwise be required. For large databases that have hundreds of millions or billions of rows in a particular table, which can be common with SAP systems, the impact can be very severe. Therefore, it is important that you have up-to-date statistics.

> **CAUTION**
>
> When you upgrade an existing database to SQL Server 2012, the statistics may become out of date and result in degraded performance. To avoid this, we recommend you update statistics immediately after upgrading your database. To do this manually, you can execute sp_updatestats. Refer to http://www.confio.com/logicalread/sql-server-post-upgrade-poor-query-performance-w02/, which contains an excerpt from *Professional Microsoft SQL Server 2012 Administration*, published by John Wiley & Sons.

There are two primary methods to deal with the problem of outdated statistics impacting your database and storage IO performance.

Trace Flag 2371—Dynamic Threshold for Automatic Statistics Update

The first method involves using trace flag 2371 by setting startup option –T2371 or DBCC TRACEON (2371, -1). This is documented in Microsoft KB 2754171 (http://support.microsoft.com/kb/2754171). This trace flag tells SQL Server to dynamically change the percentage a table needs to change before the statistics are automatically updated. In very large tables, an automatic update of statistics can now be triggered by a change of less than 1%. Using this option could result in significantly improved performance for situations where you have very large tables.

TIP

Information with regard to trace flag 2371 in SAP environments can be found in the following articles: http://scn.sap.com/docs/DOC-29222 and http://blogs.msdn.com/b/saponsqlserver/archive/2011/09/07/changes-to-automatic-update-statistics-in-sql-server-traceflag-2371.aspx.

CAUTION

Database statistics are complied against each table in your database. When SQL Server updates statistics, this information is recompiled. Automatic statistics update and trace flag 2371 may cause statistics to be updated more frequently than necessary. So there is a tradeoff between the performance benefit of doing statistics updates regularly and the cost of recompiling the statistics. The cost of doing this operation is not free, and in rare cases it can have a detrimental impact on performance. If you find any performance problems correlating to the periods of time where statistics are being updated, then you may wish to control when statistics updates occur. For the majority of customers we deal with, around 80% experience positive performance improvements and no detrimental impact by using the dynamic automatic updates for database statistics. Refer to http://technet.microsoft.com/en-us/library/ms187348.aspx.

Updating Database Statistics Using a Maintenance Plan

The second method for addressing out-of-date statistics is by using a maintenance plan. If you need more control over when database statistics updates occur, you can schedule a maintenance plan task for your databases. Ideally, the maintenance plan would be scheduled to happen when it would have the least impact on the database, and run only as frequently as needed. To determine when and how often it should run requires you to know your database workload patterns and to monitor query plan execution efficiency. Depending on your database, you may wish to schedule it to initially happen daily and adjust the schedule based on observed performance. Figure 6.10 shows the Update Statistics option in the Maintenance Plan Wizard. A full step-by-step example is provided in Chapter 11.

Figure 6.10   Maintenance Plan Wizard's Statistics Update option.

> **TIP**
>
> It's important that databases have updated statistics so that the Query Optimizer works properly. This can be done via automatic settings or scheduled maintenance jobs. Use scheduled maintenance jobs where the timing of the gathering of these statistics needs to be done to minimize impact on performance of the database during peak demand periods.

Data Compression and Column Storage

Data Compression and Column Storage (also known as xVelocity memory optimized column store indexes) are features available only with SQL Server Enterprise Edition. They are not available in other editions. (See http://technet.microsoft.com/en-us/library/cc645993.aspx for a list of which features are supported in which SQL Server editions.)

If you are licensed and using SQL Server Enterprise Edition, we would recommend you make use of these features where appropriate.

Data Compression

Data Compression was originally introduced in SQL Server 2008 and has improved markedly in 2012. One of the most important things to understand about Data Compression is that it's not just about space savings, although the savings can be significant. Using Data Compression can also have a very positive impact on storage performance and Buffer Pool usage by reducing the number of IOPS and allowing the database to store more pages in memory in the Buffer Pool in compressed form. Using compression can also dramatically reduce query execution time, as fewer pages need to be read from cache or disk and analyzed for a given query.

In SQL Server 2012, you can choose to compress either a table or index using row or page compression. By default, when you choose page compression, it automatically does row compression at the same time. Based on our experience, space savings and performance improvements of up to 75% with SQL Server 2012 can be achieved in many cases. Data Compression can be used with both OLTP and OLAP type workloads, including Data Warehouse and Batch.

CAUTION

Data Compression introduces a CPU overhead and may increase CPU utilization on your database. In most cases, this overhead is outweighed by the benefit in performance you receive. In most virtualized environments, CPU performance will not be your constraint; memory and storage IO are usually the bottleneck. However, it won't benefit every workload and is not likely suitable for small tables that change very often. The best workloads for data compression consist of large tables that are predominately read oriented. Also Data Compression can't be enabled for system tables. Refer to http://technet.microsoft.com/en-us/library/cc280449.aspx and http://msdn.microsoft.com/en-us/library/dd894051(SQL.100).aspx.

TIP

If you are using SAP with SQL Server 2012, then Page Compression is turned on by default. For detailed information about using SQL Server Data Compression with SAP, refer to http://scn.sap.com/docs/DOC-1009 and the SAP on SQL Server Page (http://scn.sap.com/community/sqlserver).

Column Storage

Column Storage, also known as xVelocity memory optimized column store index, is a new feature of SQL Server 2012 aimed at data warehouse workloads and batch processing. Column Storage is much more space and memory efficient at storing and aggregating massive amounts of data. Leveraging this feature can greatly improve the performance of data warehouse queries. However, to use it you must make some tradeoffs.

TIP

In SQL 2012, you can select from a column store index and you can also rebuild. A new feature added to SQL 2014 is the ability to select and rebuild a column store index but also directly insert, update, or delete individual rows.

When using Column Storage, you will not be able to use Large Pages and Lock Pages in Memory (trace flag 834) because this will increase the work the translation look-aside buffer (TLB, see Chapter 7) has to do. Also, the tables using the column store index will be read-only. Any time you need to write data to the table, you need to drop and re-create the column store index, but this can easily be done with scheduled batch jobs. For the types of workloads that Column Storage is well suited to, these tradeoffs are normally worth the benefits.

NOTE

For detailed information on the xVelocity memory optimized column store feature, see the following Microsoft article: http://technet.microsoft.com/en-us/library/gg492088.aspx.

The benefits of Column Storage as documented in the link in the following tip include:

- **Index compression**—Column Storage indexes are far smaller than their B-Tree counterparts.

- **Parallelism**—The query algorithms are built from the ground up for parallel execution.

- **Optimized and smaller memory structures**

From a storage perspective, the benefits of Column Storage are far less storage capacity and performance being required to achieve the desired query performance. The improvement in query performance ranges from 3X to 6X on average, up to 50X. See http://blogs.msdn.com/cfs- file.ashx/__key/communityserver-components-postattach-ments/00-10-36-36- 43/SQL_5F00_Server_5F00_2012_5F00_Column_2D00_Store.pdf.

TIP

If you are using SAP BW with SQL Server 2012 (SP1 recommended, cumulative update 2 minimum), then Column Storage is turned on by default (for SAP BW 7.0 and above) when certain support packs are applied. For detailed information about using SQL Server 2012 Column Storage with SAP BW, refer to http://scn.sap.com/docs/DOC-33129 and http://blogs.msdn.com/b/saponsqlserver/.

Database Availability Design Impacts on Storage Performance

The database availability design you choose will have a direct impact on your storage performance. The choice between the different availability types varies. In this book, we are focusing mainly on standalone instances using VMware vSphere HA, SQL Server 2012 AlwaysOn Availability Groups (AAG), and AlwaysOn Failover Cluster Instances (FCIs). Standalone instances and FCI have relatively the same storage capacity requirements (unless local Temp DB is used in the FCI case) and have the same storage performance requirements. AlwaysOn Availability Groups, which has some advantages from an availability and data protection standpoint, at least doubles the total capacity requirements as well as adds additional IO overhead, dependent on the workload, and specifies how many inserts, updates, and deletes there are, as each database change must be replicated.

TIP

No matter which availability choice you make, you need to plan for the storage performance and capacity requirements of that choice. We will cover the details of SQL Server availability design, including AlwaysOn Availability Groups and Failover Cluster Instances, in Chapter 9.

Volume Managers and Storage Spaces

When you set up storage within Windows, you have the option of using the Windows Volume Manager with Basic or Dynamic Disks or using Storage Spaces (Windows 2012 onwards). Dynamic Disks and Storage Spaces provide options that include spanning volumes, striping volumes, and fault-tolerant volumes inside the guest operating system. Managing spanned, striped, or fault-tolerant volumes inside Windows adds an unnecessary IO overhead when you are virtualizing your SQL Server—especially as you are being provided with these services through your underlying storage devices and your virtual disks can be expanded online without disruption. Because of the way that SQL Server manages its data files, and effectively accesses them and stripes the files anyway, there is no need to add any additional layers of striping for performance inside Windows. We recommend the use of basic disks in Windows and the GPT (GUID Partition Table) partition format for all SQL Server partitions. Using GPT, you will be able to expand the partitions beyond 2TB in the future (vSphere 5.5 or above required) if the need arises. As a best practice, you should configure only one partition per virtual disk for your database.

> **TIP**
>
> We recommend the use of basic disks in Windows and the GPT (GUID Partition Table) partition format for all SQL Server partitions. If you want to boot from a GPT partition that's larger than 2TB, you can use the UEFI boot features of vSphere 5.x.

SQL Server Virtual Machine Storage Design

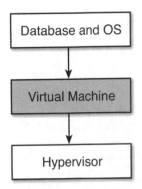

We have now covered how to optimize storage performance for SQL Server and Windows at the operating system level. Now we will look at how to optimize storage performance with your virtual machine template and discuss the different configuration options available to you. In this section, we cover different virtual machine hardware versions, virtual IO controllers, types of virtual disk, and how to size and deploy your virtual disks onto your storage devices. In this section, we start to look further at IO device queues and how they impact virtual machine storage performance.

Virtual Machine Hardware Version

The virtual machine hardware version you choose will impact the type of virtual storage IO controllers available to your virtual machine. The type of virtual storage IO controller you choose will have an impact on your storage performance, as we will cover in the next section. Table 6.3 shows the different storage IO controller options based on the different virtual hardware versions.

Table 6.3   Supported Virtual Machine Storage IO Controllers

Feature	ESXi 5.5 and Later	ESXi 5.1 and Later	ESXi 5.0 and Later	ESXi 4.x and Later	ESXi 3.5 and Later
Hardware Version	10	9	8	7	4
Maximum SCSI Adapters	4	4	4	4	4
Supported SCSI Adapters	BusLogic	BusLogic	BusLogic	BusLogic	BusLogic
	LSI Parallel	LSI Parallel	LSI Parallel	LSI Parallel	LSI Parallel
	LSI SAS	LSI SAS	LSI SAS	LSI SAS	
	PVSCSI	PVSCSI	PVSCSI	PVSCSI	
SATA (AHCI) Controllers	4	N	N	N	N

Each virtual SCSI controller (vSCSI) allows up to 15 disks to be connected, for a total of 60 vSCSI disks per virtual machine. With hardware version 10 in ESXi 5.5, VMware has introduced a new SATA (AHCI) controller. Each SATA controller allows up to 30 disks to be connected, for a total of 120 vSATA disks per virtual machine. vSCSI and vSATA can be combined on the same virtual machine for a maximum of 180 virtual disks per VM.

BusLogic and LSI Parallel are legacy controllers not suitable for SQL Server 2012 virtual machines. If you are virtualizing on ESXi 5.5 and using virtual hardware version 10, SATA may have some use if you have a need for a particularly large number of virtual disks per VM. However, for almost all cases, you will choose either LSI Logic SAS or VMware PVSCI (Paravirtualized SCSI). The reason why will become clear as we look in more detail at each of these controllers.

Choosing the Right Virtual Storage Controller

A virtual storage controller is very much like a physical storage controller in terms of how Windows interacts with it. Choosing the right virtual storage controller can have a big impact on your performance. In this section, we cover the different controller options and the performance characteristics of each type. This will help you make the right virtual storage controller choice based on your requirements and constraints.

Remember back to Principle 1: Your database is just an extension of your storage? Our goal is to maximize the parallelism of IOs from SQL Server and Windows through to the underlying storage devices. We don't want IOs to get held up unnecessarily in Windows itself. However, care needs to be taken because we don't want to issue so many IOs that the backend storage devices get overloaded and cause additional latency. Overloading your backend storage will not just impact SQL Server, but could also impact all of your other VMs. We will discuss later how you can use features of VMware vSphere to ensure quality of service to your critical databases and other virtual machines to protect them from the impact of noisy neighbors.

Table 6.4 outlines some of the key attributes of the storage controller options for your SQL Server VMs.

Table 6.4   Supported Virtual Machine Storage IO Controllers

Feature	LSI Logic SAS	VMware PVSCSI	SATA AHCI*
Maximum Disks per Controller	15	15	30
Default Adapter Queue Depth	128	256	N/A
Maximum Adapter Queue Depth	128	1,024	N/A
Default Virtual Disk Queue Depth	32	64	32
Maximum Virtual Disk Queue Depth	32	256	32
AlwaysOn Failover Cluster Instance Supported	Y	N	N
AlwaysOn Availability Group Supported	Y	Y	Y

* Supported as of vSphere 5.5 and Above, Virtual HW 10 Required

VMware's Paravirtualized SCSI controller (PVSCSI) is a high-performance SCSI adapter that allows the lowest possible latency and highest throughput with the lowest CPU overhead. In VMware vSphere 5.x, PVSCSI is the best choice, even if you don't expect your database to be issuing large amounts of outstanding IO operations. However, like SATA, PVSCSI can't be used with SQL Server AlwaysOn Failover Cluster Instances, which leverage shared disk clustering. When you are using AlwaysOn Failover Cluster Instances, your only option is LSI Logic SAS.

> **CAUTION**
>
> Changing the storage controller type after Windows is installed will make the disk and any other devices connected to the adapter inaccessible. Before you change the controller type or add a new controller, make sure that Windows contains the necessary drivers. On Windows, the driver must be installed and configured as the boot driver. Changing the storage controller type can leave your virtual machine in an unbootable state, and it may not be possible to recover without restoring from backup.

Choosing a virtual storage controller with a higher queue depth will allow SQL Server to issue more IOs concurrently through Windows and to the underlying storage devices (virtual disks). By having more virtual disks (more drives or mount points), you increase the amount of queues that SQL Server has access to. Balancing the number of data files to drive letters, to virtual disks, and to adapters allows you to maximize the IO efficiency of your database. This will reduce IO bottlenecks and lower latency.

Not all virtual disks will issue enough IOs to fill all of the available queue slots all of the time. This is why the adapter queue depths are lower than the aggregate total number of queues per device multiplied by the total number of devices per adapter. PVSCSI, for example, has 15 virtual disks, and each disk has a queue depth of 64 by default. The number of devices multiplied by their queue depth would be 960, even though the adapter default queue depth is only 256.

> **TIP**
>
> To determine the number of IO operations queued to a particular drive or virtual disk at any particular time, you can use Windows Performance Monitor to track the Average Disk Queue Length for each device. You should be recording this parameter as part of your SQL Server baseline and capacity planning to help you properly design the storage for your virtualized SQL Server systems.

In most cases, the default queue depths are sufficient for even very high performance SQL Server systems—especially when you are able to add up to four vSCSI adapters and increase the number of virtual disks per adapter. With LSI Logic SAS, you have a maximum of 32 queue slots per disk and a maximum of 128 queue slots per adapter.

Neither can be changed. In this case, your only option to scale IO concurrency is by adding virtual controllers and adding virtual disks. This is a key consideration when considering AlwaysOn Failover Cluster Instances, where LSI Logic SAS is the only vSCSI adapter option.

With PVSCSI, you can modify the disk queue depth and the adapter queue depth from their default settings. This is only required in very rare cases where your database needs to issue very large amounts of IO in parallel (>1,000). To keep things standardized and simple, we recommend leaving the default settings in your templates and only modify them if absolutely necessary. This assumes your underlying disk subsystems can support the parallelism required at low-enough latency.

Figure 6.11 shows an example of the registry entries configured to increase the maximum adapter and virtual disk queue depths for a VMware PVSCSI adapter, as documented in VMware KB 2053145.

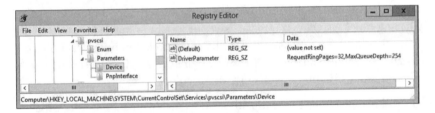

Figure 6.11   PVSCSI advanced registry parameters.

> **NOTE**
>
> If you wish to use PVSCSI as your boot controller, you need to select it when creating the virtual machine, and during the Windows installation you need to mount the pvscsi-Windows2008.flp floppy disk image from the ESXi vmimages folder. This means you will need to ensure that your virtual machine is configured with a virtual floppy disk device. Information on which versions of ESXi and Windows support PVSCSI as a boot device can be found in VMware KB 1010398.

> **CAUTION**
>
> There have been issues with using the PVSCSI driver with Windows 2008 or Windows 2008 R2 on versions of ESXi before 5.0 Update 1, as described in VMware KB 2004578. If you are using VMware vSphere 5.0, we recommend that for your SQL Server databases you upgrade to ESXi 5.0 Update 2 or later. These problems are not relevant for ESXi 5.1 or 5.5.

If you choose not adjust the queue depth or are unable to adjust the queue depth of a particular storage device or adapter, Windows will queue any additional IOs. Windows will hold up to 255 IOs per device before issuing them to the adapter driver, regardless of the devices underlying queue depth. By holding the IOs in the Windows OS before issuing them to the adapter driver and the underlying storage, you will see increased IO latency. To learn more about the Windows storage driver architecture (storport), we recommend you read the article "Using Storage Drivers for Storage Subsystem Performance" at Windows Dev Center [http://msdn.microsoft.com/en-us/library/windows/hardware/dn567641 and http://msdn.microsoft.com/en-us/library/windows/hardware/ff567565(v=vs.85).aspx].

Figure 6.12 shows the difference in IOPS and latency between PVSCSI, LSI Logic SAS, and SATA AHCI. These tests were conducted using a single drive at a time on a single VM. The VM was configured with two vCPUs and 8GB RAM. Each virtual disk was placed on the same VMFS5 data store on top of a Fusion-io ioDrive2 1.2TB PCIe flash card. IOMeter was used to drive the IO load and measure the results.

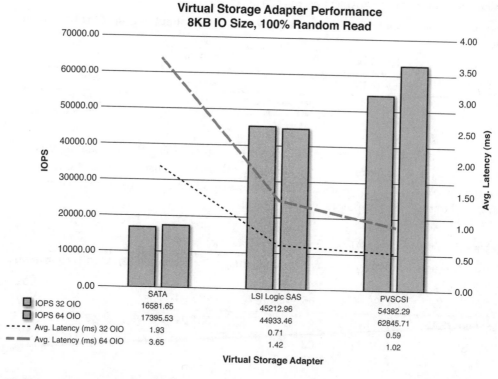

Figure 6.12 Virtual storage adapter performance.

As you can see from the graph in Figure 6.12 (published at http://longwhiteclouds.com/2014/01/13/vmware-vsphere-5-5-virtual-storage-adapter-performance/), both SATA and LSI Logic SAS have no significant performance advantage going from 32 outstanding IO operations (OIO) to 64 due to their maximum device queue depth being 32. PVSCSI, however, sees a 15% improvement in IOPS between 32 OIOs and 64, based on a single Fusion-io ioDrive2 card as the underlying storage. A storage array of multiple backend devices will potentially show a much greater improvement when queue depth is increased. This assumes the HBAs and storage processors are configured to accept a higher queue depth and not overloaded.

Table 6.5 displays the IOMeter performance results for each virtual storage adapter, including throughput and CPU utilization for the 8KB IO size. The IO pattern used was 100% random read, with a single worker thread and single virtual disk from the test virtual machine. As you can see from the results, PVSCSI shows significantly better IO performance at lower latency and lower CPU utilization compared to the other adapter types.

Table 6.5   Virtual Storage Adapter Performance (32 OIOs)

Virtual Storage Adapter	IOPS	Avg. Latency (ms)	Throughput (MB/s)	CPU Utilization
SATA	16581.65	1.93	129.54	52%
LSI Logic SAS	45212.96	0.71	353.23	45%
PVSCSI	54382.29	0.59	424.86	33%

Table 6.6 displays the IOMeter performance results of increasing the outstanding IOs from 32 to 64 to issue more IOs in parallel using otherwise similar test parameters. As was the case with the previous test, PVSCSI shows significantly improved performance compared to the other adapter types.

Table 6.6   Virtual Storage Adapter Performance (64 OIOs)

Virtual Storage Adapter	IOPS	Avg. Latency (ms)	Throughput (MB/s)	CPU Utilization
SATA	17395.53	3.65	135.90	54%
LSI Logic SAS	44933.46	1.42	351.04	43%
PVSCSI	62845.71	1.02	490.98	34%

This test also shows that a single virtual machine on a vSphere 5.5 host with a single virtual disk can provide good performance and throughput, provided the underlying storage system can support it. Using PVSCSI with vSphere 5.1 and above, a single virtual

machine can support up to one million IOPS at 4KB IO size (see http://blogs.vmware.
com/performance/2012/08/1millioniops-on-1vm.html).

CAUTION

The IOMeter performance results included in this section were created only to show the
relative difference in performance capability between the different virtual storage adapter
types. Your results will be different. These tests did not use real-world workload patterns
and should not be relied upon for sizing or capacity planning of your SQL Server databases. You should conduct your own tests to validate your environment. See Chapters 10
and 11 for details of how to validate and baseline your environment.

Choosing the Right Virtual Disk Device

You have a small number of options when choosing a virtual disk type for SQL Server,
and the choice you make may have an impact on performance. However, modern storage
systems and advancements in hypervisor technology have equalized the performance
aspects of different virtual disk types in a lot of cases. Today, the type of storage you're
using and your availability design will largely drive your virtual disk selection. Table 6.7
outlines the different virtual disk options.

Table 6.7 Virtual Disk Types

Virtual Disk	Zero on First Write	Size Limit	SQL Failover Cluster Instance Across Boxes Supported
Thin	Y	2TB–512B	N
Thick – Lazy Zero	Y	62TB (ESXi 5.5)	N
Thick – Eager Zero	N		N*
Virtual Raw Device Map (vRDM)	N		N
Physical Raw Device Map (pRDM)	N	64TB	Y
PassThrough PCI or VM DirectPath IO	N	Device Limit	Y**

*When configuring SQL Failover Cluster Across Boxes for SQL Server Failover Cluster Instances, you need to configure
the non-shared disks as Thick Eager Zero. Shared disks need to be set as either vRDM or pRDM with bus sharing set
to physical.

**It is possible to use a PassThrough PCI device or VMDirectPath IO with SQL Failover Cluster Instances to store either
non-shared disks (such as for Temp DB) or shared disks. In the case of Temp DB, you may choose to use a local
PCIe flash device and pass it through to the Cluster Node. In the case of the shared disks, you would most likely use
VMDirectPath IO to pass through a Fibre Channel HBA. A VM's memory is fully reserved automatically. Using these
options prevents VMware HA and limits other virtual machine operations. Because of the restrictions and limitations,
VMDirectPath IO is not recommended for general use. Refer to VMware Product Documentation for additional details.

NOTE

Supported Clustering Configurations are covered in VMware KB 1037959 and the VMware Product Guide: "Setup for Failover Clustering and Microsoft Cluster Services" (http://pubs.vmware.com/vsphere-55/topic/com.vmware.ICbase/PDF/vsphere-esxi-vcenter-server-55-setup-mscs.pdf).

Thin Versus Thick Lazy Zero for SQL Server

The major difference between Thin and Thick Lazy Zero disks is that Thin disks are not preallocated and start small and grow on demand, whereas Thick Lazy Zero disks are preallocated. The unit of growth of a Thin disk is the VMFS block size, which is usually 1MB for VMFS5, unless the data store was upgraded form VMFS3. On a very active VMFS data store, there is the possibility that as the Thin disk grows, the blocks allocated will not be contiguous, but in most cases, this will not negatively impact performance.

There is a myth that the performance of Thick Provisioned disks, even if using Lazy Zero, is much better than a Thin Provisioned virtual disk (VMDK). This is not the case. Thin Provisioned disks and Thick Provisioned Lazy Zero disks have similar performance characteristics. This is because each time a block of data is initially written to either a Thin or Thick Lazy Zero disk, the block must first be zeroed out. This magnifies the write IO impact of blocks that have not previously been written because two write IOs will be issued by the ESXi host for each block. This may have a noticeable negative impact on write IO latency, depending on your underlying storage.

The reason to choose between Thin or Thick Lazy Zero therefore has little to do with performance and more to do with manageability and efficiency of storage consumption. There are tradeoffs to each choice. Your choice needs to be based on your requirements and circumstances.

Using thin provisioning may allow for higher utilization of storage capacity as each VMDK, data store, and underlying storage device will have a percentage of free space unused as a safety buffer. At the same time, it will add additional management overheads to the environment because administrators have to ensure they do not excessively over-provision real storage resources in terms of both capacity and performance. You need to be aware of possible growth storms and keep on top of your storage demands.

CAUTION

Thin Provisioned VMDK growth operations on VMFS data stores generate metadata updates. Each metadata update requires a lock for a brief period of time on the VMFS data store. On some older storage arrays that do not support VMware's API for Array Integration (VAAI) and where there is an excessive number of Thin VMDKs or VMs per data store, this can cause SCSI reservation conflicts, which may result in degraded performance (additional latency). VMFS5 volumes newly created on arrays that support VAAI will use Atomic Test and Set Locking (ATS) Only. ATS addresses the problems that used to be caused by SCSI reservation conflicts. When selecting a storage array for use with VMware vSphere 5.x and SQL Server, you should ensure it supports VAAI. VMFS5 volumes that were upgraded from VMFS3 may fall back to using SCSI reservations in certain cases. See VMware KB 1021976 and http://blogs.vmware.com/vsphere/2012/05/vmfs-locking-uncovered.html.

The capacity savings from thin provisioning may well be enough to justify the management overheads because you are able to purchase more on demand instead of up front, and this could save a considerable amount of money. But you need to make sure you can get the performance you need from the capacity that has been provisioned and is used. Sizing for performance may necessitate much more capacity is provisioned on the backend storage devices and therefore diminishes any savings that may have been had when saving capacity through thin provisioning.

CAUTION

Restoring files from backup or copying files between VMs that have Thin Provisioned VMDKs will cause those disks to expand. Once the disks are expanded, they do not shrink automatically when the files are deleted. Also, since Windows 2008, if you do a Full Format on a Thin Provisioned VMDK, it will cause the disk to inflate, as a full format will zero out each block. If you use Thin Provisioned disks, you should select the quick format option when partitioning a disk in Windows. We strongly recommend that you don't over-provision storage resources to the point an out-of-space (OOS) condition could result from unexpected VMDK growth. See VMware KB 1005418 and Microsoft KB 941961.

If you don't use Instant File Initialization, then SQL Server will zero out its data files whenever they are created or extended. This will ensure you get optimal performance from the data files regardless of the underlying virtual disk format. But this comes at the cost of the time taken to zero out the file and the resulting impact in terms of storage IO to the underlying storage. As previously discussed, using Instant File Initialization allows SQL Server to act as part of Windows and not write a zero to a block before data is written to it. In certain cases, there could be substantial storage efficiencies (IO Performance and Capacity) by combining the use of Instant File Initialization, thin provisioning, and SQL Server compression. This may be especially advantageous to development and test environments. There can be a significant performance penalty if you use a non-VAAI array without using SQL Instant File Initialization on Thin and Thick Lazy Zero disks. VAAI allows the zeroing operation to be offloaded to the array and performed more efficiently, thus saving vSphere resources for executing VMs. If you use Thin Provisioned or Lazy Thick VMDKs without a VAAI-compatible array, the entire zeroing operation has to be handled solely by vSphere.

If your SQL Server and environment meets the following requirements, you may want to consider using Thin Provisioned VMDKs with Instant File Initialization and SQL Data Compression:

- The SQL Server workload will be largely read biased.

- Performance from your storage during times that blocks are initially written to and zeroed out is sufficient to meet your database SLAs.

- Performance is sufficient from the capacity required when thin provisioning is used.

- You are not planning to use Transparent Data Encryption.

- You wish to minimize the amount of storage provisioned up front and only purchase and provision storage on demand.

When you are using Thick Provisioning Lazy Zero (the default), the VMDK's space is allocated up front by vSphere, although like with thin provisioning, it is not zeroed out until it's written to for the first time (or you select full format in Windows when partitioning the disks). When you look at the data store, you may get a more accurate view of free space and there may be less variance between provisioned space and usage. The reason we say you may get a more accurate view of free space is that many modern arrays will tell vSphere the storage is allocated or consumed but won't actually do so until data is written to it, although it most likely will be reserved.

If you were considering using Thin or Thick Lazy Zero VMDKs for SQL Server, we would recommend you choose the default of Thick Lazy Zero to minimize management overheads. We would recommend using Thin where there are requirements that would benefit from it and justify the management overheads. However, before you decide on Thick Lazy Zero, you should consider Thick Eager Zero, which we cover next.

Using Thick Eager Zero Disks for SQL Server

The major difference between Thick Eager Zero and Thick Lazy Zero or thin provisioning is when the blocks on the VMDK are zeroed out. As we've covered with Lazy Zero and Thin VMDKs, blocks are zeroed on first write. With Eager Zero, the blocks are zeroed when the VMDK is created as part of the provisioning process. This means all blocks are pre-zeroed before Windows or SQL goes to access them. By doing this, you are eliminating a first write penalty in the situations where that would occur. This ensures there is no double write IO required to the VMDK after it is provisioned.

As you can imagine, it can take quite a bit longer to provision Thick Eager Zeroed disks. Additionally, provisioning and zeroing out the blocks may impact the performance of other VMs when using shared storage devices. The impact to your environment will be dependent upon the type and utilization of your backend storage devices. Some storage arrays will just throw away or ignore the zeros, and in these cases, the provisioning operations will complete relatively quickly and have minimal impact on performance.

In aggregate, over the life of a VMDK there is normally little difference in the amount of IO generated when using Thin, Thick Lazy Zero, or Thick Eager Zero VMDKs. The difference is all about the timing of when the IO is generated, either up front (in the case of Eager Zero) or on demand (first write) with Thick Lazy Zero and Thin. Once a block has been written to with Thick Lazy Zero or Thin, it has exactly the same performance characteristics as if it were Eager Zeroed. However, with Eager Zero, even if a block is never used, you have zeroed it out at the cost of a write IO operation.

TIP

When provisioning VMDKs for data files and transaction log files, we recommend you size them to allow 20% free space, which allows for any unforeseen required growth. There should be sufficient capacity for the predicted workload over at least a three-to-six-month period. By right-sizing VMDKs and holding data files and transaction log files for a reasonable period, you reduce the management and administrative burden while at the same time optimize overall performance and capacity consumption.

If you are proactively managing SQL Server data and transaction log files, and not using Instant File Initialization, then the performance of your virtual machine will be the same regardless of the virtual disk type you select. This is because SQL Server is zeroing out the blocks first before they are used. If you enable IFI, then Eager Zero will give better perfor-mance in terms of lower latency compared to Thick Lazy Zero or Thin, but only when the block is first written to. All subsequent writes or access to the same block will have exactly the same performance characteristics.

Although the aggregate amount of IO may be similar between the different virtual disk options, Eager Zero generally provides the more predictable response times because IOs will not be impacted by the additional write operation when data is written to a new block. This predictability of IO response and generally lower latency is why Eager Zero is required for the non-shared disks of a SQL Server Failover Cluster Instance. Increased latency or poor IO performance can cause unnecessary cluster failovers between nodes.

TIP

In the case of your backend storage devices supporting VAAI and the Write Same prim-itive, the operation to zero out the blocks will have a minimal impact on performance regardless of the timing of the operation, whether Eager Zero, Lazy Zero, or Thin.

With the advent of VMware's VAAI and modern arrays that support it, the impact to the environment of zeroing operations is reduced and therefore the performance impact of using Eager Zero Thick disks is also reduced during initial provisioning. If you were previ-ously thinking of using Thick Lazy Zero VMDKs and you have a VAAI-capable array that supports the Write Same primitive, we would recommend you use Thick Eager Zero instead. This provides lower management overheads and optimal performance. Regardless of whether you are using IFI or not, and in spite of the possible overhead of having written zeros to a block that may not be used, we feel this is justified for the decreased latency and increased predictability of IO responses that are provided to SQL Server. This is especially important for business-critical production databases. It is fine to use Thin or Thick Lazy Zero for your Windows OS disk, while using Eager Zero Thick for your database drives (data files, Temp DB, and transaction logs). When using SQL AlwaysOn Failover Cluster Instance, it is recommended that you configure Windows OS disks as Eager Zero Thick; shared LUNs will in this case be configured as physical RDMs.

Figure 6.13 shows a sample configuration of a virtual disk with the selection of Thick Provision Eager Zeroed.

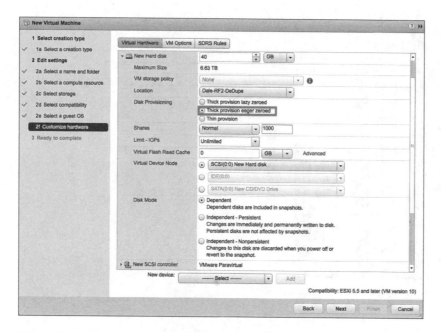

Figure 6.13   New virtual disk—Thick Provision Eager Zeroed.

Using Raw Device Maps for SQL Server

A Raw Device Map (RDM), as the name suggests, is a direct mapping of a physical LUN to a virtual machine. The main reason to choose RDM is SQL Server Failover Cluster Instances (FCI). SQL FCI uses Windows Failover Clustering (previously known as Microsoft Cluster Services), shared SCSI bus, shared disks between nodes, and requires persistent SCSI reservations. To allow the persistent SCSI reservations and the cluster to function correctly, Physical Mode or Pass-through RDM (pRDM) are required. Another reason to consider using RDMs for SQL Server is if you are leveraging physical SAN capabilities such as snapshots that you wish to present to a physical server for a purpose such as LAN-free backups, if you are not using a backup solution integrated with the VMware APIs for Data Protection. However, there are no noticeable performance differences between RDMs and virtual disks on a VMFS file system, as Figure 6.14 illustrates.

Figure 6.14 illustrates the performance comparison between VMFS and RDM using a random 50/50 mixed read-write workload pattern and the different IO sizes based on data published at http://www.vmware.com/files/pdf/performance_char_vmfs_rdm.pdf.

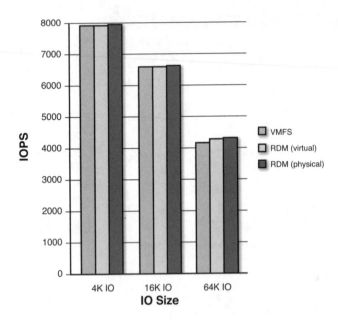

Figure 6.14   VMFS and RDM performance comparisons: IOPS vs. IO size.

NOTE

Although Virtual Mode RDMs (vRDMs) are included in Figure 6.14 for performance comparison, they are not supported for use with Windows 2008 and above failover clustering or SQL Failover Cluster Instances.

TIP

There is a common myth that you can't perform vMotion operations when using RDMs. This is not the case. VMs configured with RDMs support vMotion, but only when the virtual machine is not using SCSI bus sharing. It is the SCSI bus sharing required in a SQL Server AlwaysOn Failover Cluster Instance that prevents the vMotion operations from being supported currently, not the fact the VM is configured to use RDMs. See VMware KB 1005241.

Although there are no noticeable performance differences between a single VMDK on a VMFS data store and an RDM, there are important performance considerations and constraints with using RDMs that need to be considered, such as:

- An RDM maps a single LUN to a virtual machine, so each VM will likely consume multiple LUNs and there will be more LUNs to manage.

- More LUNs are required, which may constrain the number of VMs possible as the maximum number of LUNs per host is currently 256.

- It is not possible to perform storage IO quality of service on a pRDM; therefore, a VM configured to use a pRDM could negatively impact the performance of other VMs using the same underlying shared storage array.

- Can't leverage vSphere features such as Storage vMotion, so it can be more difficult to balance capacity and performance when using pRDMs and more difficult to resolve any storage hot spots.

Due to the management overheads, constraints, and VMware feature limitations of using RDMs, we recommend their use only when absolutely necessary, such as to deploy SQL FCI; in all other cases, VMDKs should be used. Using VMDKs future proofs your environment and allows it to benefit from any further advancements that VMware releases that pertain to VMDKs.

The IO Blender Effect

When you virtualize SQL and consolidate many SQL VMs onto fewer hosts, the amount of IO per host increases. In addition to the increase in IO per host, in most cases the IO patterns will also change. Unless you have completely dedicated storage for each SQL VM, which is not optimal from a cost or performance perspective in most cases, all IO will at some point become random.

Any time you share storage and have multiple VMs and different IO workloads, the combined IO pattern is random. Random IO, especially when write biased, can have a significant impact on storage performance, particularly when RAID (Redundant Array of Inexpensive or Independent Disks) is used. Grouping similar workloads together can help improve the blended IO pattern and reduce the burden on storage. Figure 6.15 shows the impact of combining different IO workload patterns.

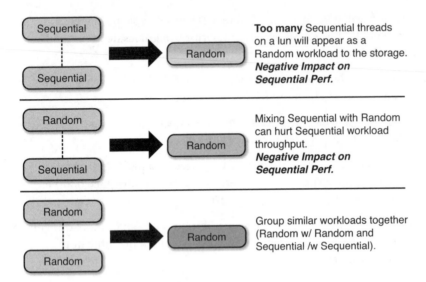

Figure 6.15   The IO Blender Effect.

This is an important concept to understand because you will need to size your storage to be able to handle the required number of IOPS with a completely random IO pattern. Random IO has a higher overhead than sequential IO in most cases, with the exception of some flash-based storage systems. Subsequent sections of this chapter will discuss IO workload performance impacts of different physical storage systems in more detail.

SQL Virtual Machine Storage Layout

Now that we have covered the various storage IO controller and virtual disk device choices, we can put it all together and discuss the design of a logical virtual machine storage layout. This layout, in turn, supports our SQL Server and Windows design and will drive the design of our underlying storage devices. We want to take our five key principles and apply these so our virtual machine storage layout meets the requirements of our database workloads in the simplest way possible, without compromising SLAs.

The example in Figure 6.16 shows a simple storage layout for a SQL Server VM that has all of its VMDKs supported by a single underlying data store. You could also have a number of SQL Server VMs and their VMDKs on the same data store. For development and test VMs, and where SQL FCI is not used, this may be a suitable design choice. It would also be suitable for the storage of your SQL Server template VM. However, it is unlikely to be a suitable choice for high-performance business-critical production SQL Server databases. The Windows C: drive, application binaries, and page file may be on the same data store or hosted on another data store.

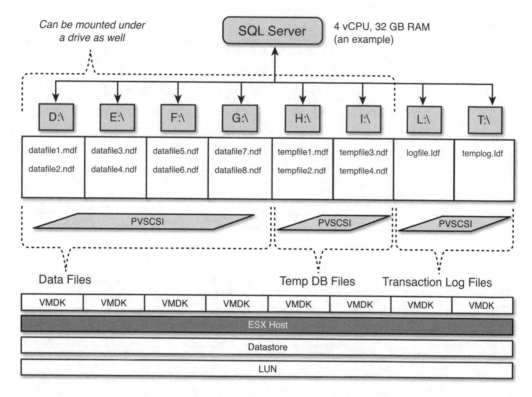

Figure 6.16 Multiple VMDK to a single data store.

The performance of SQL in this example will be limited to the performance of a single data store, and it will have access to the queue depth of a single data store, even though the individual virtual disks may be trying to issue many IOs in parallel. This example is the simplest from a management perspective, though, because there is only a single data store to manage. This sample layout assumes that not all of the virtual disks will be issuing IOs at the same time and that the aggregate amount of outstanding IOs will not exceed the available queue depth of the data store. If the available queue depth of the data store and the underlying storage device is exceeded, the result will be additional IO latency in the hypervisor and slower response times for your database. Another impact of this choice is that all IOs from SQL will be blended together and become completely random, as we show in the "IO Blender Effect."

The example in Figure 6.17 shows two VMDKs per data store. This layout may be suitable for production SQL databases, provided the underlying data store could support the performance requirements of the VMDKs. This assumes that the data store has sufficient queue depth for the peak number of outstanding or parallel IOs from the VMDKs; otherwise, additional latency will result and response times will be degraded. SQL will benefit from the combined IO performance of multiple data stores and the queue depth available from multiple data stores to allow many IOs to be serviced in parallel.

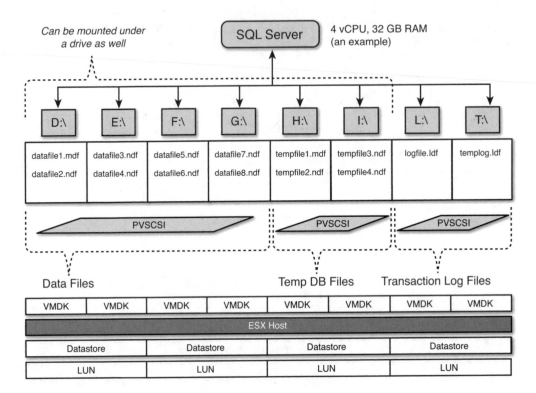

Figure 6.17   Multiple VMDK and multiple data stores.

This sample layout provides a balance between manageability and performance, because there are a relatively small number of data stores to manage per SQL VM, less than would be required for a physical SQL system or where RDMs are used. This is quite a common layout for SQL systems that have reasonable but not extreme performance requirements. The data store that holds the transaction logs would blend the otherwise sequential IO patterns and make them random. If this was a concern, the transaction log VMDKs could be separated onto their own data stores.

TIP

We recommend the VMDK for the Windows OS C: drive, application binaries, and Windows page file be hosted on a separate data store. Because the IO from the Windows OS C: drive, application binaries, and page file should be minimal, you may be able to host a number of them on a single data store, while keeping data files and transaction log disks and their data stores separate. You should take into account your availability requirements and risks, as the loss of access to a single data store in this case could impact multiple SQL systems. Backup disks can be shared with the same IO controller as the OS, and we recommend they are on their own VMDK and data store if their size and performance requirements justify it.

The example in Figure 6.18 shows each VMDK mapped to a dedicated data store. This layout is suitable for SQL systems that need extreme IO performance and scalability. It allows IO to be spread across more storage devices, and each VMDK has access to the maximum possible amount of parallel IO. The increased number of data stores and therefore LUNs will limit the total number of VMs that can be supported per host. You will have many more data stores to manage per VM, which will increase your management overheads.

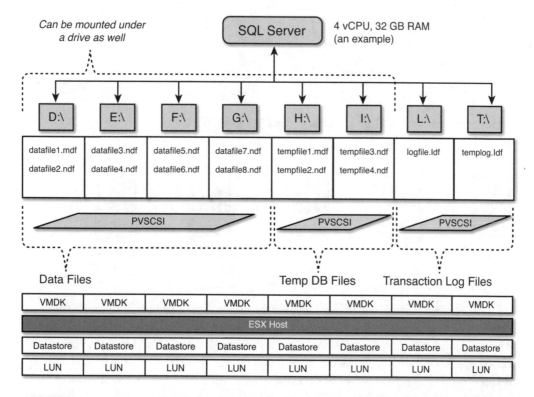

Figure 6.18   Single VMDK per data store.

If each SQL VM has 10 data stores, you could be limited to just 25 VMs per cluster, as each data store should be zoned to each host in the cluster to allow VMware HA and DRS to function correctly. It is likely that if you need this layout for storage performance, your SQL VMs will also have very large compute footprints in terms of memory and CPU. However, if this is required to meet your performance requirements, you may find that you need to design for a smaller number of hosts per cluster, and potentially have more clusters. This layout assumes that each VMDK will use the full queue depth of each data store, which is often not the case. You may find that you need to reduce the queue depth per LUN to avoid overloading your backend storage ports, which defeats the purpose of having more LUNs in the first place.

Often the need for extreme performance is driven by many database instances or schemas running on a single VM, and in these cases it may be a better design choice to split up those instances into multiple VMs. Because VMDKs (not RDMs) are used, it is possible to start with the example in Figure 6.19 and increase the number of data stores if required at a later time. You can migrate the VMDKs without any downtime by using VMware Storage vMotion.

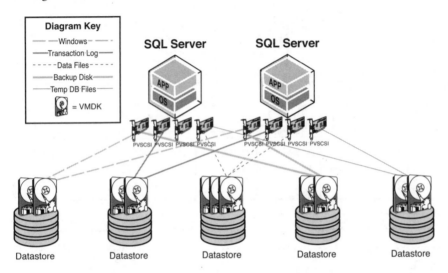

Figure 6.19 Virtual machines sharing data stores.

Up until now we have provided examples where the storage is dedicated to each SQL Server. This is a very traditional approach to SQL storage architecture. When you have a very good baseline and understanding of your inventory and workload characteristics, it is a good approach, but it has a couple of potential drawbacks. The first drawback is manageability. You must have a number of data stores supporting each VM, which produces more data stores to manage, and may not balance performance and capacity efficiently between many SQL Server VMs. You may end up with many different data store sizes for each of the different databases, which provides little opportunity for standardization. This may be more of a problem in a smaller environment because there may be fewer SQL VMs of similar size; in large-scale environments (hundreds of SQL VMs), this is generally less of a problem.

The next potential drawback is that although you may have isolated the storage logically to each VM, if you share the same storage under the covers, each VM could impact the performance of the others. When a single VM is using a storage device, you can't make use of VMware vSphere features such as Storage IO Control (SIOC) to ensure quality of service and fair IO performance between different VMs. This may place an additional burden on storage administrators to try and isolate performance at the physical storage level, which can often lead to limited and suboptimal overall performance.

Finally, the isolation approach doesn't lend itself easily to automation and policy-based administration. It is also not possible to dedicate storage devices to SQL Server VMs in this manner in most Cloud or Infrastructure as a Service environments. To make automation and policy-based administration possible, you need standardization and you need to share multiple data stores among many VMs. This then allows you to leverage the features of VMware vSphere to ensure quality of service and fairness of IO performance between the many SQL VMs if there is any contention.

The example in Figure 6.19 shows two SQL Server VMs sharing the same data stores for the different types of Windows OS and SQL disks. This layout allows the SQL VM's performance to be balanced with a standardized data store size and allows for easier automation and policy-drive provisioning and load balancing. Because the data stores are shared, VMware Storage IO Control can ensure fairness of IO and quality of service for IO performance between the multiple SQL VMs.

SQL Failover Cluster Instance Storage Layout

In this section we have shown how you can efficiently lay out your virtual machine storage for SQL and use fewer LUNs than you have VMDKs, while balancing performance requirements. This is possible when using standalone instances or when using AlwaysOn Availability Groups. However, when using SQL AlwaysOn Failover Cluster Instances, you must use pRDMs and therefore bypass the VMFS data store and the ability to share LUNs, as Figure 6.20 illustrates.

For this reason and for reduced management overheads and complexity, we recommend the use of AlwaysOn Availability Groups over Failover Cluster Instances where possible.

TIP

We recommend all non-shared disks of your SQL FCI be set to Independent Persistent to ensure they are not impacted by accidental VM snapshot operations. Any VM snapshot operations on these disks can cause unexpected cluster failovers.

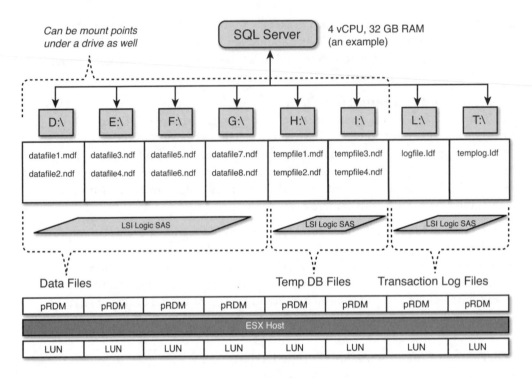

Figure 6.20   SQL AlwaysOn Failover Cluster Instance storage layout.

Expanding SQL Virtual Machine Storage

When designing your virtual machine storage architecture for SQL Server, you need to consider how the allocated storage will be expanded in the future as your databases grow. We previously discussed in "SQL Server File System Layout" the ability to expand partitions and virtual disks online without disruption. This is one way of expanding the storage available to SQL Server. An alternative approach would be to hot-add additional virtual disks to SQL Server and then balance the data files across the additional disks.

If you hot-add new disks and need to create new data files, SQL Server will stripe the data to the newly created data files as they have the more free space. For this reason, we recommend you add more than one virtual disk and data file to try and spread the IO load. This will help avoid creating hot spots. The number of VMDKs and data files you need to create will depend on your SQL workload profile.

> **TIP**
>
> Because the transaction log is written to sequentially and not striped, it is recommended that the VMDK or RDM be extended if necessary, rather than hot-adding a disk and creating a new log file. In vSphere 5.x, a VMDK can be expanded online without disruption up to a maximum of 2TB–512 Bytes.

Jumbo VMDK Implications for SQL Server

vSphere 5.5 introduced the ability to provision 62TB Jumbo VMDKs and Virtual Mode RDMs (vRDM) with a VM. Physical Mode RDMs (pRDM) are capable of being provisioned up to 64TB, as of vSphere 5.0. The VMware maximum VMFS data store size is 64TB, as it was in vSphere 5.0. This allows truly massive storage footprints to a single VM.

With Virtual Hardware Version 10, we now have the ability to provision a single VM with maximum storage capacity (see Table 6.8).

Table 6.8 Maximum Virtual Machine Storage

Virtual Disk Controller	Max # Controllers	VMDK/ Controller	Total VMDKs	Capacity VMDK/vRDM	Capacity pRDM
vSCSI Controller	4	15	60	3,720TB	3,840TB
SATA Controller	4	30	120	7,440TB	7,680TB
Totals	8		180	11,160TB (11PB)	11,520TB (11.5PB)

Just because the size of the virtual disk increases doesn't mean the performance of the virtual disk increases. With each virtual disk, the queue depth is still the same regardless of the size. This limits the parallelism of IOs to a single virtual disk, and it will also limit the throughput unless SQL is issuing incredibly large IO sizes. For this reason, the maximum capacity is largely theoretical because you would not be able to get the necessary performance.

> **TIP**
>
> The maximum theoretical SQL 2012 database size is 524PB. The maximum data file size is 16TB, and the maximum log file size is 2TB. For further maximums, see http://technet.microsoft.com/en-us/library/ms143432.aspx.

Although having lots of 62TB virtual disks is unrealistic, having a few virtual disks > 2TB is possible and potentially desirable for large SQL Servers. You can use a single virtual disk for your transaction logs (max 2TB per transaction log file), and you would be able to use a single virtual disk for your backup drive. Both transaction logs and backups are sequential in nature and could benefit from the capacity of a larger > 2TB VMDK without the performance drawbacks that would be likely for data files. Your underlying storage platform would need to support a VMFS data store of a LUN size big enough to support all of these large VMDKs. You should also consider your restore times when using large VMDKs. If you can't restore a large VMDK within your SLAs, it is not a good choice. Just because you can use Jumbo VMDKs doesn't mean you always should.

CAUTION

You can't extend virtual disks > 2TB online. You must shut down your virtual machine first, and extend the virtual disk offline through the vSphere Web Client. This is due to the disk needing to be in the GPT format. Once a virtual disk has been extended to > 2TB, each time you need to extend it further, you must shut down the VM. Alternatively, you can hot-add a new virtual disk to the VM online at any time and the new virtual disk can be > 2TB. Jumbo VMDKs can only be managed through the vSphere Web Client because the traditional VI Client (VMware C# Client) only supports VMware vSphere 5.0 features. All newer features are only available through the Web Client. We recommend you create all SQL data file, Temp DB file, transaction log, and backup drives using the GPT format.

VMFS Heap Size Considerations with Monster VMs and Jumbo VMDKs

ESXi 4.x and 5.x prior to 5.5 used a VMFS Heap value to control how much memory was consumed to manage the VMFS file system and for open or active VMDK capacity on a single ESXi host. This limit was not documented in the vSphere Maximum's product document, and by default with a 1MB block size on ESXi 5.0 GA, it would limit a host to being able to open 8TB of total VMDKs before errors could occur. The maximum on

ESXi 5.0 GA was 25TB with a 1MB block size, which required adjusting the advanced parameter VMFS3.MaxHeapSizeMB. This was later increased to 60TB by default on ESXi 5.0 by applying the latest patches and in ESXi 5.1 Update 1. The only downside of this was 640MB of RAM was consumed for the VMFS Heap.

CAUTION

For the vast majority of environments, you don't need to change the default VMFS settings, and the information in this section should be considered carefully alongside your knowledge and understanding of your particular environment, circumstances, and requirements. This really is for when you're considering virtualizing business-critical apps and Monster VMs with very large storage footprints.

In vSphere 5.5, the whole VMFS Heap size problem has been addressed. The VMFS Heap is now irrelevant as a measure of how much open and active VMDK capacity a single ESXi 5.5 host can handle. This is due to major improvements in the way the VMFS Heap and pointer blocks are managed.

VMFS pointer blocks are a pointer to a VMFS block on disk. When a VMDK is opened on an ESXi 5.5 host, all of the VMFS "pointer" blocks are cached in the Pointer Block Cache, which is not part of the main VMFS Heap (where the pointer blocks were previously stored in prior versions of ESXi). This allows the open VMFS "pointer" blocks to be addressed or accessed and managed as fast as possible without having to access metadata from the VMFS file system directly. The pointer blocks will remain in use so long as a VMDK or other file is open. However, many blocks in any individual VMDK are not often active. It's usually only a percentage of the blocks that are actively used (say, 20%). The images shown in Figures 6.21 and 6.22 display how the pointer blocks are used to refer to data blocks on the VMFS file system. Each pointer block that is active is stored in the pointer block cache to ensure the fastest possible access to the most frequently used blocks.

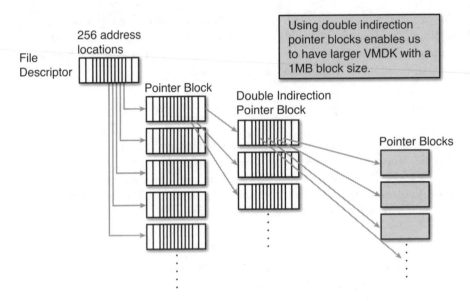

Figure 6.21   VMFS pointer block indirection—memory address mapping to physical VMFS blocks. [1]

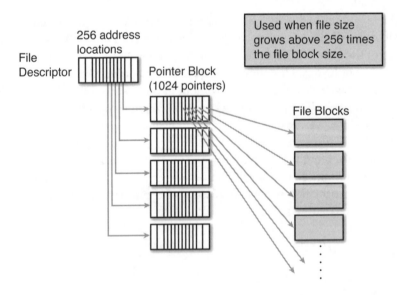

Figure 6.22   VMFS pointer block double indirection. Used for mapping very large VMFS data sets.*

---

[1] Used with permission from Cormac Hogan (http://cormachogan.com/2013/11/15/vsphere-5-5storage-enhancements-part-2-vmfs-heap/).

Pointer Block Eviction Process

This is where the new Pointer Block Eviction Process introduced in ESXi 5.5 comes in. If the number of open and active VMFS blocks reaches 80% of the capacity of the Pointer Block Cache, a Pointer Block Eviction Process will commence. This basically means the pointer blocks that are not active, or least active, will be evicted from memory and only the active blocks will remain in the cache. This new process greatly reduces the amount of ESXi host memory consumed to manage VMFS file systems and the open VMDKs capacity per host. The VMFS Heap itself in ESXi 5.5 consumes 256MB of host RAM (down from 640MB), and the Pointer Block Cache by default consumes 128MB of host RAM. You no longer have to worry about adjusting the size of the VMFS Heap at all. A new advanced parameter has been introduced to control the size of the Pointer Block Cache, MaxAddressableSpaceTB.

As with all advanced parameters, you should not change MaxAddressableSpaceTB without a good justification, and in most cases, it will not be necessary. MaxAddressableSpaceTB by default is set to 32, with a maximum of 128. This controls the amount of host RAM the Pointer Block Cache consumes. With the default setting at 32, it will consume 128MB of host RAM (as mentioned previously), and with the maximum setting of 128, it will consume 512MB of host RAM. However, it's important to note that this does not limit the capacity of open VMDKs on the ESXi 5.5 Host, just how many of the pointer blocks can stay cached in RAM. If only 20% of all VMDK blocks are active, you could conceivably be able to have 640TB or more of open VMDK capacity on the host, while still having the active pointer blocks cached without much, if any, performance penalty.

The way this new Pointer Block Eviction Process works gives you a sense of having an almost unlimited amount of open VMDK capacity per ESXi 5.5 host. But it's not quite unlimited; there is a tradeoff as the amount of active VMDK capacity on an ESXi 5.5 host increases. The tradeoff is possible Pointer Block Cache Thrashing, which may impact performance.

With the default setting of MaxAddressableSpaceTB=32, the Pointer Block Eviction Process won't kick in until the amount of open VMDKs exceeds 25.6TB. So if you aren't expecting the VMs on your hosts to routinely exceed 25TB of open and active VMDK blocks, there is probably no need to even look at adjusting MaxAddressableSpaceTB; this saves you some host RAM that can be used for other things. In most cases, you would only have to adjust MaxAddressableSpaceTB if the active part of all open VMDKs on a host exceeds 25TB. If active VMDK blocks exceed the capacity of the Pointer Block Cache, then thrashing could result from constantly evicting and reloading pointer blocks, which may have a performance penalty.

You will see signs of Pointer Block Eviction in the VMKernel logs on your hosts if it is occurring. Syslog, vCenter Log Insight, or Splunk will help you spot this type of activity. If you start to notice any sort of performance impact, such as additional storage latency visible in KAVG in ESXTOP, and a correlation to Pointer Block Eviction, then that would be a sign you should consider adjusting MaxAddressableSpaceTB. If you're planning to have 100TB of open VMDKs per host routinely, as in the case of large SQL Servers, we recommend setting MaxAddressableSpaceTB = 64 and adjusting upwards if necessary. If you're not concerned about the amount of RAM the Pointer Block Cache will consume, you could consider setting it to the maximum of 128.

Increasing MaxAddressableSpaceTB may consume host RAM unnecessarily and so should be considered along with the total RAM per host and the RAM that is likely to be consumed by all VMs. 512MB of RAM consumed for Pointer Block Cache on a host with 512GB of RAM or more is not significant enough to worry about, but could be worth considering carefully if your hosts only have 32GB of RAM.

CAUTION

Any time you change an advanced parameter in vSphere, it's something that has to be managed and considered when you are changing your environment. To "Keep It Simple and Standardized" (Principle 5), you should avoid changing advanced parameters if possible.

---

vSphere Storage Design for Maximum SQL Performance

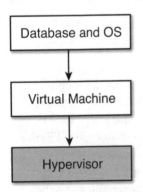

We have so far covered SQL Server VM storage architecture from the database down to the data store. We are now ready to dive into VMware vSphere storage design and physical storage design to achieve maximum performance. This section will build on what we've covered already and help you to design an underlying storage architecture that supports your high-performance SQL Server systems on top of it. We will cover the impacts of number of data stores, data store queues, storage performance quality of service (QoS), storage device multipathing, RAID, and storage array features such as auto-tiering.

Number of Data Stores and Data Store Queues

The number of data stores you specify for your SQL Servers has a direct impact on the number of VMs and hosts that you can support in a vSphere cluster. The maximum number of data stores per host is 256, and all data stores should be visible to all hosts in a single cluster to ensure features such as VMware HA and DRS function correctly. For SQL Servers that will have a low IO requirement, you may be able to host a number of them on a single data store. This is one of the great benefits of using VMFS data stores over RDMs. Ultimately the number of data stores you need depends on how many IOPS you can get from a single data store, the combined IOPS and queue depth (QD) requirement of the VMs, and the queue depth you have configured per LUN on each vSphere host. For example, if each SQL Server consumes six LUNs or data stores and you can support four SQL Servers per host, your vSphere cluster would be limited to 10 hosts, plus one host for failure.

The IOPS for a particular data store is usually measured and specified in terms of IOPS per TB. This makes it very easy to explain to application owners what performance they should expect from their storage related back to the capacity. However, the calculation can become a little more complicated when features such as array auto-tiering, compression, and de-duplication are used. As part of designing your storage environment, we recommend you specify an SLA for each type of data store that is backed by a different class of storage (or different storage policy). As part of the SLA, calculate the IOPS per TB achievable and make this known to the application owners. Knowing the IOPS per TB achievable and required will also help if you are looking to host any SQL servers in a cloud environment. Whatever the IOPS per TB is for a particular data store, it will potentially be divided by the number of hosts sharing the data store, so you will most likely not be able to run a single host to the limit, unless there is only one VM on the data store.

In many cases, you can reduce the number of data stores you need to manage by increasing the queue depth per HBA LUN on each vSphere host. This allows you to place additional virtual disks on the data store, but without sacrificing the aggregate number of available storage IO queues. We recommend you do not increase the aggregate queue depth to the storage processors. By this we mean that by reducing the number of LUNs and increasing the queue depth per LUN, the total queue depth to the storage processor ports should be the same.

CAUTION

Be aware that if your storage is under-configured or already overloaded, increasing the queue depths won't help you. You need to be aware of any queue depth limits on your storage array and processor ports and make sure that you don't exceed them. If you overload a traditional storage processor and get a QFULL SCSI sense code, the storage controller (HBA) will drop the queue depth to 1 and slowly increase it over time. Your performance during this period will suffer significantly (like falling off a cliff). We recommend that you consult with your storage team, storage vendor, and storage documentation to find out the relevant limits for your storage system before changing any queue depths. This will help avoid any possible negative performance consequences that would result from overloading your storage. Some storage arrays have a global queue per storage port, and some have a queue per LUN. Whether your storage is Fibre Channel, FCoE, or iSCSI, you need to understand the limits before you make any changes.

TIP

The default queue depth on a QLogic HBA changed from vSphere 4.x to 5.x from 32 to 64. Emulex queue depth is still 32 by default (two reserved, leaving 30 for IO), and Brocade is 32. If you didn't know this and simply upgraded, you could suffer some overloading on your backend storage processors. If your array is supporting vSphere hosts and non-vSphere hosts on the same storage processors, it is possible in some cases for the vSphere hosts to impact the performance of other systems connected to the same array. For more information and instructions on how to modify your HBA queue depth, see VMware KB 1267 and http://longwhiteclouds.com/2013/04/25/important-default-hba-device-queue-depth-changes-between-vsphere-versions/.

In Table 6.9, where the data store maximum number of VMs per host is 1, the maximum VMs on a given data store is effectively the maximum number of hosts that can be supported in a cluster. To increase the aggregate amount of active IOs per VM, you need to increase the number of LUNs and ensure VMs sharing those LUNs are split across hosts.

Table 6.9 Calculating Load on a VMFS Volume for Sample Configurations

Max Outstanding IO per LUN (n)	Avg. Active IO per VM (a)	LUN Queue Depth (d)	Max VM per Host m=(d/a)	Max VM on Data Store (n/a)
256	4	32	8	64
256	4	64	16	64
1,024	4	64	16	256
256	32	32	1	8
1,024	32	32	1	32
1,024	1	32	32	1,024
256	64	64	1	4
1,024	64	64	1	16

Table data sourced from http://www.vmware.com/files/pdf/scalable_storage_performance.pdf, with additional scenarios added.

You don't just have to worry about your maximum LUN queue depths. You also have to consider the queue depths of your HBA. Many HBAs have a queue depth of 4,096, which means you'd only be able to support 64 LUNs per host at a queue depth of 64, assuming all queues were being used. Fortunately, this is rarely the case, and overcommitting queues at the host level has less drastic consequences than overcommitting queues at the storage array level. Any IOs that can't be placed into the HBA queue will be queued within your vSphere host, and the consequence is increased IO latency, the amount of which will depend on your IO service times from your storage. Queuing inside your vSphere host can be determined by monitoring the QUED value and KAVG in ESXTOP. Recommended thresholds for average and maximum values can be found in Chapter 10.

The LUN queue depth isn't the only value that you may need to modify in order to increase performance from your data store. The LUN queue setting goes hand in hand with the VMware vSphere advanced parameter Disk.SchedNumReqOutstanding (DSNRO). DSNRO is used to control the queue maximum depth per VM when there are multiple VMs per data store. The goal of this setting is to ensure fairness of IO access between different VMs. When there is only one VM per VMFS data store, the LUN queue depth will always be used. In vSphere, Disk.SchedNumReqOutstanding is a global value up until vSphere 5.5. In vSphere 5.5, Disk.SchedNumReqOutstanding is specified on a per-device basis. This setting is modified dynamically, as is the LUN queue depth when Storage IO Control is enabled on a data store with multiple VMs that is experiencing performance constraints.

> **TIP**
>
> You can set the per-device number of requests outstanding in vSphere 5.5 by using the command
>
> esxcli storage core device set –d naa.xxx --sched-num-req-outstanding=<value>
>
> where naa.xxx is the device name and <value> is a value from 1 to 256.
>
> To list the storage devices on the system, use the following command:
>
> esxcli storage core device list
>
> By specifying the –d naa.xx option, you can confirm the setting has been changed as you expected. Also see VMware KB 1268 for further information.

Figure 6.23 shows the different queues at each level of the vSphere storage architecture. The two values that are usually worth monitoring as a vSphere admin are the AQLEN and the DQLEN. DQLEN can be adjusted up or down, depending on your requirements. For high-IO SQL Server systems where PVSCSI is used on VMDKs, we suggest you set the DQLEN to 64 as a starting point, while taking into account our previous recommendations when modifying queue depths.

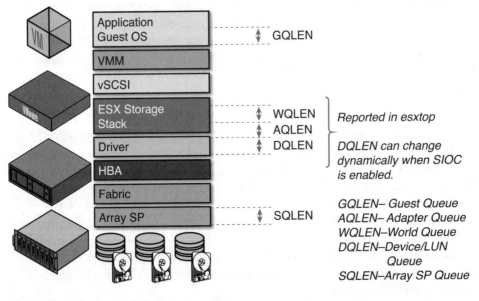

Figure 6.23   VMware vSphere storage queues.

CAUTION

If you have an under-configured storage array and insufficient individual spindles or disks to service the aggregate IO requirements, then increasing the queue depth will not improve performance. On an under-configured array, increasing queue depth will just result in the queues becoming full and increased IO latency or service times. Virtualization doesn't get around the laws of physics; you may need more disks. Our goal is to ensure the path from the guest to the underlying storage is not the bottleneck in software, so that you can get the most out of your physical storage investments and get the highest performance possible.

NOTE

If you are presenting RDMs to a VM, such as with SQL FCI, and using the LSI Logic SAS adapter, there is little benefit in increasing the queue depth to 64. Windows will only be able to issue 32 outstanding IOs before it starts queuing, and you'll never be able to make use of the additional queue depth. If you will be using a large number of RDMs on your hosts, see VMware KB 1016106.

Figure 6.24 shows the different areas where storage IO latency is measured and the relevant values inside vSphere. DAVG, which is the device latency, will indicate if you have a bottleneck in your storage array, which may mean you need to add more disks or reduce the load on that device. If you start to see KAVG constantly above 0.1ms, this means the vSphere kernel is queuing IOs and you may need to increase device queue depth, especially if the DAVG is still reasonable (< 10ms).

We want to optimize the queues through the IO stack so that the disk devices are the constraint, and not the software or queues higher in the stack. Periodic spikes in DAVG and KAVG are acceptable, provided the averages are not consistently high. Brief spikes in DAVG and KAVG are acceptable; however, high average values are a sign of a performance problem. Suggested thresholds are listed in Chapter 10.

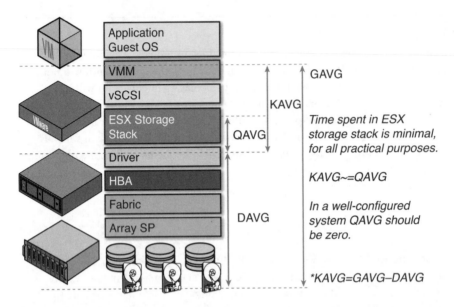

Figure 6.24   VMware vSphere storage latency.

TIP

When consolidating multiple SQL servers onto fewer hosts, there is usually an implicit assumption that SQL was not previously making full or optimal use of all of the system resources. This includes CPU and RAM, but also storage IO and HBA queues. It's your job as the architect or admin of the environment to ensure your destination vSphere platform and each host has in aggregate sufficient resources to service the blended peak IO workloads of all of the databases on a single host. Once you know what the likely blended peak is, you can design your host platforms accordingly.

"Every millisecond of storage IO latency is potentially a millisecond that SQL can't respond to an application request." —Michael Webster

---

Number of Virtual Disks per Data Store

This section is only relevant if you're building standalone SQL Server or using AlwaysOn Availability Groups with virtual disks (VMDKs). SQL FCI requires RDMs, and therefore each drive is mapped to a LUN and you can't share the LUN with multiple VMDKs. You can, however, share the LUN and drive with more data files and achieve the balance of outstanding IOs to queue depth that way.

The number of VMDKs per data store will be limited by the performance character-istics of the data store and the performance requirements of the VMs and their VMDKs. Our primary goal when we decide on the number of VMDKs per data store is to try and balance the average number of active outstanding IOs per host with the queue depth of the data store. In most cases, not all VMDKs will use all their available queue depth all of the time, and not all VMs will use their available queue depth all the time either, but they may have peaks. We need to be able to handle these peaks within a reasonable time in terms of the IO latency or service time.

The example in Figure 6.25 shows a configuration where two VMDKs are on each data store. Each VMDK has a queue depth of 64, resulting in an over-commitment in queue depth of 2:1 from the VMDKs to the data store. On average, each VMDK will be able to issue 32 outstanding IOs (assuming they're on the same vSphere host) before any additional queuing occurs in the vSphere kernel. If one VMDK is idle, the other VMDK can issue the maximum number of outstanding IOs to the data store and make use of the full queue depth. This may seem to be a rather conservative number of VMDKs per data store, but for very-high-performance systems this (or even 1:1 VMDK to data store) may be necessary to achieve the performance requirements.

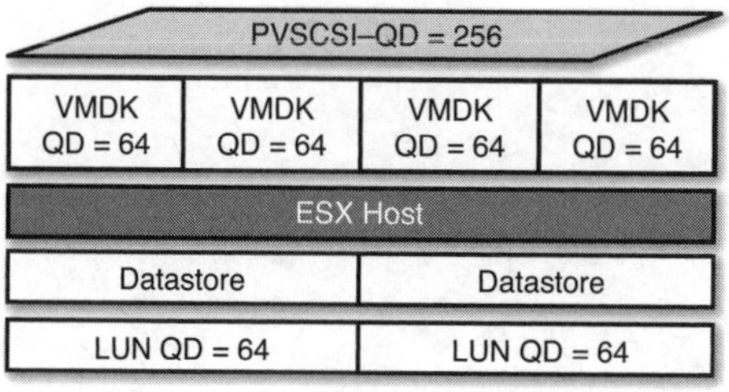

Figure 6.25 Two VMDK per data store.

The example in Figure 6.26 shows a queue depth over-commitment of 4:1, assuming all VMDKs from a single VM on the single vSphere host. Each VMDK would be able to issue on average 16 outstanding IOs, while if the other VMDKs are idle an individual VMDK will be able to fill the entire queue.

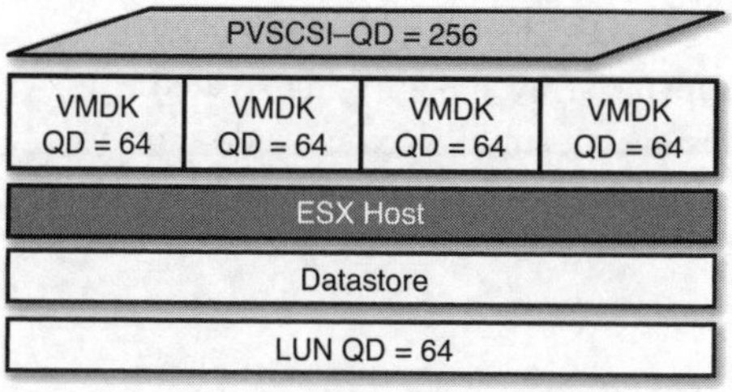

Figure 6.26 Four VMDK per data store.

This is quite possibly fine for a single host and a single VM for this data store. But a data store is shared between all hosts in the cluster. If we only host a single VM on the data store and only on a single host, we are not able to utilize all of the queue depth that is usually available at the storage array. This assumes that the physical LUN configuration can support a higher aggregate queue depth and higher IOPS at the storage array level. If your backend storage is already performance constrained by its configuration, adding more queue depth and more VMs and VMDKs to the data store will only serve to increase latencies and IO service times.

Figure 6.27 shows two SQL VMs on two different ESXi hosts accessing the same data store. In this scenario, because each host has a LUN queue depth of 64, the combined queue depth to the LUN at the storage array could be up to 128. Provided the LUN can support the additional queue depth and IOPS without increasing latency, this would allow us to extract more performance from the same LUN, while reducing the number of LUNs that need to be managed. For this reason, sharing data stores between multiple VMs and VMDKs across multiple hosts can produce more optimal performance than alternatives. But it is important to make sure that each VM gets a fair share of the performance resources of the data store.

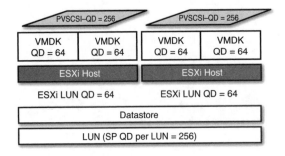

Figure 6.27   Multiple VMs on different ESXi hosts per data store.

NOTE

Prior to the introduction of VMware APIs for Array Integration (VAAI) and VMFS5, VMware used to recommend that no more than 25 VMDKs be hosted on a single data store. This no longer applies if you have a VAAI-capable array and a freshly created (rather than upgraded from VMFS3) VMFS5 data store. It's unlikely you would want to go as high as this for your SQL servers for production, but it might be applicable for Dev and Test.

> **TIP**
>
> To ensure that two VMs that are sharing the same data store do not reside on the same vSphere host, you can use vSphere DRS Rules to keep the VMs separated. This will reduce the chance of queue contention between the two SQL servers that might occur if they were on the same host. Having too many DRS Rules can impact the effectiveness of vSphere DRS and increase management complexity, so it's use should be kept to a minimum. If you get your performance calculations slightly wrong and you discover one of the VMDKs is busier than you expected, you could easily migrate it to another data store using Storage vMotion. This can be done online and is nondisruptive to SQL. Some additional IO latency may be seen during the migration process.

Storage IO Control—Eliminating the Noisy Neighbor

One of the potential impacts of working in a shared storage environment is having one VM monopolize storage performance resources to the detriment of other VMs. We call this the Noisy Neighbor Effect. If one VM suddenly starts issuing a lot more IO than all the other VMs, it could potentially slow down other VMs on the same data store, or on the same array. To combat this problem, VMware introduced Storage IO Control (SIOC) in vSphere 4.1 and has made enhancements to it in vSphere 5.x.

Where there is more than one VM sharing a data store and SIOC is enabled, if the latency exceeds a threshold (default 30ms), vSphere will take action to reduce the latency. The way it reduces the latency is by dynamically modifying the device queue depth of each of the hosts sharing the data store. What it is doing is in effect trading off throughput for latency. The result is, individual VMs may see higher latency from storage but they each get their fair share of the storage performance resources.

SIOC should be activated only to deal with unexpected peaks of IO activity and should not be stepping in all the time. SIOC should be seen as more of a last resort. If you observe higher latency in your VMs and SIOC working constantly, this is an indication that your data store or storage platform can't support the required IO workload. You may need to add more physical disks to your storage platform or reorganize some of the LUNs to reduce hot spots.

As shown in Figure 6.28, if one VM or one host begins to monopolize the available performance resources, the other VMs sharing the same data store or storage array suffer.

In some cases, it's not just that other VM's performance suffers, but other more important VMs sharing the same data store don't get the IO resources they are entitled to.

Figure 6.29 provides an example where three VMs share the same data store. One important VM and a less important VM share a vSphere host, while another less important VM is on another vSphere host. The relative importance is defined by the shares value, which uses a proportional share algorithm to carve up the performance resources. Because this doesn't work across hosts, the less important VM on its own host has full access to the available queue depth and therefore is getting more than its fair share of IO performance resources.

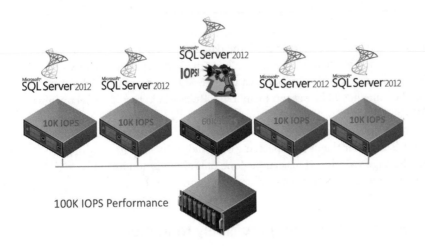

100K IOPS Performance

Figure 6.28 The Noisy Neighbor Effect.

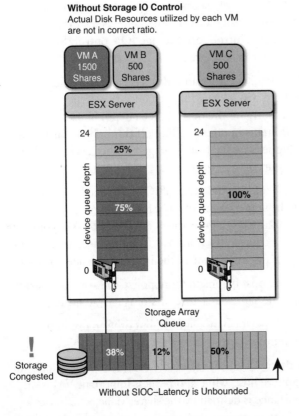

Figure 6.29 Storage congestion without SIOC.

With Storage IO Control activated, the proportional share of resources and fairness are enforced across all hosts and for all VMs that share the same data store. In the example shown in Figure 6.30, SIOC takes action to reduce the queue depth that the less important VM has access to and to ensure that the most important VM gets its full entitlement to the available IO resources of the data store. Because Storage IO Control is only going to become active when there is congestion on the data stores, it is perfectly safe to use with array auto-tiering. SIOC will simply balance out the latency while the array moves blocks around if the operations cause any latency spikes.

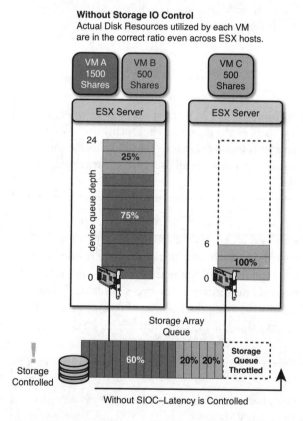

Figure 6.30   Storage controlled with SIOC.

In vSphere 5.5, Storage IO Control uses an injector that periodically tests the performance capability of a given data store and can dynamically change the thresholds it uses to determine data store congestion. If you prefer to use the traditional method of a static latency threshold, you still can. The static latency threshold will be preferable if your storage array is using sub-LUN auto-tiering, where blocks of data may be migrated to different types of storage dynamically based on the performance profile requirements. If you used the injector method to determine congestion in conjunction with an auto-tiering array, there is a high probability the injector would get inaccurate data, because sometimes it would hit high-performance blocks and sometimes it would hit low-performance blocks.

NOTE

VMware DRS does not take active queue depth or SIOC into account when considering compute-based load-balancing operations at this stage.

CAUTION

Because SIOC works only on data stores hosting multiple VMs, any data store where a single VM resides will have the full access to all of the queue depth. Usually this would be less than the aggregate queue depth used across multiple hosts to a given LUN. In some cases, this could cause a performance impact, such as when all data stores share the same RAID groups or disk groups on the array.

We recommend you enable SIOC as a standard on all of your data stores when using traditional block-based storage arrays, regardless of whether or not they are hosting more than one VM. This will ensure if things change in the future you know that your VMs will always receive their fair share of the storage IO performance resources available. If you have an auto-tiering array, we would recommend using the traditional default values of 30ms for the static latency threshold and not using the injector with vSphere 5.5.

TIP

We recommend you enable SIOC as a standard on all of your data stores, regardless of whether or not they are hosting more than one VM.

> **NOTE**
>
> The recommendations to use SIOC assume traditional block-based shared storage architecture is being used. Some modern storage systems don't suffer from the problems that caused a need to have SIOC in the first place, and therefore there is no need to use SIOC on these systems. An example is the Nutanix Virtual Computing Platform, where data access is localized per host, although it provides a distributed shared storage environment. In this case, disk shares on each host ensure fairness of IO performance. The Nutanix platform doesn't suffer from the problems that SIOC addresses, and therefore SIOC is not required.

Figure 6.31 shows the vSphere 5.5 Storage IO Control Settings dialog box. By setting SIOC to Manual, you effectively disable the injector, which is the preferred setting when using auto-tiering arrays, or storage platforms where the injector is likely to get inaccurate data.

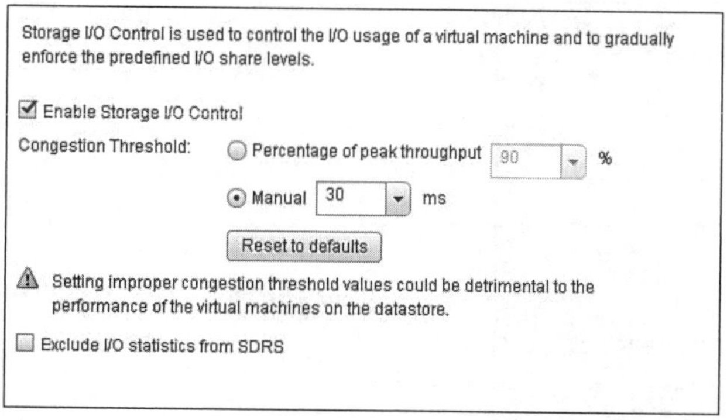

Storage I/O Control is used to control the I/O usage of a virtual machine and to gradually enforce the predefined I/O share levels.

☑ Enable Storage I/O Control

Congestion Threshold: ○ Percentage of peak throughput `90` ▼ %

                       ◉ Manual `30` ▼ ms

                       [Reset to defaults]

⚠ Setting improper congestion threshold values could be detrimental to the performance of the virtual machines on the datastore.

☐ Exclude I/O statistics from SDRS

Figure 6.31   vSphere 5.5 Storage IO Control settings.

vSphere Storage Policies and Storage DRS

With vSphere 5.x, we use Storage Policies and Storage DRS not only to reduce management overheads in a vSphere environment but also to improve performance. By using vSphere Storage Policies, you can take some of the guesswork out of provisioning your SQL Servers. By creating policies that align to the IOPS per TB and protection or availability requirements of your databases, it becomes very easy to provision new databases to the correct storage to achieve their requirements. You can manually assign storage capabilities to data stores and then create policies for those capabilities. Alternatively, you can use a storage vendor provider that leverages the vSphere API for Storage Awareness (VASA) to automatically provide visibility of the capabilities to vSphere. With VASA, when LUNs are provisioned at the physical array, the capabilities will flow through to vCenter. Storage Vendor Providers and storage capabilities are then visible when creating data stores. This allows vSphere Storage Administrators to easily include the correct storage into the correct data store, and this can later be used to create data store clusters.

Figure 6.32 shows a virtual data center where there are three possible storage policies that could be used based on the requirements of the SQL Server. You might choose Gold or Silver for different production or test database systems and you might choose Bronze for development databases. Your policies would be based on your particular requirements. To make it easy to architect for storage performance, the IOPS per TB should be known for each storage policy, and this should be communicated to all the key stakeholders until it is clear what they are getting when they provision VMs.

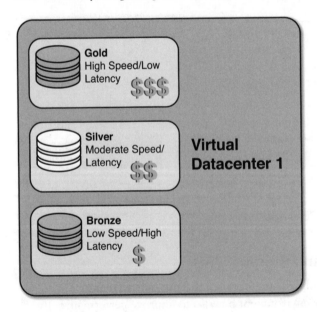

Figure 6.32   vSphere storage policies.

> **TIP**
>
> In vSphere 5.5, you assign tags to data stores and then use those tags to create storage policies. This is much like using hash tags on social media. They can easily be searched on afterward and queried or manipulated using orchestration and scripting (such as PowerCLI).

By pooling multiple (up to 32) similar data stores into data store clusters and using Storage DRS, you can ensure that initial placement of virtual disks to the best data store is automated, and this reduces the number of individual elements you need to actively manage. Storage DRS can be configured to load balance based on capacity, IO performance, or both, and can be set to simply make recommendations (manual) or be fully automated. If your array does not include automated storage block tiering, you can use Storage DRS to load balance data stores for IO performance, in addition to simply load balancing for capacity. When IO Load Balancing is enabled, Storage DRS works cooperatively with Storage IO Control and will collect IO metrics from the data stores and uses the IO injector to determine performance capabilities. The data is then analyzed periodically (by default, every 8 hours) to make IO load-balancing decisions. Importantly, the cost of any storage migrations is taken into consideration when making IO load-balancing decisions. Load balancing based on capacity or IO is achieved by performing Storage vMotion migrations between the source and destination data stores within a data store cluster.

> **TIP**
>
> If you wish to perform data store maintenance for any reason or migrate between arrays, you can put one of more data stores of a data store cluster into maintenance mode. This will enforce the evacuation of all virtual disks and files on the data stores going into maintenance mode into the remaining data stores that make up the data store cluster. Storage DRS will distribute the load and make sure that your load balancing policies is adhered to.

The example shown in Figure 6.33 is of the standard storage DRS options, including the Storage DRS Automation Level, configured for Fully Automated, and the I/O metrics settings, which are disabled. You may wish to set Storage DRS to No Automation (Manual Mode) for a period of time during operational verification testing or if you are unfamiliar with Storage DRS and data store clusters, until you are familiar and comfortable with the recommendations it makes.

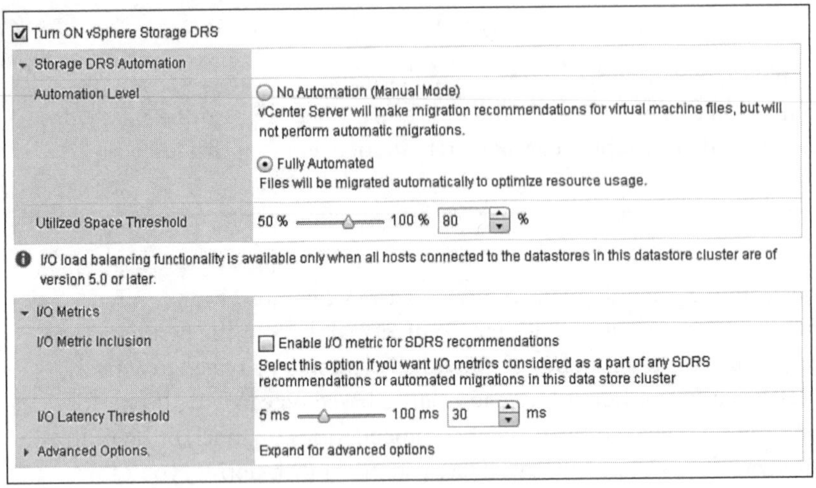

Figure 6.33 vSphere Storage DRS options.

CAUTION

Care should be taken when implementing Storage DRS on backend storage that is thin provisioned if it doesn't include data de-duplication capabilities. Traditional thin provisioned backend storage capacity could become full if a storage migration takes place between one thin provisioned data store and another if the space is not reclaimed. Because the IO injector is used to determine performance capabilities when IO metric collection is enabled, it should not be used with auto-tiering arrays because the data it gathers will be inaccurate and your array is already managing the performance of each LUN. In the case of auto-tiering arrays, you should only use Storage DRS for initial placement and capacity-based load balancing.

The example in Figure 6.34 shows the Storage DRS Advanced Options expanded. Here, you can set whether to keep VMDKs together by default and other settings. These parameters will influence how much of an imbalance there needs to be before Storage DRS will consider taking action. The most relevant settings for SQL Server are "Keep VMDKs together by default" and the advanced option shown in this figure, "IgnoreAffinityRules-ForMaintenance."

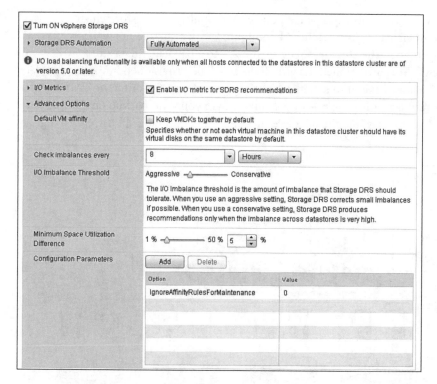

Figure 6.34 vSphere Storage DRS advanced options.

The default option for Storage DRS will keep all VMDKs from a VM on the same data store. For a high-performance database, this is not what you would want. You will want to leverage the available data stores and queue depth to get the best performance while Storage IO Control sorts out any bumps in the road and ensures quality of service. Our recommendation for SQL Server environments is to have Keep VMDKs Together unchecked. This will cause Storage DRS to spread out the VMDKs among the available data stores. If you have large numbers of SQL Servers, it may be preferable to run them in a dedicated data store cluster, because this could limit the impact they have on other workloads, and vice versa.

If at a later stage you want to add data store performance as well as capacity, you can simply add more data stores to the data store cluster and they will be used for load-balancing operations per VMDK as well as during initial placement. Separating the VMDKs among the data stores will ensure quality of service and access to performance of all the databases added to the data store cluster while making administration and management significantly easier. We would recommend you leave the IgnoreAffinity-RulesForMaintenance advanced setting at 0, unless you are willing to compromise your affinity rules and performance during data store maintenance operations.

In Figure 6.35, we have combined storage policies with multiple data store clusters. With the different virtual disks of each VM configured with a storage policy based on the required capabilities, the storage policy then maps to a particular data store cluster. Whenever a new VM is provisioned, its virtual disks will be provisioned in the correct data store cluster. The advantage of this method is that you can have the different VMDKs of a VM on a different class of storage—for example, where you want backup on a lower tier, or the OS on a lower tier, while the database files and transaction logs files are on a higher tier.

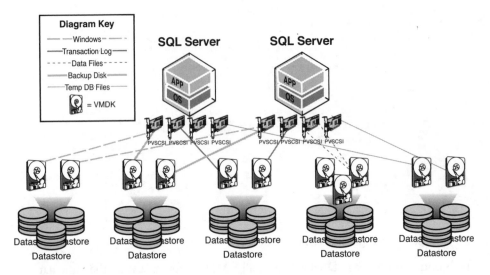

Figure 6.35   vSphere storage policies with data store clusters.

Having the flexibility of provisioning the VM to multiple storage clusters and different classes of storage sounds okay at a distance, but it also introduces additional management overheads. In storage platforms that already do automated block tiering, there is limited benefit to this approach. This approach is also difficult in Infrastructure as a Service (IaaS) environments or Cloud environments (including VMware vCloud Director or vCloud Automation Center), in which case a single VM may only be associated with a single storage profile, and automated tiering is used to manage the performance of the particular VM within the defined physical storage policy.

TIP

For a thorough understanding of Storage DRS, refer to the VMware white paper "Understanding VMware vSphere 5.1 Storage DRS" (http://www.vmware.com/files/pdf/ vmw-vsphr-5-1-stor-drs-uslet-101-web.pdf).

The sample diagram in Figure 6.36 shows multiple SQL Server VMs entirely within a single data store cluster, which would be backed by a single class of storage or single physical storage policy. Each VM's individual VMDKs would be split among the data stores of the data store cluster. Storage Policies on each VM would dictate which data store cluster the SQL Server is assigned, but an individual VM is not split between multiple data store clusters, as was the case in Figure 6.35. This is the recommended approach in environments that support automated block tiering at the storage array.

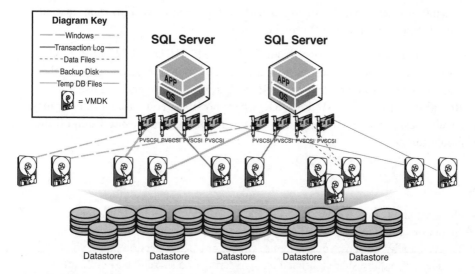

Figure 6.36   Multiple SQL Servers—single vSphere storage cluster.

This design ensures simplified management and operations while ensuring the appropriate performance of the group of SQL Servers. It is also compatible with IaaS environments and use with Cloud environments, such as VMware vCloud Automation Center and VMware vCloud Director. You may still support multiple storage policies and service levels for the storage, each being a different data store cluster. But the VMs that map to those policies would be entirely contained within the relevant data store cluster.

TIP

When you are defining your SQL Server Database Service Catalog, group your VMs not only by CPU and Memory requirements but also Storage IO requirements. The Storage IO requirements can then drive your storage policy design, at both the vSphere and physical storage layer, and the relevant data store clusters that need to be supported.

vSphere Storage Multipathing

Each block storage device (FC, FCoE, iSCSI, and so on) on the VMware Hardware Compatibility List (HCL, http://www.vmware.com/go/hcl) leverages VMware Native Multipathing (NMP) and will have a Storage Array Type Plugin (SATP) and a default Path Selection Policy (PSP). The default SATP and PSP for your storage device will depend on the vendor, and in some cases it will use a VMware generic SATP, such as VMW_DEFAULT_AA. The PSPs that are part of the built-in VMware NMP are referred to as initiator-side load-balancing or path selection policies. This is because all path selection decisions are made from the host only.

There are three built-in PSPs to choose from: VMW_PSP_MRU, VMW_PSP_FIXED, and VMW_PSP_RR. To get the best performance out of your storage and provide the highest performance and lowest latency to SQL Server, we recommend you use the VMware Round Robin PSP (VMW_PSP_RR) where possible. Your storage vendor may have a particular best practice with regard to advanced options when using Round Robin that you should follow.

> **NOTE**
>
> For vSphere 5.1 and below, VMW_PSP_FIXED and VMW_PSP_MRU are the only valid options when using SQL AlwaysOn Failover Clustering. When using SQL AlwaysOn Availability Groups, you are free to choose any path selection policy you like because it does not require shared disk failover clustering or a shared SCSI bus configuration. vSphere 5.5 introduced support for VMW_PSP_RR for SQL AlwaysOn Failover Clustering.

> **TIP**
>
> For a full list of all the supported storage devices and their associated default SATP and PSPs, refer to the VMware Storage Compatibility Guide (https://www.vmware.com/resources/compatibility/san_reports.php?deviceCategory=san). For further information on Path Selection Policies, see VMware KB 1011340.

VMware has designed vSphere's storage multipathing to be flexible and to allow storage vendors to write their own multipathing plugins. The advantage of many of the third-party vSphere multipathing plugins, such as EMC's PowerPath/VE, is that they use target-side load balancing. This is where the load on the storage array's paths, storage processors, and individual queue depths may be taken into consideration when choosing the best path for a particular IO operation. This can produce greatly improved performance and lower latency. Many vendors offer their own plugins, so you should check with your storage vendor to see if they have a plugin and what advantages it might have for your environment. Most of these plugins come at an additional cost, but in our experience it can usually be justified based on the additional performance.

> **TIP**
>
> When using iSCSI-based storage and the Software iSCSI initiator, ensure that you configure the iSCSI Port Binding in vSphere correctly so that you can get the best performance and reliability from your storage. Refer to the "VMware Multipath Configuration for Software iSCSI Using Port Binding" white paper (http://www.vmware.com/files/pdf/techpaper/vmware-multipathing-configuration-software-iSCSI-port-binding.pdf).

The VMware vSphere Native Multipathing modules eliminate a lot of the problems and complications traditionally associated with in-guest multipathing drivers. To simplify your environment further, you could choose to put your VMDKs onto NFS data stores mounted to vSphere. When using NFS, your load balancing will most likely be done on the array, or by using the correct network teaming. NFS as a data store instead of VMFS is a great solution, provided it is designed and deployed correctly to meet the performance needs of your SQL Servers. The protocol itself will not be your limiting factor for performance, especially on 10GB Ethernet. Whichever storage option or protocol you choose, you just need to design it to meet your performance requirements and verify through testing that it does. There are many situations where NFS could be a valid option, and some of the benefits are covered in the section "SQL Server on Hyperconverged Infrastructure."

vSphere 5.5 Failover Clustering Enhancements

In response to customer demands for increasing levels of database availability over and above the 99.9% easily obtainable with vSphere HA, VMware has provided a number of enhancements to the support of Windows Failover Clustering over the years. From vSphere 5.1, VMware supported five-node Windows Failover Clusters, where it previously supported only two nodes. In vSphere 5.5, VMware has again enhanced the Windows Failover Clustering support, and this is particularly relevant to high-performance SQL server databases that wish to make use of AlwaysOn Failover Cluster Instances.

Figure 6.37 shows the enhancements available when using AlwaysOn Failover Cluster Instances on vSphere 5.5.

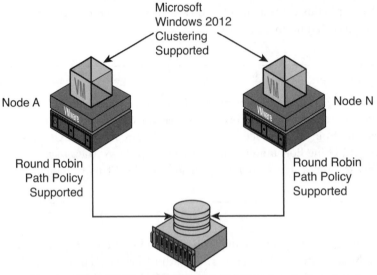

Physical Mode RDM on FC, FCoE & iSCSI Protocols Supported
Up to 5 Node Clusters Supported

Figure 6.37   vSphere 5.5 failover clustering enhancements.

The new failover clustering support in vSphere 5.5 means you can use the Round Robin multipathing policy to load-balance multiple active storage paths, Windows Server 2012 clusters are fully supported (up to five nodes when using RDMs), and FCoE and iSCSI protocols in addition to FC are supported for the RDMs.

> **NOTE**
>
> For full details of VMware's Windows Failover Clustering support, refer to VMware KB 1037959. When using large numbers of RDMs for failover clusters, you may need to perennially reserve them to ensure fast host storage rescans and boot times; refer to VMware KB 1016106. For further details on vSphere 5.5 clustering enhancements, see VMware KB 2052238.

RAID Penalties and Economics

Most storage arrays in use today use RAID (Redundant Array of Independent Disks) as a way to protect data from physical disk failures. Even though many newer storage arrays are starting to use different techniques for data protection, it's still important to understand RAID. Using the right RAID levels can have a big impact on performance and also on cost of your SQL environments and virtual infrastructures. This section more than any other will clearly demonstrate how designing for performance will take care of capacity, at least where using RAID is involved, especially as you reach for even higher performance from your SQL databases. Before we discuss RAID penalties, we will cover some IO characteristics that have a direct performance impact when used with RAID.

Randomness of IO Pattern

The randomness of IO is a very important consideration in storage design and has a direct impact on IO latency and throughput when using spinning disks. Most virtualization environments will generate a completely random IO pattern, even with sequential IO from individual VMs, as we covered previously in "The IO Blender Effect." This is because the underlying VMFS data stores are shared between multiple VMs in most cases. With SQL Server, you will have cases where VMs should still share some common VMFS data stores, as we have covered, in order to get maximum performance utilization from your arrays.

The reason that random IOs have such an impact is because the disk heads have to move between different sectors and the disk has to spin around to the correct location for a block to be read from or written to. For this reason, the average seek time and rotational speed of the disks are very important. On average, the disk heads will need to wait for 50% of the disk to spin past it prior to performing a read or write operation. Each operation is then multiplied by the RAID penalties of that operation.

The impact of randomness on reads can be worse than the randomness for writes. In most storage systems, writes will be cached (backed by battery or some other persistent form), ordered, and then written to physical disk in a way that reduces the overall impact. For reads, however, the chances of getting a cache hit in your array when the randomness increases are very low; therefore, most reads may have to come from spinning disks. The alternative would be to assign very large read cache on the array, but that is not efficient or cost effective in most cases, and still may not result in significant cache hits. The end result is that many more disks may be needed to get the best read latency and throughput for your database.

Fortunately, SQL is very good at caching, and this is why the buffer pool in a SQL Database is so big. This is also the reason there is a direct tradeoff between assigning SQL Server RAM and using it in the buffer pool and read IO from disk. This becomes especially important when things fail, such as disks in your RAID groups, which causes additional delays and additional latency.

Read/Write Bias

Just because your applications drive SQL to generate a read-biased workload doesn't mean the underlying storage system will see a read-biased IO pattern. The reason for this is the SQL buffer pool is likely to mask a lot of read IO if you have sized your VM correctly. This will mean your IO patterns may be very write biased. Writes will be going to your data files, Temp DB files, and your transaction log all at the same time. You will need to make sure you have sufficient array write cache so you don't get into a position of a force flush and a subsequent instance of the cache going write through, which will significantly degrade performance. You must have sufficient numbers of disks in the array to handle the cache flushes easily.

CAUTION

Be very careful when using 7.2K RPM SATA or NL-SAS disks on a traditional RAID array, even with automated storage tiering. Overloading a SATA or NL-SAS LUN can cause forced flush and significant periods of array cache write through (instead of the friendly cache write back), to the point where the storage processors may appear to freeze. Also, you may find LUNs being trespassed on active/passive arrays, or just lots of path flip flops on active/active arrays. With modern storage systems, including SSDs to host the active working set data and acting as a second cache area, the chances of forced flushes may be reduced. But you will need to ensure that your active working set doesn't increase to the point where it overflows the caches and SSD and causes writes directly to slow tiers.

Plan Your Performance for Failure

Your storage system at some point will experience a failure. You need to ensure that your critical SQL systems will perform at the minimum acceptable level during these failure operations. During a disk failure in certain RAID configurations, you will have significantly slower performance for both read and write operations; this is due to parity calculations and the performance required for rebuilding data on replacement disks. Disk rebuild can take a significant amount of time, and during rebuild situations you may have a risk of multiple disk failure. The bigger and slower the disk, the longer the rebuild.

NOTE

Some modern storage systems have done away with using RAID because of the performance impact and risks introduced during disk rebuild operations. If you are using a
storage platform that has a different data protection mechanism, it's important that you
understand how it works. The advantages can be significantly higher performance during
failure, significantly faster recovery from failure, and greater predictability.

RAID Penalties

Random IO patterns, read/write bias, and failure events have a big impact on performance
due to the overheads and penalties for read and write operations associated with using
RAID. This is especially so with spinning disks. Storage array vendors have come up with
many ways to try and work around some of the limitations with RAID, including the smart
use of read and write caches. In your storage design, though, we recommend you plan your
performance based on the physical characteristics of the underlying disks and plan for the
rest to be a bonus. Table 6.10 displays the IO penalties during normal operations for each
of the common RAID schemes.

Table 6.10   RAID IO Penalties During Normal Operations

RAID Level	RAID Write Penalty	Read IOPS (15K RPM)	Write IOPS (15K RPM)	Read IOPS (7.2K RPM)	Write IOPS (7.2K RPM)
RAID 0	1	175–210	175–210	75–100	75–100
RAID 1	2	175–210	88–105	75–100	38–50
RAID 5	4	175–210	44–52	75–100	18–25
RAID 6	6	175–210	30–35	75–100	12–16
RAID 1+0 (10)	2	175–210	88–105	75–100	38–50
RAID DP	2	175–210	88–105	75–100	38–50

IOPS listed in Table 6.10 are per disk. RAID 0 is included for illustrative purposes only
and is not recommended, as it is simple disk striping with no data protection.

NOTE

The basis for the IOPS calculations in Table 6.10 is the rotational latency and average seek time of each disk. These will be different depending on the latency characteristics of different manufacturers' disks. This would also not apply for solid state disks and PCIe NAND flash devices. For further information about IOPS, see http://en.wikipedia.org/wiki/IOPS and http://www.symantec.com/connect/articles/getting-hang-iops-v13.

As you can see from Table 6.10, if you have a very write-biased workload, you could get very low effective IOPS from your RAID disks. This is the primary reason why arrays have write cache—and in some cases, lots of it. This allows the array to offset much of the penalty associated with writes to RAID groups of disks. But the arrays assume there will be some quiet time in order to flush the cache; otherwise, there will be an impact to performance. The calculation for write IOPS is as follows:

```
Write IOPS = Disk IOPS / RAID Write Penalty
```

However, this only works when things are going well. If you fill your cache by having too much write IO on slow spindles, or just from general overloading, your array will stop caching writes and bypass the cache altogether (go write through). In this case, you'll get at best the raw performance of the RAID groups. This problem can be made worse when there is a disk failure and a group of RAID disks needs to be rebuilt. Depending on the type of disks, this can take many hours and severely impact performance during the rebuild operation.

Let's take the RAID penalties a bit further and look at an example where we are sizing for performance. In this example, we will look at the requirements of a SQL data store that needs to be able to deliver 5,000 IOPS. We will assume that the workload is 70% read and 30% write, which is typical for some OLTP systems.

First, we need to calculate the effective number of IOPS required. This takes the 5,000 IOPS of a 70/30 read/write workload and adjusts for the RAID penalty as follows:

```
Required Array IOPS =
(Required IOPS * Read %) + RAID Write Penalty * (Required IOPS * Write %)

Example RAID 5 Required IOPS = (5000 * 70%) + 4 * (5000 * 30%) = 9500
```

You can see from the example in Table 6.11 that to achieve 5,000 IOPS for a 70% read-biased SQL workload, we need 9,500 IOPS at RAID 5 from the array. Now that we know the required array IOPS, we can calculate the number of disks required to achieve this performance at each of the RAID levels. To do this, we divide the number of IOPS by the number of IOPS per disk. RAID penalties have already been taken into consideration due to the previous calculations.

Table 6.11 Array IOPS Required at Different RAID Levels to Achieve 5,000 SQL IOPS

RAID Level	RAID WritePenalty	Array IOPS (70% Read)	Array IOPS (50% Read)	Array IOPS (30% Read)
RAID 0	1	5,000	5,000	5,000
RAID 1	2	6,500	7,500	8,500
RAID 5	4	9,500	12,500	15,500
RAID 6	6	12,500	17,500	22,500
RAID 1+0 (10)	2	6,500	7,500	8,500
RAID DP	2	6,500	7,500	8,500

To calculate the number of disks required to meet the required IOPS of a workload, we use the following formula:

Required Disks for Required RAID IOPS = Required Array IOPS / IOPS per Disk

Example RAID 5 Disks = 9500 Array IOPS / 210 IOPS per 15K Disk = 45 Disks

As Table 6.12 demonstrates, to achieve 5,000 SQL IOPS 70% read at RAID 5 on 15K RPM disks requires 45 disks, whereas it only requires 31 disks at RAID 1, RAID 10, or RAID DP—a saving of 14 disks. If the workload is only 30% read, then we would require 74 15K RPM disks at RAID 5 and only 40 15K RPM disks at RAID 1, RAID 10, or RAID DP. This would be a saving of 34 disks to achieve the same performance. This assumes each disk can achieve the high end of the IOPS for that device. The less number of IOPS per disk, the more disks in total will be needed. In this example, we've used the high-end IOPS of each disk for the calculations. Be sure to check with your storage vendor on their recommendations for IOPS per disk when doing any calculations.

Table 6.12 Min Disks Required at Different RAID Levels to Achieve 5,000 SQL IOPS

RAID Level	15K RPM Disk 70% Read	15K RPM Disk 30% Read	7.2K RPM Disk 70% Read	7.2K RPM Disk 30% Read
RAID 0	24	24	50	50
RAID 1	31	40	65	85
RAID 5	45	74	95	155
RAID 6	60	107	125	225
RAID 1+0 (10)	31	40	65	85
RAID DP	31	40	65	85

To achieve 5,000 IOPS at RAID 6 70% read on 7.2K RPM disks, we'd need 125 disks in total. At RAID 10 on 7.2K RPM disks, the required disks falls to 65, a saving of 60 disks. The difference is even more pronounced when the workload is only 30% read. At RAID 6, we would require 225 disks, whereas at RAID 10, we would only require 85 disks—a saving of a whopping 140 disks.

TIP

RAID 6 is commonly used with SATA and NL-SAS disks because the chance of a second drive failure during a rebuild operation is quite high. This is due to the time it takes to rebuild a RAID group when using slow 7.2K RPM high-capacity disks > 1TB.

Those of you who know RAID will be thinking at this point that some of the numbers in Table 6.12 are wrong, and you'd be right. How do you get 31 disks in RAID 1 or 10, or 225 disks in RAID 6? The answer is, you don't. The numbers in Table 6.12 have not been adjusted for the minimum required for a complete RAID group, or the likely size of each RAID group that would be required to make up an entire aggregate or volume to be created from. You would need to increase the numbers of disks to be able to build complete RAID groups. For example, in RAID 5, it's common to build RAID groups consisting of 7 data disks +1 parity disk (8 total), and in RAID 6, it is common to build 8+2 or 10+2 RAID groups. RAID5 7+1 or RAID6 10+2 may be terms you've heard before when talking to storage administrators.

Now that we've adjusted the figures in Table 6.13 for the RAID groups, you can see that RAID 1 and 10 are even more efficient than RAID 5 and 6 in terms of the number of disks to achieve the same performance. This is important to understand because it also has a direct impact on the amount of capacity that will be provisioned to reach the desired performance level.

Table 6.13 Min Disks per RAID Group Adjusted to Achieve 5,000 SQL IOPS

RAID Level	15K RPM Disk 70% Read	15K RPM Disk 30% Read	7.2K RPM Disk 70% Read	7.2K RPM Disk 30% Read
RAID 0	24	24	50	50
RAID 1	32 (1+1)	40 (1+1)	66 (1+1)	86 (1+1)
RAID 5	48 (7+1)	80 (7+1)	96 (7+1)	160 (7+1)
RAID 6	60 (8+2)	110 (8+2)	130 (8+2)	230 (8+2)
RAID 1+0 (10)	32 (1+1)	40 (1+1)	66 (1+1)	86 (1+1)
RAID DP	36 (10+2)	48 (10+2)	72 (10+2)	96 (10+2)

For this part of the example, we'll imagine that our SQL database that needs 5,000 IOPS will be 2TB in size. There will be an additional 200GB for transaction logs, 200GB for Temp DB, and another 100GB for the OS, page file, and so on. In totally, the capacity required is approximately 2.5TB.

From Table 6.14, you can see the usable capacity after taking into consideration the redundant or parity disks of the various RAID types needed to achieve 5,000 IOPS based on the previous examples. The 2.5TB usable capacity requirement for our sample SQL Server can easily be met by any of the selected RAID levels based on the number of disks required to achieve 5,000 IOPS. In fact, all of the RAID levels provide a lot more capacity than is actually required—some in the extreme.

Table 6.14   Usable Capacity Deployed to Achieve 5,000 SQL IOPS

RAID Level	300GB 15K RPM Disk 70% Read	300GB 15K RPM Disk 30% Read	1TB 7.2K RPM Disk 70% Read	1TB 7.2K RPM Disk 30% Read
RAID 0	7.2TB	7.2TB	50TB	50TB
RAID 1	4.8TB	6TB	33TB	43TB
RAID 5	12.6TB	21TB	84TB	140TB
RAID 6	14.4TB	26.4TB	104TB	184TB
RAID 1+0 (10)	4.8TB	6TB	33TB	43TB
RAID DP	9TB	12TB	60TB	80TB

Table 6.14 shows that a large amount of the deployed usable capacity is actually unusable from a performance perspective. Or to put it another way, *you have way too much capacity at the end of your performance*. This clearly demonstrates Principle 3 of sizing for performance, and in doing so, capacity will usually take care of itself.

Now that we have calculated the usable capacity that needs to be provisioned to achieve the 5,000 SQL IOPS, we can calculate the IOPS per TB. As mentioned, previously using IOPS per TB is a good way to communicate with applications teams how much performance they should expect for each TB of data based on the different available storage policies available. For this example, we will take a conservative approach so that the application teams are planning on a worst-case scenario and their performance surprises will be positive. You'll remember the quote from Principle 3: "The bitterness of poor performance lasts long after the sweetness of a cheap price is forgotten."

To illustrate this, we will define three tiers of storage or storage policies:

- **Gold**—RAID10 300GB 15K RPM disks
- **Silver**—RAID5 7+1 300GB 15K RPM disks
- **Wood**—RAID6 8+2 1TB 7.2K RPM disks

We will base the IOPS per TB calculation on a 30% read-biased IO pattern. This will mean our DBAs and applications teams will likely get better performance than the defined service level.

Based on our example in Table 6.15, we could set an SLA for Gold at 800 IOPS per TB, Silver at 200 IOPS per TB, and Wood at 20 IOPS per TB. We have rounded down to take a conservative approach and ensure the SLA can always be met.

Table 6.15   IOPS per TB Based on Example 30% Read Workload at 5000 IOPS

Storage Policy	Disks Required for 5000 IOPS	Usable Capacity	IOPS per TB	Recommended SLA IOPS/TB
Gold (RAID10)	40	6TB	833 (5000 / 6)	800
Silver (RAID5 7+1)	80	21TB	238 (5000 / 21)	200
Wood (RAID6 8+2)	230	184TB	27 (5000 /184)	20

> **TIP**
>
> It is possible to achieve higher IOPS per disk by using only a small portion (say, 25%) of the disk's total capacity. This is known as short stroking or partial stroking a disk. This is because when you use the first part of a spinning disk, the rotational latency is a lot lower, as the outside of the disk platters are spinning faster than the inside, and you cover more sectors in less time. See http://searchsolidstatestorage.techtarget.com/definition/Short-Stroking.

The Economics of RAID Performance

You have seen how performance requirements can drive storage design, and how many spinning disks are required when using different RAID levels to meet performance requirements. In our example, we used a SQL Server requiring 5,000 IOPS and 2.5TB capacity. Now we will look at the economics of different RAID choices and using solid state disks (SSDs) or enterprise flash disks (EFDs) instead of spinning disks.

From Table 6.15, in order to meet a 30% read 5,000 IOPS requirement and a 2.5TB capacity requirement, the Gold storage policy is the most cost effective. It would use half the number of disks to deliver the performance required, and more than covers the capacity requirements. It would be half the cost of the Silver storage policy for this workload. Now let's take a look at how this might change if EFDs were used instead of spinning disks.

Table 6.16 shows the effective read and write IOPS after accounting for RAID penalties associated with using EFD disks with an assumed 5,000 IOPS per disk.

Table 6.16   RAID IO Penalties During Normal Operations of Enterprise Flash Disk

RAID Level	RAID Write Penalty	EFD Read IOPS	EFD Write IOPS
RAID 10	2	5,000	2,500
RAID 5	4	5,000	1250
RAID 6	6	5,000	833

Table 6.16 assumes a performance level of 5,000 IOPS for a single EFD disk. Depending on the type of EFD or SSD, these numbers could be very different. You should check with your particular vendor for their latest numbers. Also, it's quite common for the read and write performance to be different even without the RAID penalties.

Table 6.17 shows the number of EFD disks required at different RAID levels to meet the IOPS as well as the capacity requirements of our sample SQL database workload.

Table 6.17   EFDs at Different RAID Levels Required for Example SQL DB

RAID Level	RAID Write Penalty	Array IOPS (30% Read)	Required # of EFD for IOPS	# of 400GB EFD for 2.5TB Capacity
RAID 10	2	8500	2	14
RAID 5	4	15500	4	8
RAID 6	6	22500	5	9

Table 6.17 illustrates the number of EFDs required to meet both the performance and capacity requirements of our sample SQL DB. In this example, the RAID 5 option is the most cost effective from a performance and capacity perspective.

Comparing the number of 400GB EFDs required to meet the SQL requirements against the most cost effective options for spinning disks (Gold Policy RAID 10), we can see that we need five times less EFDs. For this workload, the eight EFDs may be the best option if their combined cost is less than the 40 spinning disks. In many cases, the EFDs will be less cost, especially when the reduced space, power consumption, and cooling of EFDs is considered.

Let's add a Platinum storage policy in addition to the previous defined policies and calculate the effective IOPS per TB based on our 400GB EFD example.

With the new Platinum storage policy in Table 6.18, we can easily meet the performance requirement of 5000 IOPS, but we need additional disks to meet the capacity requirement. Table 6.15 shows us that we need eight EFDs at 400GB in order to achieve the required 2.5TB. Based on provisioning 2.8TB of usable capacity, we can calculate that our achievable IOPS from that capacity at a conservative 4000 IOPS per TB at RAID5 with write penalty of 4 is 11,200 IOPS. At this point, it's likely that we'd run out of capacity well before running out of performance.

Table 6.18   IOPS per TB Based on Example 30% Read 5,000 IOPS and 2.5TB Capacity

Storage Policy	Disks Required for 5000 IOPS	Usable Capacity	IOPS per TB	Recommended SLA IOPS / TB
Platinum (400GB EFD RAID5)	4	1.2TB	4,166 (5000 / 1.2)	4000
Gold (300GB 15K RPM RAID10)	40	6TB	833 (5000 / 6)	800
Silver (300GB 15K RPM RAID5 7+1)	80	21TB	238 (5000 / 21)	200
Wood (1TB 7.2K RPM RAID6 8+2)	230	184TB	27 (5000 /184)	20

NOTE

There are many new storage platforms that include only flash as part of their architecture, meaning the entire array may become your primary tier. Some of these platforms claim to offer economics similar to spinning disks, by using advanced compression and data de-duplication techniques. These platforms are normally aimed at the highest performance workloads, such as critical SQL databases. These types of storage platforms are unsurprisingly known as "All Flash Arrays," and come from the likes of EMC, NetApp, HP, PureStorage, Violin Memory, and others.

At this point, you might consider doubling the size of each EFD to 800GB. This would halve the number of disks required to meet the capacity requirements. Assuming that each individual 800GB EFD has the same IOPS performance as the 400GB versions, you could achieve a better balance of performance and capacity. The larger EFDs would have half the IOPS per TB—in this case, to around 2,000. Five EFDs would be required to reach the required capacity. This would mean 3.2TB of usable capacity is deployed. The achievable IOPS from the deployed usable capacity would drop to 6,400. This is still a more performance than required. Also, although we are only using 5 × 800GB EFDs instead of 8 × 400GB EFDs, because they are double the capacity, they are also likely to be double or more the cost.

An EFD might be marketed at 400GB or 800GB in size, but to protect against wear of the NAND flash cells, the disk will usually have more physical capacity. This is to provide more endurance and a longer service life. This may vary between different vendors and individual SSDs, and we recommend you check with your storage vendor.

TIP

EFDs and SSDs are dollars per GB but cents per IOP, whereas spinning disks are cents per GB and dollars per IOP. In order to achieve the best balance, you need some of each. This is why many types of storage array include automatic storage tiering. Automatic storage tiering is most effective when done at the block level because individual blocks can be moved between the EFD and spinning disk storage as performance and capacity needs change. Where available, we recommend you use automatic storage tiering and seek advice from your storage vendor to ensure effective implementation and operations.

To make calculating performance and capacity based on different types of disk, numbers of disks, and RAID types easy, see the calculator at http://www.wmarow.com/strcalc/.

NOTE

There are many new types of enterprise storage systems and converged architectures on the market today that have moved away from using RAID as the main means of data protection and instead have their own methods. Often these alternative methods can achieve the same reliability and data protection levels as RAID, but without all of the complication and performance penalties. If you are using a system that doesn't rely on RAID for data protection, you can safely ignore this section. You should seek advice from your vendor with regard to sizing for capacity and performance based on their data protection methods and overheads.

SQL Performance with Server-Side Flash Acceleration

"Flash! ah-ahh! Savior of the Universe!...
Flash! ah-ahh! King of the impossible!"

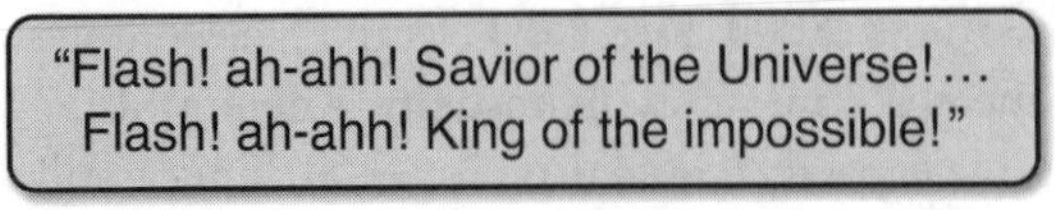

Figure 6.38   Flash acceleration and lyrics from the classic Queen song "Flash Gordon."

There is one storage technology that is currently sweeping the IT industry and revolutionizing performance, and that is NAND flash, in the form of SSDs, EFDs, and PCIe devices. When it comes to SQL performance, we think the lyrics of the Queen song "Flash Gordon" are very appropriate (see Figure 6.38). I wonder if they could see the future of enterprise and web-scale data centers when they wrote that song? Either way, as the previous section illustrated with the discussion around SSD and EFD in your storage array (including All Flash Arrays), it liberates performance for SQL from the tyranny of slow spinning disks that may no longer be economic.

But flash in an array has some limitations, and there is another location where we can use flash SSDs, EFDs, and PCIe that can greatly improve SQL performance, directly in the VMware ESXi servers hosting SQL. This is where server-side flash and associated acceleration solutions come in. Server-side flash when used as part of an IO acceleration solution can be thought of as cheap memory, rather than expensive disk. It is definitely cents per IOP and dollars per GB, but the returns on investment and performance can be substantial. Especially when it is not possible to add more RAM to the buffer cache, which would be the fastest possible storage from a performance perspective.

By using server-side flash acceleration, you can normally consolidate more SQL VMs per ESXi host, with less memory directly assigned to each SQL VM, and without sacrificing performance and user response times. Read or write IOs are offloaded to the local server flash device, and this acts as a very large cache. It can also greatly reduce the load on the back-end storage, which allows the array to improve its efficiency.

Because the flash devices are local to the server, the latencies can be microseconds (us) instead of milliseconds (ms) and eliminate some traffic that would normally have gone over the storage network. By reducing the storage IO latencies, not only are user response times improved, but overall server utilization is improved. You may see increased CPU utilization, as you are able to get more useful work done by reducing system bottlenecks.

In this section, we cover three different server-side flash acceleration solutions that are supported with VMware vSphere and can greatly improve the performance of your SQL databases. The solutions we cover are VMware vSphere Flash Read Cache (vFRC), which is included with vSphere 5.5, Fusion-io ioTurbine (IOT), and PernixData Flash Virtualization Platform (FVP). The first two solutions act as a read cache only, as all writes go directly to the backend storage while being cached and are therefore write through. PernixData FVP, on the other hand, offers a full write back cache, where both read IO and write IO can be accelerated.

VMware vSphere Flash Read Cache (vFRC)

vSphere 5.5 introduces vSphere Flash Read Cache, or vFRC, which is an infrastructure layer that aggregates flash devices into a unified flash resource pool. vFRC supports locally connected flash devices such as SAS/SATA SSDs and PCIe. The flash resource can be used to cache read IOs and is configured on a per-VMDK basis. The vFRC write policy is write through, which means that all writes go to persistent storage and are cached in vFRC simultaneously. To prevent pollution of the cache, large sequential writes are filtered out. Each VMDK flash resource allocation can be tuned based on the workload. For SQL, it's recommended that data file VMDKs and Temp DB VMDKs be configured for vFRC when used, whereas transaction log will usually have little benefit.

Figure 6.39 shows a high-level overview of the VMware vSphere Flash Read Cache architecture.

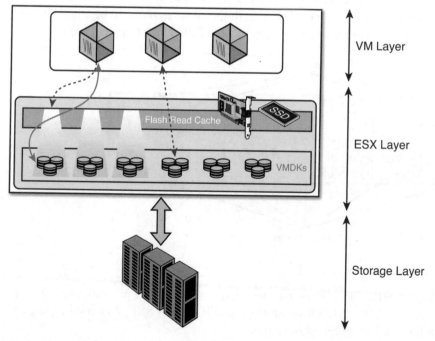

Figure 6.39 vFRC architecture overview.

The types of SQL workloads that will benefit from vFRC are read-dominated OLTP-type systems and read-dominated data warehouse queries. The ideal workload has a high repeated access of data—for example, 20% active working set that is referred to 80% of the time.

The major determinants of performance are the cache size, the cache block size, and the type of flash device used (SSD vs. PCIe). In terms of cache sizing, it is important to ensure that the cache is big enough to cover the active working set without being too big that you're wasting the valuable flash resource. The cache block size should be equal to the dominant IO size of the VMDK; for SQL, this will be predominantly between 8KB and 64KB. If you are unsure of the main IO size for your database, you can use vscsiStats for a period of time to record the IO profile. To learn more about vscsiStats, see http:// cormachogan.com/2013/07/10/getting-started-with-vscsistats/.

The type of flash device used will have an impact on the overall IOPS and latencies you can achieve. Although SATA and SAS SSDs are cheaper, they do not offer the same performance as PCIe. The right device for your environment will depend on your workload, performance, and budgetary requirements.

Having a cache block size that is too big can cause fragmentation in the cache and poor utilization. This may cause a substantial portion of the cache resource to be unutilized and therefore wasted. Figure 6.40 illustrates the impact of vFRC block fragmentation.

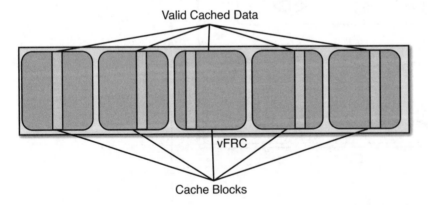

Figure 6.40   vFRC block fragmentation.

In Figure 6.40, the vFRC block is set to a much larger size than the predominant IO size—in this case, 128KB or 512KB versus the actual IO size of 8KB. As a result, a large proportion of the blocks configured is wasted.

> **TIP**
>
> If in doubt about what your cache block size should be, start at 8KB. Having the cache block size smaller than the actual IO size is better than having it oversized. Your cache block size should evenly divide the predominant IO size to ensure best performance and lowest latency. If your predominant IO size were 64KB, then having a cache block size of 8KB or 16KB would be fine because it can evenly divide the IO size.

The cache size and block size are manually set when you enable vFRC on a VM, and they can be changed at runtime without disruption. Having the cache too small will cause increased cache misses, and having it too big is not just wasteful, it will impact your vMotion times. By default, when vFRC is configured, the cache of a VM will be migrated when the VM is vMotioned. If it's set too big, this will increase the vMotion times and network bandwidth requirements. You can, if desired, select the cache to be dropped during a vMotion, but this will have an impact on SQL performance when the VM reaches its destination while the cache is being populated again.

> **CAUTION**
>
> Make sure a large enough flash resource exists on each server in your vSphere cluster. If you have an insufficient vFRC resource on a server, you may not be able to migrate or power on a VM.

> **NOTE**
>
> Performance tests conducted by VMware using the Dell DVD Store to simulate an ecommerce site with vFRC showed up to a 39% performance improvement with certain configurations. A number of statistics can be useful for monitoring and tuning vFRC. For detailed information on vFRC, performance test results from VMware, and vFRC stats, refer to http://www.vmware.com/files/pdf/techpaper/vfrc-perf-vsphere55.pdf.

Fusion-io ioTurbine

ioTurbine is caching software from Fusion-io that leverages the Fusion-io ioMemory range of high-performance flash devices, such as the SLC- and MLC-based ioDrive and ioScale PCIe cards. ioTurbine creates a dynamic shared flash pool on each ESXi server that can be divided up between cache-enabled VMs based on proportional share algorithm. By default, each VM is assigned the same shares and thus get an equal proportion of the available flash cache resource pool.

Like VMware's vFRC, ioTurbine is a read cache, and all writes are sent through to persistent storage while simultaneously being cached. Unlike vFRC, there are no manual parameters to set on a per-VM basis to size the cache or the blocks that are cached. This automatic and dynamic sizing of the flash cache of each VM is useful where you have lots of VMs that can benefit from caching or where you have flash devices of different sizes on different hosts. It reduces the management overhead.

Figure 6.41 displays a high-level overview of the ioTurbine architecture, including Fusion-io's Virtual Storage Layer (VSL) driver. As of ioTurbine 2.1.3, which supports vSphere 5.5, the VSL SCSI driver is used by default instead of the VSL block driver. This can provide improved performance and better resiliency.

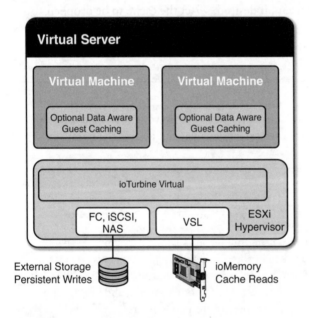

Figure 6.41   ioTurbine architecture overview.

In addition to being able to cache a VM, ioTurbine is capable of caching disks, files, and entire volumes. With the optional in-guest agent, the caching becomes data and application aware. This means particular files within the OS can be cached while others are filtered out. This is very useful for SQL where we only want the data files and Temp DB files cached while the transaction logs are not cached.

ioTurbine is fully compatible with VMware features such as DRS, HA, and vMotion. ioTurbine also works in environments where not all ESXi hosts contain a flash device, in which case the flash cache of a server would be set to 0.

In the example in Figure 6.42, if one of the VMs in the left ESXi host is migrated to the right ESXi host, all VMs will be allocated one third of the flash cache capacity of each host because there will be three cached VMs on each host.

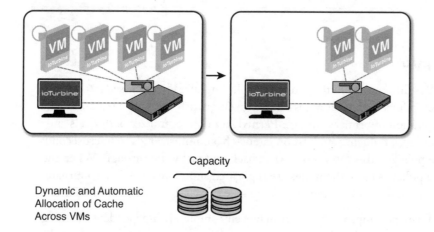

Figure 6.42   ioTurbine dynamic and automatic allocation of flash cache.

TIP

Fusion-io has a tool called the ioTurbine Profiler that allows you to observe the effects of caching on production or staged systems prior to investing in the ioTurbine software and necessary hardware. The ioTurbine Profiler simulates the effects of storage acceleration on a Linux or Windows system. For more information, see http://www.fusionio.com/products/ioturbine-virtual/.

Table 6.19 was obtained from Fusion-io performance test results published at http://www.fusionio.com/blog/performance-of-a-virtualized-ms-sql-server-poor-ioturbine-to-the-rescue. The results demonstrated that by offloading reads to the ioTurbine flash cache, write performance also increased by just over 20%. This test was based on TPC-E workload. This demonstrates that read caching can also improve write performance to a certain extent.

Table 6.19   ioTurbine SQL Server Performance Example (TPC-E)

	ioTurbine Off	ioTurbine On	Improvement
Avg. Duration (us)	146,861	29,800	400%
Avg. CPU Time Consumed	22	22	None
Total Reads	95,337,525	127,605,137	34%
Total Writes	34,901	43018	23%

PernixData FVP

PernixData FVP is different from the other two solutions already discussed in that it aggregates server-side flash devices across an entire enterprise to create a scale-out data tier for the acceleration of primary storage. PernixData FVP optimizes both reads and writes at the host level, reducing application latency from milliseconds to microseconds. The write cache policy in this case can be write back, not just write through. When the write back cache policy is used, the writes are replicated simultaneously to an alternate host to ensure persistence and redundancy in the case of a flash device or host failure.

Application performance improvements are achieved completely independent of storage capacity. This gives virtual administrators greater control over how they manage application performance. Performance acceleration is possible in a seamless manner without requiring any changes to applications, workflows, or storage infrastructure.

Figure 6.43 shows a high-level overview of the PernixData Flash Virtualization Platform architecture.

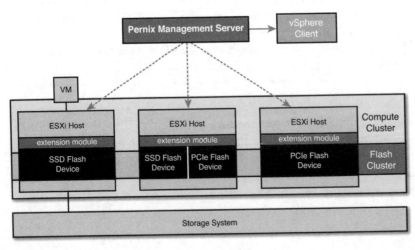

Figure 6.43   PernixData FVP architecture overview.

The flash devices in each ESXi host are virtualized by FVP, abstracted and pooled across the entire flash cluster. As a result, you can have flash devices of differing types and sizes in different hosts. Ideally though, you will have a homogenous configuration to produce more uniform performance acceleration. Hosts that don't have local flash devices can still participate in the flash cluster and benefit from read IO acceleration. This is termed a "non-uniform configuration," when some hosts have local flash devices and some don't.

In the case of a non-uniform flash cluster configuration, when a VM on a host without a flash device issues a read operation of data already present in the flash cluster, FVP will fetch the data from the previous source host and send it to the virtual machine. Because there is no local flash resource present, it cannot store it locally; however, FVP will continue to fetch data from the flash cluster to keep the latency to a minimum while reducing the overall stress and load on the storage array.

With PernixData FVP, it may be possible to delay the need for costly forklift upgrades of existing primary storage investments that have reached the end of their performance, well before the end of their capacity. As we've seen with our RAID calculations, this can be common for high-performance workloads. FVP can provide much more efficient use of the deployed capacity and may allow the breathing space required for you to determine the best next steps for your future storage and virtualization strategies.

> **NOTE**
>
> PernixData has a demonstration of how it accelerates SQL performance available at http://blog.pernixdata.com/accelerating-virtualized-databases-with-pernixdata-fvp/. The PernixData FVP Datasheet is available at http://www.pernixdata.com/files/pdf/ PernixData_DataSheet_FVP.pdf.

The examples in Figures 6.44 and 6.45 show a SQL 2012 database driving around 7,000 IOPS consistently and the resulting latency both at the data store and at the VM level. The total effective latency is what the virtual machine sees, even though the data store itself is experiencing drastically higher latency. In this case, in spite the latency of the data store being upwards of 25ms, the SQL VM response times are less than 1ms.

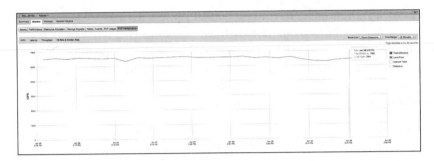

Figure 6.44   PernixData FVP acceleration for SQL Server 2012 IOPS.

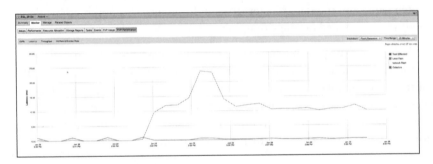

Figure 6.45   PernixData FVP acceleration for SQL Server 2012 latency.

When FVP cannot flush the uncommitted data to primary persistent storage fast enough—that is, when more hot data is coming in than there is flash space available—FVP will actively control the flow of the new data. This means that FVP will artificially increase the latency, ultimately controlling the rate at which the application can send, until the flash cluster has sufficient capacity and returns to normal. FVP does not transition to write through, even when it is under heavy load. Applications normally spike and are not continuously hammering the data path 100% all time, so FVP flow control helps smooth out the "spikey" times, while providing the most optimized performance possible.

CAUTION

Migrating a VM in an FVP flash cluster, in certain network failure scenarios, or when the local or replica flash device fails, FVP will automatically change the write back policy to write through. This ensures data protection, while degrading write performance. However, reads may still be accelerated by requests being serviced from the remainder of the flash cluster. When the issue is resolved the policy will be automatically returned to write back. For more information, see the "Fault Tolerant Write Acceleration" white paper on http://pernixdata.com and http://frankdenneman.nl/2013/11/05/fault-tolerant-write-acceleration/. This is a standard part of the FVP Fault Tolerant Write Acceleration Framework.

SQL Server on Hyperconverged Infrastructure

If there is one technology trend that is revolutionizing the enterprise data center more than just flash alone, it is hyperconvergence. This is where storage and compute (CPU and RAM) are provided in a single package and connected by standard Ethernet networks. By far the leader in this sector of the market is Nutanix, with its Virtual Computing Platform. This section covers key aspects of SQL Server performance and architecture of the Nutanix Virtual Computing Platform.

The Nutanix Virtual Computing Platform is built for virtualization and cloud environments, with the idea of brining the benefits and economics of web-scale architectures from companies such as Google, Facebook, and Amazon to the masses. The Nutanix solution includes storage and server compute (CPU and Memory) in a platform building block. Each building block is 2 RU and based on standard x86 server technology. The platform architecture is designed to deliver a unified, scale-out, shared-nothing cluster with no single point of failure (SPOF). Hyperconverged platforms don't require SAN or NAS storage, or fibre channel networks, but can sit along side existing environments.

A general aspect of hyperconverged platforms and Nutanix in particular is a reduction in the number of components that need to be managed and a reduction in the overall solution complexity. The reduction in complexity and increased simplicity translates into ease of deployment and operations, such as when dynamically increasing a cluster's size, and ease of designing and architecting successful solutions, even for business-critical applications such as SQL Server.

For designing a SQL Server environment, a Nutanix platform is arguably simpler because there are no LUNs, no RAID, no FC switches, no zoning, no masking, no registered state change notifications (RSCN), and no storage multipathing required. All management is VM and VMDK centric. An advantage of being VM and VMDK centric is that storage IO from a VMDK is seen as what it is: sequential is sequential and random is random. This allows the platform to optimize for that IO pattern without the impact of the IO Blender Effect.

This doesn't mean you have to throw away the assets you've already got and that still have a book value. You can use a hyperconverged platform to offload some capacity and performance from your existing systems. This can improve your overall performance and reduce management complexity.

With Nutanix, you have one pool of storage across a distributed file system cluster called the Nutanix Distributed File System (NDFS), which includes SSDs for high performance and low latency and HDDs for cheap capacity. The different types of storage devices in the storage pool are automatically tiered using an intelligent information life cycle management (ILM) engine to ensure the most frequently used data is available in memory or in flash cache. This assumes you have sufficient capacity in your high-performance tier for the most active working set of your VMs. If you are deploying SQL Server on Nutanix, the sections of this chapter you need to follow closely are "SQL Server Database and Guest OS Design" and "Virtual Machine Storage Design," in addition to "The Five Key Principles of Database Storage Design," which appears at the start of this chapter.

Nutanix has a small number of model options available to try and make it easy to choose the right one and to make it easy to support. Depending on the model of platform selected, a single 2U building block can include up to four nodes, combining up to 80 CPU cores (two sockets, 10 cores each per node), 2TB RAM (512GB per node), and 8TB of high-performance storage. These building blocks can be scaled out without any artificial limits and provide linear performance as you add more VMs. If more capacity is required per node, a different building block type with up to 16TB–20TB per 2RU can be mixed and matched into a single NDFS cluster to balance both compute capacity and storage capacity and performance. Typical performance from a 2RU building block is up to a combined 100K 4KB Random Read IOs, up to 50K 4KB Random Write IOs, 1.4GBps sequential write throughput, and 3GBps sequential read throughput across four NDFS nodes. These numbers were produced using the built-in Nutanix Diagnostics Tool; actual application performance with mixed workloads will vary. You should benchmark your particular applications and seek advice from Nutanix on your particular virtualization scenarios. It should be noted that SQL Database predominant IO size will be 64KB or above if you have followed the guidance so far in this chapter.

Figure 6.46 shows an overview of the Nutanix Virtual Computing Platform Architecture, including each hypervisor host (VMware ESXi), SQL VMs (User VMs), Storage Controller VM (Controller VM), and its local disks. Each Controller VM is directly connected to the local storage controller and the connected disks using VMware DirectPath/IO. By using local storage controllers on each ESXi host access to the NDFS file system, the data access path is localized and doesn't always require transport over the network, thereby reducing network traffic and potentially improving performance, predominantly for read operations. NDFS ensures that writes are replicated and distributes data within the cluster for data protection. The local storage controller on each host ensures that storage performance as well as storage capacity increase when additional nodes are added to a Nutanix NDFS cluster.

Figure 6.47 shows an overview of a single Nutanix NDFS cluster combining many different workloads, including SQL Server VMs, into different VMware vSphere clusters.

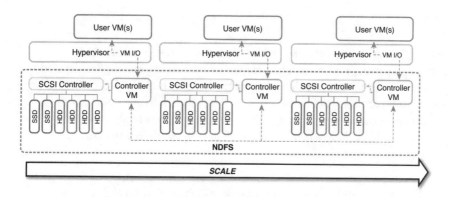

Figure 6.46 Nutanix Virtual Computing Platform Architecture overview.

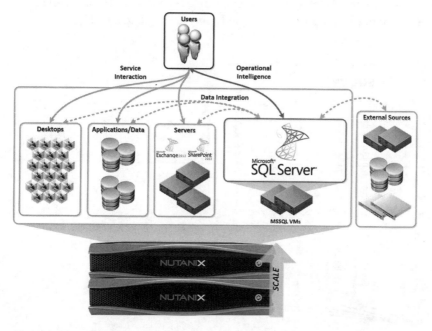

Figure 6.47 SQL Server on the Nutanix Virtual Computing Platform.

Although the storage is local to each node, NDFS makes it appear to the hypervisor as shared storage and therefore integrates with VMware DRS, HA, and fault tolerance. The combination of SSD and HDD local storage in addition to automated tiering is aimed at balancing both cost and performance. Also, NDFS data protection techniques remove some of the performance penalties associated with RAID. The localization of data allows for performance and quality of service to be provided per host, so noisy VMs can't greatly impact the performance of their neighbors. This allows for large mixed workload vSphere clusters that may be more efficient from a capacity and performance standpoint, while being resilient to failure.

> **TIP**
>
> Nutanix has a "SQL Server Best Practices" white paper and reference architecture available at http://go.nutanix.com/rs/nutanix/images/sql-on-nutanix-bp.pdf. For detailed information on the entire Nutanix architecture, see the Nutanix Bible by Steven Poitras at http://stevenpoitras.com/the-nutanix-bible/. The "VMware vSphere on Nutanix Best Practices" white paper (available at www.nutanix.com) covers in detail each vSphere feature and how it should be designed and configured in a Nutanix environment.

Due to the simplified nature of the Nutanix storage architecture and NDFS, we can simplify the storage layout for SQL Server. Figure 6.48 includes a sample layout, which is standard in a Nutanix environment, consisting of a single NFS data store and single storage pool. We do not need to configure multiple LUNs or calculate LUN queue depths.

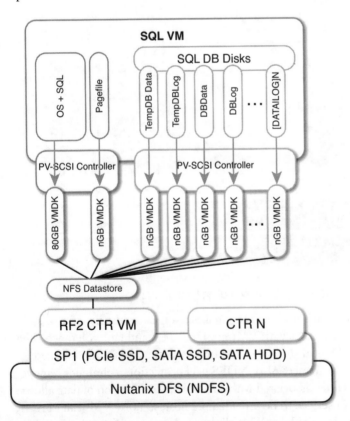

Figure 6.48 SQL Server VM disk layout on the Nutanix.

For high-performance, critical databases we would recommend you include 4 × PVSCSI controllers and split up the data files, Temp DB, and transaction logs similarly to that described in the section on SQL VM storage layout. With the four PVSCSI adapters available, we recommend that you start with two VMDKs per controller and expand the number of virtual disks per controller as evenly as necessary.

The simplified storage layout potentially provides a number of benefits to each type of SQL Database. Table 6.20 outlines some of the benefits you may be able to expect.

Table 6.20 Nutanix Benefits for OLTP and OLAP SQL Databases

	Nutanix Benefits
SQL OLTP	Localized I/O for low-latency operations
Transactional Database	SSD for indexes and key database files
	Ability to handle random and sequential workloads without the impact of the IO Blender Effect
SQL OLAP	Local read I/O for high-performance queries and reporting
Analytical Database	High sequential write and read throughput
	Scalable performance and capacity

To demonstrate the capability of the Nutanix platform for SQL Server, a number of SQLIO benchmarks were performed as part of the "SQL on Nutanix Best Practices" white paper (http://go.nutanix.com/TechGuide-Nutanix-SQLBestPractices_Asset.html), reproduced here with permission. Figures 6.49 through 6.52 resulted from the benchmarks.

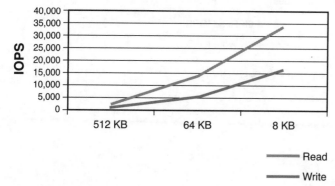

Figure 6.49 SQL Server SQLIO single VM random IOPS by block size.

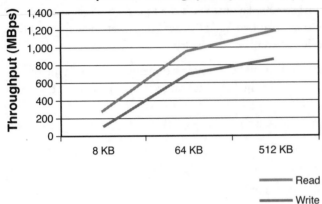

Figure 6.50   SQL Server SQLIO single VM throughput by block size.

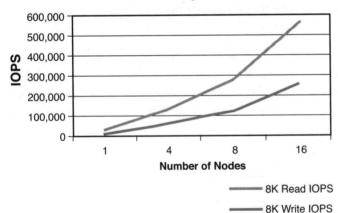

Figure 6.51   SQL Server SQLIO multiple VM IOPS scalability.

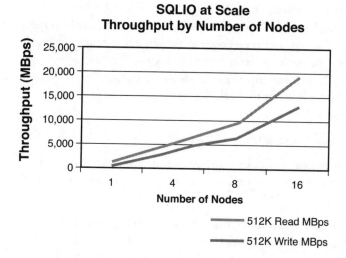

Figure 6.52 SQL Server SQLIO multiple VM throughput scalability.

Figures 6.49 through 6.52 show different performance profiles of the Nutanix Virtual Computing Platform for SQL Server VMs based on the "Nutanix SQL Best Practices" white paper, which includes the detailed configuration and testing details as well as individual IO pattern scenarios. Because most environments consist of mixed IO workloads, you should baseline your environment and consider the impact of IO mix and different IO sizes. The Nutanix platform can coexist with existing storage investments and offload workloads from existing storage platforms, thus freeing up both capacity and performance. It is a valid consideration for SQL Databases that fit within the performance envelope of the scale-out platform.

Summary

Throughout this chapter, we have provided architecture examples based on real-world projects that you can adapt for your purposes. We've tried to explain all the relevant considerations and best practices you need to worry about when architecting your environment for high-performance and critical SQL Server databases. We covered the key aspects of SQL Server storage architecture for all environments as well as the differences you need to understand when architecting storage specifically for virtual SQL Server databases, such as the IO Blender Effect and the way IO queues work across hosts on the same data store.

We provided guidance on important database storage design principles and a top-down approach covering SQL Server Database and Guest OS design, Virtual Machine Storage design, VMware vSphere Storage Design, and then down to the physical storage layers, including RAID and using server-side flash acceleration technology to increase performance and provide greater return on investment. We concluded the chapter by covering off one of the biggest IT trends and its impact on SQL Server: hyperconvergence and scale-out, shared-nothing architectures.

Let's briefly recap the key SQL design principles:

- **Your database is just an extension of your storage**. Make sure you optimize all the IO paths from your database to storage as much as possible and allow for parallel IO execution.

- **Performance is more than just the underlying storage devices**. SQL Buffer Cache has a direct impact on read IO, whereas virtual IO controller device queues and LUN, HBA, and Storage Processor queues can all impact performance and concurrency of IO before anything touches a physical storage device.

- **Size for performance before capacity**. If you size for performance, capacity will generally take care of itself. Much of this is due to the overheads associated with RAID storage needed to provide enterprise-grade data protection and resiliency. Use flash storage and automatic tiering to balance the performance and capacity requirements to get a more cost-effective solution overall.

- **Virtualize, but without compromise**. This involves reducing risk by assessing current performance, designing for performance even during failure scenarios, validating your design and its achievable performance, and ensuring storage quality of service, such as Storage IO Control. These all contribute to a successful SQL virtualization project. Make sure project stakeholders understand what performance to expect by having SLAs aligned to achievable IOPS per TB.

- **Keep it standard and simple**. Whatever design decisions you make for your environment, keep them as consistent as possible and have defined standards. Design for as few options as possible in your service catalog that cover the majority of system requirements. Only deviate from defaults where required.

We have covered storage performance in depth, as it is one of the most critical resources for a SQL Database. The next chapter will drill into how SQL memory allocation impacts the performance of your database, and how SQL and memory might change in the future.

TIP

Throughout this chapter, we have referred to SQL Server trace flags. A full list of the trace flags can be viewed at http://social.technet.microsoft.com/wiki/contents/articles/13105.trace-flags-in-sql-server.aspx. To enable trace flags when using Windows 2012, you need to run the SQL Configuration Manager, which doesn't appear in the list of applications. To do this, enter **sqlservermanager11.msc** in the application search box on the Apps screen.

Chapter 7

Architecting for Performance: Memory

In Chapter 5, "Architecting for Performance: Design," we introduced the concept of the "IT food group," shown in Figure 5.1. We discussed how important it is to provide your database the right balance of memory, disk, CPU, and network. Without enough of any single one of these essential resources, you will never have a properly performing system. We also stressed how important it is for you to balance these resources to ensure you get optimal performance from your virtualized database. All this must be done in the context of a shared resource environment.

In this chapter, we focus on leveraging memory as a resource, with the goal being to optimize the performance on your virtualized SQL Server database. Topics to be discussed in this chapter include the following:

- How to properly set SQL Max Memory

- Benefit of locking pages in memory

- NUMA (non-uniform memory access)

- Memory reservations

- Swapping, ballooning, and transparent page sharing

- Large memory pages

- How many VMs can you put on a physical host?

- SQL Server 2014 in-memory database

Memory

One of the most critical resources a database has is memory. You want to speed up a SQL Server database; the quickest way to do this based on my experience is to allocate more memory to it. By allocating more memory, you are minimizing the amount of physical I/O your database will have to perform. In other words, when the SQL Server database does not have enough memory, the database will move more of its workload to the physical I/O. A physical I/O request is still one of the slowest actions a database can perform.

As mentioned before, a database is just an extension of your disk drives. A slow disk array typically means a slow database. To speed up a database quickly, you need to minimize the physical I/O the database has to perform. In a perfect world, you would read all your data into memory, and the only time the database would have to go out to the storage array is to record a transaction.

> **CAUTION**
>
> When a SQL Server database does not have enough memory, the database will move more of its workload to physical I/O. Physical I/O is many orders of magnitude slower than memory access. Remember that RAM operations are measured in nanoseconds, whereas disk operations are measured in milliseconds.

Memory Trends and the Stack

If you think back over the past 20 years, one of major trends that have taken place in Information Technology is that vendors are finding ways to introduce memory into the entire stack. Starting with the CPU vendors and moving all the way down to the storage array vendors, they keep putting bigger and bigger memory caches at every possible level as a way to boost performance. This is illustrated in Figure 7.1, which shows the many levels of memory you would typically see in an environment.

At the server/physical host level and above, the CPU interacts with the array of memory associated with the CPU. Vendors started creating a separate array of memory associated with each CPU socket to prevent the performance hit associated with several processors attempting to access the same memory at the same time. A CPU is able to access its own local memory associated with the socket faster than nonlocal memory. Nonlocal memory is memory local to another processor or shared between processors. NUMA is another example of the trend of introducing memory into the stack to speed performance. NUMA stands for non-uniform memory access. We will discuss non-uniform memory access in great detail in the section of this chapter titled Non-Uniform Memory Access (Numa).

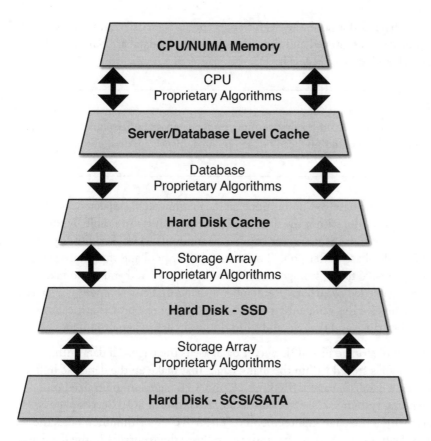

Figure 7.1 Memory trends and the stack.

Database Buffer Pool and Database Pages

At the server level, the SQL Server engine deals with the database cache, more commonly called the database buffer pool. The SQL Server engine uses a Most Recently Used (MRU) algorithm to determine which database pages to leave in memory and which database pages to swap back out of disk if there is not enough room in the database buffer pool to hold all the data in memory. By using this algorithm, it attempts to hold the data in memory that you are most likely to request next. Remember the important point we made earlier in the chapter: When a SQL Server database does not have enough memory, the database will move more of its workload to physical I/O.

An important point to make here is that the only way the SQL Server can access data is if it's residing within the database buffer pool. When a request is made within SQL Server for data, it first looks within the database buffer pool. If the database cannot find what it needs within the database buffer pool, the SQL Server engine then calls out to the storage to go retrieve it. The data is retrieved and then placed within the database buffer pool, at which point the database is able to access it.

IMPORTANT

SQL Server can only access data if it's first residing in the database buffer pool. Only data that resides in the database buffer pool can be manipulated, inspected, or altered by SQL Server.

Only data that resides in the database buffer pool can be manipulated, inspected, or altered by SQL Server. Until it resides within the database buffer pool, it is not usable by the database. Without memory, the SQL Server engine cannot do its work. As a DBA, you control the size of the database buffer pool. Too small a buffer pool and the database will constantly be calling outside to the storage array. Too large a pool and you could take away valuable memory needed elsewhere. Remember a virtualized environment is a shared resource pool of resources. How efficiently you use memory as a resource is critical to overall database performance and the overall health of the virtualized environment.

The fundamental unit of storage in a SQL Server database is the page. All data within the database buffer pool is stored within the many pages that make up the database buffer pool. In SQL Server, a database page is 8KB in size, and 8KB pages are optimized for the Windows operating system and are not adjustable. Each time a SQL Server page is touched, a counter within the page in incremented. The MRU algorithm then takes the hottest pages, those with the highest count, and tries to keep them current in the database buffer pool.

Paging and Swapping: A DBA's Nightmare

Quick question: *Paging* and *swapping* are common terms used by database administrators and system administrators. So what is the difference between paging and swapping?

Both paging and swapping are methods of moving the contents of data in memory to another storage device. That storage device is typically a disk drive, and the contents are placed within what is commonly called a swap file or page file. For example, in VMware vSphere, the file is called a vSwap file.

Swapping is when you move all the memory segments belonging to a particular process that's running onto another storage device. The important word here is *all*. When this happens, all execution on that process stops, until enough space exists for all the memory segments owned by that process to be brought back into memory. Remember, it's an all-or-nothing proposition.

Paging is when a subset of the memory segment IE: individual pages are able to be swapped in and out as needed. In this case, the SQL Server database would look within the page table. If the page needed is already in memory, SQL Server accesses the contents of that page. If the page needed by the process is not in memory, you get a page fault. Processing is temporarily suspended until the operating system is able to bring the needed page into memory. The key here is that this is *not* an all-or-nothing proposition. The coming in and out from the secondary storage device is done at a more granular level. In this example, the paging in and out is at the individual page level.

CAUTION

When paging or swapping occurs, the performance of your virtualized database is severely impacted. This should be avoided at all cost.

Continuing further down the stack, when the data the SQL server database engine needs is not available within the database buffer pool, it must make a request to the storage array for the needed information.

The storage array looks within its cache to see if the data needed is available to it. It also uses proprietary algorithms to keep the storage array data cache populated with the information you are most likely to need. Notice how memory is being used once again to boost performance by helping to minimize I/O. When the storage array cannot resolve the request, it then makes a request to retrieve the information from the physical drives.

Newer storage arrays, such as the EMC VMAX, IBM V7000, and NetApp FAS6200, would look within the SSD drives. (I am using flash and SSD interchangeably for purposes of this example.) According to Wikipedia (http://en.wikipedia.org/wiki/Solid-state_drive), a solid-state drive (SSD) "is a data storage device using integrated circuit assemblies as memory to store data persistently." As mentioned previously, solid-state storage should be thought of as cheap memory rather than expensive disks.

As you can see from the definition at Wikipedia, SSD drives are just another form of memory cache. The storage array uses additional proprietary algorithms to keep the SSD drives populated with the information you are most likely to need. When the SSD drives cannot resolve the request, they then look to the SATA/SCSI drives for the data. Depending on the storage array, it might contain SATA drives or SCSI drives. Blending SSD drives with SATA or SCSI drives together gives you better performance at a much more reasonable cost.

As this example illustrates, the trend within storage arrays is to minimize the amount of physical I/O that might be needed by leveraging memory. Any time you have memory-to-memory access happening, your database will perform faster.

Database Indexes

Another powerful tool we use to speed up a database's performance is the strategic placement of indexes. Indexes can greatly reduce the amount of physical I/O needed to retrieve the necessary data to resolve a query. This is an overly simplified way of explaining how a database retrieves data, but it illustrates the point I am trying to make.

When a database retrieves data, it can do so in one of two ways. The database performs a full table scan or an index seek. A full table scan is the equivalent of starting at the beginning of a book and reading every page of the book until the very end. An index read is the equivalent of using the index in the book and jumping right to the page you need. The index has the effect of greatly minimizing the amount of I/O the database has to perform. Unlike a book index, which points you to the page you need to go look up, a database index can sometimes provide all the data that is needed to resolve a query without going out to the actual source table itself for the data. We will provide an example of how an index works in the next section of this chapter.

> **NOTE**
>
> Indexes are an important tool in a DBA or developer's toolbox for improving overall database performance. It's important that periodic maintenance routines be put in place to keep those indexes operating optimally.

Database Indexes and Memory

Earlier in this chapter, we talked about database pages. For the purposes of this example, I am going to simplify things by not taking into account the overhead associated with a table or index within the SQL Server database.

Let's imagine you have a table within SQL Server with 10 columns, and each column is defined as char (100). As you can see in Figure 7.2, each column uses 100 bytes, which in turn means each row of data in that table requires 1,000 bytes. A 1KB page contains 1,024 bytes, and an 8KB page contains 8,024 bytes. Each page in the database buffer pool will contain up to a maximum of eight rows of that table. One hundred pages of that same table within the database buffer pool will contain up to a maximum of 800 rows of data.

Think of an index as a subset of the table itself. If you create an index on the first two columns of the table used in the example (and assuming no compression), then each row of the index would use 200 bytes. As you can see in Figure 7.2, each 8KB page within the database buffer pool would contain up to 40 index rows. One hundred pages would contain up to a maximum of 4,000 rows of data.

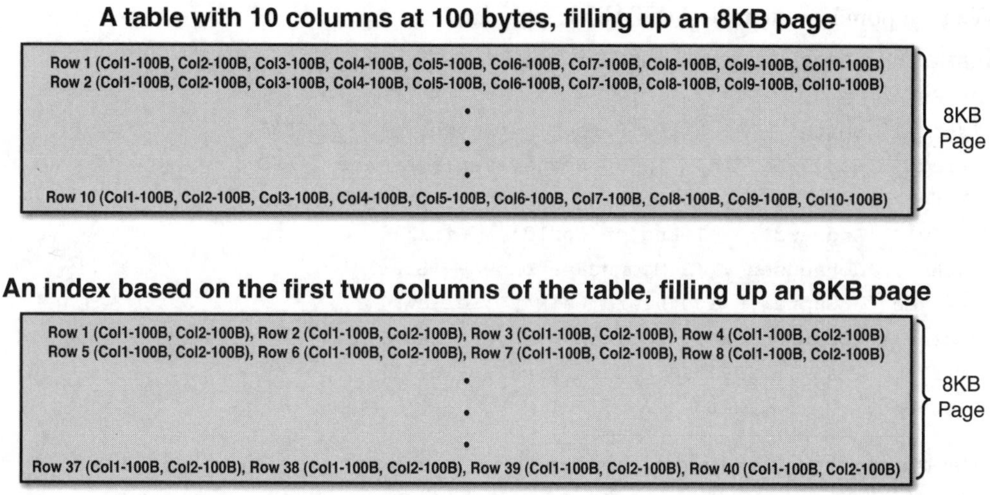

A table with 10 columns at 100 bytes, filling up an 8KB page

Row 1 (Col1-100B, Col2-100B, Col3-100B, Col4-100B, Col5-100B, Col6-100B, Col7-100B, Col8-100B, Col9-100B, Col10-100B)
Row 2 (Col1-100B, Col2-100B, Col3-100B, Col4-100B, Col5-100B, Col6-100B, Col7-100B, Col8-100B, Col9-100B, Col10-100B)

•
•
•

Row 10 (Col1-100B, Col2-100B, Col3-100B, Col4-100B, Col5-100B, Col6-100B, Col7-100B, Col8-100B, Col9-100B, Col10-100B)

8KB Page

An index based on the first two columns of the table, filling up an 8KB page

Row 1 (Col1-100B, Col2-100B), Row 2 (Col1-100B, Col2-100B), Row 3 (Col1-100B, Col2-100B), Row 4 (Col1-100B, Col2-100B)
Row 5 (Col1-100B, Col2-100B), Row 6 (Col1-100B, Col2-100B), Row 7 (Col1-100B, Col2-100B), Row 8 (Col1-100B, Col2-100B)

•
•
•

Row 37 (Col1-100B, Col2-100B), Row 38 (Col1-100B, Col2-100B), Row 39 (Col1-100B, Col2-100B), Row 40 (Col1-100B, Col2-100B)

8KB Page

Figure 7.2   A table filling an 8KB page, and an index based on the first two columns filling the 8K page.

As you can see, the index is able to pack substantially more rows of data into each page of memory within the database buffer pool. This means substantially less I/O is physically required to bring those rows of data into the database buffer pool. Less I/O means faster performance of your virtualized database.

An Index Provides All the Data Needed to Resolve a Query

To demonstrate the point of an index answering the results of a query without having to go back to the source table, let's create a really simple table. In this example, we create a table called MYTABLE that has four columns, named A, B, C, and D. In this example, the columns are type char, in keeping with the previous example. In the real world, you would more likely use nvarchar or varchar to conserve space.

```
Create Table MYTABLE
(A Char(100) not null,
 B Char(100) not Null,
 C Char(100) not null
 D Char(100) not null)
Go
```

We then populate the table MYTABLE with data:

```
INSERT dbo.PEOPLE (FNAME, LNAME)
VALUES
('John', 'Smith', '70 Kilby Street', 'Anywhere', 'BLUE'),
('Fred', 'Harglebargle', '1600 Pennsylvania Avenue','RED'),
('Mary', 'Johnson'), '10 Downing Street', 'Orange'),
('Andy', 'Andrews'), '1 End of World', 'Pink'),
('John', 'Johannsen', '2 Moonscape Lane', 'Black'),
('Ranjan', 'Gupta', '100 Board Walk', 'Yellow'),
('Susan', 'Brandonson', '10 Yawkey Way', 'Red'),
('Mark', 'Chan', '9999999 Ocean Drive','Blue')
GO 50000
```

After loading the table with data, we then create an index on the table. The index we create will be a compound/composite index on the first two columns of the table:

```
Create Index IX Myindex mytable on dbo.mytable (A,B)
```

We then issue a basic select statement against the table we created. The select statement we issue will only retrieve data from columns A and B:

```
Select A,B from dbo.MYTABLE where A='Mary'
```

In this example, the SQL Server database will be able to resolve this query without ever looking within the source table itself. Think of the index as a mini copy of the table, only containing data from the columns referenced in the index.

In the select statement, we only reference columns A and B. The index was created using columns A and B. Therefore, everything the query has requested is contained within the index itself, so the query never has to go back to the source table for any data.

Once this select statement is modified to include column C or D, the query can no longer resolve the request just using the index. Remember how we said the index is a mini copy of the table. In the mini copy of the table, those columns do not exist. Therefore, we must go back to the source table for the contents of C or D. This means that retrieving what is stored in the other columns of the table requires looking within the contents of MYTABLE itself. The following three select statements use the index to help speed the query along, but also have to look at the source table ultimately to retrieve all the data requested:

```
Select A,B,C from dbo.mytable where A='Mary'
```

```
Select A,B,D from dbo.mytable where A='Mary'
```

```
Select A,B,C,D from dbo.mytable where A='Mary'
```

What is clear is that whatever you can do to minimize physical I/O, the faster your database will perform. Storage array vendors do this by putting intelligence into the physical hardware (storage array) and how it utilizes memory to minimize physical I/O. Database vendors such as Microsoft do this by putting intelligence into the software (database engine) itself, the operating system, and how it leverages memory. Server vendors do it by putting memory associated with the CPU sockets. At every level—from the physical hardware (such as storage arrays) to the software (such as the SQL Server database)—vendors are finding ways to use memory to speed up performance.

As DBAs, we are constantly in a balancing act of how much of the IT food group (disk, CPU, memory, and network) we feed our database. It is clear that memory is one of the most powerful levers we have in our toolbox to optimize database performance. The choices we make will have a huge impact on overall database performance.

Host Memory and VM Memory

We as people have two types of memory: short-term and long-term memory. As we experience life, our short-term memory is recorded. Over time, it then feeds our long-term memory. When people lose their short-term memory, they would then lose the ability to obtain new long-term memory. As you can see, short-term memory and long-term memory are interconnected; this is true for your virtualized database as well, and it's important to understand the distinction between the two.

In your virtualized environment, memory exists at three levels that are also interconnected. As you can see, Figure 7.3 illustrates this point. You assign memory to the individual virtual machines that the SQL Server database resides on, and you also have memory at the hypervisor level, which is then mapped to the actual physical memory on the machine itself.

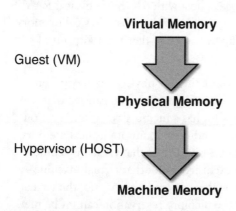

Figure 7.3   The three levels of memory.

The demand on the physical host is the aggregate demand of all the VMs running on the host. For example, if you had 10 VMs running on a physical host that each demanded 20GB of virtual memory (vRAM), the total aggregate demand on the physical host would be 200GB of virtual memory.

If your database is sitting on a physical host that only has 64GB of RAM available to it, 64GB is the entire amount of memory the physical host will ever be able to provide the many individual virtual machines residing on the host, no matter what the total demand is. In this example, you have oversubscribed memory or virtual memory. Oversubscribing is a common practice when virtualizing, but one we do not recommend for hosts that contain production databases—that is, until you have a thorough understanding of the total memory demands on the physical host your production databases are located on.

It is important that a database has access to the resources its needs when it needs them. When the database does not have access to the memory it needs, performance can be severely impacted, which is why we recommend that you don't oversubscribe memory for mission-critical SQL Server databases. A memory reservation will ensure that those critical applications always have the memory they need available to them. For now, think of a memory reservation as setting aside a certain amount of physical RAM that can only be used by a single virtual machine.

Mixed Workload Environment with Memory Reservations

One of our recommendations is to separate your production database from your development and test environments, if you are able. We also realize this is not always practical or feasible. Therefore, many times you will have a mixed environment. A mixed environment is one where you have both your production and nonproduction SQL server databases on the same physical host.

Figure 7.4 illustrates a mixed environment on a physical host with 64GB of physical RAM. No matter how many virtual machines are on this physical host, the most physical memory that will ever be available is 64GB. When you add up the memory demand footprint of all the VMs, you get 74GB.

To help ensure that production workloads are not competing for physical memory from nonproduction workloads, a memory reservation is set. In Figure 7.4, you can see that 40GB has been reserved. As each VM is first started, if it has a memory reservation set on it, a check is made by the hypervisor to see if a corresponding amount of physical memory on the host is available so it can be set aside for the exclusive use of that virtual machine. If the answer is yes, the memory is set aside for the exclusive use of that virtual machine and is no longer available for use by other virtual machines. If the answer is no, the virtual machine will not start because the requirement for the memory reservation cannot be met.

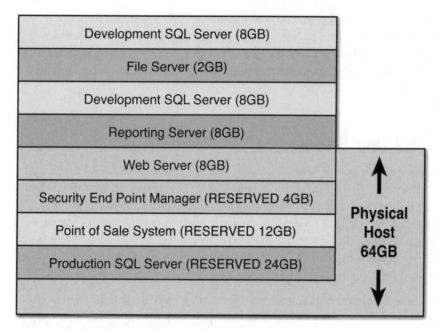

Development SQL Server (8GB)

File Server (2GB)

Development SQL Server (8GB)

Reporting Server (8GB)

Web Server (8GB)

Security End Point Manager (RESERVED 4GB)

Point of Sale System (RESERVED 12GB)

Production SQL Server (RESERVED 24GB)

**Physical
Host
64GB**

40GB out of 64GB is reserved, and total virtual memory demand is 74GB.

Figure 7.4   Mixed workload environment with virtual memory oversubscription.

In Figure 7.4, if we doubled the amount of physical memory on the host from 64GB to 128GB, there would be enough memory set aside for all the virtual machines with memory reservations plus any additional demand the other VMs listed would ever put on the physical host, as configured. That would be an example of a system where memory is not overcommitted. There is more than enough memory to meet the demands of all the virtual machines that reside on the physical host.

It's important to remember that when a database cannot get the resources it needs when it needs them, database performance will be negatively impacted as the database waits for those needed resources.

CAUTION

When you first start virtualizing your production databases, its important you don't overcommit memory. When there is not enough physical memory to meet the demands of the VMs, excessive paging and swapping will occur, which will impact database performance.

If the physical host is memory starved, then the individual VMs are at risk of being memory starved, which will induce paging and swapping. The one exception to this rule is memory reservations. To help prevent memory shortages, the hypervisor has tools available to it, such as transparent page sharing and ballooning, that can help lessen the strain on the physical host.

Transparent Page Sharing

To paraphrase the Scottish poet Robert Burns, the best laid plans of mice and men often go astray. No matter how well you plan the memory usage, there may come a time when the physical host becomes oversubscribed. One of the tools available to the hypervisor is transparent page sharing (TPS). TPS enables the hypervisor to remove redundant pages of memory to free up memory that is needed elsewhere. In Figure 7.2, we talked about how memory management happens at three levels: the guest VM level and the hypervisor level and physical host. TPS happens at the hypervisor level or physical host level.

Where there are idle CPU cycles, the hypervisor is running hash algorithms to generate "hints" so that it knows the location of the redundant pages of memory. Redundant pages of memory could occur when virtual machines are running the same applications, running the same guest operating systems, or working with the same datasets, but they actually happen at a level below application and operating system awareness, so redundant pages can still be found even if all workloads are unique. Only when there is actual memory contention at the physical host level does the hypervisor start using transparent page sharing.

TPS won't stop paging and swapping from happening; it actually allows them to happen. What it will do is allow the paging and swapping to happen with the least possible amount of performance impact.

Recognizing the fact that many of the virtual machines running may have identical sets of memory content, TPS invokes the hypervisor to identify those duplicate contents of memory and allows them to be shared. It does that by keeping a single read-only copy, and it uses a copy-on-write mechanism to ensure the security and integrity of the data.

If you had three guest VMs running the Windows 8 operating system, the hypervisor would only need to keep one copy of the operating system in memory for all three VMs to share. The memory would be reclaimed and made available to the hypervisor, which would give it back to the guest virtual machines to take advantage of on the physical host.

In this example, one copy of the OS would be placed in memory. The other two virtual machines would have pointers to the spot.

> **TIP**
>
> Transparent page sharing is more effective the more similar the VMs are. When possible, put like operating systems on the same physical host.

> **TIP**
>
> A great resource for better understanding transparent page sharing in more detail, as well as other memory management techniques, is the VMware performance study titled "Understanding Memory Resource Management in VMware vSphere 5.0," found at http://www.vmware.com/resources/techresources/10206.

Internet Myth: Disable Memory TPS

There is a myth circulating that TPS is an expensive process in terms of overhead, the consequences of using it far outweigh the benefits, and it should be disabled.

In Figure 7.5, you can measure the impact of having transparent paging disabled compared to having it enabled. You see that enabling page sharing introduces a negligible performance overhead when run in the default setting. When Mem.ShareScanTime is set to 10 minutes for all workloads, there is still less than 1% percent overhead experienced.

Mem.ShareScanTime specifies the time in minutes within which an entire virtual machine is scanned for page-sharing opportunities. The default setting is 60 minutes. So even when this happens six times an hour, the overhead is minimal.

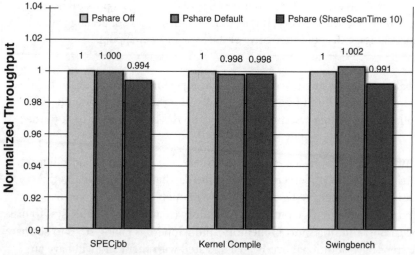

Figure 7.5 Dispelling the myth surrounding TPS.

TIP

To learn more about this study and why you do not want to disable transparent page sharing, review the performance study from VMware titled "Understanding Memory Resource Management in VMware vSphere 5.0." The URL is http://www.vmware.com/resources/techresources/10206.

BEST PRACTICE

We recommend that you keep the default setting for Mem.ShareScanTime and do not disable transparent page sharing. This is a far more efficient way to deal with memory constraints than the alternative of paging and swapping.

Memory Ballooning

Transparent page sharing is a process that is constantly running on the hypervisor when there are spare CPU cycles, looking for opportunities to reclaim memory. Ballooning is a memory-reclamation technique that only kicks in when the physical host is running low on physical memory. Because TPS is scanning all the time, it will be activated before ballooning in most cases. Memory ballooning happens at the guest virtual machine level versus the hypervisor (host) level.

CAUTION

Never shut off the balloon driver. This is your first line of defense for a physical host that is running low on physical memory. It is a far more efficient way of dealing with a physical memory shortage than the alternative of the hypervisor swapping.

When memory ballooning is taking place, there can be a performance impact. In the case of a virtual machine that has a lot of free memory, ballooning might have no impact on performance at all. The operating system will just give up the free memory back to the hypervisor.

In the case of your virtualized SQL Server database, there will be a performance impact. Ballooning is detrimental to SQL Server because of the database buffer pool. As the balloon inflates and the operating system doesn't have enough pages on its free list, the operating system may choose to page out its own memory (that is, use pagefile.sys) to disk. You have a physical host running short of memory, and vSphere is taking steps to alleviate the issue. Those steps have additional overhead associated with them and will have an impact on database performance. Yet, the alternative to those steps would be paging and hypervisor swapping—a DBA and system administrator's worst nightmare.

In a perfect world, it's best you never overcommit memory for your mission-critical workloads and avoid the possibility of memory ballooning completely. However, none of us lives in a perfect world.

For example, if you have a physical host with 30GB of physical memory and 45GB of memory is in demand by the different virtual machines running on the physical host, the balloon driver (known as vmmemctl.sys) might be invoked. There is not enough physical memory available from the physical host after TPS has already done what it could to alleviate the shortage, so the balloon driver now attempts to help. In Figure 7.6, step 1 shows the balloon driver sitting idle. The host is now experiencing memory shortages. In step 2, the balloon driver inflates itself inside the guest virtual machines if it has identified spare memory. That forces the memory to be paged out, which in turn frees the memory back to the hypervisor so it can be used by other more demanding virtual machines. Later on in step 3, when the host no longer has a memory shortage, the balloon driver within the guest OS deflates, allowing the guest OS to reclaim the memory.

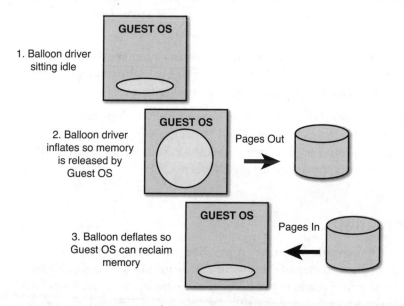

Figure 7.6   Balloon driver in action.

A great analogy to describe the balloon driver is Robin Hood: It steals available free memory from the rich virtual machines by inflating the balloon driver, freeing up that memory back to the hypervisor so that memory-constrained (poor) VMs can use it temporarily when there is not enough physical memory to go around.

Why the Balloon Driver Must Run on Each Individual VM

Because the hypervisor is completely decoupled from the virtual machines running on it, the hypervisor has no idea how memory is actually being used within the individual virtual machines. The balloon driver is a process that runs on each individual virtual machine, communicating with the guest operating system to determine what is happening with memory within the guest OS. The balloon driver has the ability to allocate and pin unused memory and communicate what it has done back to the hypervisor.

Working with the hypervisor, the balloon driver then reclaims pages of memory that are considered less valuable by the guest operating system. In other words, the balloon driver works with the hypervisor to allocate memory from the guest operating systems and return it back to the hypervisor for use.

If you think about the many VMs running within your host, many of them may not use all the memory allocated to them. As a DBA, how many of the tables in your database do you think are actually using all the space allocated to them? This is the same idea we find, for example, when a 4GB virtual machine is actually only using 2GB. The balloon driver frees that 2GB of unused memory back to the hypervisor for use where it is needed most. A virtualized infrastructure shares resources, so this ability to free up resources for use elsewhere is critical.

By engaging the balloon driver, we hope to avoid the hypervisor swapping, which is a much more resource-intensive way of dealing with the physical memory shortage. When the database buffer pool is sized properly, this unused memory will not exist.

An excellent resource for a detailed discussion on how the VMware balloon driver works is the technical white paper published by VMware titled "Understanding Memory Resource Management in VMware vSphere 5.0." For your convenience, you can also use the URL http://www.vmware.com/files/pdf/mem_mgmt_perf_vsphere5.pdf.

Memory Reservation

As you learned earlier in this chapter, a memory reservation provides the ability to guarantee a set amount of physical memory to a particular virtual machine and only this virtual machine. No other virtual machine will have access to the memory that is reserved. For mission-critical workloads such as a production database, we recommend you use memory reservations. This is especially important when you have mixed workloads of production and nonproduction databases and you want to maintain quality of service.

Once you have set a memory reservations, when you first start the virtual machine, a check is made by the vSphere hypervisor to see if enough physical RAM is available to meet the memory reservation requirement. If there is not enough physical RAM available to meet the memory reservation requirement, the virtual machine will not start. We discuss in the next section ways to override this default behavior.

No matter what the workload is on the physical host, this amount of memory is guaranteed to the virtual machine that has the memory reservation set, which is why it will not start if the memory is not available.

> **TIP**
>
> You should use memory reservations for the VMs that contain your tier-1 SQL Server databases. The memory reservation should be for 100% of the VM's configured memory size. At a minimum, it needs to cover the SQL Server database buffer pool and the overhead of the operating system.

Memory Reservation: VMware HA Strict Admission Control

As mentioned, when using VMware HA strict admission control, you are not able to power on a virtual machine if it would violate the availability constraints. In the example of using a memory reservation, a VM would not be allowed to power on if there was not enough physical memory available to commit. However, the setting "Allow virtual machine power-ons that violate availability constraints" enables the virtual machine to power on even if the memory reservation could not be met.

There are many valid reasons why you might allow this to happen. For example, you have a two-node cluster, and one of the nodes fails; you would want your business to keep on functioning. Therefore, as the virtual machines fail over the remaining functioning node, you would want to ignore the memory reservation during this critical time. To quote the VMware documentation: "Your particular usage scenario might make disabling VMware HA strict admission control desirable."

Memory Reservations and the vswap File

When a VM host is first powered on, it creates a swap file for that virtual machine that is equal in size to the difference between the virtual machine's configured memory size and its memory reservation. For production SQL Server databases, we recommend that the memory reservation be 100% of the configured size. Don't forget to include the overhead of the operating system. When this is done, an interesting thing happens with the vswap file.

In Figure 7.7, we created a memory reservation for 100% of what the VM could ever use, so the database will never have to use the vswap file. The hypervisor recognizes this fact.

You will notice the vswap file is 0.00KB in size. The hypervisor knows it will never use this swap file, so it is able to create the swap file in name only.

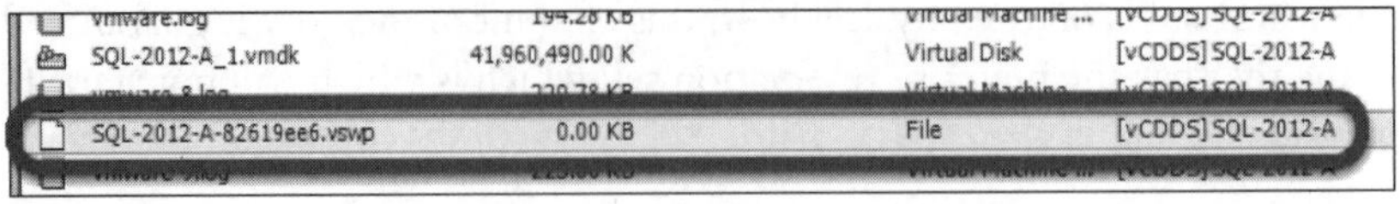

Figure 7.7   Setting a reservation creates a 0.00KB vswap file.

Throughout this chapter, we have talked about the importance of making sure the database has the resources it needs when it needs them. Memory is a critical resource for the database, and we strongly recommend that you use a memory reservation to ensure the database does not contend with other VMs for memory that could severely impact database performance. Being able to reserve memory for all your mission-critical workloads may not be possible given the constraints of your physical environment. As you get more comfortable with the resource demands of the VMs over time, then overcommitment of memory can be considered as a viable option in the management of your virtualized databases.

CAUTION

If you plan to overcommit memory, make sure you have enough disk space to create the vswap file; otherwise, the VM will not start.

Throughout this chapter, we have talked about how important it is not to overcommit memory. In the real world, the customers that get the most out of their VMware environment routinely overcommit resources. They only overcommit once they understand how resources such as memory are needed and used. Coming out of the gate, follow our guidelines and don't overcommit. Let at least a full business cycle go by. Once you understand the resources that are needed and when they are needed, it is okay to introduce overcommitment into your environment. It is the key to making sure your mission-critical virtual machines have the resources they need when they need them.

SQL Server Max Server Memory

When you configure how SQL Server uses memory, you have two options available to you:

- Use Max Server Memory.
- Use Min Server Memory.

These two options establish the upper and lower limits for the amount of memory used by the buffer pool within the database. Min Server Memory controls the minimum amount of physical memory that the database engine will try to keep committed. When you set Min Server Memory, the buffer pool does not immediately acquire the memory you specify. When the database starts, it only acquires the minimum amount of memory that is needed to start the database. It grows over time, as the database needs more. If the Windows operating system needs the memory for itself, the database may never reach the setting you established for Min Server Memory.

Max Server Memory is the opposite of Min Server Memory. Max Server Memory establishes the high water mark for how much memory the SQL Server database can consume. Max Server Memory is the amount of memory in megabytes that is managed by the SQL Server memory manager.

Both of these values can be set using sp_configure. The more important of these two choices is to configure Max Server Memory.

> **CAUTION**
>
> When configuring the database, you have two choices: Max Server Memory and Min Server Memory. Doing nothing is not an option. It is important that you set Max Server Memory to prevent the database from negatively impacting the operating system.

As DBAs, we know firsthand that databases by their nature will consume as much memory as we give them. When a database consumes all the available memory, database performance will be severely impacted. By the database consuming all available memory, it starves the operating system from the resources it needs, causing the OS to page and swap. To prevent this from happening, it's important that you configure Max Server Memory properly. So even though we say you have two options, you really only have one.

SQL Server Max Server Memory: Common Misperception

A common misperception is that when SQL Server starts, it grabs all the memory allocated to it with Max Server Memory. In reality, SQL Server will only request the memory it needs to initialize the database and will acquire additional memory as required. The SQL Server engine will not release memory until the minimum threshold has been reached, and it will not acquire memory above and beyond the Max Server Memory setting.

An excellent Microsoft TechNet article titled "Effects of Min and Max Server Memory" can be found at http://technet.microsoft.com/en-us/library/ms180797%28v=sql.105%29. aspx.

Formula for Configuring Max Server Memory

At Ntirety, our consulting services team has developed a simple formula based on our experience that gets you to an appropriate setting for Max Server Memory. Before I share the formula, it's important to remember there are no hard-and-fast rules. Each particular situation has nuances you have to account for. Also, a number of other factors impact how much memory you need to leave for the Windows operating system. Here are some examples:

- Are big copy jobs being performed periodically?

- Are a lot of extended stored procedures in use? Remember, they operate in the free memory segment.

- Is the virtual machine also acting as a web server or application server?

This formula is a starting guideline that should be appropriate for the majority of situations. Once it is implemented, we recommend following up by reviewing SQL buffer pool performance (page life expectancy) and the available system RAM to see if any tweaks are needed (up or down) for Max Server Memory.

Based on our experience, we recommend you use the following formula:

Assigned VM Memory – (2GB + Additional 1GB per 16GB Physical Memory) = SQL Max Memory

To make this a little easier, Figure 7.8 serves as a quick reference guide for where to start your settings for Max Server Memory. It's important to remember that with Server Max Memory set, the balloon driver's ability to reclaim memory will be affected. Because all the memory is accounted for, there will be no memory available for the balloon driver to reclaim, which is why for non-mission-critical systems this may not be advantageous, especially if you are trying to achieve high consolidation rates. As DBAs and system administrators, we know managing the infrastructure is all about weighing the pros and cons of each choice. With a tier-1 production database, it's pretty cut and dry. Make sure it gets the resources it needs, when it needs them.

The settings in Figure 7.8 are appropriate for a SQL Server database on a physical server. In a virtualized environment, it's important to remember that you are in a shared environment. So when you use the quick reference guide in Figure 7.8, it should be done within the memory size of the virtual machine that houses the database, not within the memory of the physical server that hosts all the virtual machines. Therefore, if you are sitting on a physical server with 128GB of RAM and the mission-critical database is housed within a 32GB virtual machine, the setting for Max Server Memory should be 28GB.

Total System RAM	Formula 2GB + Additional 1GB per 16GB Physical Memory	SQL MAX MEM Setting
16GB	16GB – (2GB + 1GB)	13GB
32GB	32GB – (2GB + 2GB)	28GB
48GB	48GB – (2GB + 3GB)	43GB
64GB	64GB – (2GB + 4GB)	58GB

Figure 7.8   SQL MAX MEM settings.

Large Pages

Another place where you can squeeze additional performance from your virtualized tier-1 SQL Server database is through the use of large pages. For SQL Server to use large pages, you must first enable it through the trace flag –T834.

Figure 7.9 illustrates how you enable large pages for SQL Server using trace flag –T834.

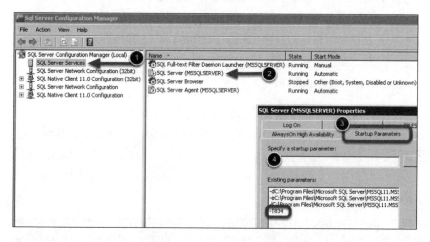

Figure 7.9   Enabling large pages.

What Is a Large Page?

All operating systems have a page size with which they work in memory. With Windows, the normal page size for a X64 system is 4KB. That means all work within memory happens in 4KB increments. This means all access to the buffer pool happens in 4KB chunks. When you enable large pages, the size is moved up to 2MB. A large page is many orders of magnitude larger than the default page size. The difference in page sizes is like the difference between moving your data with a pickup truck versus a very long cargo train. The immediate gain is that address translations happen much faster. This is because there are many fewer memory pages to manage. In other words, memory can be allocated quicker to the virtual machine, which translates into faster performance for your database.

Upon database startup when large pages are enabled, the database will immediately allocate all memory for the buffer pool rather than grow it dynamically. By having all pages allocated up front, SQL Server avoids the risk of memory fragmentation or out-of-memory conditions later. Another added benefit: Because the allocation of large pages can take some time if it happens dynamically, you now avoid a performance hit that would happen later when your database queries are first initiated.

Large pages must be in contiguous space within memory, which is why it's important that they be implemented with many of the other suggestions we made earlier in this chapter. For example, memory reservations will help ensure you have a large chunk of contiguous space.

Large pages cannot easily be swapped out, nor are they candidates for transparent page sharing. There are two reasons large pages are not candidates for TPS:

- There is very low likelihood that two large pages would ever be identical. VMware recognizes this fact and does not consider them candidates for TPS.

- It would be very resource intensive to perform a bit-by-bit comparison of a large page to determine if it was a candidate for TPS.

Large pages cannot easily get the benefit of ballooning, which is why it's important that you make sure there is sufficient memory on the physical host to meet the demands of your mission-critical SQL Server databases.

Large Pages Being Broken Down

When the physical host is under memory constraints and it has exhausted all other alternatives, it will begin the process of breaking large pages into the default page size—which for a X64 system would be 4KB. Earlier in Figure 7.3, we talked about how memory is managed. In this example, large pages are broken down at the hypervisor (host) level, not at the guest VM level. Remember, large pages cannot be swapped out as they are by the hypervisor.

The large pages must first be broken down into the default page size. In addition, large pages are not candidates for transparent page sharing. Once those pages are broken down into the default size of 4KB, the hypervisor can start to invoke TPS to help free up memory.

In the case of ballooning, the balloon driver would make a request of the guest VM to see if it is able to free up memory to help deal with the physical memory shortage the host is struggling with. If the balloon driver is able to identify excess memory, it would free that memory back to the hypervisor. By using memory reservation with the VM your SQL Server database is on, you avoid any of this happening to your database.

Lock Pages in Memory

Within the Windows operating system, there is a policy that enables you to authorize an account in order to lock pages in memory. When dealing with a mission-critical SQL Server database, we recommend that you lock pages in memory, which is illustrated in Figure 7.10. This provides a guarantee from the operating system to your SQL database that it will always get the memory it has allocated. When the Lock Pages in Memory policy and large pages are used together, the hypervisor will not be able to request the guest VM attempt to balloon memory from the virtual machine on which your SQL Server database is housed.

Give it the rights ⟶

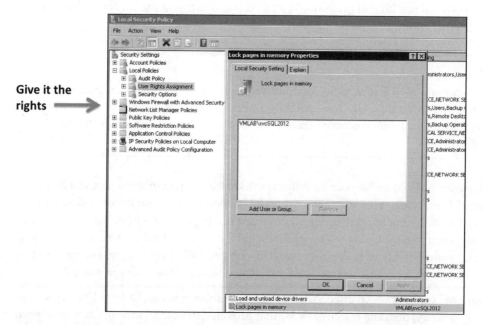

Figure 7.10   Lock Pages in Memory rights.

At the vSphere level, it is still possible that the hypervisor could break down its large pages into small pages, making them a candidate for transparent page sharing. This backing of guest operating system large pages with hypervisor small pages is not optimal and leads to the recommendation to reserve 100% of the guest virtual machine's memory.

This combination of large pages and lock pages in memory prevents the SQL Server buffer pool from being paged out by the Windows operating system. It should also be noted that it prevents the balloon driver from being able to reclaim memory to hand back to the hypervisor for use in other virtual machines. In the case of your production database, this is desirable because the primary objective is to make sure the mission-critical database has the resources it needs to get the job done when it needs them and is not waiting on others. This will ensure that memory is not taken away from the database.

A database will consume as much memory as you give it, which is why we always reserve head room for the operating system and any other applications running on that virtual machine that may need memory. The performance of memory is magnitudes faster than the performance of disks, and your database is just an extension of your storage.

There is a school of thought that Lock Pages in Memory is not needed with the newer versions of the Windows operating system, which have improved memory management capabilities. Our experience has taught us to limit this practice to your most mission-critical SQL Server databases and limit Max Server Memory to the confines of the overall size of the virtual machine in question. We recommend that you should always lock pages in memory.

TIP

For your mission-critical SQL Server databases, we recommend you lock pages in memory to prevent the SQL Server buffer pool being paged out by the Windows operating system. Make sure you have a reservation for the amount of memory at the hypervisor layer.

The opposite is also true for your noncritical workloads; we recommend that you do *not* lock pages in memory. This will then enable the balloon driver to do its job and reclaim memory for use by the hypervisor for other virtual machines on the host. This is important especially when you are trying to consolidate a number of workloads onto a single physical host. The assumption here is that they won't always need all of the assigned resources at the same time. Never forget a virtualized infrastructure is a shared infrastructure.

You want to avoid the yo-yo effect, where the reclamation process (Balloon Driver) is recovery memory, then the resource (VM) that provided the excess memory is now in need of it, so the reclamation process gives it back to the VM, then the balloon driver recovers the memory again and so on and so on and so on. Every time the system thrashes as resources ebb and flow, other resources are impacted, such as CPU and disk. For example, as paging and swapping occur, the storage array is impacted.

How to Lock Pages in Memory

In order to lock pages in memory, it is important that the appropriate account has rights. There is a Windows policy that determines which accounts are able to lock pages and which accounts cannot. The account in your environment that has privileges to run sqlservr.exe is the account you want to give the ability to lock pages in memory. For SQL Server databases before 2012, you should also make sure this account has the awe_enabled configuration set to on. AWE stands for "address windowing extensions." This allows a 32-bit SQL Server to address more memory. Note that awe_enabled is not needed on the 64-bit versions of SQL Server.

Non-Uniform Memory Access (NUMA)

When you're building your virtual machines, we recommend that you size each one to fit within a single NUMA node so that you get optimal performance for your virtual machines.

Throughout this chapter, we have talked about how both the hardware vendors and the software vendors have found ways to introduce memory to speed up processing. NUMA is another example of that trend of introducing memory into the stack to speed performance.

Today's CPUs are faster than the main memory they use. Therefore, these CPUs can become stalled due to a lack of memory bandwidth while waiting for data they needed to arrive from main memory. To prevent this from happening, the vendors started creating a separate array of memory associated with each CPU socket to prevent the performance hit associated with several processors attempting to access the same memory at the same time.

In Figure 7.11, we illustrate a four-CPU system with six sockets each, and a cache of memory associated with each physical CPU socket. Each one of those memory caches linked to a physical CPU socket in this illustration is a NUMA node.

In a perfect world, you could size each virtual machine to fit within a single NUMA node and you would have optimal performance. When a CPU needs to access memory not within its own NUMA node, the data must be transferred over from the other node. This is slower than accessing memory within the NUMA node itself. Memory access times are non-uniform and depend on the location of the memory and the particular node it is coming from—thus the term "non-uniform memory access."

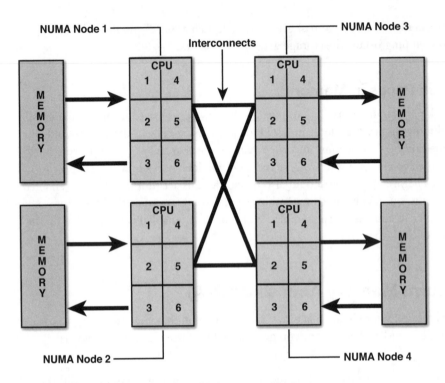

Figure 7.11 NUMA nodes: a four-CPU system with six cores.

If the system illustrated in Figure 7.11 has a total of 128GB of RAM associated with it, then each NUMA node would consist of 32GB of RAM. For optimal performance, the total size of each virtual machine should be less than 32GB. This would ensure optimal performance because you would never have to take the performance hit associated with spanning NUMA nodes. If you don't know the NUMA node size, ask your server vendor.

Just as a database page has a certain percentage of each page reserved for page management, the same holds true for vSphere memory management. Within that 32GB NUMA node, a very small percentage of the 32GB will be utilized by the hypervisor for memory management. You should always size your VM's knowing a little off the top is reserved for memory management, so in this example, the maximum size a VM can be to fit within the NUMA node is slightly less that the 32GB. An excellent blog article from VMware that talks about this overhead can be found at http://blogs.vmware.com/vsphere/2012/05/memminfreepct-sliding-scale-function.html.

It's worth noting here that the remote access penalty is the same for a physical implementation as it is for virtual implementations.

> **TIP**
>
> To avoid NUMA remote memory access, size your virtual machine memory to less than the memory per NUMA node. Don't forget to leave a little room for memory management overhead.

VMware is NUMA aware. When a virtual machine first powers on, it is assigned a home NUMA node. Think of a NUMA node as a set of processors and memory. It will keep a particular VM running on the same NUMA node. If the hypervisor detects that the NUMA node the VM is running on is busy, it will migrate the VM to another NUMA node to get better performance. It is important to note that when you hot-plug a CPU, you affect vSphere's ability to utilize NUMA. The two capabilities do not work well together. When vSphere first starts up, it establishes the NUMA home nodes based on the number of CPUs. When a CPU is hot-plugged, it affects these settings. In effect, it disables vSphere's ability to use NUMA. Our experience has taught us that NUMA is much more beneficial to the performance of your SQL Server database than the ability to hot-plug a CPU.

vNUMA

Even though vSphere has been "NUMA aware" for a very long time, in vSphere 5 VMware introduced vNUMA. vNUMA helps optimize the performance of a virtual machine too large to fit within a single NUMA node and must span NUMA boundaries by exposing to the guest operating system the actual physical topology so that it can make its own NUMA decisions. This is good news for large-scale SQL Server workloads that are virtualized that cannot fit within a single NUMA node.

A great blog article titled "vNUMA: What It Is and Why It Matters" can be found at http://cto.vmware.com/vnuma-what-it-is-and-why-it-matters/.

As we discussed earlier, NUMA and the ability to hot-plug a CPU should not be used in combination with each other.

> **TIP**
>
> vNUMA is disabled if vCPU hot plug is enabled. The link to the VMware knowledge base article is http://kb.vmware.com/kb/2040375.

To learn more about NUMA nodes, see the VMware technical white paper, "The CPU Scheduler in VMware vSphere 5.1," which can be found at https://www.vmware.com/files/pdf/techpaper/VMware-vSphere-CPU-Sched-Perf.pdf.

Sizing the Individual VMs

Memory is a very valuable resource that, as you have learned in this chapter, can greatly affect the performance of your database in a number of ways. When you build out the virtual machines, it's important to keep them as lean as possible. This will help you with your NUMA boundaries. This will also help make sure you are efficiently using the resources you have available to you. In this shared environment, it will help ensure adequate memory is available for the hypervisor to share among the many individual virtual machines running on the physical host.

Your virtualized database is sitting on a shared environment. To ensure quality of service means making sure the database has the resources it needs in the context of a shared environment. This is why we put so much emphasis on resource guarantees for resources such as memory. By building your VM as efficiently as possible, you help make sure there are enough of the shared resources for everyone.

CAUTION

When you create your virtual machines, keep the footprint as lean as possible. Don't install database and Windows operating system features you will not need. Make sure you disable all unnecessary foreground and background processes.

When you build the virtual machines, keep this in mind as you make the many choices you have available to you. Don't install features of the Windows operating system you will never need, and don't install features of the database you will never need. Also, disable all unnecessary foreground and background processes you don't need; by doing so, you will keep the VM as lean as possible.

When building a virtual machine that will house a production database, it is recommended that you build it from scratch, not using the P2V converter. A database is a very complex environment, and experience has taught us that over time the environment can be become very cluttered with components that are no longer needed. Use this opportunity to create the new database environment as lean and clean as possible.

More VMs, More Database Instances

One of the questions we get asked at conferences by database administrators is, "Is it better to have more virtual machines, or one or two virtual machines that house a number of database instances?"

In Figure 7.12, we illustrate the two configurations. On the left side, we have one virtual machine that hosts three SQL Server instances, whereas on the right side, we have three separate virtual machines, each hosting an individual SQL Server instance. There may be licensing issues that require you to use one configuration over the other. But if we take licensing out of the equation, our experience has shown us that it is better to implement with more distinct virtual machines, as illustrated on the right in Figure 7.12.

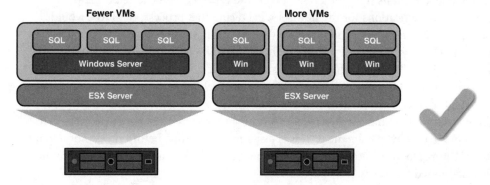

Figure 7.12   More VMs versus more database instances.

A SQL Server database is one of the most resource-intensive applications you will ever virtualize. By implementing each production SQL Server database as a separate virtual machine, you will have much better control over how resources such as memory are utilized.

For example, if you had three SQL Server databases on one virtual machine—let's assume two of them are nonproduction and one of them is production—you would want to implement the many techniques we have talked about in this chapter for the mission-critical database, but not for the non-mission-critical databases. That is not be possible if they are all hosted on a single VM.

You have greater ability to fine-tune how resources are allocated to a particular virtual machine. Another consideration is your ability to deal with a failed host or critical time for the business. Let's say you're an online retailer, and it's Cyber Monday, the busiest day of the year. You could, on that particular day, power down all non-critical virtual machines, thus freeing up resources needed for mission-critical virtual machines.

Having more virtual machines offers a number of benefits:

- Better resource isolation
- Better security management
- Better patch management
- Better performance

Thinking Differently in the Shared-Resource World

In a virtualized environment, we keep talking about how it's a shared-resource environment. This is something that takes getting used to for the typical database administrator. Traditionally, the database would sit on a physical server whose resources were 100% dedicated to only that production database.

Every few years, when its time for a new server, the DBA would be asked to help determine the specifications for the new server. During that process, the DBA would go through an exercise to determine the new server configuration needed. During this exercise, the DBA would always pad the request. If 64GB of RAM were needed, the DBA would ask for 128GB of RAM. If four CPUs were needed, the DBA would ask for eight CPUs. Any good DBA would pad his request for as much as he thought he could convince management to buy. This was done for the DBA's self-preservation. Whichever server was purchased was going to have to last the DBA until a new server was purchased. No matter what was purchased by management, it was just a matter of time before it was not enough and the DBA would be spending a lot of time he did not have doing performance tuning to stretch the limited resources.

In this shared-resource world, where your database is virtualized, you have to learn to ask for just the amount of resources you really need. If you ask for too much, you are wasting resources and also potentially preventing other virtual machines from having access to the resources they may need.

When your database sits on a physical server, your ability to add resources dynamically does not exist. That is not the case when your database is virtualized. You now have the ability to dynamically hot-add memory.

If your virtual machine that houses the database is configured at 32GB of memory, you can dynamically allocate an additional 32GB to it. After a slight delay, the virtual machine will have access to 64GB of RAM.

Using the SP_Configure command within SQL Server, you can also dynamically adjust Server Max Memory. With a virtualized database, resources such as vCPU (virtual CPU) and virtual RAM are just a click away. If you choose to use the capability to hot-plug a CPU, remember it affects your ability to use NUMA.

SQL Server 2014 In-Memory Built In

The Microsoft website talks about SQL Server 2014 and the new in-memory capabilities built in to the core database engine for online transaction processing (OLTP) and data warehousing (http://www.microsoft.com/en-us/sqlserver/sql-server-2014.aspx). As stated before, the slowest action a database performs is reading from the storage array. If we could keep all our needed data in memory, the database performance improvement would be enormous.

According to the Microsoft data sheet titled "SQL Server 2014 & The Data Platform," you will see up to a 30× performance gain using SQL Server 2014 in-memory capabilities. It claims you will see in average of 10× performance gains for existing SQL Server applications. When we think about the speed of reading from memory versus physical I/O, a 10× or more improvement seems very attainable. It's important to note that as of the writing of this book, SQL Server 2014 was in General Release, so your individual mileage with the product may vary. However, our experience tells us that the numbers quoted should be very attainable.

Summary

In this chapter, we discussed the IT food groups with a focus on memory. Memory is one of the most critical resources you have available. Everyone from hardware vendors to software vendors are finding new ways to leverage memory to speed up performance. The newest version of SQL Server will have an in-memory database that is able to perform magnitudes faster than its predecessors by levering memory as a resource.

We stressed how important it is that you have the right balance of resources if you want to optimize the performance of your virtualized SQL Server database. This is especially important in a shared environment. By using techniques such as setting memory reservations, you can ensure that mission-critical resources have the resources they need when they need them, even in a shared-resource environment.

We discussed the many tools available to the hypervisor, such as TPS and ballooning, to help ensure the hypervisor is getting the most leverage out of the physical memory available to it. We also discussed NUMA and a number of other things you need to take into consideration when you virtualize your production SQL Server database.

Chapter 8

Architecting for Performance: Network

We have now reached the final IT food group—the network. Although SQL Server is generally not very network intensive, the network is very important as the means of access for all clients and applications, as well as the means of access to storage in a SAN environment. When you are using advanced configurations such as SQL AlwaysOn Failover Cluster Instances and AlwaysOn Availability Groups, the network becomes even more important because it is the means of data replication and cluster failure detection. A fast, reliable, low-latency network will improve the speed of response to your applications and clients. In a virtualized environment, the network is also heavily used to provide greater flexibility and manageability through the use of VMware vMotion and VMware DRS. Providing the appropriate quality of service for different network traffic types—such as client traffic, cluster traffic, replication traffic, management, and vMotion traffic—is important to ensure you can meet application service levels.

TIP

For SQL Server DBAs, operating virtualized databases is simpler than physical or native database servers from a network perspective. There is no need to configure network teaming or VLAN drivers inside Windows. There is also no need to configure storage multipathing drivers—the only exception being where you are using in-guest iSCSI connectivity to storage. Network teaming and storage multipathing are handled transparently, reliably, and simply through VMware vSphere. No longer will a misconfigured or misbehaving teaming driver or Windows multipathing problems cause an issue for your database.

This chapter covers how to get the required network performance from your SQL Server VMs—from using the right network adapter type, cluster network settings, and the benefits of jumbo frames, to designing and configuring your hypervisor and your physical network for performance, quality of service, and network security.

SQL Server and Guest OS Network Design

This section focuses on getting the best network performance out of SQL Server and your Windows virtual machines when running in a VMware vSphere environment. A number of options and best practices that can be used to improve network performance and reliability, which we cover in this section. It is recommended that you consider the options during your design process and come up with a standardized configuration that can be applied to your templates. This will reduce operational complexity. Remember to "keep it standardized and simple."

Choosing the Best Virtual Network Adapter

The three main virtual network adapter choices for configuring your virtual machines are described in Table 8.1. E1000E was introduced with vSphere 5.0 and is the default for Windows 2012 and above. However, the recommended network adapter is VMXNET3. VMXNET3 consistently shows the best performance, lowest latency, and highest throughput for the best CPU cost efficiency and is optimized for a VMware environment. Unless there is a problem that prevents you from using VMXNET3, it should be the standard vNIC configured in all your VM templates.

Table 8.1 Virtual Network Adapters

Virtual NIC	Description	Support OS	Virtual HW
E1000	An emulated version of the Intel 82545EM Gigabit Ethernet NIC.	Windows 2003 and newer	Version 4 and newer
E1000E	An emulated version of the Intel 82574 Gigabit Ethernet NIC. It is the default vNIC for Windows 2012 and newer Windows guest operating systems.	Windows 2003 and newer	Version 8 and newer
VMXNET3	VMware paravirtualized NIC designed for performance. It offers lower latency, higher throughput, and reduced CPU usage compared to E1000 and E1000E. (VMware tools required.)	Windows 2003 and newer	Version 7 and newer

NOTE

When VMXNET3 was released with vSphere 4.0, VMware published a performance evaluation that compared it to other network adapter choices. You can review this paper at http://www.vmware.com/pdf/vsp_4_vmxnet3_perf.pdf.

Figure 8.1 shows the relative performance between the different virtual network adapter options. The tests used the default maximum transmit unit (MTU) size of 1,500 bytes as well as Windows 2012 running on vSphere 5.5 on a 10Gbps network between hosts. The hosts had two eight-core Intel E5-2650 v2 (Ivy Bridge) CPUs, 256GB RAM, and an Intel 82599EB 10G SFP+ dual-port NIC. Multiple test iterations were measured using the netperf tool (http://www.netperf.org/netperf/) and a single TCP stream. The graph shown in Figure 8.1 uses the average results of the multiple tests. The same hosts were used for all network performance tests for data in this chapter.

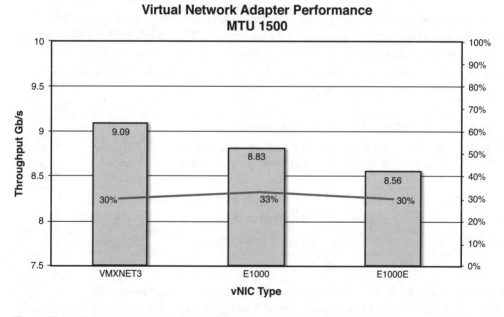

Figure 8.1 Virtual network adapter performance with default settings.

> **CAUTION**
>
> There is a known issue with regard to E1000 and E1000E network adapters that can cause high packet drop rates. See VMware KB 2056468, "High rate of dropped packets for guests using E1000 or E1000E virtual network adapter on the same ESXi 5.x host." There is also a known issue with vSphere 5.1 and UDP performance with Windows. For more information, see VMware KB 2040065.

Virtual Network Adapter Tuning

For most cases, the default settings for the selected network adapter will work well. We recommend that you keep the default settings unless you experience a performance problem or there is a strong justification to adjust them. If you need to deviate from the defaults, it's important to make sure any changes are documented and thoroughly tested.

In some cases, adjustments are needed, especially where systems send or receive large numbers of small packets. This is often the case with OLTP databases, where there are many small transactions, or where a lot of program code or configuration is stored in database tables. Table 8.2 displays some of the common parameters that may need to be adjusted based on particular workload requirements.

Table 8.2 Virtual Network Adapter Advanced Settings

Virtual NIC	Jumbo Frames Support	RX Buffers (Default/Max)	TX Buffers (Default/Max)	Interrupt Moderation	Receive Side Scaling	Multiple TX / RX Queues
E1000	Y	256 / 4,096	512 / 2,048	Enabled (Adaptive)	N	N
E1000E	Y	256 / 4,096	512 / 2,048	Enabled (Adaptive)	Y (Enabled)	N
VMXNET3	Y	512 / 4,096	512 / 4,096	Enabled	Y (Disabled)	Y

A number of applications can be very network intensive when communicating with SQL Server databases and send many thousands of small packets per second (for example, SAP). For these types of applications, increasing receive and transmit queues on the SQL Server can improve performance and reduce packet retransmissions.

TIP

If you have an application server that is particularly network intensive when communicating with the database, you may be able to locate it on the same host and on the same port group to greatly improve network communications responsiveness and throughput. The reason for this is that *VMs on the same host and on the same port group communicate at memory speed and are not limited by the physical network.* The network traffic does not have to go outside of the host.

By default, virtual network adapters are optimized for high throughput, and not for the lowest latency. In addition to adjusting queues, interrupt moderation may need to be disabled to reduce latency. Interrupt moderation reduces the number of CPU interrupts that the virtual network adapter issues in order to reduce CPU utilization and increase throughput, but by doing this it also increases latency.

TIP

Power management policy of your hosts and the guest operating system of your virtual machine can have an impact on network latency and throughput. Generally, the BIOS setting of OS Control Mode and the vSphere Power Management policy of Balanced (default) are recommended. However, if you have particularly latency-sensitive VMs, we recommend configuring your host power policy for high performance or static high performance. We recommend in all cases that your Windows Power Management policy be set to High Performance. For further information on tuning for latency-sensitive workloads, see http://www.vmware.com/files/pdf/techpaper/VMW-Tuning-Latency-Sensitive-Workloads.pdf.

In some situations, adjustments of the virtual network adapter inside the guest operating system may not be sufficient to achieve the required performance. In these cases, interrupt coalescing may need to be disabled on the virtual network adapter, either in the virtual machine configuration or on the host. To disable interrupt coalescing on a virtual Ethernet adapter, you need to modify the advanced parameter `ethernetX.coalescingScheme` (where X is the number of the Ethernet adapter, such as 0 or 1) and set it to `disabled`. The following example shows how you would add the required advanced setting to disable interrupt coalescing for virtual Ethernet adapter 0 in a virtual machine configuration using VMware PowerCLI:

```
Get-VM <VMName> | Set-AdvancedSetting -Name ethernet0.coalescingScheme
-Value disabled
```

Alternatively, you can add a line to the VM's advanced settings using the vSphere Client or vSphere Web Client, as shown in Figure 8.2.

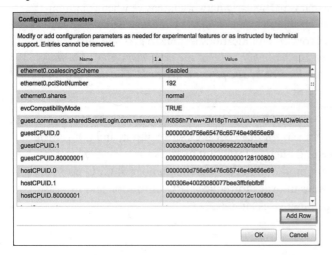

Figure 8.2   Disable the virtual Ethernet adapter coalescing scheme.

If the VM was powered on at the time, the advanced setting is added, but the VM will need to be shut down and powered back on in order for the setting to take effect.

CAUTION

If you decide to tune your virtual network adapters, it can make performance worse. It is recommended that any changes to default settings are thoroughly tested in your environment and only made if they are absolutely necessary to meet business requirements.

Windows Failover Cluster Network Settings

When you use SQL Server AlwaysOn Failover Cluster Instance or AlwaysOn Availability Groups in a virtualized environment, adjustments are necessary to the default failover cluster network settings. AlwaysOn Availability Groups allows you to continue to use VMware DRS and vMotion without causing unnecessary interruptions or failovers. In most cases that use AlwaysOn Failover Cluster Instance, vMotion is not possible because shared RDM devices will be used. However, in cases where direct in-guest iSCSI access is used for AlwaysOn FCI shared cluster disks, you will be able to continue to leverage VMware DRS and vMotion, provided the recommended adjustments are made. Figure 8.3 displays an example of the Windows Failover Cluster settings, with the network settings highlighted.

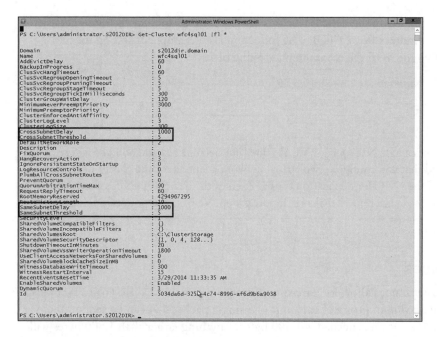

Figure 8.3   Windows Failover Cluster network settings.

Table 8.3 displays each of the important Windows failover cluster network settings along with their default, maximum, and recommended values based on Windows Server 2012 and above. If you are running an earlier version of Windows, the default or maximum values may be different.

Table 8.3   Windows Failover Cluster Heartbeat Settings

Setting	Description	Default Value	Maximum Value	Recommended Value
CrossSubnetDelay	Value in milliseconds of the cluster heartbeat frequency across different subnets	1000ms	4000ms	1000ms
CrossSubnetThreshold	Number of missed heartbeats tolerated across subnets before a failover occurs	5	120	10
SameSubnetDelay	Value in milliseconds of the cluster heartbeat frequency within the same subnet	1000ms	2000ms	1000ms
SameSubnetThreshold	Number of missed heartbeats tolerated within the same subnet before a failover occurs	5	120	10

The easiest way to modify the default cluster network settings to their recommended values is to use Windows PowerShell. The following is an example of setting the SameSubNetThreshold to the recommended value of 10:

```
(Get-Cluster).SameSubnetThreshold=10
```

> **TIP**
>
> To ensure that a single NIC port or VLAN does not become a single point of failure, it is recommended that you configure two virtual network adapters for the cluster heartbeat, separate from the vNIC for application traffic. Each of the heartbeat vNICs should be configured to use a different virtual switch port group, VLAN, and physical NIC port.

Jumbo Frames

Standard Ethernet frames allow for a maximum transmission unit (MTU) of 1,500 bytes. This means the maximum protocol data unit of a single packet that can be sent at one time before fragmentation is needed is 1,500 bytes. Anything larger than 1,500 bytes will need to be fragmented on the source, sent in multiple packets, and then reassembled on the destination. Although this has been perfectly acceptable in the past with up to 1Gbps networks, it introduces overheads when transmitting large amounts of data and on high-speed networks, such as 10Gbps and above.

Modern 10Gbps and above network adapters include features such as Large Segment Offload and Large Receive Offload to try and alleviate the overhead of dealing with many standard-size packets when using a 1,500 byte MTU. However, this doesn't address the entire overhead, and as a result both source and destination systems experience lower throughput, higher latency, and higher CPU usage than is necessary. Using jumbo frames can address these problems and provide the best performance for high-bandwidth networks and where you are using features such as SQL AlwaysOn Availability Groups.

Using jumbo frames allows for protocol data units above 1,500 bytes to be transmitted and received without fragmentation, thereby reducing the total number of packets and the amount of overall packet processing required to send large amounts of data. The MTU and jumbo frame size can vary across different network vendors, but they commonly allow for up to six times the size of a standard-sized packet.

Figure 8.4 displays the throughput and CPU utilization between Windows 2012 VMs on different hosts when configured with jumbo frames.

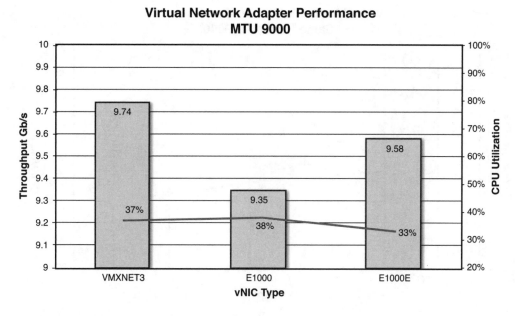

Figure 8.4   Virtual network adapter performance with jumbo frames.

CAUTION

The version of VMXNET3 shipped in VMware Tools as part of VMware vSphere 5.0 GA had a bug that prevented jumbo frames from working. It is recommended that you have the latest version of VMware Tools installed, and that you are on at least Update 2 if you are using vSphere 5.0. See VMware KB 2006277 for further information.

When compared to Figure 8.1, the E1000E adapter shows an improvement in performance of greater than 1Gbps when using jumbo frames, and VMXNET3 shows an improvement of slightly more than 0.5Gbps. A much greater improvement in network performance is demonstrated when two VMs are on the same host, as shown in Figure 8.5.

Although throughput is higher in Figure 8.5, so is CPU utilization. This is due to the hypervisor not being able to make use of the physical network adapter offload capabilities when transmitting between the two VMs on the same host. However, the CPU cost is lower per Gbps of throughput compared to the test between hosts in Figure 8.4.

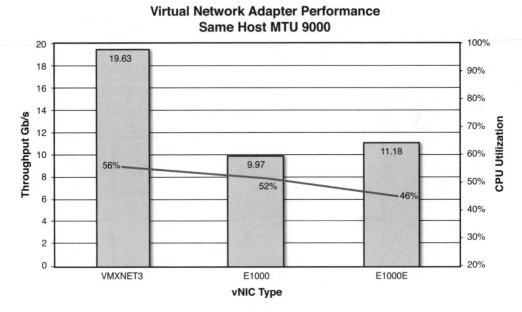

Figure 8.5   Same host virtual network adapter performance with jumbo frames.

In order for you to use jumbo frames, it must be configured consistently from the source to the destination system. This means you need to configure support for jumbo frames in Windows for the virtual network adapter, on the virtual switch within VMware vCenter or ESXi, and on the physical network. Jumbo frames configuration needs to be enabled on any network devices between the source and destination systems that will carry the packets. As a result, it can be much easier to configure jumbo frames when implementing new network equipment, although with proper planning and verification, it is easily achievable in an existing network environment.

CAUTION

Some network device vendors, such as Arista, ship their equipment from the factory with jumbo frames enabled. However, other vendors and some older network devices, if not properly configured, may not allow jumbo frames to pass and will simply drop the packets instead of fragmenting them. Some devices will break the packets down to a smaller size (fragment the packets) and allow them to pass, but the cost of breaking the packets down will severely slow down your network. Some network devices may only allow jumbo frames to be set globally, and the settings may only take effect after a reboot. Because of this, it is important that you check the support of jumbo frames on your network devices with your vendor and have a thorough implementation and test plan to ensure desired results.

The types of network traffic that will benefit most from using jumbo frames on 10Gbps and above networks include SQL Database Mirroring, Log Shipping, AlwaysOn Availability Groups, Backup Traffic, VMware vMotion (including Multi-NIC vMotion), and IP-based storage, such as iSCSI and NFS. In order for SQL Server to use jumbo frames effectively, the Network Packet Size Advanced option should be increased from its default setting. This is in addition to configuring jumbo frames in Windows and on the virtual and physical networks. The Network Packet Size setting should be increased from its default value of 4096 to 8192, as shown in Figure 8.6.

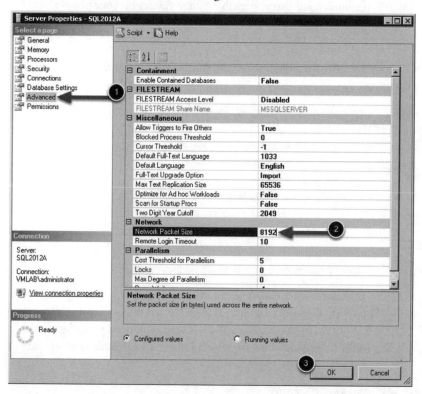

Figure 8.6   SQL Server Network Packet Size advanced setting.

Configuring Jumbo Frames

As previously mentioned, you need to configure jumbo frames in Windows, on your virtual switch, and also on your physical network. Because each physical network switch has a slightly different configuration, it will not be covered here. Usually the physical switch maximum MTU will be 9,216 or thereabouts. You should check with your vendor documentation. The figures in this section were captured from Windows 2012, the vSphere Web Client, and vSphere 5.5, and would be similar to vSphere 5.1. If you are using a different version of Windows or vSphere, refer to the product documentation for details on configuring jumbo frames.

CAUTION

You may notice a brief period of interruption to virtual machine network traffic when enabling jumbo frames in Windows. To ensure the least amount of traffic disruption to your environment, it is recommended that you enable jumbo frames on your physical network, then on your virtual switches, followed finally by your virtual machines.

Figures 8.7 and 8.8 show the Edit Settings button and jumbo frames configuration, respectively, for a virtual standard switch.

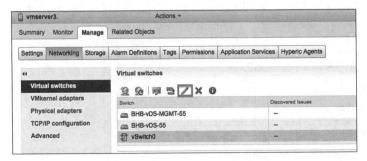

Figure 8.7   vSphere Web Client virtual standard switch Edit Settings button.

In order to enable jumbo frames on a virtual standard switch, you need to configure each host individually. Each virtual standard switch that needs to support jumbo frames needs to be modified on each host. In the vSphere Web Client, you need to navigate to a vSphere host and click the Edit Settings button, which looks like a pencil, as shown in Figure 8.7.

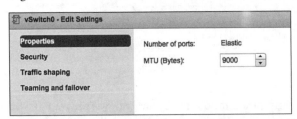

Figure 8.8   vSphere Web Client virtual standard switch jumbo frames setting.

Figure 8.8 shows the virtual standard switch that is enabled for jumbo frames with an MTU of 9000.

Configuring jumbo frames on a vSphere distributed switch is slightly different because it is centrally managed. This means there is only one place to configure this and it applies automatically to all hosts connected to the switch. To get to the Edit Settings dialog for a vSphere distributed switch, navigate to **Network** in the vSphere Web Client, right-click on **vSphere Distributed Switch**, and then click **Edit Settings**. Figure 8.9 shows the configuration of jumbo frames on a vSphere distributed switch.

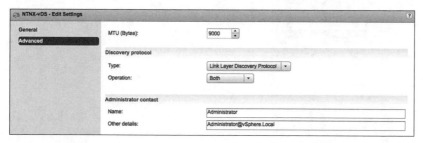

Figure 8.9 vSphere Web Client vSphere distributed switch jumbo frames setting.

Now that jumbo frames are configured on the physical network and the virtual switches, we can configure Windows. Figure 8.10 shows the Windows network properties page of a VMXNET3 vNIC. You need to click **Configure** to display the advanced vNIC properties.

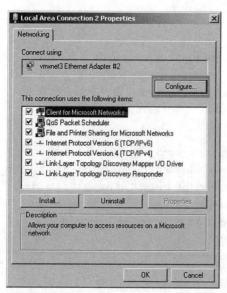

Figure 8.10 Windows vNIC properties page.

Figure 8.11 shows the advanced vNIC properties page with the **Jumbo Packet** option highlighted. By setting the value to **Jumbo 9000**, you are enabling jumbo frames.

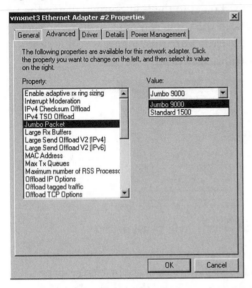

Figure 8.11   Windows VMXNET3 vNIC advanced properties page.

Testing Jumbo Frames

Now that you have configured jumbo frames, you need to verify everything is working correctly. To do this, you need to test the network path from the source to the destination where jumbo frames are used. This could be from a primary server of an AlwaysOn Availability Group to its secondary server. We will now discuss two examples of how to verify correct jumbo frames configuration.

One of the easiest ways to verify the network path is configured correctly for jumbo frames is to use ping. This method works regardless of whether you chose to use a virtual standard switch (vSS) or a vSphere distributed switch (vDS). Instead of using the standard ping without any options, you need to specify the packet size and specify that no packet fragmentation should occur. You need to make sure you use the correct packet size; otherwise, you will get an error.

As shown in Figure 8.12, even though we have configured our network to accept 9,000-byte packets, we still have to account for the necessary headers (ICMP and IP) when we are testing the jumbo frames configuration.

Jumbo Ping Packet

Figure 8.12   Jumbo ping packet.

If you tried to just do a ping of 9,000 bytes with the "do not fragment" option (-f in Windows), you would receive a message saying, "Packet needs to be fragmented but DF Set." Therefore, the number of bytes specified for the ping command needs to match the payload of the jumbo frames packet, which is 8,972 bytes with the -l option. Here is an example of a ping command from Windows to check the correct jumbo frames configuration:

```
ping -f -l 8972 SQL2012A

Pinging SQL2012A (10.17.33.31) with 8972 bytes of data:
Reply from SQL2012A (10.17.33.31): bytes=8972 time<1ms TTL=63
Reply from SQL2012A (10.17.33.31): bytes=8972 time<1ms TTL=63
```

In addition to ping, if you are using vSphere 5.1 or above, with an Enterprise Plus license and a vSphere distributed switch, then you can make use of the vSphere distributed switch health check feature to verify your jumbo frames configuration. The vSphere distributed switch health check periodically checks the configuration of the physical and virtual network, including the configured VLANs, MTU, network teaming, and failover settings. Figure 8.13 shows the results of a vSphere distributed switch health check configured on a sample vSphere distributed switch from the vSphere Web Client.

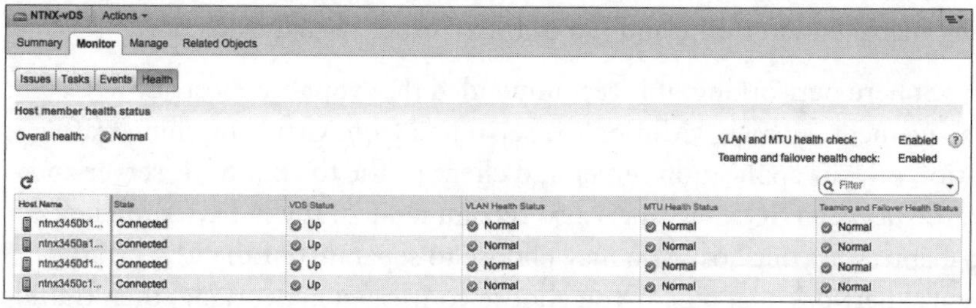

Figure 8.13   vSphere distributed switch health check status.

Figure 8.14 shows the configuration of a vSphere distributed switch health check on a sample vSphere distributed switch from the vSphere Web Client.

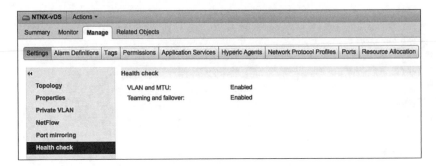

Figure 8.14   Configuration of a vSphere distributed switch health check status.

Once a vSphere distributed switch health check is configured, it will alert you to any misconfigurations that occur with your setup.

TIP

For additional information about the vSphere distributed switch health check, including a video of the configuration settings, see VMware KB 2032878.

VMware vSphere Network Design

As we covered in Chapter 5, "Architecting for Performance: Design," because the SQL Server databases are now sitting on a hypervisor, we must manage the different traffic types that exist, for both the virtual machines and the hypervisor. SQL Server will have to manage traffic bound for the Windows OS, possibly in-guest iSCSI, the database application, and replication traffic (if using AlwaysOn Availability Groups, database mirroring, or log shipping). In addition, other ESXi host traffic must also be accounted for and managed, including management traffic and the traffic of other virtual machines.

When you design vSphere networking, it is recommended that vSphere Host (ESXi) traffic, such as management, storage, vMotion, be separated from virtual machine traffic. Additional separation of your application server and client traffic to your SQL server and any replication traffic between SQL servers is also recommended. If you have sufficient physical network adapters in your host, you may choose to separate out the ESXi traffic onto separate physical network adapters. If you choose converged networking, then traffic should be separated logically using VLANs. This section covers how to design your VMware vSphere host networking, including storage networking, for performance, quality of service, and availability. Because there are many network design options, this section covers the most common and recommended designs based on our experience.

Virtual Switches

Virtual switches (vSwitches) connect virtual machines to virtual networks, as well as to each other, on the same host. When a virtual switch is configured with a physical adapter, it can connect virtual machines to the physical network and the outside world. Each virtual machine connects to a virtual switch port on a port group. The port group forms the boundary for communications on a virtual switch. This is an important concept to understand, especially for security.

A virtual switch and a port group are layer 2 only; they do not perform any routing, and there is no code that allows a VM connected to one port group to communicate with another VM on another port group. Communications between different port groups is prevented even if they are on the same virtual switch, unless the traffic goes via a router or firewall VM or if traffic is sent out to the physical network and routed back into the host.

A port group is where you define VLAN tags and other properties of the virtual networks that are connected to the virtual switch. Communications between VMs that are connected to the same port group and virtual switch remain within a host and are performed at memory speed. They are not limited to the speed of any network adapter, but instead are limited only to the speed of the host CPUs and memory bus.

There are two main types of virtual switch, as Table 8.4 shows.

Table 8.4 Virtual Switches

Virtual Switch	Description	Features
vSphere standard switch (vSS)	Defined and managed on a per-ESXi-host basis. Detects which virtual machines are logically connected to each of its virtual ports and uses that information to forward traffic to the correct virtual machines. Can be connected to physical switches by using physical Ethernet adapters, referred to as uplink adapters, to join virtual networks with physical networks.	All license editions Simple network teaming and failover (including static Etherchannel) Traffic shaping Simple port security VLAN support Jumbo frames

Virtual Switch	Description	Features
vSphere distributed switch (vDS)	In addition to the properties of a vSphere standard switch, a vDS acts as a single switch across all associated hosts in a data center to provide centralized provisioning, administration, and monitoring of virtual networks. You configure a vSphere distributed switch on the vCenter Server system and the configuration is populated across all hosts that are associated with the switch. This lets virtual machines maintain consistent network configuration as they migrate across multiple hosts.	Enterprise Plus license All vSS features plus the following: Advanced network teaming and failover (including LACP and load-based teaming) Network health check Flow monitoring (NetFlow) Per virtual port policy Network IO control (QoS) 802.1p priority tags CoS and DSCP tagging Private VLAN Network Discovery Protocols Port mirroring Virtual switch backup and recovery Multiple uplink port groups

In addition to connecting VMs to virtual switches, you also connect vSphere Host VMKernel Services, for things such as vMotion, management, NFS, and iSCSI.

> **TIP**
>
> When you are running business-critical SQL Server systems, using Enterprise Plus licenses and the vSphere distributed switch is recommended. This allows you to take advantage of the advanced quality of service features provided by VMware vSphere to ensure you can meet your database SLAs. This is especially important with very large databases, where network-based storage (NFS or iSCSI) or database replication is being used.

Figure 8.15 shows an example of what a vSphere distributed switch configuration may look like for a vSphere host with two 10Gb Ethernet NICs.

vSphere Distributed Switch: vDS-Production

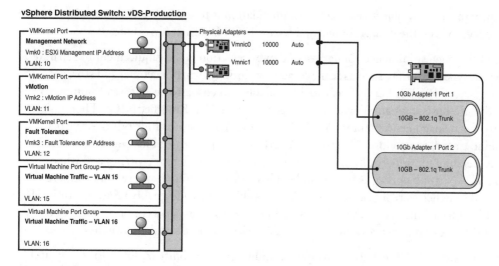

Figure 8.15 Example of vSphere host networking with a vSphere distributed switch.

We are often asked how many vSwitches should be used. The answer is simple: as few as possible to meet your requirements. We recommend using a single vSwitch unless you have a reason (such as security and physical separation across different switches) to use more. There are no extra points for configuring more than one vSwitch.

> **NOTE**
>
> It has been common practice in the past to configure vSphere host management networking on vSphere standard switches to avoid any configuration errors impacting network availability and therefore host management on a vSphere distributed switch. vSphere 5.1 and above include features to protect against and detect vSphere distributed switch configuration errors, and these features allow you to back up and restore your vSwitch configuration. It is therefore much safer now to use a vSphere distributed switch for all virtual networking, which allows all traffic to benefit from the advanced features.

Number of Physical Network Adapters

A number of factors influence the number of physical network adapters required, including vSphere License level, bandwidth requirements, latency and response time requirements, whether database replication or AlwaysOn Availability Groups are used, security policy for traffic separation, and storage networking requirements. The sizing of your databases and hosts in terms of memory can also impact network adapter choice due to vMotion requirements. It is important to balance these different requirements and come up with a design that best meets your objectives. Our recommendation is to use as few network adapters as necessary, to keep the design simple, and to use 10Gb Ethernet if possible.

One of the biggest influences of network adapter selection is the requirement to separate different types of traffic, such as management, vMotion, virtual machine, and storage traffic. Before 10Gb Ethernet was widely available and cost effective, it was common to see vSphere hosts configured with six or eight or more 1Gb Ethernet NICs. There might be two for management, two for vMotion, and potentially two or four NICs for virtual machine traffic, or two for VM traffic and two for storage traffic. This could have been due to needing to support physical network separation to different switches and where using VLAN trunk ports was not possible. This was also common where only vSphere standard switches were in use and it was not possible to provide quality of service or intelligent load balancing across the NIC ports. Figure 8.16 shows an example of a common 1Gb Ethernet virtual networking configuration with vSphere standard switches.

With the cost of 10Gb Ethernet dropping rapidly, the availability of 40Gb Ethernet, and the increasing popularity of convergence, it is much more common to see two or four NICs total per host. The reduced number of ports reduces complexity and cost. However, this means that separation of traffic through VLANs and quality of service control become much more important and hence the increasing popularity of using vSphere distributed switches.

Our recommendation is to use 10Gb Ethernet NICs wherever possible. Two 10Gb Ethernet for SQL Server, vMotion, and/or storage, with two 1Gb Ethernet for management, can be a good solution. With mega-monster SQL VMs (512GB RAM and above) or where additional availability is required, we recommend the use of two dual-port 10Gb Ethernet NICs per host, especially in the case of Ethernet-based storage (iSCSI, NFS, or FCoE).

> **NOTE**
>
> Depending on the server and network adapter type being used, the physical NIC adapters could be presented as multiple virtual adapters to the vSphere host, such as a single 40Gb Ethernet interface being displayed in the vSphere host as four 10Gb Ethernet NICs.

> **TIP**
>
> If you start to see a high number of pause frames on physical network interfaces or dropped packets in ESXTOP or in guest operating systems, you will need to investigate further. For ESXTOP, the key metrics to watch are %DRPTX and %DRPRX.

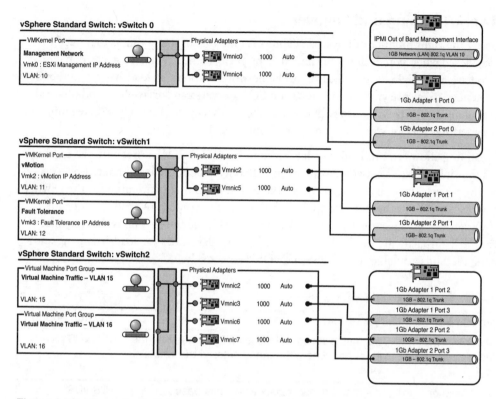

Figure 8.16   Example of vSphere host networking with vSphere standard switches.

TIP

In some cases, you may need more than two 10Gb Ethernet NICs for an extremely large database. During the Software-Defined Datacenter Panel for Monster VM Design at VMworld in 2013, a customer told a story of a SQL data warehouse with 32 vCPUs, 512GB RAM, 60% read IO requiring 40K IOPS, using iSCSI storage and CPU utilization of between 50% and 100%. The customer was having difficulty when trying to perform vMotion operations for maintenance, because only one 10Gb Ethernet NIC was being used. The recommended solution in this case was to configure jumbo frames and use multi-NIC vMotion across at least two 10Gb Ethernet NICs and use network IO control to ensure quality of service. Each vSphere host had four 10Gb Ethernet NICs configured. To watch the session, see https://www.youtube.com/watch?v=wBrxFnVp7XE.

Network Teaming and Failover

Selecting the right number of physical adapters is only one of many things that need to be considered when you design your network for performance. You also need to make sure you are maximizing the utilization of the network adapters by load-balancing them, and you need to ensure your applications and SQL Servers can survive host and physical network failures. With VMware vSphere, we achieve this by configuring NIC teaming and failover settings for our vSwitches and port groups.

NIC teaming allows you to load-balance VM and ESXi host VMKernel network traffic across multiple physical network adapters and effectively pool them together. The load balancing is performed in accordance with the teaming method configured for the vSwitch (in the case of vSS) or the port group. When using a vSS, you can override the default vSwitch settings on a per-port-group basis. With a vDS, the port group is the only place where the load-balancing method is configured. Table 8.5 shows the load-balancing and teaming methods available for the vSS and vDS, respectively.

Table 8.5 Virtual Switch Teaming Methods

Teaming Method	Description	vSwitch Support
Route Based on Virtual Port ID (default policy)	This method load-balances uplinks based on the virtual port where the traffic entered the virtual switch.	vSS/vDS
Route Based on IP Hash (Static EtherChannel)	This method load-balances uplinks based on a hash of the source and destination IP addresses of each packet. For non-IP packets, whatever is at those offsets is used to compute the hash. Load-balances on outbound traffic only.	vSS/vDS
Route Based on Source MAC Hash	This method load-balances uplinks based on a hash of the source MAC.	vSS/vDS
Use Explicit Failover Order	Always uses the first available connected uplink from the list of active adapters.	vSS/vDS
Route Based on Physical NIC Load	Evaluates physical uplink utilization every 30 seconds. If utilization exceeds 75%, the load is balanced based on both inbound and outbound utilization across available physical uplinks.	vDS only
LACP and Enhanced LACP	LACP (Link Aggregation Control Protocol) support (802.3ad) allows multiple uplinks to be bonded using dynamic link aggregation. Limited support for LACP in the vDS was introduced in vSphere 5.1, and a broader feature set is introduced in vSphere 5.5. This method load-balances only on outbound traffic.	vDS only

For a vSphere standard switch, the recommended load-balancing method is Route Based on Virtual Port ID. This is the default setting and the simplest method to use. When you use this method for SQL Server VM traffic, it is recommended that management and vMotion traffic be separated onto a different uplink NIC. This can be done easily by specifying different adapters as active or standby. Figure 8.17 shows the configuration of a vSphere standard switch with the recommended active and standby configuration.

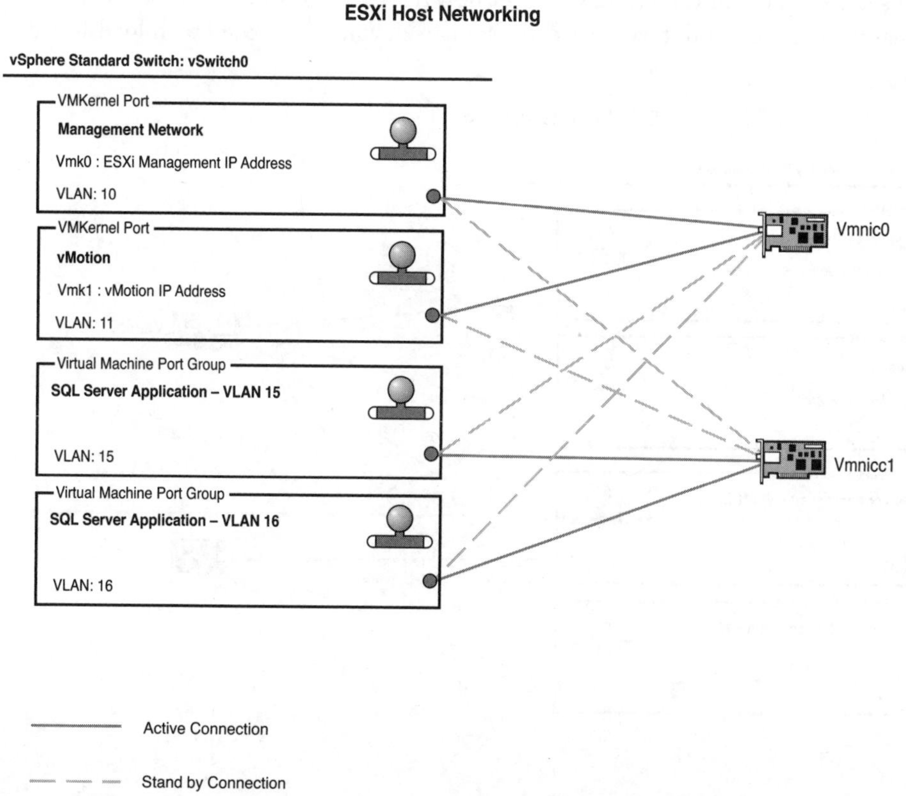

ESXi Host Networking

Figure 8.17 Example of vSphere host active and standby NIC configuration.

For a vSphere distributed switch, the recommended load-balancing method is Route Based on Physical NIC Load (load-based teaming). This method is very simple to configure, works with or without switch stacking or clustering configurations, and dynamically load-balances traffic based on inbound and outbound utilization. For management traffic, it is recommended that the port group be configured with one active uplink NIC, with the remaining configured as standby, and that you use Route Based on Virtual Port ID. This ensures predictability of where the management traffic is routed. Figure 8.18 shows a vSphere distributed switch configured with the Route Based on Physical NIC Load setting for the vMotion and virtual machine port groups.

One of the biggest benefits of using the vSphere distributed switch and Route Based on Physical NIC Load (load-based teaming) is that you can increase the quality of service at the same time as you reduce the number of total NIC ports per host. This can have a big payback in reduced capital and operational expenditure. It also means far fewer cables are required per host, making your data center easier to manage. However, at the same time as reducing the number of NIC ports per host (minimum 2), you need to ensure the quality of service. In the next section, we cover how network IO control can be used to ensure quality of service, and it works exceptionally well when combined with load-based teaming.

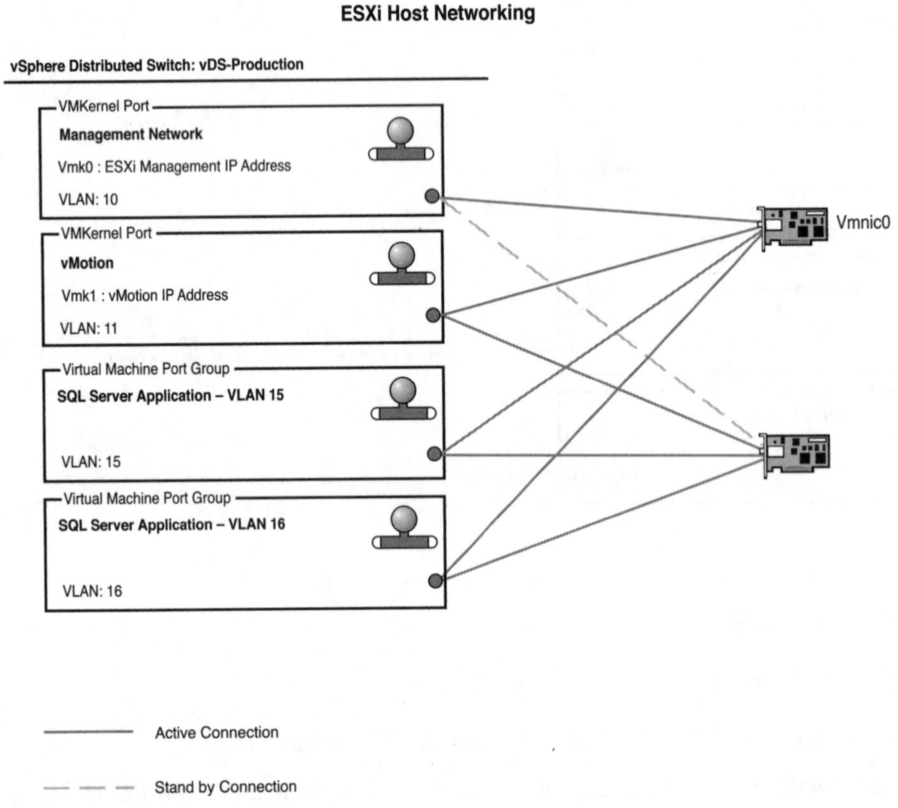

Figure 8.18   Example of vSphere host networking using load-based teaming.

> **TIP**
>
> LACP and static EtherChannel with the Route Based on IP Hash setting are not generally recommended due to their configuration complexity and limitations. Further information on LACP support and limitations can be found in VMware KB 2051307, 2034277, and 2051826. Further discussion of the pros and cons of EtherChannel, LACP, and load-based teaming can be found at http://longwhiteclouds.com/2012/04/10/ether-channel-and-ip-hash-or-load-based-teaming/.

In addition to high performance and resilient vSphere host networking, you should aim to design a high-performance, scalable, and resilient data center network with no single point of failure. Some oversubscription of network links may be possible to improve efficiency and cost effectiveness, provided your throughput and latency requirements can still be met. When you use virtualization, your network will experience higher utilization, especially at the edge where vMotion, backup, replication, and virtual machine traffic all combine. Where possible, Leaf-Spine network architecture is recommended. Figure 8.19 shows an example of a simple Leaf-Spine architecture with a vSphere host redundantly connected using two dual-port NICs.

> **NOTE**
>
> For more information on Leaf-Spine architecture, see the following references: http://www.cisco.com/c/en/us/td/docs/solutions/Enterprise/Data_Center/MSDC/1-0/MSDC_Phase1.pdf and http://go.arista.com/l/12022/2013-11-05/jt893/12022/97352/Arista_Cloud_Networks.pdf.

Figure 8.19 uses Multi-Link Aggregation Group (MLAG) between the spine switches, which is suitable on a small scale. Larger-scale designs would typically utilize Equal-Cost Multi-Path (ECMP) between the Leaf and Spine nodes.

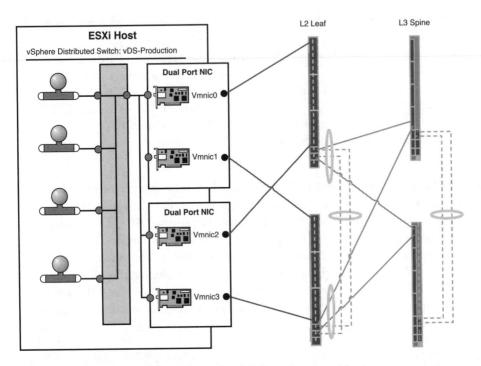

Figure 8.19 Example of vSphere host Leaf-Spine network architecture.

Network I/O Control

As we covered in Chapter 5, the Network IO Control (NIOC) feature of the vSphere distributed switch allows for different traffic types to be prioritized at the host level to ensure that each type of traffic gets its fair share of network resources. It is based on a proportional share algorithm, which allows it to adjust to different traffic patterns dynamically and not limit any one type of traffic if there is no congestion. This avoids having to set any hard limits and allows much more effective pooling of network resources across physical NICs and hosts. Figure 8.20 shows an NIOC configuration with a user-defined resource pool for SQL Server replication traffic.

Table 8.6 shows a sample configuration of NIOC resource pools with a user-defined resource pool for SQL Server replication. It includes the share's values and calculation for the percentage entitlement of bandwidth of each of the different resource pools. Although it is possible to tag each resource pool with a class of service (or 802.1p priority tag, in this example), we are happy for the vSphere hosts to control traffic priority.

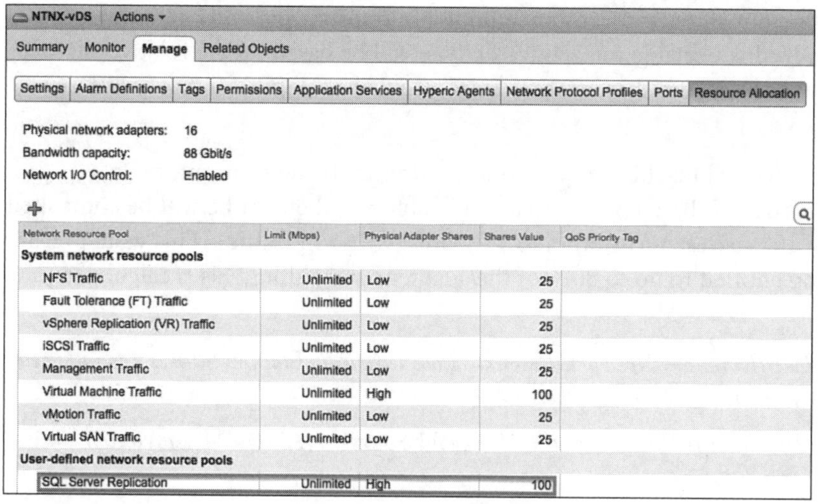

Figure 8.20 Network I/O Control resource pools.

Table 8.6 Sample Network I/O Control Resource Proportional Shares

Resource Pool	Physical Adapter Shares	Shares	Min. Entitlement
NFS Traffic (System)	Low	25	6.25%
FT Traffic (System)	Low	25	6.25%
vSphere Replication (System)	Low	25	6.25%
iSCSI Traffic (System)	Normal	50	12.5%
Management Traffic (System)	Low	25	6.25%
Virtual Machine Traffic (System)	High	100	25%
vMotion Traffic (System)	Low	25	6.25%
Virtual SAN Traffic (System)	Low	25	6.25%
SQL Server Replication Traffic (User-Defined)	High	100	25%
Total Shares		400	100%

The shares and the minimum percentage bandwidth entitlement comprise the worst-case scenario of the total bandwidth a network resource pool will be allocated in times of contention. This guarantees quality of service when a network adapter is saturated. The share of transmit bandwidth available to a network resource pool is determined by the network resource pool's shares and what other network resource pools are actively transmitting. Where not all network resource pools are transmitting and competing, the proportion of bandwidth available to each traffic type will be based on the relative shares. We recommend you always use shares rather than specific host limits for bandwidth per resource pool.

For example, if only virtual machine and vMotion traffic are being transmitted on a congested physical adapter, based on the shares in Table 8.6, their traffic will be controlled in a proportion of 100 shares (VM traffic) to 25 shares (vMotion traffic). This would result in VM traffic being entitled to up to 80% of the adapter bandwidth. This is calculated as follows:

> *Bandwidth Entitlement = Network Resource Pool Physical Adapter Shares / Combined Shares of Transmitting Resource Pools*
>
> *VM Traffic Bandwidth Entitlement = 100 (VM Shares) / 125 (VM + vMotion) = 80%*

However, if VM traffic didn't need all the bandwidth it is entitled to, then vMotion would be free to use whatever available bandwidth remains, but would be entitled to a minimum of 25%. Frank Denneman shows many different additional scenarios in his primer on NIOC (see http://frankdenneman.nl/2013/01/17/a-primer-on-network-io-control/).

> **NOTE**
>
> Network I/O Control requires a virtual distributed switch. To learn more about NIOC, read the "vSphere Networking for 5.5" white paper: http://pubs.vmware.com/vsphere-55/topic/com.vmware.ICbase/PDF/vsphere-esxi-vcenter-server-55-networking-guide.pdf and http://www.vmware.com/files/pdf/techpaper/VMW_Netioc_BestPractices.pdf.

> **CAUTION**
>
> When a dependent or independent hardware iSCSI adapter or physical Converged Network Adapter (CNA) is used for FCoE, none of the traffic will be visible to vSphere, nor can it be managed or guaranteed by using NIOC. Physical network-based quality of service, limits, or reservations may be needed to ensure each type of traffic gets the bandwidth it is entitled to and that application SLAs are met.

Multi-NIC vMotion

Multi-NIC vMotion, as the name implies, allows you to split vMotion traffic over multiple physical NICs. This allows you to effectively load-balance any vMotion operation, including single vMotions. This doesn't require any special physical switch configuration or link aggregation to support because it's all built in to VMware vSphere. This feature is available from vSphere 5.0 and above and allows vMotion to be load-balanced across up to sixteen 1Gb Ethernet or four 10Gb Ethernet NICs. This is particularly important when you have incredibly large memory configurations per host (512GB and above) or where you have mega-monster VMs, because it will allow you to migrate VMs or evacuate a host using maintenance mode much faster, while reducing overall performance impacts.

Although Multi-NIC vMotion doesn't require a vSphere distributed switch, using it in conjunction with a vSphere distributed switch and the Network I/O Control feature is recommended. This will reduce the amount of configuration effort required per host. vMotion will consume all bandwidth available to it, so using it with a vSphere standard switch can negatively impact other traffic types because you aren't able to guarantee quality of service. If you intend to use Multi-NIC vMotion with a vSphere standard switch, then dedicated physical adapters for vMotion traffic are recommended.

You configure Multi-NIC vMotion by creating multiple VMKernel port groups, each with a different active adapter, and any remaining adapters configured as standby or unused. You need to ensure that vMotion is enabled for each of the VMKernel ports assigned to the port groups. Figure 8.21 illustrates the configuration of Multi-NIC vMotion on a host with two physical NICs using a vSphere distributed switch.

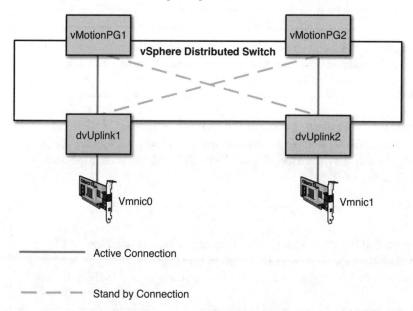

Figure 8.21   Multi-NIC vMotion on a vSphere distributed switch.

The load-balancing method chosen for each vMotion port group should be Route Based on Virtual Port ID. A sample configuration of a vMotion port group for Multi-NIC vMotion, as displayed in the vSphere Web Client, is shown in Figure 8.22.

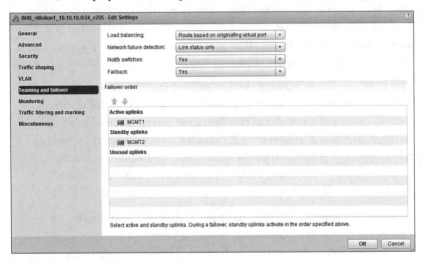

Figure 8.22   Multi-NIC vMotion port group on a vSphere distributed switch.

CAUTION

Multi-NIC vMotion is only supported on a single nonrouted subnet, so you must ensure that all vMotion VMKernel ports that are to participate in the vMotion network have an IP address on the same network subnet.

As mentioned in the "Jumbo Frames" section of this chapter, Multi-NIC vMotion can benefit from the increased MTU that jumbo frames provide. Figure 8.23 shows the performance characteristics of single NIC vMotion and Multi-NIC vMotion recorded during a performance test of vSphere 5.0.

TIP

Each 10Gb Ethernet NIC worth of vMotion requires approximately one physical CPU core of CPU utilization on the vSphere host. To get optimal performance, you need to ensure that you have sufficient physical CPU resources for the vMotion traffic and virtual machines.

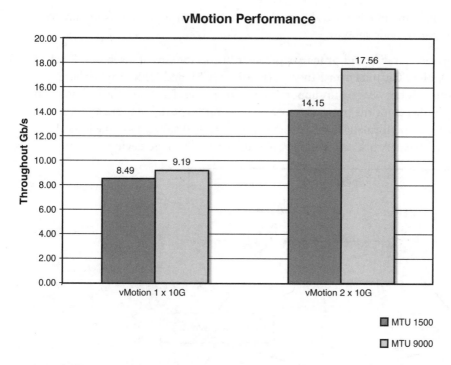

vMotion Performance

Figure 8.23   Single-NIC and Multi-NIC vMotion performance.

> **CAUTION**
>
> In the original release of vSphere 5.0, there was an issue that could impact the wider network when Multi-NIC vMotion was used, due to one of the MAC addresses timing out. This issue was fixed in vSphere 5.0 Update 2. For further information, see http:// longwhiteclouds.com/2012/07/15/the-good-the-great-and-the-gotcha-with-multi-nic-vmotion-in-vsphere-5/.

Storage Network and Storage Protocol

In order for you to achieve the best possible SQL Server performance as well as meet your SLAs and business requirements, you need to have a fast and reliable storage network. Your storage network is a key component that delivers performance and also data protection and integrity. You need to ensure that your storage network is scalable, highly available, and that it can meet the performance needs of all your databases and applications. When it comes to storage protocol choice, the determining factors are much less about performance and much more about other business requirements, existing investments, and storage vendor support.

VMware supports four different primary storage protocols for virtual machines: Fiber Channel (FC), Fiber Channel over Ethernet (FCoE), iSCSI, and NFS. Any of these supported protocols can be used to support your SQL Server databases. Each protocol has different requirements for the physical network; however, logically they are architected similarly to provide performance and availability. Figure 8.24 shows a sample logical diagram of a storage network connecting vSphere hosts and storage devices.

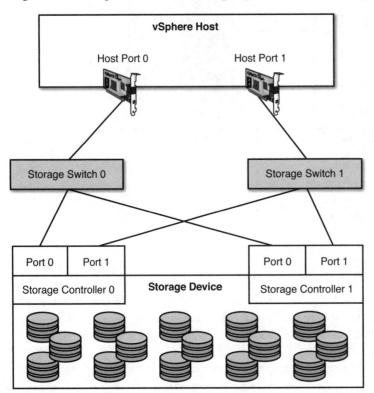

Figure 8.24   Traditional vSphere storage logical network architecture.

Figure 8.24 shows a traditional logical storage network architecture. As we covered in Chapter 6, "Designing for Performance: Storage," there are other options today with the growth of hyperconverged solutions, such as the Nutanix Virtual Computing Platform and others. The important aspects of Figure 8.24 are the resilient connection of the vSphere host to the storage network and of the storage device and storage controllers through to the storage network. This ensures that there is no single point of failure. To improve performance, multipathing of storage paths can be used, or link aggregation in the case of NFS. Ideally, the storage devices are connected to the vSphere hosts no more than one network hop away and on a nonblocking lossless network fabric.

TIP

For information on configuring iSCSI port binding, see VMware KB 2038869. For a comparison of supported storage protocols, see http://www.vmware.com/files/pdf/tech-paper/Storage_Protocol_Comparison.pdf and http://www.netapp.com/us/media/tr-3916.pdf.

Network Virtualization and Network Security

John Gage, who was the fifth employee of Sun Microsystems, is credited for coining the phrase "The network *is* the computer" in 1984. He foresaw the future, and this became the vision for Sun Microsystems. Prior to the dot-com bust and the rise of VMware and x86 virtualization, you would have thought Sun was going to be in a commanding position to deliver upon this vision (or at least a dominant player). However, that was not to be. If you look at the growth rates of virtual server access ports in Figure 8.25, you can see Gage's statement has come true—the network is the computer. However, it is VMware vSphere that provides the network, and it has more server access ports than any other company on the planet.

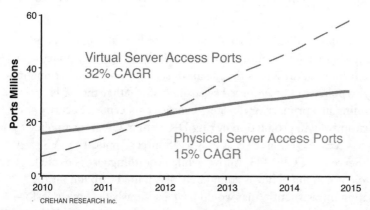

Figure 8.25 Network port growth rate (VMware analyst briefing, VMworld 2013).

According to Crehan Research, virtual server access ports are increasing at a compound annual growth rate (CAGR) of 32%, versus physical server access ports of only 15%. Also, virtual server access ports surpassed physical server access ports in 2012. This isn't really surprising when you look at the explosive growth of virtualization and virtual machines, and the required virtual and physical access ports that are required to support them. Virtual machines surpassed physical servers for the first time in 2012 according to VMware as well.

Why is this important? There are two primary reasons. First, the network is the computer, and more switching of network traffic is being done inside hypervisors now than anywhere else, not all of which has to flow out to the physical network (communication between VMs on the same port group remains within the host). Second, this makes VMware (even before the acquisition of Nicira, and the availability of NSX) the dominant global networking company, at least in terms of server access ports—not Cisco, HP, Juniper, or anyone else. This means that in the new world of the software-defined data center, the point of traffic aggregation and security is the hypervisor and the virtual switch, not the physical network.

The existence of network virtualization and network security within the hypervisor and virtual switch means the physical network architecture will become more simple, while databases and applications can be provisioned on demand and be much more agile. Instead of the physical network and other devices performing all the network- and security-related services, they will become mostly just a fast access layer to move traffic from place to place, whereas the hypervisor leverages distributed switching, routing, and firewalling (from VMware and integration partners) to provide per-virtual-machine and per-logical-group security policy. When you virtualize, your networking and security performance will increase in line with Moore's Law via Intel releasing new server equipment and network adapters, and you can benefit from technology upgrades completely in a nondisruptive manner.

With the security policy applied on individual virtual machines or logical groups, VMs can be mobile and move anywhere while retaining the same consistent security policy. You will no longer be reliant on IP addresses as the means of security policy enforcement. The same consistent security policy can be enforced regardless of whether the VMs or virtual applications are running in a primary or disaster recovery data center. Security policy can be tested nondisruptively in production during DR testing. Creating a policy to allow applications servers to access SQL Server is as easy as "Source: Application A Server Group, Destination: SQL Server A, TCP:1443, Allow" while everything else is denied. The processing required to enforce the policy is completely distributed throughout the environment, thus eliminating infrastructure that would have previously become a performance chokepoint. More importantly, security policy can be applied automatically when your SQL Server databases or virtual applications are provisioned from your service catalog, thus removing any risk of manual security configuration errors and the weeks of delays that can often follow.

Figure 8.26 shows a logical architecture with virtualized network security between the application servers and database servers that ensure that production application servers can only access production SQL databases and that test and dev application servers can only access test and dev SQL databases.

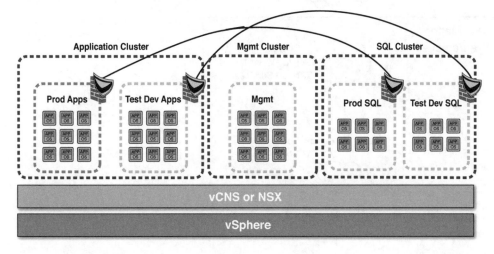

Figure 8.26   Application and database server virtualized security zones.

Figure 8.27 shows the logical network architecture of a traditional three-tier application with completely virtualized networking and security services.

Figure 8.27 (which comes from VMworld 2013's NET5266, "Bringing Network Virtualization to VMware Environments with NSX") shows how completely the networking and security virtualization can be when using VMware NSX. Each component of the three-tier application is separated from a security perspective with routing and firewall rules implemented and enforcement distributed to each vSphere host. Additionally, if applications or servers on a physical VLAN need to access the environment, NSX can provide a bridge to the physical VLAN.

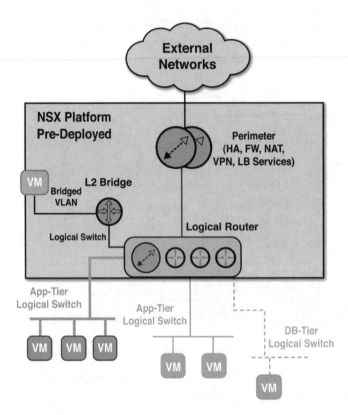

Figure 8.27   Completely virtualized networking and security with VMware NSX.

With network virtualization, your security can become context aware. By this we mean instead of just being based on source and destination constructs, security policy can include physical access location, time of day, and user identity. This allows you to secure access to certain areas based on where and when a user logs in, where they are physically located, and what identity and method they have authenticated with, all in real time. This makes auditing and compliance much more simple because you can track everything back to an individual and their location.

Figure 8.28 (from VMworld 2013's SEC5891, "Technical Deep Dive: Build a Collapsed DMZ Architecture for Optimal Scale and Performance Based on NSX Firewall Services") demonstrates this concept showing a typical three-tier application and the security access for web admins and DBAs from secured virtual desktops, based on their user credentials.

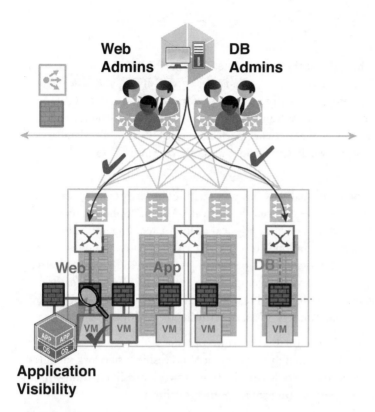

**Application
Visibility**

Figure 8.28   Virtualized networking security with context awareness.

By creating security policy based on user identity and location, you can ensure access only from authorized groups of users, prevent insider attacks, and gain access into which users are accessing which applications and when. You can provide greater security to your DMX, applications, and SQL databases, while providing greater visibility and auditability to your security teams. All of this combined means you don't have to sacrifice SQL Server and application network performance when implementing compliance and security.

TIP

If you own VMware vCloud Suite licenses, you already have everything you need to get started with virtualized networking and security with VMware's vCloud Networking and Security. This is not as feature rich as VMware NSX, but many of the same concepts apply. To learn more about vCloud Suite and vCloud Networking and Security, see http://www.vmware.com/products/vcloud-suite/. To learn more about VMware NSX, see http://www.vmware.com/products/nsx/.

Summary

In this chapter, we covered how to get the required network performance from your SQL Server VMs by choosing the right virtual network adapter, VMXNET3, and how using jumbo frames, where appropriate, can greatly increase performance and reduce CPU utilization. We showed you some of the advanced tuning options that may be required in certain situations to optimize the virtual network performance of SQL Server databases, including when using AlwaysOn Availability Groups and other forms of database replication.

You can't have a high-performing virtual network without a high-performance, scalable, and reliable physical network. We have covered the critical VMware vSphere network design components, including virtual switches, physical adapters, teaming and failover, and the physical network. Our recommendation is to use vSphere distributed switches and port groups with the Route Based on Physical NIC Load setting to ensure SQL Server network performance. To provide quality of service, leverage the Network I/O Control feature, and to enhance availability, use vDS Network Health Check and vDS Backup and Restore. When required for large hosts and monster VMs, use Multi-NIC vMotion.

Your storage network is also critical to the performance of your SQL databases and their data availability and integrity. Having a high-performance and resilient network includes your storage network. Your objective is to design the best network possible within your constraints, while minimizing or eliminating single points of failure.

We concluded this chapter by discussing network virtualization and virtualized network security and how security can be greatly enhanced in a virtualized environment. VMware is the biggest company for virtual server access ports in the world. By virtualizing your networking and security, you benefit from the performance of distributed virtualized computing and web-scale architectures, with performance increasing in line with Moore's Law.

Chapter 9

Architecting for Availability: Choosing the Right Solution

There are many choices when it comes to protecting your database, but the database is not the only application to consider. Too often individuals become too focused on a technology and not a solution. This chapter will not provide a "silver bullet solution" for database availability. The goal of this chapter, and the philosophy of the authors, is to provide the right solution for the right use case based on customer discussions. Although there are many "right" solutions, it is important to design the right solution for the right use case.

This chapter will walk through options available to DBAs and vSphere administrators for high availability, business continuity, disaster recovery, and backing up their databases and their infrastructure. What value have you provided the business if the database is up and running but the rest of the application stack is down?

Determining Availability Requirements

It should not come as a surprise that one area of database virtualization that can lead to hours of discussion, with both vendors and internally with the customers, is protection of the database. DBAs have been entrusted with protecting the company's most important information. It is often said that the database is the heart of a company. Lose the wrong database, and the company cannot make business decisions. So, naturally, DBAs tend to be very conservative and will go with a solution that provides the highest availability and provides them with granular data protection. And why not? Lose the data, lose your job.

However, what about the rest of the application stack? Does it matter if the web servers are down but the database is available to accept incoming requests? Actually, years of experience and meeting many customers has proven the answer to be a resounding, "It depends." It depends because for some customers, DBAs are measured and compensated independently of the web and application tier administrators. For these DBAs, we have found their primary concern is making sure the database is available. And this is okay, because by placing a database on ESXi, we can make it more available than in the physical world.

For other customers—and we have found this to be an increasing trend—the stack is being measured for availability. Therefore, the entire supporting cast is measured against whether the application is working or not working. You either get full credit or no credit. This ensures that all teams are working together to support the business. The business only cares that the entire stack is working, not your individual part of the stack. Sounds a bit harsh, but this is the truth.

Providing a Menu

A noticeable trend seen across industries is that the budget for IT initiatives is slowly moving away from IT and into the business. Shadow IT is now getting a budget. So what does this mean for IT administrators? This means that we are going to need to become better at communicating to the business the capabilities of the infrastructure and the options the business units and application owners have when it comes to protecting their applications. Remember the "everything as a service" comments we made in previous chapters? If this trend continues, over time the business and application owners are going to want a menu to choose from when it comes to their applications—much like the menu they get when they go to a cloud provider.

Based on the previous trend information and as part of your database virtualization project, it is important to quantify and qualify the availability options available to the business. As we will discuss throughout this chapter, a variety of options are available to protect applications and the application stack. As this chapter unfolds, you will begin to place the availability options into buckets, such as disaster recovery, business continuity, high availability, hypervisor-level protection, operating system-level protection, application-level protection, and others. Based on your business and the trends going on inside your organization, it is important to understand and present the right options to the application owner.

It is important that the business understands what the options are and how those options translate in terms of availability, recovery, cost, and accountability. It is important that they understand what is included and what is not included with their selections. Interview the business to get a full picture as to the importance of the application.

> **TIP**
>
> You want the business to define the application's requirements for availability, recoverability, downtime, and so on. It is easier to justify the cost of an availability solution when the business is driving the requirements.

Come at this from multiple angles. The application itself may not be that important on the surface, but the systems it interacts with may be very important and therefore change how the application should be protected. It is your job to be consultative during this process.

How to get started? Simple, generate a list of questions you need the answers to in order to provide a consultative recommendation to the business. Make this a living document, and do not be afraid to go back and interview an application owner again. Questions to ask the business include the following:

- Do people's lives depend on this application? (This would be the case for a healthcare application, for example.)
- Is this a revenue-generating application?
- What other applications interact and/or depend on this application?
- How long can the application be down before it affects the business? (You must quantify the cost of the downtime.)
- Is a crash-consistent copy acceptable? (Define this for them.)
- Is this application (database) cluster aware? (Direct them to the vendor, if necessary.)
- Is this application subject to any regulatory regulations? If so, which ones?
- What is your budget for this application?

As you become more familiar with scoping and providing solutions, your list will grow and become more refined. An important point: The list should not be designed so there is only one right answer.

With the interviews complete, you should have an idea of the importance of the application as well as the availability, continuity, and recoverability requirements. You can now provide a menu of options to the application owner along with your consultative recommendation. In a world where you are competing with cloud providers for "better, faster, cheaper," do not forget that great customer service goes a very long way.

SLAs, RPOs, and RTOs

For some, the heading of this section is nothing more than a bunch of four-letter words. For the rest of us, these terms are important because they drive the service levels for virtualized SQL servers. They ensure that the business and IT are in agreement about the service levels for the application. Therefore, set expectations early and remind people of them often—like every time you send them a bill.

A service-level agreement (SLA) can be a contractual or informal agreement between departments or companies. An example of a contractual agreement would be an agreement between an external supplier, such as an Internet provider, and a business. An example of an informal agreement would be an agreement between the IT department and the finance team for keeping key accounting systems online. We are not going to get into the depths of what comprises an SLA here; other resources are available that cover this subject in detail.

The business's willingness to invest financially should drive SLAs. IT should not sign up for SLAs that are impossible to meet based on the budget allocated to them by the business. Communication between IT leaders and business leaders is crucial.

It is much easier to gather requirements from the business, put together a solution, and ask the business to fund a solution that meets their requirements than to put together a solution and ask the business to fund the project.

Recovery point objectives (RPOs) are tied to how much data can be lost and operations still continue. This will vary widely within and among organizations. The RPO will drive the availability solution applications require. For example, a database that holds configuration information for an application may be able to sustain a 24-hour period of data loss because the data does not change frequently, whereas a database managing stock trades made for customer portfolios cannot lose more than one minute of data. Many factors can drive the RPO for an application, so be sure to ask the application owner exactly how much data can be lost.

Recovery time objectives (RTOs) determine how much time an application can be down before it is returned to operation (brought back online). Like RPOs, this will vary within and among organizations. The answer to this question will drive the availability requirements for the application. For example, a database that holds patient allergy information for the anesthesiology department cannot be down for long, because it is important to administer the right anesthesia for patients. Therefore, the RTO for this application may be 15 minutes.

It is important to flesh out both the RPO and RTO of an application because these are important when it comes to making a consultative recommendation on the appropriate availability solution. Finally, it is important that the business define an application's RPO and RTO requirements. (Notice a theme here?) It is important that the business dictate the SLAs, RPOs, and RTOs to IT and that IT meet these requirements. Be sure to have a reporting mechanism in place to ensure adherence to the SLAs, RPOs, and RTOs set forth and agreed upon.

Business Continuity vs. Disaster Recovery

Often we have found there to be confusion between business continuity and disaster recovery. It is important to understand both terms. Have a business continuity plan and a disaster recovery plan in place for your applications and your organization. This is not meant to be an exhaustive review of business continuity and disaster recovery, but rather an overview.

Business Continuity

Business continuity is the planning done by a company to ensure their critical business functions remain operational or can resume shortly after some sort of service interruption, whether minor or major. An example of a minor outage would be the loss of a motherboard inside a physical server. An example of a major outage would be the loss of a data center due to a natural disaster. What goes into developing the business continuity plans are business impact analysis (BIA) studies to understand the impact systems have and their importance to the company. BIAs often have recovery priority assignments for applications. The company's business continuity plan should include how to recover the environment, resume operations, ensure asset relocation (this includes people), and have testing and validation of the plan included. The goal of a business continuity plan is to ensure critical operations of the business despite the outage incurred. It answers the question, "How can the company be rebuilt after a massive outage?"

> **NOTE**
>
> For more information, the National Institute of Standards and Technology (NIST) has created some recommended practices that can be found by searching for the most recent revision of NIST Special Publication 800-34: Continuity Planning Guide for Information Technology Systems.

Disaster Recovery

Disaster recovery involves activities executed during a disaster, whether minor or major. Disaster recovery encompasses the actions taken by individuals during the actual event. Disaster recovery operates at the micro level, whereas business continuity operates at the macro level. One additional difference is that a disaster recovery plan tends to focus more on technology, whereas business continuity takes into account the entire scope of resumption from an outage.

For the virtualized SQL Server environment, it is important to understand the pieces and parts that make up the virtualized SQL Server stack and the applications these databases support, because this will dictate their recovery procedure and priority. The disaster recovery plan contains the steps necessary to recover the virtualized SQL Server after the outage.

Disaster Recovery as a Service

First and foremost, the declaration of a disaster is a business decision. Someone within the company must make a decision to declare the disaster. There are financial and other ramifications that must be taken into account prior to enacting the recovery plans. It is important to understand who within the organization has the power to declare that a disaster has occurred. We have worked with large, multinational organizations that have CIOs for individual business units. These CIOs each have the ability to declare a disaster. If this is representative of your organization, it is important to ensure that if someone declares a disaster, the enactment of this plan does not disrupt services of other business units.

It is important to remember a disaster recovery plan must entail the entire organization, not just your system. As we have stated, and will state again: So what if your system is up and available? There are no gold stars for being first when the rest of the organization is down or your server needs to be rebooted because it came up in the wrong order. Guess what? Rebooting your server just extended the RTO.

Many products can aid in disaster recovery. However, what you need is a solution. A solution, from our experience, is a combination of multiple products that when put together provide a disaster recovery solution. Find a solution that takes into account the entire data center, not just a single application. Key pieces of any solution are orchestration and automation. Remember, this is a disaster, and the resources with the necessary knowledge to restore systems may not be available, so orchestrate and automate as much of the recovery as possible. For the orchestration and automation, we recommend reviewing VMware's Site Recovery Manager (SRM). SRM allows for the orchestration and automation of your disaster recovery plans while also providing the ability to execute nondisruptive tests of your plans.

> **NOTE**
> More information on SRM can be found at https://www.vmware.com/products/site-recovery-manager/.

"Fragmented" is the one-word answer we get from the majority of our customers when we ask them to define their disaster recovery plans. They tell us they have 37 different procedures and methods for recovering applications in their environment. Customers are looking for simplification of their disaster recovery plans. This is where we suggest implementing a tiered solution. The tiered approach involves providing four or five tiers, each offering different capabilities. Take these capabilities, place them in a menu format, and present them to the application owners after the interview process. Table 9.1 has an example of what this solution might look like. The first tier (Tier 1) leverages synchronous replication at the storage layer, provides multiple point-in-time rollback capability, and is tied to an orchestration and automation tool. This solution is tied to RPOs and RTOs. Each tier is composed of multiple technologies to achieve the most cost-effective solution possible. The tiering of solutions also simplifies and reduces the fragmentation of recovering systems during an event.

Table 9.1   DRaaS Tiered Offering

Tier	Technologies	RPO	RTO
Tier 1	Synchronous/asynchronous replication Multiple point-in-time recovery Orchestrated and automated recovery	1–15 minutes	1 hour
Tier 2	Asynchronous replication Multiple point-in-time recovery Orchestrated and automated recovery	15 minutes–12 hours	12 hours
Tier 3	Asynchronous replication Software-based backup Orchestrated and automated recovery	24 hours	1–3 days
Tier 4	Software-based backup	24 hours	4–7 days
Tier 5	Tape backup	Best reasonable effort (BRE). No RPO provided in the event a disaster is declared. If systems are available and staff is available, IT will make a BRE to restore the system.	Best reasonable effort (BRE). No RTO provided in the event a disaster is declared. If systems are available and staff is available, IT will make a BRE to restore the system.

Tiering the solution accomplishes many objectives. The first is that it simplifies the disaster recovery planning process. It reduces the cost of disaster recovery while making cost more predictable and manageable. It flushes out noncritical systems from the recovery plan, accomplished via Tier 5. Providing zero RPO/RTO in the event of a disaster provides for the use of an existing technology (for example, tape) that investments have been made in but does not plan into the future direction of the organization.

Finally, remember that we work in IT. Murphy (aka Murphy's Law) has a cubicle three down from where you sit. Despite your best efforts—flawless designs, impeccable implementations—something, somewhere will go wrong. Make sure you have plans to recover and be sure to regularly test these plans.

vSphere High Availability

vSphere has been designed with performance and availability in mind. VMware has designed vSphere to be the most performant (yes, I know that is not a word) and highly available platform on which to run your enterprise applications. We will now discuss features within vSphere that provide high availability to the virtual machines that run on top of vSphere.

Hypervisor Availability Features

The hypervisor itself has been built and designed to provide performance and protection. Many features exist within vSphere that make vSphere the platform on which to run your most demanding applications. For example, what happens when one virtual machine—say, a test/development virtual machine—begins to consume precious I/O on the array and begins to interfere with the production SQL Server virtual machine on the same host? Storage I/O control kicks in and ensures the production SQL Server receives the proper I/O distribution.

What makes vSphere the desired platform on which to run your applications is VMware's core philosophy on the virtualization, which is evident in the products and solutions they provide customers. The four core tenants are as follows:

- Partitioning
- Isolation
- Encapsulation
- Hardware independence

Partitioning is defined as the ability to run multiple operating systems on one physical device and provide a means by which this device's physical resources are divided among the virtual machines resident on this device.

Isolation is defined as providing fault and security isolation at the hardware level while providing advanced resource controls to ensure availability and performance of the virtual machine running on the physical hardware. This is the "one virtual machine blue screen does not affect other running virtual machines on the same host" philosophy.

Encapsulation is the ability to save an entire virtual machine's system state into a set of files. We have all been working with files for many years, so we understand how to copy and paste files. How much easier is disaster recovery if we are copying files versus ensuring firmware versions are identical on each server.

Hardware independence is the philosophy that administrators should be able to provision or migrate a virtual machine to any similar or different piece of physical hardware. The ability to pry a vendor's label off the physical asset and to seamlessly slide in the right solution from the right vendor is a strong value proposition. For the DBAs, this is the "I can move my database to the new, shiny, and more powerful server every time it is added to the cluster versus running SQL on the same piece of hardware for five years" feature.

Moving past philosophy and into the hypervisor itself, there are features present within the hypervisor that provide for high availability. As discussed in Chapter 6, "Architecting for Performance: Storage," the storage stack has been built to seamlessly and transparently handle hardware failure. If one of the HBA cards in your ESXi host fails, I/O operations are automatically routed out another HBA card. If a path to the storage array becomes inaccessible, the hypervisor will reroute the I/O down another path to the array. In addition, to handle situations in which there is an overallocation of storage resources, vSphere will leverage storage I/O control to ensure proper distribution of I/O to the virtual machines. Review Chapter 6 for more information on these features.

Chapter 8, "Architecting for Performance: Network," discusses the networking high availability VMware has built in to their networking stack. The vSphere distributed switch removes the complexity of manually configuring each individual virtual switch on every ESXi host. Let's face it, having to do something manually over and over opens the door for errors. One central location to manage a configuration and have this configuration remotely applied reduces errors and makes the environment more available by reducing downtime due to administrative error.

Much like storage I/O, VMware introduced network I/O control into the vSphere stack to ensure the delivery of critical network services—for example, NFS and iSCSI performance when a vMotion is initiated, and proper distribution of network bandwidth when an overallocation of network resources occurs on a physical network card. Just as important as availability is performance. The phone rings whether the system is slow or if the system is down, so leverage technologies built in to vSphere to ensure performance for virtual machines. Read Chapter 8 for more information on these and other features within the vSphere hypervisor that will allow you to architect a performant (yes, there is that word again) and highly available network stack.

The previous storage and network examples are just a few of the built-in features of the hypervisor. We will now move on to discussing configurable features within the hypervisor and the vSphere platform.

vMotion

Do you remember your first vMotion? I sure do. There are few things in our lives that we remember exactly when and where we were when they occurred. Throughout our travels, one question that always gets a resounding "yes" is when we ask about people's first vMotion moment. vMotion provides the ability to migrate (move) a powered-on virtual machine from one physical host to another physical host with no downtime or interruption to the services provided by that virtual machine.

MEMORY LANE

My first vMotion moment occurred in a data center in Akron, Ohio. My VMware SE, Bob, came on site and we updated ESX (long live the MUI!) to the appropriate version and we tested vMotion. I was sure it was a trick. I watched as a nonbuffered video played in a virtual machine and was migrated from ESX01 to ESX02. In fact, I was so sure it was a trick, I shut down ESX01. I cannot recall the video that was playing, but I do recall that moment in time. What was yours?

---

vMotion migrates the entire state of a virtual machine from one physical host to another physical host. State information includes current memory content, BIOS, devices attached to the virtual machine, CPU, MAC address, and other properties that make up the virtual machine.

For your standalone SQL Servers, the value this brings is if there is an issue with the underlying hardware (for example, the NIC goes bad) in a virtual environment, the SQL Server virtual machine network traffic is seamlessly routed out another physical NIC and the SQL Server VM can then be vMotioned to another physical host. There is no downtime incurred by SQL to fix the failed NIC. From an SLA perspective, SQL continues to provide services. In the physical world, you will have to shut down the SQL Server, replace the NIC, and then power on the SQL Server. This is a service interruption, or this means you are staying around to fix the NIC and ensure SQL boots and resumes services during a change window. I know which option I like better: vMotion the SQL Server, and let someone on the infrastructure team deal with the failed NIC. vMotion is a battle-tested, tried-and-true core feature of the vSphere platform; there is no reason not to use it (unless you are running SQL Server AlwaysOn Failover Cluster Instances—more on that later).

Distributed Resource Scheduler (DRS)

DRS leverages vMotion technology to balance virtual machine workloads across multiple ESXi hosts in a cluster. DRS pools the physical CPU and memory resources of an ESXi cluster together and uses this aggregate information to make decisions on where to best run the virtual machine workloads within the cluster; for a virtual SQL Server, this is important. Some SQL Servers may sit dormant for two and a half months but then, at the end of every quarter, will ramp up and consume all the resources assigned to them. As these SQL Servers ramp up, DRS will move other virtual machines that may conflict with CPU and memory resources off the ESXi host to another ESXi host, thus freeing up the necessary CPU and memory resources for the SQL Server requiring those resources.

Storage vMotion

Storage vMotion allows an administrator to migrate the storage of a virtual machine from one data store to another data store while the virtual machine is powered with no disruption in service. For the SQL Server virtual machines running on vSphere, this provides many benefits. The first is if the data store the virtual machine is running on is running out of room and action cannot be taken to grow the current data store, the SQL Server's virtual disks can be relocated onto a data store that has sufficient room. Another use case is when the SQL Server virtual machine's I/O requirements exceed the capabilities of the data store on which it resides, the virtual machine's disk files can be relocated onto a data store that will satisfy the performance requirements.

> **NOTE**
>
> Storage vMotion operations are greatly enhanced when using VAAI-compliant subsystems. For more information on VAAI, refer to Chapter 6.

Storage DRS

Much like how DRS pools together CPU and memory resources, Storage DRS pools together storage resources. Storage DRS provides a means by which the management of a group of data stores is automated based on variables such as latency and utilization.

As virtual machines are placed into a Storage DRS–enabled cluster, Storage DRS will monitor the individual data stores and make appropriate migration decisions based on how Storage DRS is configured. The benefit for a virtualized SQL Server is that policies can be put in place to manage the SQL Server virtual machines to protect against a poor-performing data store as well as a data store that is running out of capacity.

Enhanced vMotion X-vMotion

X-vMotion is the combination of vMotion and Storage vMotion within a single operation. This means that a virtual machine is able to change the ESXi host it is running on and the data store (storage) the virtual machine is running on at the same time, even if the storage is not shared between hosts.

> **NOTE**
>
> For more information on X-vMotion, see http://blogs.vmware.com/vsphere/2012/09/vmotion-without-shared-storage-requirement-does-it-have-a-name.html.

vSphere HA

vSphere HA provides protection when running multiple virtual machines on the same host. vSphere HA is designed to monitor the physical ESXi hosts for availability. If an ESXi host experiences an outage, it is vSphere HA's job to restart the affected virtual machines on another ESXi host in the cluster. This provides a recovery time measured in the reboot of a virtual machine. vSphere HA is turned on by a check box for an entire vSphere cluster: no complex configuration or special skill sets required. The value this brings for SQL Server virtual machines is twofold.

First, by virtualizing standalone SQL Servers, this automatically provides them hardware-level protection. In the physical world, if there is a hardware failure, there is a service interruption until the hardware issue is resolved. This usually translates to downtime measured in hours, not minutes. When the ESXi host a SQL Server virtual machine is running on experiences a hardware failure, vSphere HA detects this outage and restarts the SQL Server virtual machine on another host. Based on the ACID properties of the SQL database (discussed in section "vSphere App HA," later in this chapter) and the storage I/O crash-consistency properties within ESXi, the SQL Server virtual machine is powered on, the Windows operating system boots, and SQL Server loads and resumes operation. This is quite a handy feature if the failure occurs at 3 a.m.

> **NOTE**
>
> ESXi will maintain the correct order of writes to allow for a proper restart after a crash. ESXi acknowledges a read or write to the guest operating system only after the read or write is verified by the hardware controller to ESXi. When reading the following KB article, be sure to note the difference between a Type 1, bare-metal hypervisor (ESXi) versus a Type 2, hosted hypervisor (VMware Workstation): http://kb.vmware.com/kb/1008542. The exception is if vFRC is involved, then reads originate from cache and writes are sent to storage.

The second benefit vSphere HA is the introduction of a new, cost-effective availability option for the business that is not available in the physical world. If the application can sustain a reboot (say, one to five minutes) and the business is okay with crash-consistent copies, then vSphere HA is an effective solution to provide increased availability. The database will protect itself according to ACID properties, but you should also consider other tiers of the application stack.

But wait, there's more! vSphere HA does not just work at the physical host level. vSphere HA also has the ability to monitor the guest operating system and applications running inside the guest operating system. Disabled by default, but configurable, vSphere HA has the ability to monitor the virtual machine for heartbeat traffic from VMware tools, network traffic generated by the virtual NIC, and storage traffic originating from the virtual SCSI adapter. If these three conditions are not present, vSphere assumes the virtual machine has blue screened and can reboot the virtual machine. How vSphere monitors applications running inside the guest operating system will be covered in the next section.

vSphere App HA

vSphere App HA allows for the monitoring of applications running inside virtual machines. vSphere App HA allows an administrator to monitor the location and status of these applications, define remediation actions to take place if a service (sqlserve.exe, for example) becomes disabled, and generate alerts and notifications that a monitored service has been impacted. As of the writing of this chapter, vSphere App HA supports SQL Server 2005 through 2012. To learn more or to check for updated information, check http://www.vmware.com/products/vsphere/features-application-HA.

We have worked with a lot of customers who have reevaluated their existing SQL Server clusters to determine which SQL Server databases could run on a standalone SQL Server running on the vSphere platform. There are valid reasons to move and not to move SQL Server databases off a clustered instance, but customers have used vSphere HA and vSphere App HA to drive complexity and cost out of their infrastructure while maintaining and improving the availability of their SQL Server databases.

vSphere Data Protection

vSphere Data Protection (vDP) is an appliance-based backup and recovery solution developed by VMware for your virtual infrastructure. vDP provides deduplication of data across all virtual machines running against the same vDP appliance and utilizes Changed Block Tracking for both backup and restore operations. vDP can perform file-level or virtual machine-level restores.

For some of your virtual infrastructure, vSphere Data Protection will meet your requirements. There is also another version called vSphere Data Protection Advanced that brings additional capabilities to the table. Because we are discussing SQL Server virtualization, it is worth mentioning that vDP Advanced provides application-aware agents. For SQL Server, this provides the ability to perform granular backup and restores of individual databases and/or logs. Oh, and as an added bonus, it can be used to back up your physical SQL Servers as well. For more information on vSphere Data Protection and vSphere Data Protection Advanced, go to https://www.vmware.com/ca/en/products/vsphere/features-data-protection.

vSphere Replication

VMware's vSphere Replication is a hypervisor-integrated replication engine. vSphere Replication is integrated into the kernel of the ESXi hypervisor. vSphere Replication enables the protection of virtual machines by replicating them from one ESXi host to another ESXi host. vSphere Replication is hardware independent, so the target server can be different from the source server. In addition to being hardware independent, vSphere Replication is also storage independent. This means you can run your production virtual machines on a high-performing storage array and replicate your virtual machines to a remote facility running three-year-old servers with direct attached disks. vSphere Replication also allows an administrator to select the VMDK file type. For example, on the production side, the VMDK file type can be Thick Provisioned Eager Zeroed and on the recovery side the VMDK file type can be Thin Provisioned.

vSphere Replication integrates with Microsoft Windows Volume Shadow Copy Service (VSS) via VMware tools. Once this has been configured for the virtual machine, writers are flushed and the application and operating system are quiesced to ensure full application consistency for backups. If VSS fails for some reason, vSphere Replication continues despite the failure and will provide OS-consistent backup and generates a notification that a VSS-level backup was not achieved.

Why is this important for SQL Servers? This provides a hypervisor-level replication of your SQL Server virtual machines. For some (maybe not all) SQL Servers, the recovery procedure is "restore from backup." With vSphere Replication, the ability exists to replicate this virtual machine to a remote site. A company can buy standalone physical servers, install ESXi on the direct attached storage, enable vSphere replication, and now DR exists for all SQL Servers. Finally, for additional cost savings, the VMDK file format can be changed to Thin Provisioning for increased density and utilization of the physical assets at the alternate site.

> **NOTE**
>
> vSphere Replication works against powered-on VMDKs, requires Virtual Hardware 7 or later, and has an RPO of 15 minutes to 25 hours. For more information on vSphere Replication, VMware published this white paper: http://www.vmware.com/files/pdf/vsphere/VMware-vSphere-Replication-Overview.pdf.

vCenter Site Recovery Manager

vCenter Site Recovery Manager (SRM) is a product from VMware that allows for the automation and orchestration of your disaster recovery plans. SRM automates your disaster recovery run book. SRM allows for frequent, nondisruptive testing, whether against the entire run book or a portion of the run book. SRM does require an underlying replication technology, and it can provide an RPO equal to the underlying replication technology. SRM provides support for both array-based replication and vSphere Replication. Need to re-IP your servers at your recover site? SRM can handle this request. SRM also offers the ability to reprotect and reverse replication once a plan has been executed.

Why is this important for SQL Servers? As discussed in the "vSphere Replication" section, some SQL Servers have a "restore from backup tape" recovery plan. In addition, just because my database is available at the remote site, it does not mean my application is available or working. SRM provides the ability to bring up your infrastructure in a reliable and predictable manner. For example, when initiated, SRM will boot critical application servers, such as Active Directory Domain Servers, DNS servers, DHCP servers, and so on. Once these servers are up and responding, SRM will move on to either booting or verifying key infrastructure servers, such as database servers, are up and operational before moving on to starting application-level servers, web servers, and finally virtual desktops for the end users. This is just one example of the capabilities of SRM. SRM is a powerful tool that should be evaluated as part of your disaster recovery plan.

VMware vCloud Hybrid Service

vCloud Hybrid Service, or vCHS, is an offering from VMware that extends your on-premise vSphere infrastructure into the Cloud. vCHS bridges the divide between on-prem and off-prem cloud services. vCHS is built on vSphere, so there is tight integration between your infrastructure and the vCHS infrastructure. No need to convert your virtual machines to adhere to a cloud provider's infrastructure.

What is the use case for SQL Server virtual machines? As we move toward the mobile cloud era, vCHS provides the ability to extend your on-prem data center into the cloud. This provides a location for a portion or the entire application stack. One example is you can use vCHS to power on additional SQL Server virtual machines for end of quarter processing and only pay for the compute used. vCHS can house running SQL Servers that are participating in SQL Server AlwaysOn Availability Group replication. vCHS also offers a disaster recovery solution based on vSphere Replication. As the mobile cloud era evolves and you are asked to evaluate options, we highly recommend evaluation of vCHS.

Microsoft Windows and SQL Server High Availability

Now what we have covered the availability features present within the vSphere platform and how these benefit a SQL Server installation, we will move on to discussing capabilities that exist within Windows and SQL Server. We will discuss these features and how they provide high availability and disaster recovery options for your virtualized SQL Server deployments. It is important that many of the vSphere high availability options can be used alongside functionality provided by Microsoft. Often individuals make this a "this versus that" conversation versus a "best of both worlds" discussion. Remember, you are building a menu of services to offer the business and your job as a technician is to provide the right solution for the business requirement.

We will focus this discussion SQL Server AlwaysOn Failover Cluster Instances and SQL Server AlwaysOn Availability Groups. These are two unique offerings available for SQL Server deployments. But, before we get to that, as promised earlier we will begin our discussion with an overview of ACID, what it is and why it is important, and what this means for a virtualized SQL Server versus a physical SQL Server.

ACID

In the 1970s, Jim Gray defined the properties of a reliable transaction system.[1] ACID is an acronym that represents a method by which database transactions are processed reliably, and defined a transaction as a single logical transaction on the data.[2]

---

[1] http://en.wikipedia.org/wiki/ACID
[2] http://en.wikipedia.org/wiki/ACID

ACID stands for Atomicity, Consistency, Isolation, and Durability. Atomicity can be equated to all or nothing. This means that if any part of a transaction fails, then the entire transaction fails. For SQL Server, this means that if part of a transaction fails, then the database itself is left unchanged; sometimes this involves rolling back changes made to the database returns to the original state.

Consistency refers to the state in which the system is in before and after a transaction begins. If for any reason a transaction would cause the system to enter an invalid state upon its completion, the transaction is stopped, any changes made to the system are rolled back, and the system returns to a consistent state once again. The system will start and end a transaction in a consistent state.

Isolation allows a transaction to believe it is has sole access to the system, which may not be the case. SQL Server is designed to be accessed by multiple individuals, and it is imperative these individuals and their transactions believe they have exclusive use of the system. Transactions may occur at the same time. If these transaction do not believe they have dedicated use of the system, the system may not be deemed consistent, thus causing a roll back. It is the isolation property that protects against the consistency violation.

Durability is the last of the four transaction properties. Durability states that once a transaction is committed, it is permanent. In other words, no matter what happens to the system after a successful transaction, the transaction will persist. This includes hardware failures, software failures, and so on. For SQL Server, this is accomplished by writing information into a transaction log file prior to releasing the transaction. Writing the transaction to physical media meets the durability requirement for a transaction.

How does the introduction of ESXi affect the ACID properties of a transaction? The short answer is, it does not. The reason is that ESXi will only acknowledge a read or write to the guest operating system after the read or write is verified by the storage controller; if vFRC is involved, then reads are from the cache and writes go to the storage. Once this read or write is verified, it is handed off to the guest operating system to process, and this now becomes a Windows and SQL operation. From a physical server or virtual server perspective, it is exactly the same when dealing with a Type 1 hypervisor such as vSphere.

NOTE

If you want to read Jim Gray's paper on the transaction concept, it can be found at http://research.microsoft.com/en-us/um/people/gray/papers/theTransactionConcept.pdf.

SQL Server AlwaysOn Failover Cluster Instance

SQL Server AlwaysOn Failover Cluster Instance (FCI) is a high availability solution for SQL Server instances. This protection is provided at the same site or across sites. It should be noted that for SQL Server AlwaysOn FCI that span multiple sites, array-based replication technology is required. This is the clustering solution most of us are familiar with and that has been around for years. SQL Server AlwaysOn FCI does leverage Windows Server Failover Clustering (WSFC) functionality. SQL Server AlwaysOn FCI requires two instances of Windows Server to be connected to the same backend storage. Once configured, SQL Server AlwaysOn FCI will protect against hardware, operating system, or application issues and fail over services to the standby SQL Server. Another popular use for SQL Server AlwaysOn FCI is for rolling upgrades of SQL Server itself and patching of the underlying operating system. There is minimal downtime while services transition from the failed server to the standby server. These failovers can be automatically or manually initiated either by fault detection or administrative interaction. With SQL Server AlwaysOn FCI, only one of the SQL Servers can own the resource at a time, and the shared disk represents a single point of failure.

SQL Server AlwaysOn FCI is a solid solution that provides high availability for SQL Server databases. With Windows Server 2012 and SQL Server 2012, Microsoft has done a nice job in hiding the complexities of configuration and have eased administrative overhead associated with this implementation.

For a virtualized SQL Server implementation, there are valid reasons to run SQL Server AlwaysOn FCI. There are also limitations to running SQL Server AlwaysOn FCI that must be accounted for during the decision process as whether to virtualize these SQL Servers.

When it comes to critical databases that support the business and business operations, we have historically seen these implemented on SQL Server clusters. As new technologies and solutions enter the market, by both Microsoft and other vendors such as VMware, we will see a shift from this technology to others.

When a purely physical implementation of SQL Server AlwaysOn FCI is being run, one variable that is often missed or not considered is the time it takes to replace the failed hardware. When the underlying hardware fails, SQL Server AlwaysOn FCI will detect this failure and restart the services on the standby node. However, at this point, the SQL Server database hosting the business's most critical workloads now has two single points of failure: the first being the shared storage, and the second being the hardware it is running on. So the question to ask is, how long will it take to replace the physical hardware, install, configure, and patch the Windows operating system, and then install, configure, and patch the standby node of SQL Server? From our travels, the best any customer has ever said is six hours, with hardware onsite. Not having hardware onsite is a different story, and the vast majority of customers do not have standby servers.

When you virtualize SQL Server AlwaysOn FCI, you get the best of both worlds. SQL Server protects the application and provides rolling patch upgrade capabilities. vSphere HA watches and protects against hardware failure. How does this work? In a virtualized implementation of SQL Server AlwaysOn FCI, when there is a hardware failure, SQL Server AlwaysOn FCI will transfer services to the standby node and resume servicing requests, exactly the same as it would in the physical world. vSphere HA will detect the hardware failure and reboot the downed SQL Server on another node in the vSphere cluster. The virtual machine will boot, Windows will start, and SQL Server will initialize and reestablish quorum. Your database is protected once again, in the time it takes vSphere to detect the hardware failure and reboot the virtual machine. Protection is reestablished in minutes versus hours.

Although this may seem like a panacea, you must consider operational overhead when implementing SQL Server AlwaysOn FCI on vSphere. The first is a firm requirement by VMware to use raw device mappings, or RDMs, when doing SQL Server AlwaysOn FCI between ESXi hosts.

SQL Server AlwaysOn FCI uses a shared SCSI bus between the virtual machines. Because of this, there are certain actions that cannot be performed on these virtual machines. Anything that involves a hot change to the virtual machine can disrupt the heartbeat between virtual machines and will cause a node to failover. Some of these actions include the following:

- vMotion migration
- Hot memory add
- Hot CPU add
- Increasing disk size
- Utilization of vSphere snapshots
- Pausing/resuming of a virtual machine
- Memory overcommitment leading to virtual swapping or memory ballooning

Yes, for SQL Server AlwaysOn FCI, VMware does not support vMotion of the SQL Server nodes. In addition, VMware does not support the use of the paravirtualized SCSI adapter, and customers should follow the support and configuration guidance provided in the SQL Server Clustering Guides for the version of vSphere running in your environment. For more information on what is and is not supported by VMware, bookmark http://kb.vmware.com/kb/1037959. For a link to the Clustering Guide specific to your version of vSphere, bookmark http://kb.vmware.com/kb/1004617.

From an operational perspective, it is important to set the automation level of all virtual machines in an AlwaysOn FCI to Partially Automated. This will allow for the automatic placement of the virtual machines during creation and will also serve to provide migration recommendations, but it will not migrate the virtual machines. The vSphere Clustering Guide for MSCS will contain more information on how to configure this setting for your SQL Server AlwaysOn FCI virtual machines. We do want to stress that vSphere HA is supported; however, it is important that SQL Server virtual machines participating in the SQL Server AlwaysOn FCI never—and we mean *never*—reside on the same host. There are several methods by which to configure this option, but we recommend using vSphere DRS groups and VM-Host affinity rules. How to configure this is detailed out in the Setup Guide for MSCS available for your version of vSphere (use http://kb.vmware.com/kb/1004617 to obtain the guide).

If you have an ESXi host with 10 or more RDMs used in the SQL Server AlwaysOn FCI implementation, a reboot of the ESXi host may take a long time. Therefore, VMware recommends marking the passive MSCS LUNs as perennially reserved. This will reduce the time it takes the ESXi host to boot. For more information on how to configure a perennially reserved LUN for your version of vSphere, KB 1016106 (http://kb.vmware.com/kb/1016106) contains the answers.

The final item to discuss concerns increased operational coordination between the vSphere team and the SQL Server team. Due to the fact SQL Servers participating in an AlwaysOn FCI implementation cannot be vMotioned, any actions that require the vSphere team to evacuate an ESXi host, such as applying an update, require the SQL Server team to fail over the services from one SQL Server node to the other node. Some customers view this as high operational overhead and as a reason not to virtualize SQL Server. Other customers view this as a minor inconvenience to providing a more resilient and reliable infrastructure for their customers.

SQL Server AlwaysOn Availability Groups

SQL Server AlwaysOn Availability Groups (AGs) were introduced with SQL Server 2012 and provide a new solution for customers seeking a highly available SQL Server implementation. SQL Server AlwaysOn AGs differ from SQL Server AlwaysOn FCI in that they do not rely on a shared disk. A shared disk represent a single point of failure. SQL Server AlwaysOn AGs utilize replication built in to SQL Server to replicate between SQL Servers. Although SQL Server AlwaysOn AGs eliminate the single point of failure at the disk level, they do, at a minimum, double the storage requirements for your SQL Server implementation. We did say an AG doubles the requirements, but we did not say it doubles the cost. Storage costs associated with a SQL Server AlwaysOn AG will change depending on the design implemented.

SQL Server AlwaysOn AG also differs from SQL Server AlwaysOn FCI in that SQL Server AlwaysOn AG groups databases together and fails these databases over as a group, whereas SQL Server AlwaysOn FCI works at the SQL Server instance level.

SQL Server AlwaysOn AG is similar to SQL Server AlwaysOn FCI in that it too relies on Windows Server Failover Clustering (WSFC). Both these solutions require the Windows Server administrator to create a WSFC instance prior to their creation. Although they differ in their WSFC requirements and configuration, they are both based on and require WSFC to be installed and configured.

SQL Server AlwaysOn AG supports up to five availability replicas. A replica is a copy database, or a group of databases. There is one primary replica and up to four secondary replicas. The replicas can be configured to support two commit modes. These modes are synchronous and asynchronous.

Consider using synchronous commit mode when the SQL Servers are well connected because enabling this option increases transaction latency. Synchronous commit solves the high availability solution in that every transaction is replicated to all synchronous members, which at the time this chapter was written was limited to three (the primary and two secondary replicas). Synchronous commit mode allows for an RPO of zero, meaning zero data loss.

The asynchronous commit replica should be used when the replicas are separated by great distance. Asynchronous mode does not have the transactional overhead associated with the synchronous commit model; however, this means there is a potential for data loss.

The availability modes—synchronous and asynchronous—can be mixed per SQL Server AlwaysOn AG. In addition, AlwaysOn AGs provide the ability to create a read-only connection into the replicas as well as the ability to run backup operations off these secondary replicas. Be sure to read, understand, and implement the correct licensing options for the secondary replicas.

NOTE

For more information on the availability modes for SQL Server AlwaysOn AGs, read http://technet.microsoft.com/en-us/library/ff877931.aspx.

SQL Server AlwaysOn AGs support an Availability Group Listener (that is, a DNS name and IP address) for each Availability Group. Point clients to the AG Listener for them to access your SQL Server AG implementation, and the AG Listener will direct them to the appropriate replica. The AG Listener is responsible for redirecting requests when a SQL Server participating in a SQL Server AG is no longer available.

So what does a SQL Server AG implementation look like on vSphere? Pretty much any way you want it to look. Whereas a SQL Server FCI uses a shared SCSI bus, a SQL Server AG does not, which frees us from the tyranny of the shared SCSI bus. Because the shared SCSI bus is not a factor, VMware will support the use of VMDK files, vMotion, DRS, Storage vMotion, Storage DRS, Enhanced vMotion, vSphere HA, and other features. In short, this is a great stack on which to run your mission-critical SQL Server databases.

For the most current, up-to-date information on what is supported by VMware for SQL Server AlwaysOn AGs, reference http://kb.vmware.com/kb/1037959 and review the "Non-Shared Disk and SQL AlwaysOn AG" section in the link.

Putting Together Your High Availability Solution

Now that we have reviewed the features available within the vSphere platform and those provided by Microsoft with SQL Server, it is time to have availability discussions with the appropriate teams. We have found education is the key. vSphere administrators do not know all the intricacies involved with maintaining a healthy, highly available, disaster-resilient SQL Server. And DBAs are unaware of the plethora of features available within the vSphere platform and how they enhance a SQL Server implementation. Cross-education between groups is essential. Once these teams agree upon a strategy, remember that both teams need to support the SLA. It is now time to put together the menu for your end users. Table 9.2 provides an example of what your offer sheet might look like. Put something down in writing that everyone can agree upon prior to talking with the application owners and then share the document with them. This way, everyone is working from the same document and there are no misunderstandings about the services provided and the service levels associated with these services.

Table 9.2 Sample High Availability Chart

Database HA Strategy	Granularity	Storage Type	File Type	vSphere HA	vMotion	SRM	RPO Data Loss	RTO Down Time	Notes
Log shipping	Database	Local/shared	VMFS/RDM	Yes	Yes	Yes	Based on transaction log capture frequency. Every 15 Minutes Transaction Log Interval means you could lose 15 minutes worth of data.	Manual recovery, one hour on average.	Must switch over manually.
Database mirroring	Database	Local/shared	VMFS/RDM	Yes	Yes	Yes	None (when transaction safety mod set to full) and synchronous replication.	Less than three seconds (Automated with Witness Server) or manual recovery.	Microsoft has stated DB Mirroring will be depreciated and removed in a future releases of SQL.
SQL Server clustering (Pre-SQL 2012)	Instance	Shared	RDM	Yes	No	Yes	Based on transaction log capture frequency. Every 15 Minutes Transaction Log Interval means you could lose 15 minutes worth of data.	Less than 30 seconds.	SRM requires manual scripting.
AlwaysOn Availability Groups (2012+)	Database	Local/shared	VMFS/RDM	Yes	Yes	Yes	None (with synchronous commit mode).	Less than three seconds or manual recovery.	Can vMotion active/passive nodes.
AlwaysOn Failover Cluster Instances (2012+)	Instance	Shared	RDM	Yes	No	Yes	None.	Less than three seconds or manual recovery.	SRM requires manual scripting.
VMware Snapshot*	VM Level	Local/shared	VMFS/RDM	Yes	Yes	Yes	Recovery point back to when snapshot is taken.**	On average, under 30 minutes.	Manual (not recommended for database backup).
vSphere HA	VM Level	Shared	VMFS/RDM	Yes	Yes	Yes	In-flight transactions are rolled back (not committed).	The time it takes to reboot the OS and start SQL Server Services plus any database instance recovery needed. Note: By default, it is not application aware.	In the event of physical server failure, a VM hosting database is restarted on another physical server with spare capacity.

Summary

In this chapter, we have discussed how to put together the right high availability solution for your environment. As we said at the start of this chapter, we never send a customer a white paper and say this is the right solution for their environment. Instead, we work to understand the business requirements and map those to the features and functionality present in products to derive the right solution for the customer.

We discussed how shadow IT is now getting a budget. We discussed the growing importance to understand the features and functionality present in the entire stack: VMware and SQL Server. We talked about cross-education so that each team understands the pros and cons of each solution as well as the creation of a menu to simplify the offering for the business.

This marks the last of the architecting chapters. Chapter 10, "How to Baseline Your Physical SQL Server System," will discuss the importance of baselining your SQL Servers and provide examples of how to baseline SQL Server.

How to Baseline Your Physical SQL Server System

> *"Check it before you wreck it."*
> —Jeff Szastak

> *"The bitterness of poor performance lasts long after the sweetness
> of a cheap price is forgotten."*
> —Unknown

The title of this book is *Virtualizing SQL Server on VMware: Doing IT Right*. An
essential part of "doing it right" is having a good understanding of the workload characteristics and configuration of the existing physical source systems that are to be virtualized.
Remember that unlike in a physical environment, where it's common practice to oversize
the server, in a virtualized infrastructure it's important you "right-size" the VM that
houses your SQL Server database. You can always hot-plug a vCPU and hot-add memory
if more is needed.

TIP

As a DBA, it is very important you embrace this new way of managing the environment,
one where you right-size for today, knowing that in the future if you need more
resources, such as CPU, memory, and disk, they are just a click away. In fact, oversizing
VMs can actually degrade performance.

You can get this understanding of what is needed to properly configure the virtualized environment by recording and analyzing a performance baseline of your existing physical systems. This is one of the most critical success factors for physical-to-virtual SQL Server migrations, so that you can prove the same or better performance characteristics after virtualization.

> **TIP**
>
> It's very important to baseline your important physical systems. This is one of the most important steps—if not *the* most important step—you need to take if you want to properly virtualize your critical SQL Server databases.

This chapter covers both infrastructure and application baseline activities related to SQL Server 2012 and provides you with the **why**, **when**, **what**, and **how** of measuring the baseline successfully, as well as how to ensure you at least meet (if not exceed) your system's required performance once it is virtualized. This applies even if the database is being implemented first as a virtual machine—although in that case, you will design a valid benchmark or load-test for that particular database to prove it meets your requirements.

What Is a Performance Baseline?

A *performance baseline* is a measurement of a system with a known configuration under known conditions that can be used as a reference point for further measurements as configurations or conditions change. A baseline is often used to document "normal" behavior under a known set of conditions. When you're developing a new system, the performance baseline will normally include critical system metrics that give an indication of good or bad performance as measured against a reference of the nonfunctional requirements. An example of a nonfunctional requirement might be the system achieves 450 transactions per second, with 95% of transactions serviced within 25ms latency.

When you're considering virtualizing an existing system, the process of recording the baseline is more concerned with measuring what the current system performance is and the critical metrics that make up that performance, rather than determining whether the existing system's performance is good or bad.

> **TIP**
>
> The baseline is a measurement of what the current system performance is as well as the critical metrics that make up that performance.

Before you begin to baseline your existing system, ask yourself this question: Are you happy with how the system performs today? If the answer is "no," then what makes you think that moving it to a virtualized infrastructure alone will make it better? Virtualization is not a silver bullet that solves all problems. When you virtualize a poor-performing system, you should expect poor performance unless something changes. This is one of the many reasons establishing a proper baseline is so important.

To better illustrate the value of a proper baseline, let's talk about a situation we had happen earlier this year. We had as a client a very large engineering firm that went out and purchased state-of-the-art hardware (both a new server and storage array) to run their entire environment on. They moved just the database onto the new infrastructure. They expected everything to get faster, yet the opposite happened. The new infrastructure ran substantially slower than the older infrastructure that was running the database and a number of other applications. After several failed attempts to correct the problem with the new infrastructure, the firm called us in to determine why.

The first thing we did was to baseline the existing system. We then baselined the database sitting on the new infrastructure. When we compared the two baselines, what jumped right out at us was the fact that the new disk storage array was substantially slower than the old disk storage array. Slow disk drives always mean a slow database. This is why it is so very important to baseline before you begin the journey of virtualizing a database.

> **TIP**
>
> Over 80% of the problems in a virtualized environment have to do with storage. The storage is either misconfigured, misused, or mis-sized.

The baseline is used as a reference to determine whether the virtualized systems meets or exceeds the performance of the physical system it was migrated from. You need to capture a baseline of the existing live production system to act as this reference while at the same time not impacting production performance.

> **TIP**
>
> It is important to capture a baseline of the existing production system while at the same time not impacting production performance.

Later in this chapter, we show you what tools to use and how to properly baseline the performance of your production system while not impacting performance. An example of some of the metrics to consider that make up the performance baseline are displayed in Figure 10.1. In this figure you see many other things you need to consider, from security to operations, but they are not the focus of this chapter.

It's very important to gather a baseline that is representative of the workload. There is no point in baselining a system at night when all the real work happens during the day, and vice versa.

> **TIP**
>
> It's very important that the baseline sample you take is a representative workload.

In addition to system and application performance metrics, the baseline should include time reference data, such as time of day, day of week, week of month, and month of year. This is to ensure that seasonal or cyclic anomalies in workload patterns are captured and understood. If the analysis period doesn't include critical cyclical system peaks, adjustments will need to be made based on a risk factor during the design and validation of the virtual infrastructure. System logs can be useful to help provide the delta of system performance between the baseline during the analysis period and historical peaks. It is also important to understand the workload. If your sampling interval is every 5 minutes, and you have the system ramp up every 3 minutes, you might not capture this peak in your sample set and you will not identify this until you are in production.

> **TIP**
>
> Work with both the DBA and the application owners to understand the workload and determine an appropriate sampling period and duration.

Our experience has taught us that when sampling a SQL Server database, the sampling interval should be 5 minutes or less. We typically recommend 15-second intervals.

When sampling T-SQL, we recommend using a 1-minute interval. A lot can happen in a database in a short amount of time.

TIP

When sampling a SQL Server database, we highly recommend using a very frequent sampling interval of 5 minutes or less—with 15 seconds being the recommendation.

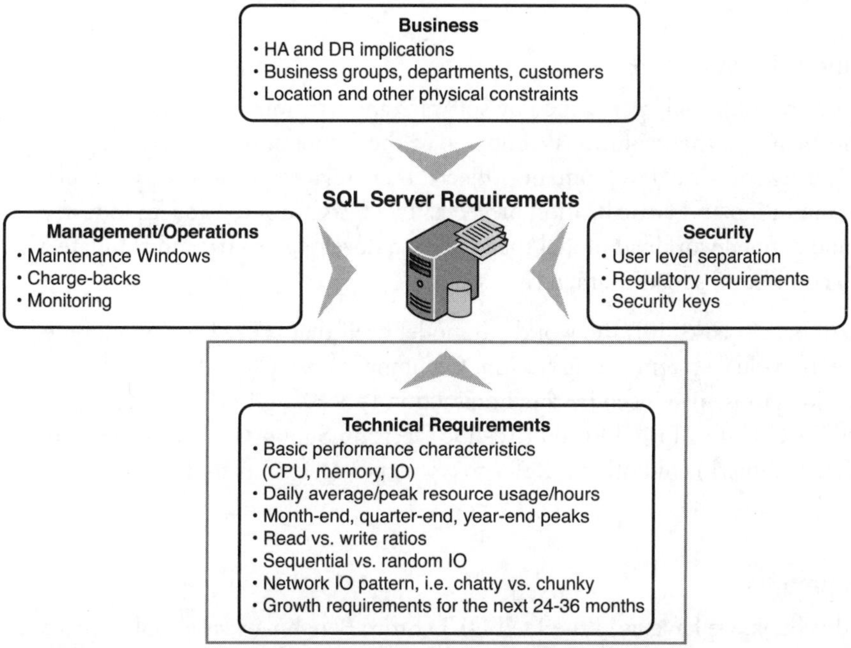

Business
- HA and DR implications
- Business groups, departments, customers
- Location and other physical constraints

SQL Server Requirements

Management/Operations
- Maintenance Windows
- Charge-backs
- Monitoring

Security
- User level separation
- Regulatory requirements
- Security keys

Technical Requirements
- Basic performance characteristics (CPU, memory, IO)
- Daily average/peak resource usage/hours
- Month-end, quarter-end, year-end peaks
- Read vs. write ratios
- Sequential vs. random IO
- Network IO pattern, i.e. chatty vs. chunky
- Growth requirements for the next 24-36 months

Figure 10.1 SQL server migration—the big picture.

Difference Between Performance Baseline and Benchmarks

A performance baseline is not the same as a benchmark, although you can record a baseline during a benchmark. A *benchmark* is where you apply a standardized synthetic or simulated (that is, not real-world) workload model to the system under test and then measure the results. A key difference of a benchmark is that it's a synthetic simulation against a non-production system, rather than a recording of actual performance of a real production system. There are three main types of benchmarks:

- Industry-standard benchmarks, which are created by a standards body of some sort. Examples of this type of benchmark include TPC, TPC-C (OLTP), and TPC-H (Decision Support).

- Vendor benchmarks, which are created by an application or system vendor.

- Custom benchmarks, which you create based on your own system workload models or recordings from actual production systems.

Industry-Standard Benchmarks

Benchmark tests are commonly performed by software and hardware vendors to demonstrate the performance of their solutions compared to the competition, as well as by project teams during software development projects. Benchmarking is also very useful during system migration and virtualization projects. The tests are run using an industry-standardized and defined workload model that has been developed to try and simulate a certain type of application's load characteristics.

In these types of benchmarks, it is the workload model itself that is used as the reference, rather than the individual system configuration. Common industry-standard database benchmarks include those produced by the Transaction Processing Performance Council (TPC), such as TPC-C (OLTP), TPC-H (Ad-hoc Decision Support), TPC-VMS (virtualized database benchmark), and others. Refer to www.tpc.org for a complete listing of benchmarks and their results.

Vendor Benchmarks

Throughout this book, we have used the Dell DVD Store Benchmark as a tool to provide consistent, repeatable performance test results. This is a good example of a vendor benchmark and is a well-defined standard repeatable benchmark that is relatively quick and easy to set up and use.

Another example of a vendor benchmark, which is useful for comparison, is the SAP SD Benchmark. Although designed primarily to compare SAP ERP systems across all types of different system architecture, including Unix and x86 systems as well as different databases, it is a great OLTP workload and a well-defined standard test. You can find SAP-certified benchmark results for Windows systems using Itanium, Intel, and AMD processors and different versions of MS SQL Server. We discuss later in this chapter how these benchmark results can be useful in comparing performance metrics from different systems as part of your baseline and design process.

Developing Your Own Performance Benchmarks

Using industry-standard or vendor benchmarks can be useful to get a general idea of the performance of your virtual infrastructure and design, as compared to other examples of the same benchmark being run. However, this is not a valid representation of what you should expect for your specific workloads when they are virtualized. In order to get a valid performance benchmark for your workloads during your virtualization project, you will need to develop your own workload model or benchmark. The workload model or benchmark you develop needs to take into account your environment and its unique requirements, characteristics, and constraints.

There are two primary methods for developing your own benchmarks to be used during your virtualization project. Both methods are briefly discussed here. Examples of the second method are given later in this chapter.

An easy way to get a good understanding of your workload is to pick the business day of the month that is busiest and record all the relevant application and infrastructure metrics so that you can reproduce the workload during your benchmark testing. You should take seasonality into account as well, if you have a seasonal or cyclical business. Also, make sure you adjust any numbers to meet expected cyclical peaks. If you have this existing data available already through monitoring systems, it will make your job of getting an accurate benchmark much easier.

Benchmark Workload Model Based on System Nonfunctional Requirements

The first method can be used if you developed the system originally. In this case, you may have a copy of the nonfunctional requirements that need to be met, and the original testing team should have documented the workload model. Over time the workload model and nonfunctional requirements will likely have changed, and hopefully your capacity planning team has kept them up to date as part of their standard operating procedures. If this is the case, you can use this model, in combination with a load generator, to perform system benchmarks as part of your virtualization project. If the model and nonfunctional requirements have not been kept up to date, you will need to modify them to make them as valid and realistic as possible. This type of benchmark isn't as accurate as a benchmark based on recorded production performance.

Benchmark Workload Model Based on Recorded Production Performance

The second method of developing your benchmark involves recording a baseline from actual production transactions or system performance metrics and then replaying the baseline against an equivalent virtualized non-production copy. The recording and replaying may be achieved by using a specialized tool that has been developed for this purpose. Alternatively, you may take the recorded system baseline and create a workload model from it manually that can then be fed into a load generator such as Apache Jmeter or HP Load Runner.

Baseline Your Performance Benchmark

You would normally baseline the configuration of your benchmark testing by running a series of simulations and recording the results to ensure they are consistent. When the test results have stabilized or normalized, you have a baseline of your performance benchmark. This baseline can then be used as a reference for further benchmark testing where the configuration has been modified. This is an important step to ensure the validity of your results and so you have a control you can measure further tests against.

Using Your Baseline and Your Benchmark to Validate Performance

You would use your chosen benchmark to try and simulate the production load against the non-production version of the system prior to migrating it. This is to ensure the virtualized system can meet the performance characteristics that were recorded during the baseline of the production system. Depending on the results of your performance benchmark tests compared to your production baseline, you may need to make design or configuration adjustments.

Once you're satisfied with your performance benchmark compared to the baseline, you may want to modify the workload characteristics. You would do this to increase system load in order to find the maximum system performance or headroom that can be expected of the system once it is virtualized. This is very important during validation of your virtual infrastructure and virtual machine design prior to migrating your production systems. A relatively small amount of effort now can return you greater performance and stability later when your business and your workloads change. Figure 10.2 shows the strategy of baselining and benchmarking to ensure valid performance comparisons.

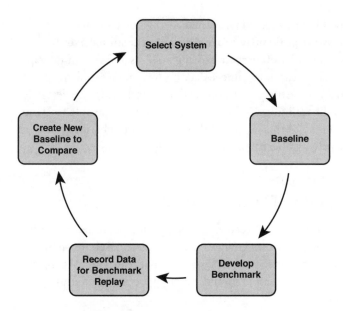

Figure 10.2 Baselining and benchmarking life cycle.

Why Should You Take a Performance Baseline?

Your performance baseline will be used to validate that the virtual infrastructure and the design of the virtual machines meet or exceed the requirements of the source physical systems, both before and after they are virtualized.

The following are the most important reasons for taking a performance baseline of your source and destination systems:

- Reduced risk of not meeting requirements

- Increased ROI by being able to optimize infrastructure utilization

- Reduced risk of over- or under-investment

- Prevention of performance problems during database and infrastructure configuration changes

- Significantly easier, more accurate, and quicker architecture design process

Failure to accurately baseline your source and destination configurations could lead to the failure of your overall database virtualization project in the worst case, and in the best case not knowing what the acceptable or expected performance and behavior are. **Not baselining makes troubleshooting significantly more difficult and subjective.** It is very common for customers that do not baseline their existing systems and do not do gap analysis between physical and virtual to run into unnecessary performance problems that then take significant time and effort to resolve. Our hope is that by following the design guidance provided in this book and baselining your performance, you will be able to avoid performance problems that would result otherwise, and that when things change, you'll be able to much more quickly and easily resolve them and identify the root causes.

When Should You Baseline Performance?

It is good performance management practice to record baseline performance periodically, and especially before and after any major system changes. Performance baselines should be measured for both production and non-production systems as part of standard project and operations processes. A performance baseline should generally be recorded in the following situations:

- As part of the design validation of a new infrastructure, including new vSphere designs and changes to existing designs or environments

- As part of normal business-as-usual activities, before and after any major system configuration or software changes

- When migrating an existing system from one platform to another, either at the application level or when doing a physical-to-virtual or virtual-to-virtual migration

- As part of introducing a new database to production

- During proof of concept or pilot implementation

Regular baselining of your system at key points is one way of managing system performance to ensure it meets service-level agreements (SLAs).

What System Components to Baseline

This section covers the metrics you should collect at a minimum when baselining your SQL Server databases. You may choose to collect additional metrics as part of your baseline as well.

Existing Physical Database Infrastructure

> **NOTE**
>
> Per-database stats on a consolidated database server are not easy to measure when you are recording physical infrastructure performance metrics. For this reason, you need to collect application-level performance metrics in addition to the infrastructure.

A number of important metrics that are relevant to all SQL servers are available to baseline. Table 10.1 illustrates the metrics you should monitor and the recommended thresholds for them.

Table 10.1   SQL Server Baseline Infrastructure Metrics

Resource	Metric	Physical Host / VM	Description	Threshold
CPU	Processor (_Total): Privileged Time	Both	Percentage of time that the process threads spent executing code in privileged mode.	Avg +10% indicates possible CPU pressure.
	Processor (_Total): Processor Time	Both	Percentage of elapsed time that all process threads used the processor to execute instructions.	Avg +80% indicates possible CPU pressure.
Memory	Pages/Sec	Both	Rate at which pages are read from or written to disk to resolve hard page faults.	Less than 20.
	Available Mbytes	Both	Shows amount of memory available to processes that are running on the computer.	Greater than 128MB.
	Free System Page Table Entries	Both	Shows the number of page table entries that are not currently in use by the system.	Greater than 3,000.
	Paging File (_Total): %Usage	Both	Amount of the page file instance that is in use.	Less than 70%.
Disk	LogicalDisk: Disk Bytes/sec		Rate at which bytes are transferred (used to determine disk throughput).	

Resource	Metric	Physical Host / VM	Description	Threshold
	LogicalDisk(*): Avg Disk Sec/ Read	Both	Average time, in seconds, of a read of data from disk. Every ms here is a ms your user is not getting a response.	<10ms = good. 10ms = okay. 20–50ms = slow, needs attention. >50ms = serious I/O bottleneck.
	LogicalDisk(*): Avg. Disk Sec/ Write	Both	Average time, in seconds, of a write of data back to the disk. Every ms here is a ms your user is not getting a response.	<10ms = good. 10ms = okay. 20–50ms = slow, needs attention. >50ms = serious I/O bottleneck.
Network	Bytes Total/sec		Rate at which the network adaptor is processing data bytes.	

While you are collecting and analyzing the various infrastructure metrics, you need to pay attention to averages and peaks. Ideally you will be capturing the existing system's performance during a cyclical system peak workload period, which might be end-of-month, end-of-quarter, or end-of-year processing. You need to determine when the likely peaks are based on your business and your particular systems. However, if you are not able to capture the peaks and the averages during a peak business and system period, you will need to make adjustments based on your knowledge of those times. In some organizations, peaks of system volumes can range from 20X to 100X normal system volumes.

If your system is supporting an Internet-facing application, you will have to take unexpected peak loads and spikes into account. This can be very hard to predict, so you should take a conservative approach based on what you think the worst-case scenario is, or the maximum that has been observed in the past. You can then, based on your workload model and business knowledge, extrapolate what may be required, taking into account known future activities.

> **NOTE**
>
> A vCPU of a virtual machine is only single threaded. Unlike a physical CPU core, it does not include a hyper-thread. If you want to get the most out of your system and do like for like comparisons with the physical source system, you will need to configure your VM with as many vCPUs as you have CPU threads on your physical platform.

Database Application Performance

When you are recording your SQL Server baselines and benchmarks, you should be capturing application-level performance metrics that give a valid representation of acceptable performance for the system. These are the types of metrics that will have a direct and immediate impact on your users if there is a problem. Some items to consider monitoring are as follows:

- Transactions per second or per minute
- Concurrent users and sessions
- Transaction latency average and peaks
- End-user experience and end-user response times for business transactions
- Batch job duration
- Report duration

You should also make use of the SQL Server 2012 Performance Dashboard Reports. This is a quick and easy way to get an understanding of how your database is performing.

SQL Server 2012 Performance Dashboard Reports can be found at this URL:

http://www.microsoft.com/en-nz/download/details.aspx?id=29063

Table 10.2 outlines specific SQL Server Perfmon and SQL Profiler counters and metrics that are useful for your baselining and benchmarking process. These will allow you to perform a valid comparison before, during, and after virtualization of your SQL Server systems.

Table 10.2 SQL Server Perfmon Counters

Resource	Metric	Phys / VM	Description
SQLServer: Buffer Manager	Buffer Cache Hit Ratio	Both	Percentage of time that the pages requested are already in cache.
	Page Life Expectancy	Both	Time, in seconds, the data pages stay in SQL cache, on average. Low page life of <300 can indicate: (1) SQL cache is cold, (2) memory problems, or (3) missing indexes. Correlates to Lazy writes/sec and Checkpoint pages/sec.
	Cache Hit Ratio	Both	Percentage of time that the procedure plan pages are already in cache (for example, procedure cache hits). That is, how frequently a compiled procedure is found in the procedure cache (thus avoiding the need to recompile).

Resource	Metric	Phys / VM	Description
SQLServer: Memory Manager	Memory Grants Pending	Both	Memory resources are required for each user request. If sufficient memory is not available, the user waits until there is adequate memory for the query to run.
	Target Server Memory (KB)	Both	Total amount of dynamic memory the server is willing to consume.
	Total Server Memory (KB)	Both	Total amount of dynamic memory the server is currently consuming.
SQLServer: General Statistics	Logins/sec	Both	Number of logins per second.
	Logout/sec	Both	Number of logouts per second.
	User Connections	Both	Number of user connections.
SQLServer: Databases	Log Flush Wait Time	Both	Waiting for transaction log writes (ms).
	Log Flush Waits/sec	Both	This is the number of commits waiting on a log flush.
	Transactions/sec	Both	SQL Server transactions per second.
SQLServer: Latches	Average Latch Wait Time(ms)	Both	Latches are short-term lightweight synchronization objects. Latches are not held for the duration of a transaction. Typical latching operations occur during row transfers to memory, controlling modifications to row offset table, and so on.
SQLServer: Locks	Average Wait Time(ms)	Both	Transactions should be as short as possible to limit the blocking of other users.
SQLServer: SQL Statistics	Batch Requests/sec	Both	SQL Server batch requests per second.
	SQL Compilations/sec	Both	Number of SQL compilations. Compilations/sec includes both initial compiles and subsequent recompiles.
	SQL Re-Compilations/ sec	Both	Number of SQL recompiles.

Table 10.3 shows the metrics for individual query performance. The Profiler data log can grow pretty quickly. Only use it when a defined set of queries is being tested.

Table 10.3 SQL Server Profiler Counters

Resource	Metric	Phys / VM	Description
Store Procedures --> RPC: Completed	Duration	Both	Elapsed time taken
	CPU	Both	Amount of CPU used
	Reads	Both	Number of logical reads
	Writes	Both	Number of physical disk writes
TSQL --> SQL: StmtCompleted	Duration	Both	Elapsed time taken
	CPU	Both	Amount of CPU used
	Reads	Both	Number of logical reads
	Writes	Both	Number of physical disk writes
TSQL --> SQL: BatchCompleted	Duration	Both	Elapsed time taken
	CPU	Both	Amount of CPU used
	Reads	Both	Number of logical reads
	Writes	Both	Number of physical disk writes

Existing or Proposed vSphere Infrastructure

It is important as part of your baselining and benchmarking exercise that you record the relevant statistics from your existing or proposed VMware vSphere environment. These statistics will include virtualization-specific counters that can be used to determine whether there are any problems with your configuration or design that need to be investigated now or at a later stage.

During your baselining process, you should be monitoring and recording performance using the counters from ESXTOP for your vSphere environment, as shown in Table 10.4.

Table 10.4 ESXTOP Counters

Resource	Metric	Host / VM	Description	Threshold
CPU	%USED	Both	CPU used over the collection interval (%).	
	%RDY	VM	CPU time spent in ready state.	<5% / vCPU
	%SYS	Both	Percentage of time spent in the ESXi Server VMKernel.	20

Resource	Metric	Host / VM	Description	Threshold
	%CSTP	VM	Percentage of time the world spends in ready, co-descheduled state. (Make sure larger SMP VMs are effective and not under contention.)	<3%
	%VMWait	VM	A derivative of %WAIT, without including %IDLE time, but includes %SWPWT and the time the VM is blocked for when a device is unavailable.	<10%
Memory	Swapin, Swapout	Both	Memory ESX host swaps in/out from/ to disk (per VM) or cumulative over host.	0
	MCTLSZ (MB)	Both	Amount of memory reclaimed from resource pool by way of ballooning.	0
	N%L	Host	Percentage of memory that is local to the NUMA home node.	>80% to 100% preferred
	%SWPWT	Host	VM waiting swapped pages to be read from disk.	0
	CACHEUSED	Host	Compressed memory.	0
Disk	READs/s, Writes/s	Both	Reads and writes issued in the collection interval.	
	CMDS/s	Both	Number of IOPS being sent to or coming from the device or virtual machine being monitored.	
	DAVG/cmd GAVG/cmd for NFS Datastores	Both	Average latency (ms) of the device (LUN).	Target is <10ms for ESX Hosts running DBs
	KAVG/cmd	Both	Average latency (ms) in the vmkernel (aka queuing time). For databases, we want this at or below 0.1ms (no queuing); other workloads OK at 2ms.	1.0
	ABRTS/s	VM	Aborts issued by guest (VM) because storage is not responding. For Windows VMs, this happens after 60 seconds by default. Can be caused for instance when paths failed or array is not accepting any IO for whatever reason.	0

Resource	Metric	Host / VM	Description	Threshold
	RESETS/s	Host	The number of storage commands reset per second.	0
Network	MbRX/s, MbTx/s	Both	Amount of data transmitted per second.	
	PKTRX/s, PKTTX/s	Both	Packets transmitted per second.	
	%DRPPX, %DRPTX	Both	Dropped packets per second; should not be above 0%.	0

Before you virtualize your first mission-critical database—whether it's being migrated or being freshly provisioned—you should benchmark your vSphere environment while collecting the preceding metrics. This will give you assurance that your vSphere infrastructure is operating as expected, is likely to support the SQL database workloads, and that at least at the infrastructure level the performance is acceptable. This will also give you a baseline of the core vSphere environment performance that can be used as a comparison when you have put your databases on top of it. Any issues that come out of this baselining and benchmarking exercise can be resolved before the first real SQL Server database is ever migrated, which can save a lot of time and effort at a later stage.

The following tools can be used to help you benchmark your vSphere environment:

- **SQLIOsim**—http://support.microsoft.com/?id=231619.
- **IOBlazer**—http://labs.vmware.com/flings/ioblazer.
- **IOMeter**—http://www.iometer.org/.
- **Dell DVD Store**—https://github.com/dvdstore.
- **I/O Analyzer**—http://labs.vmware.com/flings/io-analyzer. I/O Analyzer is a great fling. It's a vApp, has multiple distribution points, uses IOMeter, and integrates with ESXTOP metrics. (See http://wahlnetwork.com/2013/02/01/testing-multiple-workloads-with-the-vmware-io-analyzer-video/ for a video of how it works.)

Comparing Baselines of Different Processor Types and Generations

The infrastructure metrics covered in Table 10.1 are standard metrics that are collectable across all systems, even if they are a completely different system architecture. If your source system is Itanium based, although the metrics themselves are the same, they will not all directly translate to your destination x86 systems. The same is true if you are comparing across system generations. The CPU performance in particular is one main area where you will have to do some adjustments when baselining and comparing systems based on different CPUs, including Intel Itanium-based Windows and SQL Server environments to x86-based SQL Server virtual machines.

As described briefly in the previous section on vendor benchmarks, the SAP SD 2 Tier Benchmark is a standard, repeatable, publicly published benchmark that can be used for comparing different systems quickly. It is an OLTP-type benchmark, and the results are available to view and download at http://www.sap.com/solutions/benchmark/sd2tier.epx. The results available include systems covering Intel Itanium, Intel Xeon, and AMD processor types, across multiple CPU generations and multiple versions of SQL Server.

Using the SAP SD Benchmark allows you to figure out what system processor utilization on your source system during baselining is likely to equate to in terms of processor utilization on your destination system during your performance testing, baselining, or benchmarking. This is very useful when comparing dissimilar source and destination processor generations or processor types. So if you're going from Intel Itanium on your physical system to Intel Xeon on your destination virtual machine, or switching from AMD Opteron to Intel Xeon, or vice versa, this gives you a quick and easy way of comparing CPU utilization.

The main unit of measure provided by the SD Benchmark is SAPS. By comparing the SAPS between different processor types, you can get an idea of the relative performance differences between those processors. The next section gives you some examples.

Comparing Different System Processor Types

Table 10.5 shows examples based on data from the SD Benchmark 2 Tier results comparing performance between different CPU types. Because some business-critical databases currently run on Intel Itanium processors on HP Integrity Superdome systems, we have included an example as part of this comparison.

Table 10.5 SAP SD Benchmark Examples Between Different Processor Types

SAP SD Benchmark Examples	HP Integrity Superdome 16	HP DL385 G8	Cisco UCS B22 M3
SAP Certification ID	2006090	2012036	2012028
SAPS	28200	33320	33150
Concurrent Users	5600	6100	6070
Processors and Type	16 x Intel Itanium 2 9050	2 x AMD Opteron 6386SE	2 x Intel Xeon E5-2470
Processor Cores and Clock Speed	32 cores @ 1.6GHz	32 cores @ 2.8GHz	16 cores @ 2.3GHz
CPU Threads	64	32	32
RAM	256GB	128GB	96GB
SQL Server Version	2005	2012	2012
SAPS per CPU Socket	1762.5	16660	16575
SAPS per CPU Core	881.25	1041.25	2071.88
SAPS per CPU Thread	440.63	1041.25	1035.94
Transaction Response Time	1.91 seconds	0.99 seconds	0.99 seconds

As you can see from this table, the HP AMD Opteron-based system is only 18% more powerful, core for core, compared to the HP Itanium system. However, the Cisco Intel Xeon-based system is more than 2.35 times more powerful, core for core, than the HP Itanium system.[1] What this also shows is that an Intel Hyper-thread is almost as good as an AMD core, even with the Intel CPU having a lower clock speed. Based on these results, we can now compare a percentage of CPU utilization from a baseline taken on an Itanium system and estimate the expected percentage CPU utilization on an AMD or Intel-based system. As in these examples, 50% CPU utilization of a single Itanium core would be approximately 21% CPU utilization on the Intel Xeon E5-2470 core, and would be approximately 41% CPU utilization on a single AMD Opteron 6386SE core. This is determined by dividing the CPU utilization of the source system by the relative performance of the destination system, as shown in the following calculation example:

```
Destination CPU Utilization = Source CPU Utilization *
(Source SAPs per Core / Destination SAPs per Core)

Destination CPU Utilization = 50% * (881.25 / 2071.88) = 21.27%
```

---

[1] Based on Gartner's RPE2 benchmark results published in March 2013, the latest Intel Xeon E7 family of processors is about twice as fast as the latest Intel Itanium 9500 series.

If you happen to be reading this book in advance of virtualizing an SAP system using SQL Server 2012, you may be interested to know that the largest SAP system we're aware of using SQL Server as its database platform running on VMware vSphere is approximately 10.2 million users and around 8 million SAPS, including production and non-production environments. This is a substantial system for a very large government department.

Comparing Similar System Processor Types Across Generations

The same sort of calculations can be done to compare processors within the same type but between different processor generations. Table 10.6 presents the SAP SD Benchmark results for three different HP Server and Intel Xeon processor generations.

Table 10.6   SAP SD Benchmark Examples Between Different Processor Generations

SAP SD Benchmark Examples	HP DL380 G6	HP DL380 G7	HP DL380 Gen8
SAP Certification ID	2009004	2011005	2012012
SAPS	18030	28480	42920
Concurrent Users	3300	5220	7865
Processors and Type	2 x Intel Xeon X5570	2 x Intel Xeon X5690	2 x Intel Xeon E5-2690
Processor Cores and Clock Speed	8 cores @ 2.93GHz	12 cores @ 3.46GHz	16 cores @ 2.9GHz
CPU Threads	16	24	32
RAM	48GB	96GB	128GB
SQL Server Version	2005	2008	2008
SAPS per CPU Socket	9015	14240	21460
SAPS per CPU Core	2253.75	2373.33	2682.5
SAPS per CPU Thread	1126.88	1186.67	1341.25
Transaction Response Time	0.98 seconds	0.99 seconds	0.99 seconds

From this table, we can see the progression of performance, core for core, socket for socket, and thread for thread, across three HP server generations taken from the SAP SD 2 Tier benchmark results. Even for relatively the same CPU Core clock speed, the core-for-core performance varies significantly between the G6 and Gen8 systems. This is as you would expect with the advances being achieved regularly with modern processor technology.

If you don't want to use SAPS and you simply want to compare between different x86 processor types and generations, you can also use publicly available SPECInt benchmarks. Table 10.7 presents the SPECInt (www.spec.org, CINT2006) results for the same processor types as listed in Table 10.6.

Table 10.7   SPECInt Benchmark Examples Between Different Processor Generations

CINT2006 Rates	HP DL380 G6	HP DL380 G7	HP DL380 Gen8
CPU	Intel Xeon X5570 @ 2.93GHz	Intel Xeon X5690 @ 3.46 GHZ	Intel Xeon E5-2690 @ 2.90 GHz
Result	251	435	693
Baseline	233	421	668
Cores	8	12	16
Chips	2	2	2
Cores per Chip	4	6	8
Result per Core	31.38	36.25	43.31

NOTE

When using SPECInt or SAPS Benchmarks as a comparison between CPUs of different generations or types, you should take into consideration that they were determined at close to 100% system utilization. This means they are only good as a relative comparison and to translate a CPU utilization figure on one system to another. You should allow some headroom for peaks when doing your calculations.

Non-Production Workload Influences on Performance

Your performance testing, benchmarking, baselining, and validation needs to consider non-production workload influences that may impact performance. The performance of your environment might be influenced by some or all of the following activities:

- AV updates
- Backups
- Database Consistency Check (DBCC) processes
- Index defragmentation
- Database statistics update

You will need to consider how frequent these types of activities are and how much impact they have on your SQL Server databases. If the impact is high, you will want to include these activities in your workload modeling and testing. This will ensure that your systems performance is still acceptable even while these important non-production activities take place.

TIP

Don't forget to exclude your data files and log files from your antivirus (AV) scanning. It can have a huge impact on performance, especially when real-time AV scanning is used.

Producing a Baseline Performance Report

A performance baseline report is a useful tool for recording the outcomes of a baselining and benchmarking exercise and to set expectations with project sponsors and key stakeholders, such as DBAs and application owners. The performance baseline report is the evidence that proves what the required system performance is and whether systems will likely perform to expectations or not, based on the proposed design and proposed infrastructure. This report captures the point in time before the systems were virtualized and can be used in the future when changes are made or if end users are not satisfied with system performance. Earlier in this chapter, we discussed the example of the large engineering firm. If they had performed a proper baseline up front, they would have not experienced the many weeks of problems they had.

If you are virtualizing a small number of relatively low-importance database systems, you might not need to go to the trouble of formally documenting the baselining and benchmarking of the systems. However, if you are virtualizing one or more large or mission-critical SQL Server systems, then this report should be considered a critical part of your project deliverables. Remember that good performance now becomes expected performance later. The performance bar is always moving, and without an objective point of reference you have no way to determine whether your databases are performing well or otherwise.

Here are our suggestions for the sections you should cover and the content you should include at a minimum in your baseline performance report. This example was taken from a baseline performance report created during a large database migration project.

- Executive summary, including Report Overview and Baseline Assessment highlights (assessment period, critical business cycles covered, data centers, contributors, and summary of activities)

- Baseline performance summary (system processor load for business hour average and peak load, top-5 CPU consumers, top-5 IO consumers, and top-5 lowest memory available during peak)

- Baseline performance comparison between physical and virtual systems showing application metrics, such as database transactions per second and transaction latency for top systems during validation benchmark testing

- Baseline analysis of physical systems, including database transactions per second, latency, and throughput metrics for the top-5 systems

- Detailed findings (detailed system metrics for each system baselined)

- Processor load by system, business hours average, and peak load

- Disk transactions/s, throughput and latency, % disk busy, and disk queue length

- Memory metrics by system, including configured RAM, available RAM Mbytes, and % business hour average and peak consumption

- Detailed Database Transaction metrics by database instance and schema, including transaction SQL, average reply bytes, average latency, max latency, hits per second, and total hits

- System inventory by system name, including OS and version, # CPUs, CPU MHz, Total MHz, Installed RAM, # SCSI controllers, # disks, # NICs, and NIC speed

All of this information will play an important part in your design and implementation of your SQL Server databases running on VMware vSphere.

Performance Traps to Watch Out For

This section will cover some of the common performance traps that you need to watch out for during your SQL Server and vSphere infrastructure baselining and benchmarking exercises. Some of the topics covered might be more obvious than others, but all are important when you want to ensure performance and availability of your SQL Server databases when they are virtualized.

Shared Core Infrastructure Between Production and Non-Production

If there are any shared core infrastructure components between production and non-production that might become saturated or overloaded, this could cause your baselines and benchmarks to be invalidated in the best case, or, worse, potentially cause production outages during performance benchmarks. As part of your analysis and design process, you should evaluate what shared core infrastructure components there are that might impact your baselining and benchmarking, such as shared storage arrays, network components, and firewalls.

You need to determine if any of the links in the chain where you will be monitoring and testing will likely exceed their capacity. It could be something as simple as exceeding the maximum number of concurrent connections through a shared firewall, which leads to dropped connections and application instability in test or production. It could be a shared storage array that gets overloaded or experiences performance degradation during performance benchmarks, which then impacts other workloads. The reality is that many organizations can't afford to have completely separated and isolated production and non-production environments. Often the costs are simply not justified. In those cases, you need to take a risk-based approach and understand what the limits are, what the impacts might be on your testing or on production while you're testing, and come up with a plan to mitigate those risks.

Invalid Assumptions Leading to Invalid Conclusions

Often during baselining and benchmarking exercises or database migration projects, you will need to make assumptions where there is no clear information. Sometimes these assumptions could prove incorrect, and this might cause some or all of your conclusions to be invalidated. An example of an assumption that could lead to invalid performance conclusions is if you assumed an existing shared storage array, the same as is being used for your physical databases, would be used once the databases are migrated to virtual machines. If this is correct, you may expect similar storage performance as the physical database systems currently enjoy, assuming the infrastructure design is similar. If this proves incorrect and you made an assumption about storage performance based on this, it could be completely invalid. You would potentially need to repeat some tests to determine what the actual performance will be.

Lack of Background Noise

Often you might find if you do benchmarking in an isolated test environment that your performance results are actually better than production, even though your test environment might be configured similarly to production. This can be caused by the lack of background activity or background noise of other systems in the test environment. In production, you would have a multitude of different systems and many users pounding away day and night. This type of background noise is often very hard to simulate in a test environment, but it is important to at least consider it as part of your benchmarking and baselining activities and, if necessary, make assumptions (often called an educated guess) and make adjustments to your results.

Failure to Considering Single Compute Unit Performance

Single Compute Unit (SCU) Performance refers to the execution performance of a single thread or single unit of work and is impacted by the clock speed of the system CPUs. The levels of cache within a CPU can also influence SCU Performance. The higher the SCU, the faster queries will execute and the faster response times may be for certain workloads.

Clock for Clock performance between CPU generations is important to compare when evaluating a Single Compute Unit Performance comparison. Often between CPU generations, the same clock speed can achieve up to 15% increase in performance. Many SQL queries will benefit from a higher system clock speed, especially when they are CPU intensive, single threaded, and long running. However, applications and queries that are generally very parallel in nature and combine lots of small execution payloads will run just fine on a system with a lower clock speed but many processors.

The Max Degree of Parallelism setting on your SQL Server database is one setting that will impact the degree of parallelism for your SQL queries, in addition to the individual query execution plan. It is recommended this parameter be set equal to 1 for OLTP workloads and only changed from 1 if testing shows a benefit. The tradeoff when increasing this value is that one user or one connection could monopolize the resources of the database.

Blended Peaks of Multiple Systems

When you virtualize multiple systems, you will most likely be consolidating them onto a fewer number of physical servers. Although there are cases where customers choose to consolidate 1:1, this is by no means the norm. As a result of this, you need to ensure that the peaks of all of the systems that will be running on a particular host combined do not exceed the resources of that host. This is something you should be capturing during your baselining, benchmarking, and validation of the virtual infrastructure.

If all of your virtualized SQL Server databases have log shipping, backup, or maintenance tasks scheduled to run at exactly the same time, this may reduce the consolidation ratios that are possible. Failure to consider blended peak workloads of multiple systems per host could result in your databases not meeting their SLAs during peak times. If you get your estimates slightly wrong and there is spare capacity within your clusters, VMware DRS will load-balance VMs across the cluster automatically. It is recommended that you have DRS enabled and set to fully automatic. Figure 10.3 shows a blended workload of an OLTP database and a batch-driven data warehouse–type database virtualized on the same host to demonstrate how two different workloads can coexist happily and improve overall utilization.

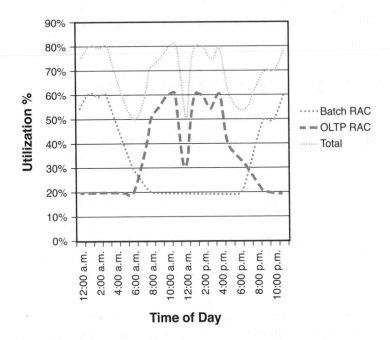

Figure 10.3 Example of compatible blended database peak workloads.

vMotion Slot Sizes of Monster Database Virtual Machines

vMotion Slot Size is a term coined to describe how much compute capacity is required in order for the largest VM to migrate from one host to another in a VMware DRS cluster or for the largest VM to restart in the case of a VMware HA event. The vMotion Slot Size should not be confused with a VMware HA Slot Size because it needs to be considered regardless of whether your VMware HA Admission Control Policy is set to Number of Host Failures or Percentage of Resources Reserved for Failure. It is especially applicable to large database servers that will likely have large memory reservations.

If there is enough overall compute capacity in your cluster for maintenance or HA events but this capacity is fragmented across the hosts, it may impact your ability to put hosts into maintenance mode. It may also extend the time it takes for HA to restart your largest VMs. In the case of an HA event, DRS will kick in and attempt to defragment the cluster's resources in order for the VMs to be able to restart; however, there is no guarantee it will be able to free up enough resources.

In order to ensure you always have enough free resources in your clusters to perform maintenance and restart in the case of an HA event, it is recommended as a general rule of thumb that your ESXi hosts are twice the size of the largest VM you plan to support. This will ensure that in a cluster with N+1 hosts locally (to allow for HA), you will always be able to restart the largest VMs and perform maintenance.

Figure 10.4 illustrates this point. On the fourth host is a VM with 48GB RAM. Overall, the cluster has sufficient resources for HA Admission Control. Assuming all the memory of each VM is reserved, there is nowhere for the large VM on the fourth host to restart if that host were to fail. The fourth host in this case would also not be able to enter maintenance mode.

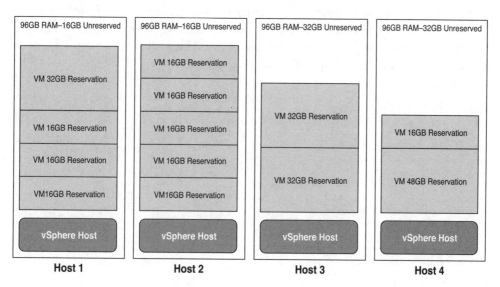

Figure 10.4   vMotion Slot Size example.

Summary

This chapter covered both infrastructure and application baseline activities related to SQL Server 2012. Much of the information covered could be applied to other versions of SQL Server, or even completely different applications. It provided you with the **why, when, what,** and **how** of measuring the baseline successfully, and how to ensure you at least meet if not exceed your system's required performance when virtualized. When virtualizing SQL Server databases, especially large and business-critical databases, it's important that you reduce risk and eliminate guesswork as much as possible. You want to virtualize but you don't want to compromise—be it performance, availability, recoverability, or any other SLA. If that is your goal, then baselining your workloads is critical.

The real measure of your success will be when your databases are virtualized and meet or exceed the requirements set out at the start of the project. You will never know that without a good baseline to measure from. If you do this part of your job well, your operational teams will also thank you for it. They will be able to leverage the data during system maintenance and troubleshooting. It will form part of the ongoing database capacity and performance management processes.

This chapter has given you the essential tools with which to successfully baseline any SQL Server 2012 system. You now know how to compare between generations of hardware platforms, even different hardware architectures, so you can "right-size" the design and architecture of your systems, based on your requirements. This will allow you to achieve optimal performance with service quality assurance.

Chapter 11

Configuring a Performance Test—From Beginning to End

To this point, we have provided deep dives into individual topics for virtualizing SQL Server. We are often asked, "How do I test SQL on vSphere?" In this chapter, we are going to put it all together and walk you, the reader, through setting up SQL 2012 on Microsoft Windows Server 2012. We will configure the AlwaysOn Availability Groups, and using an open source load-generation tool, Dell DVD Store, we will simulate workload. Furthermore, it should be noted this configuration has also been shown to work with Windows 2008 R2 as the operating system supporting SQL 2012 and Windows 8 as the desktop generating the workload.

Introduction

Before we begin discussing what is needed for the test, let's cover *why* we are running this test:

- Is this a test to show the DBAs in the organization how well virtualized SQL can perform on a vSphere infrastructure?

- Is the test part of a bakeoff between physical and virtual configurations?

- Is this simply a test of functionality?

Once we understand the "why," we can set proper expectations for the test. This means creating the proper documentation, detailing the test plan, identifying and monitoring of key performance indicators, ensuring consistency between tests (for example, if measuring physical versus virtual performance), and ensuring proper sponsorship.

So that we are on the same page, we are creating a performance test in this chapter that has the ability to stress the infrastructure beyond its limits. Be mindful of where this configuration is being stood up, the time of day, and the duration of the testing. We have seen individuals set up performance tests using production equipment and bring the production environment to its knees. Don't be that person.

CAUTION

To be clear, run the following test configuration against non-production equipment.

It should be noted that some of the configuration options presented in this chapter do not follow production best practices for implementing SQL Server. Be mindful of this when you are configuring your implementation and make the appropriate changes to ensure adherence to your company's policies. Be cognizant of the settings that are being chosen and understand their impact so as not to generate any REGs (résumé-generating events). It is important to know *why* you are making a particular setting change before you make that change. What may initially be a harmless configuration change can have serious downstream implications to the environment.

TIP

Do not work on these performance tests in a vacuum. Depending on the goals, size, and configuration, assistance and buy-in may be necessary from the DBA, Network, and SAN teams—and critical to the success of this initiative. Use this as an opportunity to educate your coworkers on the benefits of virtualizing SQL Server.

We are creating this test in total isolation in our vSphere 5.5 environment. The vSphere 5.5 lab we used for this configuration consists of two IBM x3650 M2 hosts, each with 128GB of RAM. These hosts are connected via fiber channel to an EMC VNX. The LUNs are configured in a Data Store Cluster configuration. Each data store is approximately 1TB in size. Each physical host has seven 1GB NICs available, and we are using distributed virtual switches on the ESXi hosts. We have carved out a dedicated VLAN for the purposes of this test so as not to affect other workloads running on these hosts. We stood up the Active Directory Domain Services Server, SQL Servers, and Windows 8.1 virtual machines from Microsoft ISOs. We downloaded vCOPs, Hyperic, and Virtual Infrastructure Navigator (VIN) virtual appliances and have these running to provide us telemetry of our virtual environment. VMware vCenter Server is running as a virtual machine in our configuration.

What We Used—Software

Here is a list of all the software used:

- vCenter Server 5.5
- Two ESXi 5.5 hosts
- One Windows Server 2012 Standard running Active Directory Domain Services (AD DS) along with DNS
- Two Windows Server 2012 Datacenter Edition Servers, each running SQL Server 2012 Enterprise Edition Service Pack 1
- One Windows 8.1 x64 desktop
- Dell DVD Store 2.1
- Strawberry Perl for x64 Windows
- Unix-to-DOS conversion utility

What You Will Need—Computer Names and IP Addresses

You will need the following computer names:

- AD DS virtual machine name
- Two SQL Server 2012 virtual machine names
- Windows 8.1 virtual machine name
- Windows Failover Cluster name (shows up as a Computer Name is AD)
- SQL Server Listener name (shows up as a Computer Name is AD)

The following is a bulleted list of the IP addresses needed to stand up the lab. We also included Table 11.1, which represents the name, operating system version, SQL version, and IP addresses of all the virtual machines used in our lab:

- One IP address for the Windows Server 2012 AD DS virtual machine
- Four IP addresses for the SQL Server 2012 virtual machines
- One IP address for the Windows 8.1 virtual machine
- One IP address for the Windows Failover Cluster
- One IP address for the SQL Server 2012 Listener

Table 11.1 Virtual Machine Name, OS, and IPs

Name	Windows Version	SQL Version	IP Address
AD_2012	Windows Server 2012 Standard		172.26.109.10/24
SQL_2012_a	Windows Server 2012 Datacenter	SQL Server 2012 Enterprise Edition SP1	172.26.109.20/24 5.5.5.1/ 24
SQL_2012_b	Windows Server 2012 Datacenter	SQL Server 2012 Enterprise Edition SP1	172.26.109.30/24 5.5.5.2/24
LoadGen	Windows 8.1 Enterprise		172.26.109.200/24
Cluster Name – wfc4sql01			172.26.109.150
Listener Name – sql2012agl01			172.26.109.160

Additional Items for Consideration

Ensure the proper resources are assigned to this project. Work with your extended team to ensure the configuration built will meet the test objectives. For example, ensure you have enough storage allocated to the project as part of enabling AlwaysOn, which requires taking full database backups. If you are looking at doing a 20GB database, this space needs to be calculated into your storage request.

Getting the Lab Up and Running

We have two ESXi 5.5 hosts we will be using for the test. Prior to building our virtual machines, it is important to have the base foundation for the infrastructure configured. We have vCenter Server running as a virtual machine. We have already downloaded and configured the vCOPs, Hyperic, and Virtual Infrastructure Navigator virtual appliances. We installed and configured these virtual appliances according to best practices, which can be found in each product's Installation and Configuration documentation available on VMware.com. Once our foundation was configured, we installed the following virtual machines on our ESXi hosts (see Figure 11.1):

- AD_2012, which is the Windows Server 2012 virtual machine configured with AD DS, domain name s2012dir.domain

- SQL_2012_a and SQL_2012_b, both running Windows Server 2012 Datacenter Edition and SQL Server 2012 Enterprise and are members of the s2012dir.domain

- LoadGen, which is the Windows 8.1 virtual machine and also a member of the s2012dir.domain

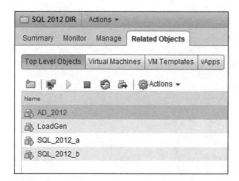

Figure 11.1   Snapshot of the lab.

Using vCenter Infrastructure Navigator, we can display and understand the relationships between these systems. We will revisit vCenter Infrastructure Navigator after we have installed and configured SQL Server 2012 with AlwaysOn Availability Groups to identify the changes. vCenter Infrastructure Navigator automatically generates the visual shown in Figure 11.2 and automatically updates this as dependencies evolve. At the end of our configuration, you will see an updated screenshot of Figure 11.2 that shows how vCenter Infrastructure Navigator automatically updated the configuration and connections based on our implementation of clustering, AlwaysOn Availability, and the virtual machine driving the test workload.

Next, we will install vCenter Hyperic agents inside these virtual machines so we can begin monitoring these systems. We are using Hyperic as our in-guest agent to gather OS- and SQL-level data. This step is optional, and you can leverage tools you already have; however, vCenter Hyperic can provide valuable telemetry into what the virtual machines are doing from an operating system, middleware, and application perspective. When we combine this level of introspection with vCOPs, we are able to paint a picture of the entire infrastructure.

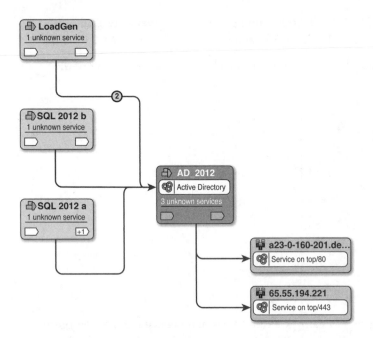

Figure 11.2   Using vCenter Virtual Infrastructure Navigator to display dependencies.

We have installed and configured vCenter Hyperic, which is outside the scope of this book. However, for more information on vCenter Hyperic, visit http://www.vmware.com/products/vcenter-hyperic. With vCenter Hyperic installed, browse to the folder containing the virtual machines that are part of this configuration (in this case, the SQL 2012 DIR folder). Highlight all the virtual machines that the vCenter Hyperic Agent is targeted to be deployed on and click the **Install Hyperic Agent on the selected VMs** icon, as shown in Figure 11.3.

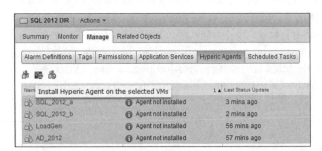

Figure 11.3   Deploying the Hyperic agent to a group of virtual machines.

Once the agents are pushed out to each individual virtual machine and they start as a service, you will receive an "Agent running" status for these virtual machines, as represented in Figure 11.4.

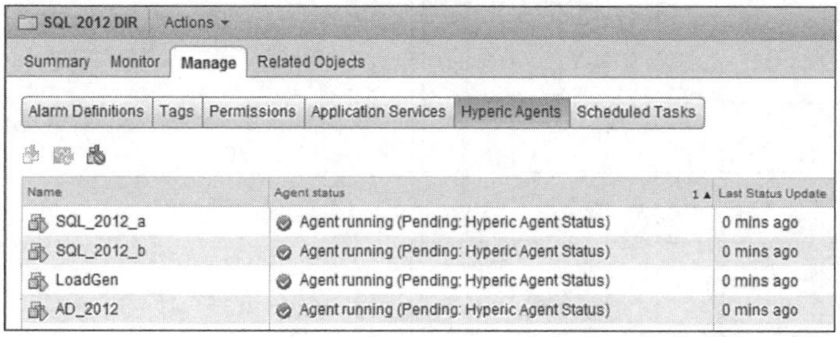

Figure 11.4 Successful deployment of the Hyperic agent to a group of virtual machines.

Now that we have successfully installed the vCenter Hyperic agent inside our virtual machines, we will move onto configuring their VMDK files.

VMDK File Configuration

Per the VMware Knowledge Base Article 1037959 titled "Microsoft Clustering on VMware vSphere: Guidelines for Supported Configurations" (http://kb.vmware.com/kb/1037959), the following is true for non-shared disk clustering (per KB update on 11/20/2013): SQL AlwaysOn Availability Groups have vSphere support, VMware HA support, vMotion DRS support, and Storage vMotion support, and scale is the same as operating system and application limits (so you can run the same number of nodes on vSphere 5.5 as you can in the physical world). This is visible in the bottom line of Figure 11.5. Make sure you read the table notes of this KB article because it goes into further detail regarding what VMware will support.

> **NOTE**
>
> The difference between "shared disk" and "non-shared disk" in VMware KB 1037959 is based on Microsoft's requirement for a disk to be "shared" among multiple systems. For SQL 2012 AlwaysOn Availability Groups, this is not a requirement; however, SQL 2012 AlwaysOn Failover Cluster Instances (FCIs) do have this requirement.

VMware vSphere support for Microsoft clustering solutions on VMware products

This table outlines VMware vSphere support for Microsoft clustering solutions:

| | Microsoft Clustering on VMware | vSphere support | VMware HA support | vMotion DRS support | Storage vMotion support | MSCS Node Limits | Storage Protocols support | | | | | Shared Disk | |
							FC	In-Guest OS iSCSI	Native iSCSI	In-Guest OS SMB	FCoE	RDM	VMFS
Shared Disk	MSCS with Shared Disk	Yes	Yes[1]	No	No	2 5 (5.1 and 5.5)	Yes	Yes	Yes[6]	Yes[5]	Yes[4]	Yes[2]	Yes[3]
	Exchange Single Copy Cluster	Yes	Yes[1]	No	No	2 5 (5.1 and 5.5)	Yes	Yes	Yes[6]	Yes[5]	Yes[4]	Yes[2]	Yes[3]
	SQL Clustering	Yes	Yes[1]	No	No	2 5 (5.1 and 5.5)	Yes	Yes	Yes[6]	Yes[5]	Yes[4]	Yes[2]	Yes[3]
	SQL AlwaysOn Failover Cluster Instance	Yes	Yes[1]	No	No	2 5 (5.1 and 5.5)	Yes	Yes	Yes[6]	Yes[5]	Yes[4]	Yes[2]	Yes[3]
Non shared Disk	Network Load Balance	Yes	Yes[1]	Yes	Yes	Same as OS/app	Yes	Yes	Yes	N/A	Yes	N/A	N/A
	Exchange CCR	Yes	Yes[1]	Yes	Yes	Same as OS/app	Yes	Yes	Yes	N/A	Yes	N/A	N/A
	Exchange DAG	Yes	Yes[1]	Yes	Yes	Same as OS/app	Yes	Yes	Yes	N/A	Yes	N/A	N/A
	SQL AlwaysOn Availability Group	Yes	Yes[1]	Yes	Yes	Same as OS/app	Yes	Yes	Yes	N/A	Yes	N/A	N/A

Figure 11.5   VMware KB 1037959.

As discussed in Chapter 6, "Architecting for Performance: Storage," the number, type, and queue depth settings of virtual SCSI adapters can have an impact on the performance of the virtual machine. This section will discuss configuration of four virtual SCSI adapters and the placement of VMDKs for the SQL Server 2012 virtual machines. We will use the default settings so we have an understanding of vSphere 5.5's out-of-the-box capabilities. This will allow for the generation of a baseline, so if necessary we can make adjustments and measure their impact.

> **NOTE**
>
> Although additional settings can be made to increase performance of the system, you should weigh the impact of these setting versus running a close to a default configuration as possible. Remember the "Keep It Simple" rule—it scales better than having a bunch of one-off configurations. But if you need it, use it.

To add additional virtual SCSI adapters to a virtual machine, browse to the virtual machine and click **Edit Settings**. When the virtual machine's dialog box pops up, click the down arrow next to **New device:** and select **SCSI Controller** (see Figure 11.6) and then click **Add**.

Figure 11.6   Adding a virtual SCSI controller to a virtual machine.

After you click **Add**, you will notice a new entry for New SCSI controller has appeared in the dialog box. Click the down arrow to expand this selection, and select **VMware Paravirtual** as the controller type, as shown in Figure 11.7.

Click **Add** and repeat this process until three new SCSI controllers have been added.

For the purposes of this lab, we striped the VMDKs across the three available datastores in our datastore cluster. All three of our datastores have the same performance characteristics and are roughly the same size. We attempted to distribute them as much as possible to spread out the load. When looking at VMDK placement on the disk subsystem, it is important to match the VMDK's purpose (OS and binary versus log drive) to the underlying storage. For more information on the VMDK-to-datastore mapping, read Chapter 6, which goes into various configuration options available for your configuration.

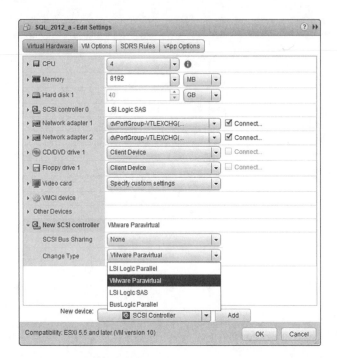

Figure 11.7   Changing the virtual controller type to VMware Paravirtual.

Next, we are going to add VMDKs to the virtual machine and strategically place them on the new SCSI controllers. Click the down arrow next to **New device** and select **New Hard Disk** and click **Add**. A new line will appear in the dialog window labeled New Hard Disk. Click the down arrow and make the following changes:

- Correct VMDK size based on the size of the test. Note that each VMDK may be a different size based on its function (database, logs, tempdb, backup).

- Select **Thick provision eager zeroed**.

- Set **Virtual Device Node** (see Table 11.2 for information on how we striped them the VMDKs for these two virtual machines).

Figure 11.8 displays a screenshot of the preceding bullet points and how we configured them for our lab.

Repeat this process until the required number of VMDKs has been added to the virtual machine, as depicted in Figure 11.9, and then click **OK** to commit the changes to the virtual machine. Repeat this process on all SQL Server 2012 virtual machines that will participate in the AlwaysOn Availability Group. For the purposes of our configuration, we configured both SQL_2012_a and SQL_2012_b with the configuration detailed in Table 11.2. If you are a visual type, see Figure 11.10 for a visual representation of the SCSI controller and VMDK layout.

Figure 11.8   Adding and configuring the VMDK file.

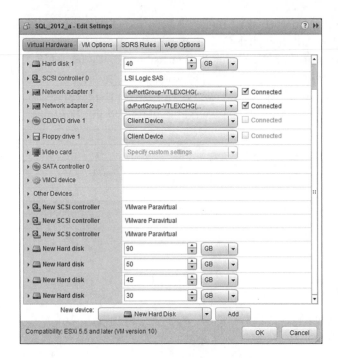

Figure 11.9   Review the added SCSI controllers and VMDKs.

Table 11.2   VMDK File Layout on Virtual Machines

Virtual Machine Name	VMDK Size	Disk Name	Virtual Device Node
SQL_2012_a	40GB	OS and SQL Binaries	0:0
SQL_2012_a	90GB	backup	0:1
SQL_2012_a	50GB	logs	1:0
SQL_2012_a	45GB	database	2:0
SQL_2012_a	30GB	tempdb	3:0
SQL_2012_b	40GB	OS and SQL Binaries	0:0
SQL_2012_b	90GB	backup	0:1
SQL_2012_b	50GB	logs	1:0
SQL_2012_b	45GB	database	2:0
SQL_2012_b	30GB	tempdb	3:0

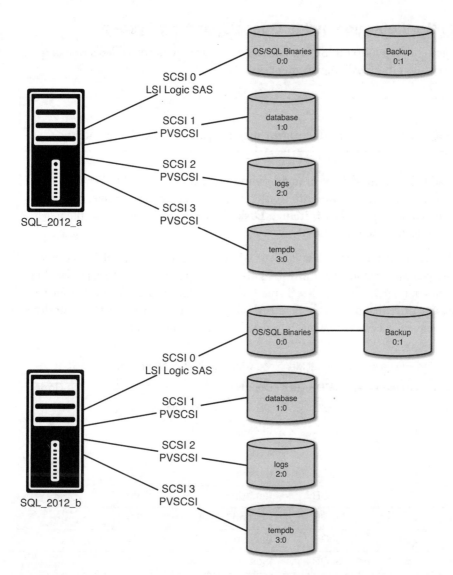

Figure 11.10   Layout of VMDK files for SQL_2012_a and SQL_2012_b.

NOTE

SCSI0 is LSI Logic SAS since we are only putting the OS and backup VMDKs on this adapter. For configurations in which we would put a VMDK-hosting DB or log data, we would make this a Paravirtual SCSI adapter. For more information on the differences between the LSI Logic SAS and Paravirtual SCSI adapter and when to use them, read Chapter 6.

VMDK File Configuration Inside Guest Operating System

Now we are going to log in to our SQL VMs and configure the newly added storage. After logging in, navigate to the Disk Management utility.

> **TIP**
>
> From a PowerShell prompt, type **diskmgmt.msc** to open the Disk Manager utility.

The recently added disks need to be brought online and initialized. Right-click each of the newly added disks and select **Online**. After bringing all the added disks online, right-click one of newly added disks and select **Initialize Disk**. A wizard opens; ensure all the newly added disks are selected and select **OK**.

After the disks have been initialized, it is time to assign them drive letters. Before clicking a disk, make sure you understand what the disk's purpose is so you can ensure proper labeling to coincide with your VMDK layout. See Table 11.3 for the layout used. You will notice we are using the same drive mapping for both virtual machines; ensure that whatever your drive-letter-naming scheme is, both virtual machines are identical to one another.

Table 11.3   VMDK File Layout on Virtual Machines with Drive Letter Mappings

Virtual Machine	Drive Letter	VMDK Size	Disk Name	Virtual Device Node
SQL_2012_a	C:\	40GB	OS and SQL Binaries	0:0
SQL_2012_a	R:\	90GB	backup	0:1
SQL_2012_a	L:\	50GB	logs	1:0
SQL_2012_a	K:\	45GB	database	2:0
SQL_2012_a	T:\	30GB	tempdb	3:0
SQL_2012_b	C:\	40GB	OS and SQL Binaries	0:0
SQL_2012_b	R:\	90GB	backup	0:1
SQL_2012_b	L:\	50GB	logs	1:0
SQL_2012_b	K:\	45GB	database	2:0
SQL_2012_b	T:\	30GB	tempdb	3:0

It is important as you go through this process that you understand which disk inside Windows is related to which VMDK file. As you can see from Figure 11.11, SQL_2012_a and SQL_2012_b added the VMDK files in a different order, assigning them as different disks. For example, SQL_2012_a added the 45GB drive as Disk 2 whereas SQL_2012_b added the 50GB drive as Disk 2.

> **TIP**
>
> To help identify which virtual disk is used by Windows, see this KB article: http://kb.vmware.com/kb/1033105.

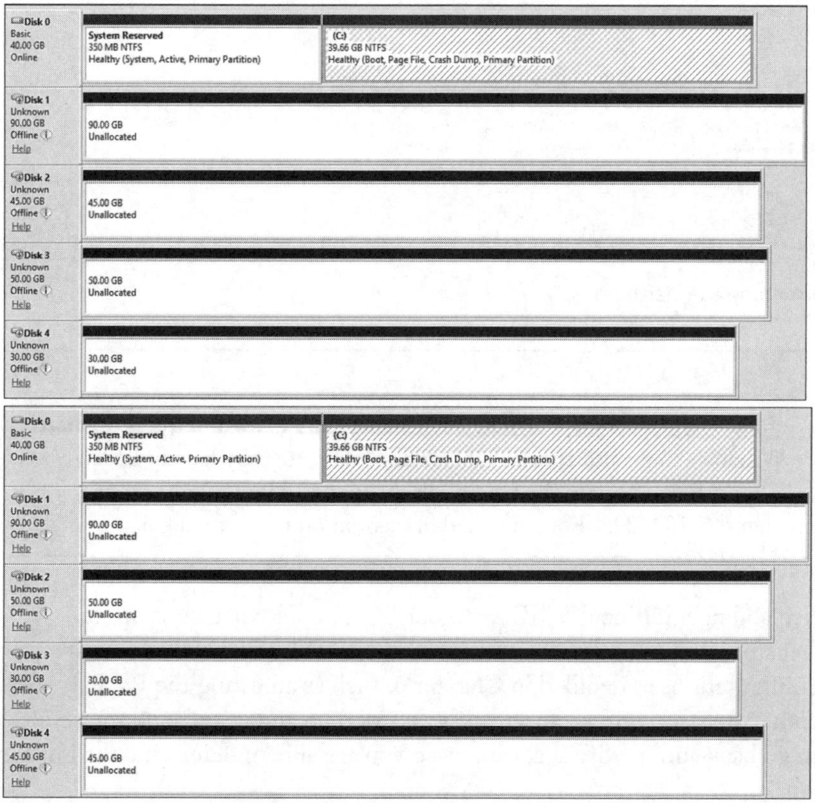

Figure 11.11 Disk assignment discrepancies.

Once the disks have been initialized and brought online, right-click the appropriate disk and select **New Simple Volume** to bring up the New Simple Volume Wizard. In the wizard, click **Next** to begin. Click **Next** on the Specify Volume Size page. On the Assign Drive Letter or Path page, select the correct drive letter and click **Next**. On the Format Partition page, change the **Allocation unit size** to **64K**, label the volume appropriately, and click **Next** (see Figure 11.12). On the final page of the wizard, the Completing the New Simple Volume Wizard, click **Finish**. Repeat these steps until all the disks have been added for both SQL Servers' virtual machines.

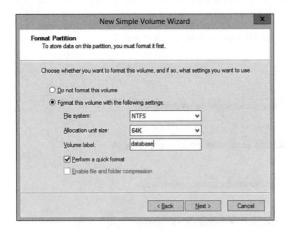

Figure 11.12 Formatting the partition.

TIP

If Eager Thick Zeroed was not selected earlier, unchecking the **Perform a quick format** option will force Windows to go and check every block of disk, thereby having ESXi touch every block. For information on the type of disks supported by ESXi hosts, see http://kb.vmware.com/kb/1022242. For a detailed discussion on these, read Chapter 6.

We have completed adding additional VMDKs to our SQL Server virtual machines and configured that storage appropriately (see Figure 11.13). We will not be doing any of the advanced configurations as detailed in Chapter 6, such as adjusting the PVSCI adapter queue depth. After the configuration has been stood up and tested, and the results documented, then go back and modify accordingly so you are able to determine the impact of the modifications.

Volume	Layout	Type	File System	Status	Capacity	Free Space	% Free
(C:)	Simple	Basic	NTFS	Healthy (Boot, Page File, Crash Dump, Primary Partition)	39.66 GB	27.02 GB	68 %
backup (R:)	Simple	Basic	NTFS	Healthy (Primary Partition)	90.00 GB	89.90 GB	100 %
database (K:)	Simple	Basic	NTFS	Healthy (Primary Partition)	45.00 GB	44.90 GB	100 %
logs (L:)	Simple	Basic	NTFS	Healthy (Primary Partition)	50.00 GB	49.90 GB	100 %
System Reserved	Simple	Basic	NTFS	Healthy (System, Active, Primary Partition)	350 MB	109 MB	31 %
tempdb (T:)	Simple	Basic	NTFS	Healthy (Primary Partition)	30.00 GB	29.90 GB	100 %

Figure 11.13 Disk layout completed.

Memory Reservations

Protecting memory around certain applications can have a positive impact on their performance. VMware best practices have stated that for production, latency-sensitive systems, reserve memory for the virtual machine. This setting can be enabled or disabled while the virtual machine is running. There are two options when setting a memory reservation. A fixed setting can be configured, and this is the amount of memory for this virtual machine that will be reserved for that virtual machine. The second option is for a dynamic setting that will adjust as the memory assigned the virtual machine changes. For a detailed explanation, refer to Chapter 7, "Architecting for Performance: Memory."

To enable memory reservations for the full virtual machine, open the properties of the virtual machine, expand **Memory**, check the **Reserve all guest memory (All locked)** box (see Figure 11.14), and then click **OK**. Repeat these steps on all SQL Server virtual machines participating in this test.

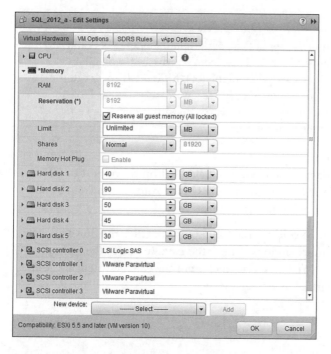

Figure 11.14   Enabling memory reservations.

NOTE

Because this setting is dynamic, during the test, enable, disable, and adjust the size of the reservation to observe the impact of the setting.

Enabling Hot Add Memory and Hot Add CPU

One of the many benefits of virtualizing SQL 2012 on vSphere is the ability to add memory and CPU resources to the SQL Servers while they are running. This configuration setting must be set while the VM is in a powered-off state, so shut down both SQL Server virtual machines. If you try to enable these settings while a virtual machine is powered on, they will be grayed out.

CAUTION

As discussed in Chapter 5, "Architecting for Performance: Design," when enabling hot plug for virtual machines, you will disable vNUMA. There are benefits to using vNUMA and there are benefits to using hot plug capabilities, so choose appropriately. This KB article contains more information: http://kb.vmware.com/kb/2040375.

NOTE

Make sure the operating system and the application *both* support adding CPU and memory while the system is running. Go to VMware.com's VMware Compatibility Guide website, select Guest OS (What are you looking for), ESXi 5.5 (Product Release Version), Microsoft (OS Vendor), and under Virtual Hardware, select either Hot Add Memory or Hot Plug vCPU. OS vendors will also only support this option at certain license levels for both the OS and the application.

Right-click the virtual machine you want to change. Click the drop-down next to CPU and check the box next to **CPU Hot Plug / Enable CPU Hot Add**, as shown in Figure 11.15, and before clicking OK, proceed to the next step.

Click the down arrow next to CPU to collapse the CPU options. Click the down arrow next to Memory to expose the memory options. Check the **Enable** box to the right of **Memory Hot Plug** (see Figure 11.16). Click **OK** to commit the changes. Repeat these steps on the second SQL Server virtual machine.

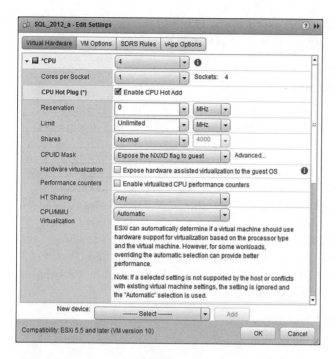

Figure 11.15   Enabling CPU Hot Add.

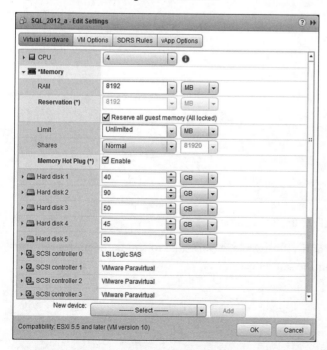

Figure 11.16   Enabling Memory Hot Plug.

We have successfully configured Hot Add for CPU and Hot Add for Memory. In the next section, we are going to configure affinity rules for the virtual machines.

Affinity and Anti-Affinity Rules

Since we are in still in the vSphere web client, we are going to stay here and configure rules to ensure that the SQL Server virtual machines do not reside on the same physical host.

These settings are configured at the cluster level. If necessary, click the **Host and Cluster** view within the vSphere web client. Locate the cluster in which you want to enable this option and click it. Next click the **Manage** tab, and then click **DRS Rules**. Under the DRS Rules heading, click the **Add** button. In the Create DRS Rule Wizard, enter a name for the rule, ensure the check box next to **Enable rule** is checked, and select **Type: Separate Virtual Machines**. Then click the **Add** button to locate and select the SQL Server virtual machines and click **OK** (see Figure 11.17). Verify the rule has been configured correctly and then click **OK** to create the rule.

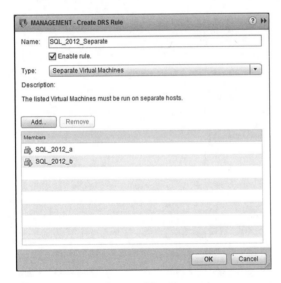

Figure 11.17   Creating an anti-affinity rule.

Now that we have configured the anti-affinity rule, we are able to simulate failures during our testing and ensure the VMs on the same host.

Validate the Network Connections

This section covers validating that we have the binding order of our network adapters correct for our virtual machines. We want to ensure our routable IP address has the highest priority.

We have labeled our network adapters **LAN** and **Heartbeat**. The LAN network is connected to the routable network and the Heartbeat network is a nonroutable network. It should be noted that for our Heartbeat network, we only configured the IP address and subnet mask.

To validate the setting, open **Control Panel, Network and Internet, Network Connections**. Then press the **Alt** key and select **Advanced, Advanced Settings...** to open the Advanced Settings dialog box. On the **Adapters and Bindings** tab, locate Connections and ensure the routable network (LAN) is listed at the top (see Figure 11.18). Perform this on all virtual machines that are part of this configuration.

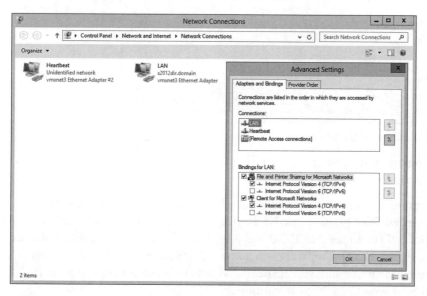

Figure 11.18 Validating the network adapter binding order.

Configuring Windows Failover Clustering

This section covers installation of the Windows .NET Framework 3.5.1 and Failover Clustering.

From the Windows 2012 Server Manager Dashboard, click the **Add roles and features** hyperlink. Click **Next** on the **Before you begin** page. Ensure the **Role-based or feature-based installation** radio button is selected (see Figure 11.19) and click **Next**.

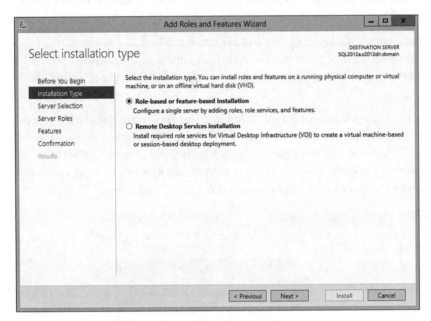

Figure 11.19   Selecting the installation type.

On the **Select destination server** page, ensure the correct SQL Server virtual machine is selected, as shown in Figure 11.20, and click **Next**.

On the **Select server roles** page, do not select any boxes and click **Next**. On the **Select features** page, expand **.Net Framework 3.5 Features** and check the box adjacent to **.Net Framework 3.5 (includes .NET 2.0 and 3.0)**. Further down the list, click **Failover Clustering** (see Figure 11.21). This will open a new dialog box prompting you to install additional features that are required for managing Windows Failover Clustering; on this page, click **Add Features**. Click **Next** to continue.

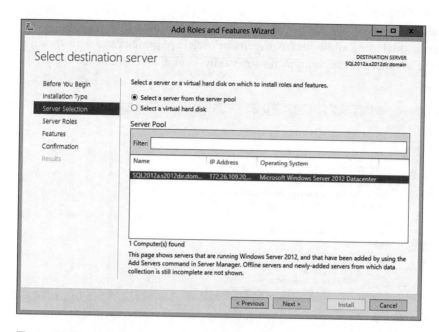

Figure 11.20   Selecting the virtual machine to modify.

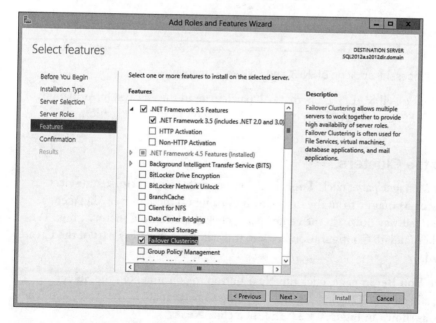

Figure 11.21   Selecting the right features.

On the **Confirm installation selections** page, confirm .NET Framework 3.5 and
Failover Clustering (including additional management tools) are present and then click
Install. When the installation has completed successfully, click **Close** to exit the wizard
(see Figure 11.22).

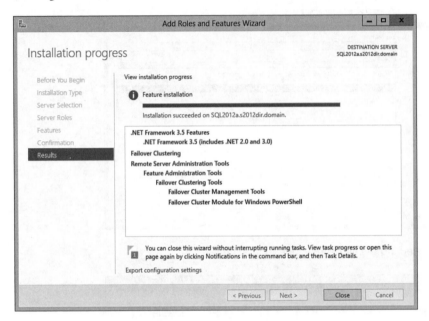

Figure 11.22   Successful addition of .NET and Failover Clustering.

Repeat these steps on all SQL Servers that will participate in the AlwaysOn Availability
Group. Once all the servers have been configured, move on to the next section.

Setting Up the Clusters

On the Server Manager page, click **Tools** in the upper right, click **Tools**, and select
Failover Cluster Manager from the drop-down to bring up the Failover Manager
interface. About halfway down, in the center pane, click the **Create Cluster...** link. We
are skipping the Validate Configuration because this will be included as part of the Create
Cluster Wizard.

On the **Before You Begin** page, click the **Next** button to continue. On the **Select
Servers** page, add all the SQL Servers that are going to participate in the AlwaysOn Availability Group, as shown in Figure 11.23, and then click **Next**.

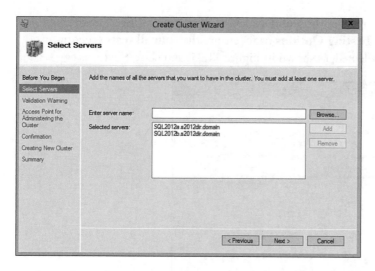

Figure 11.23 Adding the SQL Server virtual machines.

On the Validation Warning page, shown in Figure 11.24, select **Yes. When I click Next, run configuration validation tests, and then return to the process of creating the cluster.**

> **NOTE**
>
> For more information on the Cluster Validation Wizard, see http://technet.microsoft.com/library/jj134244.

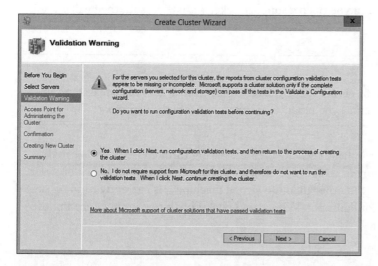

Figure 11.24 Launching the Cluster Validation Wizard.

On the **Before You Begin** page of the **Validate a Configuration Wizard** page, click **Next** to continue. On the **Testing Options** page, ensure the **Run all tests (recommended)** radio button is selected, as shown in Figure 11.25, and click **Next**.

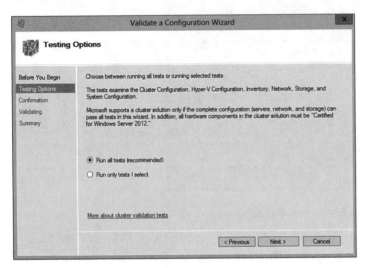

Figure 11.25   Run all tests for a cluster validation.

On the **Confirmation** page, verify the settings are correct and click **Next** to begin the testing. After the test is finished, it will provide a status detailing the results of the analysis. It is important for production environments that a copy of this report is retained (somewhere other than the default location of the report). In addition, anytime you modify the cluster, you should always rerun the report and save this report as well. The reason for retaining these reports is if you open a support ticket with Microsoft, they will ask for these validation reports.

TIP

It is important a copy of the cluster validation report is retained. Also remember to rerun the cluster validation each time you modify the cluster and save the new report.

This information can come in handy when you are working through issues. You can do this by clicking **View Report** (see Figure 11.26), and when the report opens in a browser, save the report off to a location other than the virtual machine it is currently running on. Return to the Validate a Configuration Wizard and click **Finish** to continue creating the cluster.

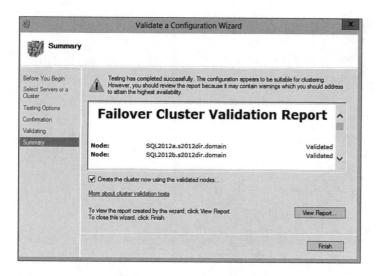

Figure 11.26   Completing the validation wizard.

On the **Access Point for Administering the Cluster** page, type in a unique name for the cluster (wfc4sql01) and a valid IP address. As shown in Figure 11.27, you can see we used 172.26.109.150 for our configuration.

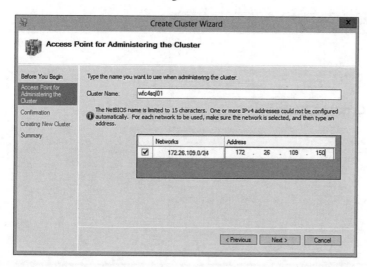

Figure 11.27   Naming and IPing the cluster.

On the **Confirmation** page, verify the settings, uncheck the **Add all eligible storage to the cluster** box (see Figure 11.28), and then click **Next** to continue.

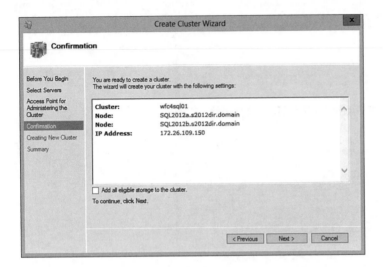

Figure 11.28   Confirmation and unchecking the option to add storage to the cluster.

After the wizard completes, you should see the **Summary** page, shown in Figure 11.29, and it should contain a message indicating you have successfully completed the Create Cluster Wizard. Click **Finish** to close the wizard.

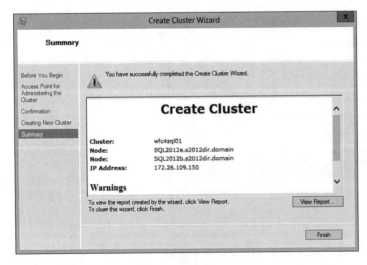

Figure 11.29   Successfully completing the Create Cluster Wizard.

Open the Failover Cluster Manager and verify the cluster is up and functioning properly.

If you open the Failover Cluster Manager and receive an error like the one in Figure 11.30, this is a known issue and there is a patch available. The patch is located at http://support.microsoft.com/kb/2803748. The patch can be applied manually or you can perform a Windows Update after installing Windows Failover Clustering. Install this patch on all servers participating in the Windows Failover Cluster. For this setup, we ran a Windows Update.

Figure 11.30 Weak event error.

We will verify that Active Directory has been populated with the name of our cluster and DNS has the correct IP address. On the AD DS virtual machine, open **Active Directory Users and Computers** and click the **Computers** OU. In this OU, locate the cluster name configured in a previous section (WFC4SQL01). Next, open DNS Manager and locate the corresponding DNS entry (wfc4sql01 172.26.109.150). In Figure 11.31, we see the Failover Cluster virtual network name account as well as the DNS entry for this account.

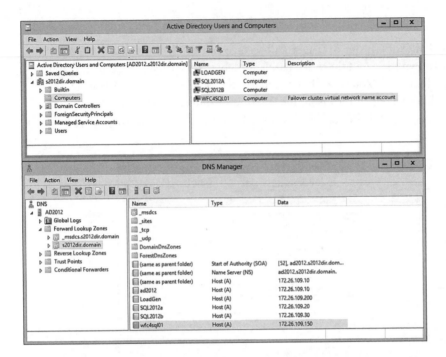

Figure 11.31   Validating Active Directory and DNS have the correct cluster information.

This concludes the setup and configuration of Windows Failover Clustering. In the next section, we will validate the network configuration for the cluster.

Validate Cluster Network Configuration

Next, we want to verify the network configuration for the cluster is correct and we are allowing client communication on the right network, our routable network (LAN), and not down our nonroutable network (Heartbeat). To do this, open the **Failover Cluster Manager** from Windows Server Manager (under **Tools** in the upper right). Connect to the newly created cluster (wfc4sql01.s2012.domain) and expand **Network**. Click **Cluster Network 1** and then **Properties**. For Cluster Network 1, we see this contains our routable network and there is a check box next to **Allow clients to connect through this network**. Close the dialog box and repeat for Cluster Network 2. On the Cluster Network 2 dialog box, we identify this is using our nonroutable network and there is no check mark next to **Allow clients to connect through this network**. Figure 11.32 shows Cluster Network properties for Network 1 and Network 2 in a side-by-side comparison.

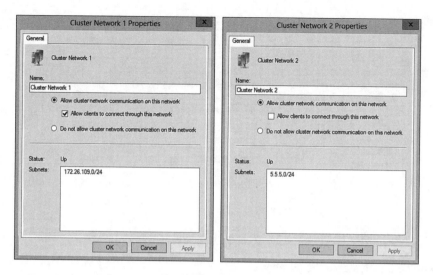

Figure 11.32   Validating clustering network configuration.

Changing Windows Failover Cluster Quorum Mode

We are now going to change the cluster's quorum configuration mode from its current setting, Node Majority, to Node and File Share Majority. Because we are going to create a file share witness, we need to create a share the SQL Servers will be able to access. We will create this share on the Windows 8.1 virtual machine.

On the Windows 8.1 virtual machine, we have created an additional VMDK. The reason we added the additional storage is if we need to dynamically grow this VMDK file because we are running low on available disk space.

After we added the additional storage, we presented it as the **R:** drive and created a folder called **MSSQL**. Then we created and nested a folder called **WFCFS01** inside **MSSQL**.

On the folder that was created for the file share (WFCFS01), right-click the folder and select **Properties**, click the **Sharing** tab, click the **Advanced Sharing** button, check **Share this folder** on the Advanced Sharing dialog box, and click the **Permissions** button. On the Permissions for (WFCFS01) dialog box, under **Group or user names:**, click the **Add:** button. On the Select Users, Computers, Service Accounts, or Groups dialog box, click the **Object Types** button. On the Object Types dialog box, check **Computers** and click **OK**. On the Select Users, Computers, Service Accounts, or Groups dialog box, in the **Enter the object names to select** section, enter the name of the cluster that has been created (wfc4sql01). Once the cluster name has been added, click **OK** in the Select Users, Computers, Service Accounts, or Groups dialog box. On the Permissions for (WFCFS01) dialog box, ensure the cluster name has **Change** permissions. Figure 11.33 shows what these steps look like on a Windows 8.1 operating system.

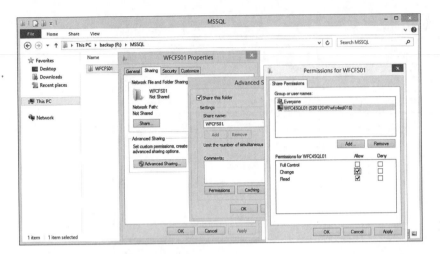

Figure 11.33   Adding the cluster to the file share.

Click **OK** to close out the Permissions for (WFCFS01) dialog box, click **OK** to click out of the Advanced Sharing dialog box, and finally click **Close** to exit the (WFCFS01) Properties dialog box. We are done with the Windows 8.1 virtual machine for the moment. We are now going to switch over to our SQL virtual machine where the Windows Failover Cluster has been configured.

From the Failover Cluster Manager interface on our SQL Server, right-click the cluster (wfc4sql01.s2012dir.domain) and select **More Actions**, **Configure Cluster Quorum Settings…**, as shown in Figure 11.34.

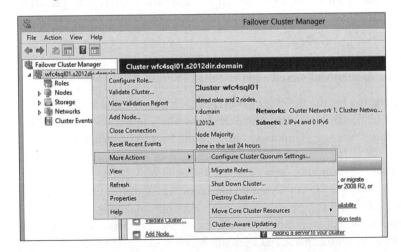

Figure 11.34   Opening the Configure Cluster Quorum Wizard.

On the Before You Begin page, click **Next**. On the Select Quorum Configuration Option page, select the **Add or change the quorum witness** radio button (see Figure 11.35) and click **Next**.

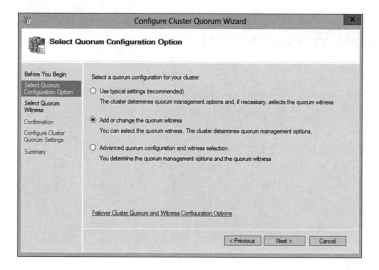

Figure 11.35   Changing the quorum witness.

On the Select Quorum Witness dialog box, select **Configure a file share witness (recommended for special configurations),** as shown in Figure 11.36, and click **Next.**

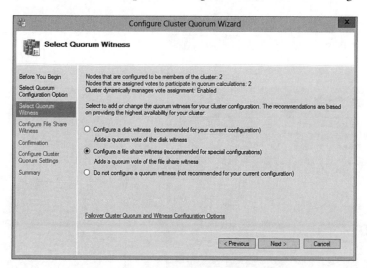

Figure 11.36   Choosing the file share witness option.

On the **Configure File Share Witness** dialog page, enter the path to the file share that was created earlier in this section (for our configuration, **\\LOADGEN\WFCFS01**) and click **Next**. See Figure 11.37 for our configuration. After you click **Next**, the file share path will be validated.

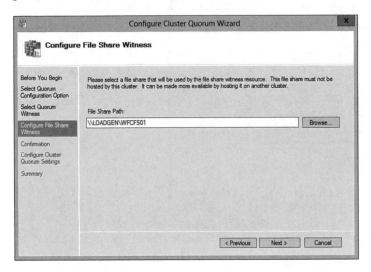

Figure 11.37   Entering the file share path.

On the **Confirmation** page, shown in Figure 11.38, verify the information is correct and then click **Next**.

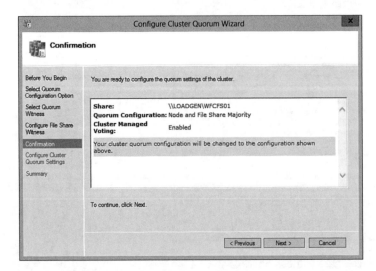

Figure 11.38   Confirming the configuration.

On the **Summary** page, shown in Figure 11.39, review the report to ensure all settings were configured properly and then click **Finish** to exit the wizard.

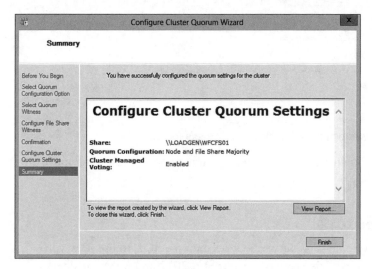

Figure 11.39   Configuration complete.

On the Failover Cluster Manager, in the summary section, **Quorum Configuration** should now reflect the updated setting of **Node and File Share Majority,** as depicted in Figure 11.40.

Figure 11.40   Viewing the configuration change.

In addition, back on the Windows 8.1 virtual machine, in the folder that was used for the File Share Majority, we can see a new folder was created, and when we open this folder, we see that two files have been created, **VerifyShareWriteAccess.txt** and **Witness.log,** as shown in Figure 11.41.

Figure 11.41   Viewing files written inside the file share witness folder.

This completes the section on changing the cluster quorum mode. Next, we will move on to installing SQL Server 2012.

Installing SQL Server 2012

The first thing we are going to do is create a service account for SQL to use. We will create a service account in Active Directory named **svcSQL2012** and we will uncheck **User must change password at next logon**, check **User cannot change password**, and check **Password never expires**, as shown in Figure 11.42.

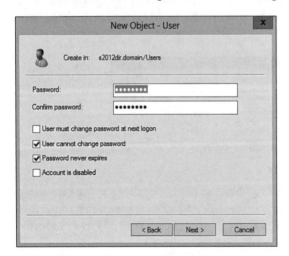

Figure 11.42   Creating a SQL service account.

On the first SQL Server, mount the SQL Server 2012 ISO and launch the installation wizard. On the **SQL Server Installation Center**, on the left-hand side, click **Installation**, and then on the right, click **New SQL Server stand-alone installation or add features to an existing installation**. Figure 11.43 represents the installation screen.

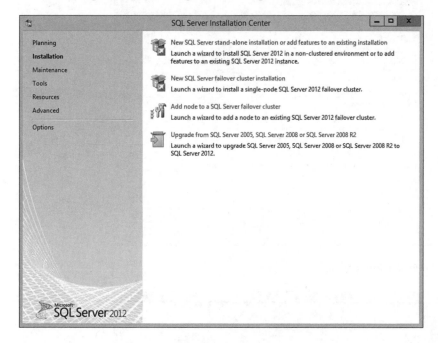

Figure 11.43   Starting the installation of a new SQL Server.

The install will run through a preflight check (see Figure 11.44). If any issues are identified, remediate them now. When ready, click **OK** to continue the installation.

On the **Product Key** page, shown in Figure 11.45, specify if you are using the free edition or if you have a product key, either validate or enter the product key, and click **Next**.

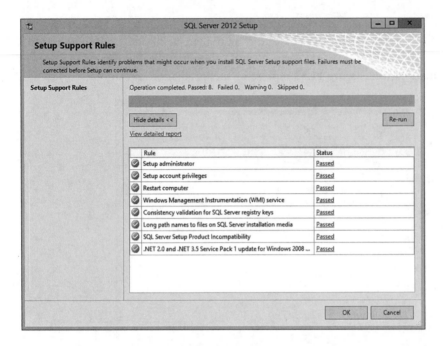

Figure 11.44   Setup preflight check.

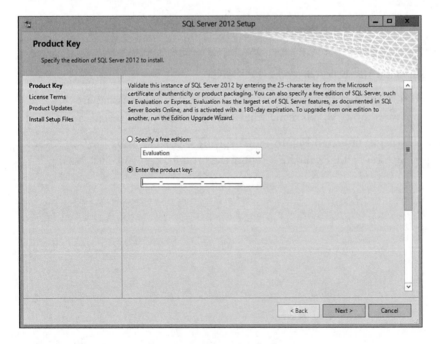

Figure 11.45   Entering the appropriate product key.

On the **License Terms** page, shown in Figure 11.46, check the box next to **I accept the license terms** and then click **Next** (only after reading through and understanding the license terms).

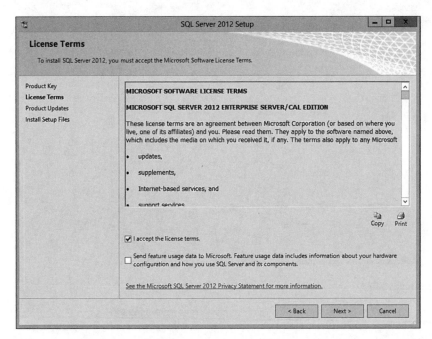

Figure 11.46   Reviewing the license terms.

On the **Product Updates** page, shown in Figure 11.47, click **Next** to install the latest updates. The installer will now run through several tasks and report the status of each task's progress.

After the previous tasks have finished, another analysis is performed to identify any issues that may prevent a successful installation. If there are any issues, remediate them at this time (see Figure 11.48). When ready, click **Next** to continue.

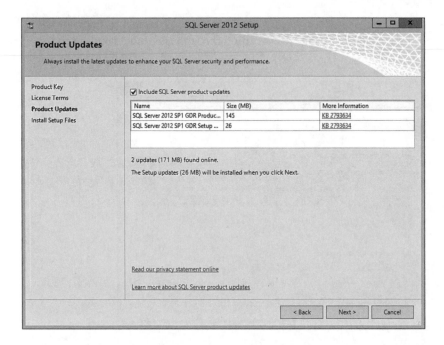

Figure 11.47 Updating SQL.

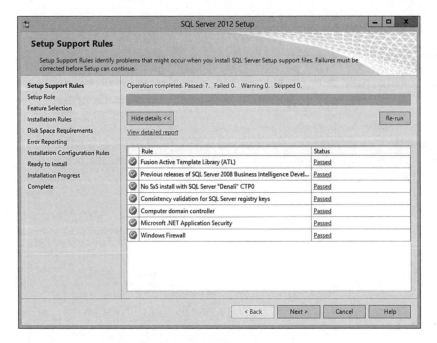

Figure 11.48 Preflight checks, part deux.

On the **Setup Role** page, shown in Figure 11.49, ensure the **SQL Server Feature Installation** radio button is selected and click **Next**.

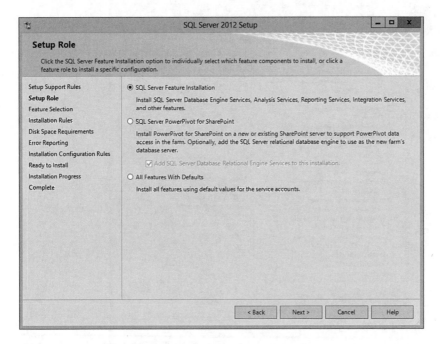

Figure 11.49   SQL Server feature installation.

On the **Feature Selection** page, shown in Figure 11.50, select the following eight features, configure the installation directory if necessary, and click **Next** when finished.

- Database Engine Services
- SQL Server Replication
- Full-Text and Semantic Extractions for Search
- SQL Server Data Tools
- Client Tools Connectivity
- Documentation Components
- Management Tools - Basic
- Management Tools - Complete

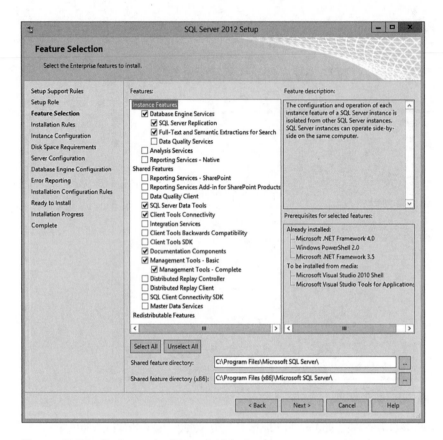

Figure 11.50   Feature selection—eight features.

On the **Installation Rules** page, shown in Figure 11.51, a series of checks will be performed. If there are any issues identified, remediate them now. When ready, click **Next** to continue.

On the **Instance Configuration** page, shown in Figure 11.52, for purposes of this installation, we are going with the defaults provided; therefore, click **Next** to continue.

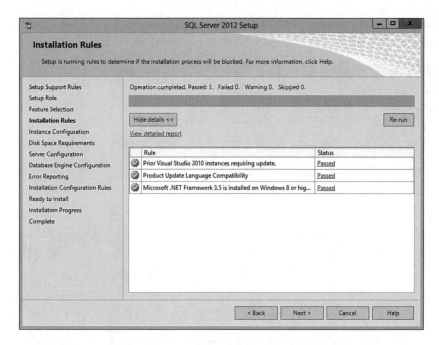

Figure 11.51   Installation rules validation check.

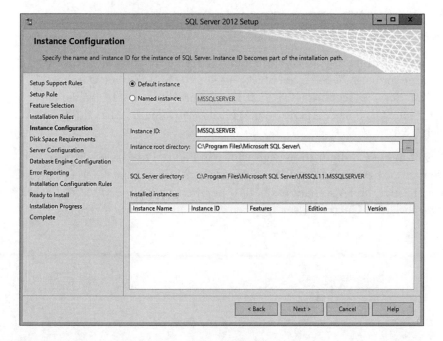

Figure 11.52   Instance Configuration—Default.

On the **Disk Space Requirements** page, shown in Figure 11.53, verify there is enough disk space available for the installation and click **Next** to continue.

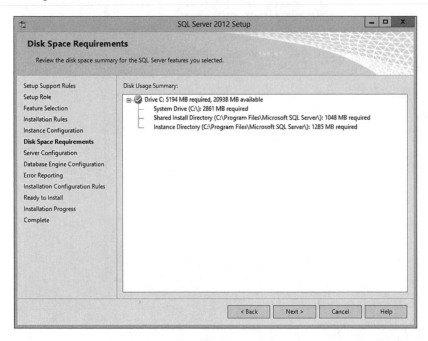

Figure 11.53   Validating disk space requirements.

On the **Server Configuration** page, shown in Figure 11.54, we are going to change the **Account Name** for both the **SQL Server Agent** and the **SQL Server Database Engine** to the **SQL Service Account** (svcSQL2012). We are also going to change the **Startup Type** for the **SQL Server Agent** from Manual to **Automatic**. After this has been configured, click **Next**.

On the **Database Engine Configuration** page, shown in Figure 11.55, select **Mixed Mode (SQL Server authentication and Windows authentication)** and enter a password for the SA account. After the SA account has been configured, under **Specify SQL Server administrators**, click **Add Current User** and then click the **Data Directories** tab.

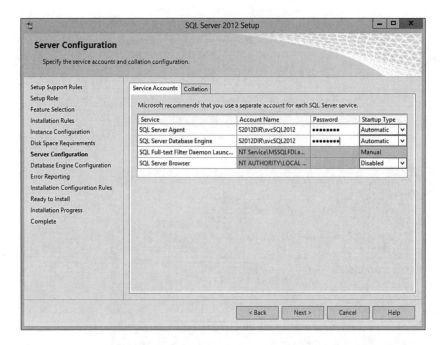

Figure 11.54 Configuring the server.

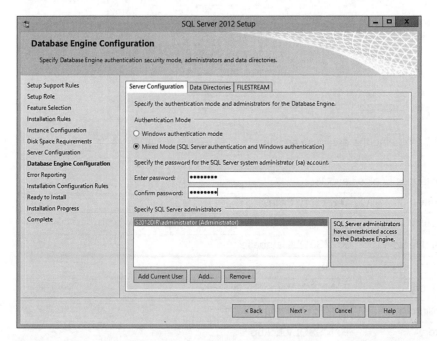

Figure 11.55 Configuring Mixed Mode and the SQL Server administrator.

On the **Data Directories** tab, shown in Figure 11.56, configure the proper location for the database, log, temp DB, and backup directories. Table 11.4 details how we have configured them in our lab.

> **NOTE**
> Be sure to configure all the SQL Servers with the exact same storage layout.

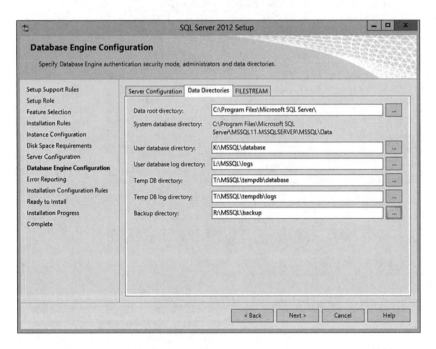

Figure 11.56   Configuring the database engine.

Table 11.4   Database Engine Layout

Directory Name	Directory Path
Data root directory	C:\Program Files\Microsoft SQL Server (default)
User database directory	K:\MSSQL\database
User database log directory	L:\MSSQL\logs
Temp DB directory	T:\MSSQL\tempdb\database
Temp DB log directory	T:\MSSQL\tempdb\logs
Backup directory	R:\MSSQL\backup

After configuring the directory paths, click **Next** to continue the installation.

On the **Error Reporting** page, shown in Figure 11.57, click **Next**.

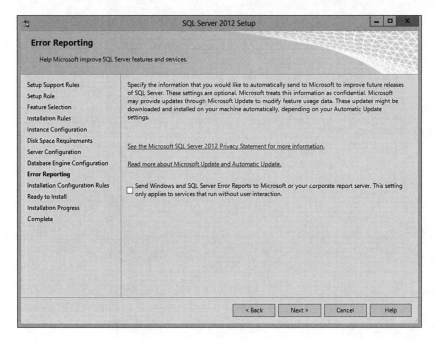

Figure 11.57   Determining the Error Reporting setting.

On the **Installation Configuration Rules** page, shown in Figure 11.58, another set of preflight checks will be run. If there are any issues identified, remediate them at this time. When ready, click **Next** to continue.

On the **Ready to Install** page, shown in Figure 11.59, review the settings to ensure they are correct. If they are correct, click **Install** to begin the installation.

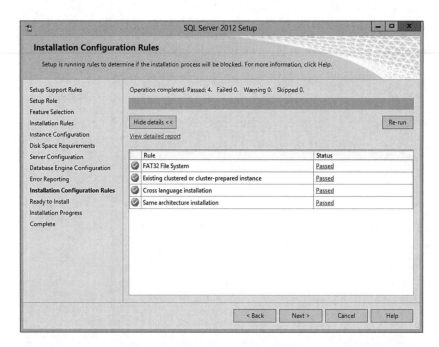

Figure 11.58   Further validation, one last time.

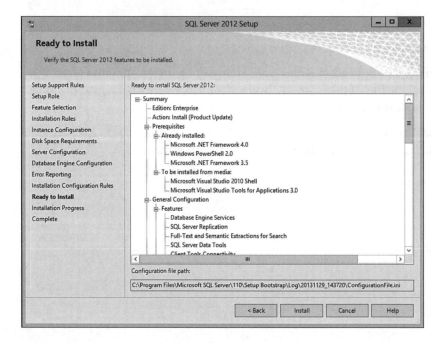

Figure 11.59   Almost there—validate the settings.

On the **Complete** page, shown in Figure 11.60, click **Close** to finish the installation and close the wizard. Repeat this section for all SQL Servers. Once you have installed SQL Server 2012 on all relevant virtual machines, proceed on to the next section.

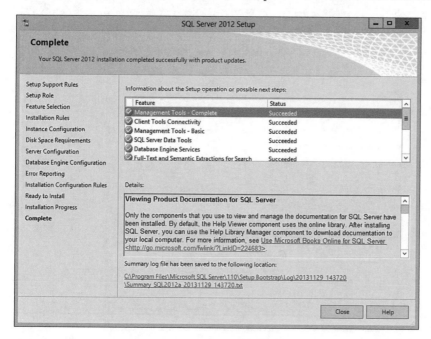

Figure 11.60   SQL Server installation complete.

This completes the installation of SQL Server 2012 on our virtual machines. The following section will cover the configuration of SQL Server for AlwaysOn Availability Groups.

Configuration of SQL Server 2012 AlwaysOn Availability Groups

In this section, we will configure various SQL Server 2012 settings, enable SQL Server 2012 AlwaysOn Availability Groups, and create a test database to ensure everything is working as expected.

The first step in the process is we are going to create a shared folder on our Windows 8.1 virtual machine. This share must be accessible to both of our SQL Server virtual machines. We are going to use our SQL Server account created in the previous section (svcSQL2012).

Figure 11.61 shows how we created a folder named **aobackup** inside of the MSSQL folder. We shared **aobackup** using the **SQL service account** (svcSQL2012) giving it

Read/Write access to the share. When you have everything configured appropriately, click **Share**, and take note of the share path because we will need this information in a future step. For our setup, the share is **\\LOADGEN\aobackup**.

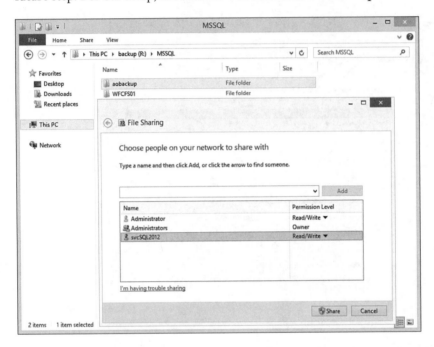

Figure 11.61   Creating a shared folder on the Windows 8.1 virtual machine.

We are done with the Windows 8.1 virtual machine for the time being; now let's get back to our SQL Servers.

Next, open the SQL Server Configuration Manager. Once this is open, click **SQL Server Services**, **SQL Server (MSSQLSERVER)**. Then right-click **SQL Server (MSSQLSERVER)** and select **Properties**. When the dialog box opens, click the **AlwaysOn High Availability** tab. On the AlwaysOn High Availability tab, place a check mark next to **Enable AlwaysOn Availability Groups** and then click **Apply**. Click **OK** to acknowledge the warning message stating the SQL Server service requires restarting prior to the setting taking effect. Figure 11.62 displays what this looks like on a Windows Server 2012 operating system.

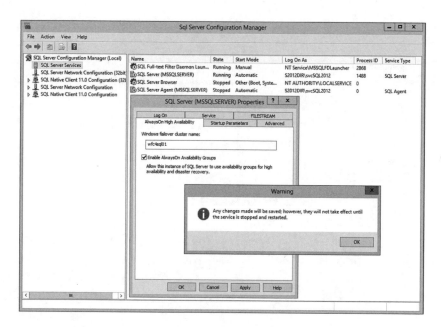

Figure 11.62   Enabling AlwaysOn High Availability.

Now we are going to enable large pages for SQL Server. This is an optional parameter that can be part of your functional testing to determine the impact of enabling Large Pages with SQL Server. This feature is automatically enabled in SQL 2012 when you give the service account running sqlservr.exe **Lock Pages in Memory** permissions. For versions previous to SQL 2012, you must enable this trace flag along with the **Lock Pages in Memory** permission (configuration details in next step). Figure 11.63 shows how to enable the trace flag. Click the **Startup Parameters** tab. After the tab opens, type **–T834** and then click **Add**, click **OK**, and then click **OK** again to acknowledge the warning message. It should be noted this setting can only be turned on during startup and requires the Lock Pages in Memory user right to be configured (we do this in the next step).

NOTE

Microsoft does not recommend using this Large Pages trace flag when using the Column Store Index feature, per http://support.microsoft.com/kb/920093.

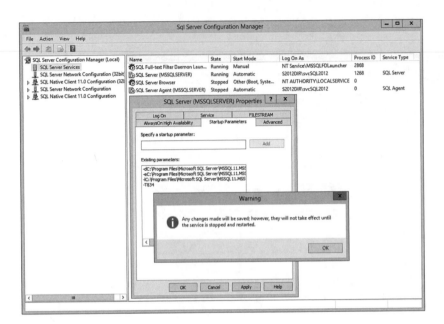

Figure 11.63   Enabling Large Pages in SQL Server.

> **NOTE**
>
> For more information on this and other trace flags available for SQL Server, visit Microsoft's KB article on the topic: http://support.microsoft.com/kb/920093.

Open the **Local Security Policy** management console. A quick way to do this is to open **PowerShell** and type **secpol.msc**. Once the console is open, locate and expand **Local Policies** and then click **User Rights Assignment**. Under the Policy column, locate **Lock pages in memory**. Right-click **Lock pages in memory** and select **Properties**. Add the SQL Service account (svcSQL2012) and click **OK** to configure the setting. Figure 11.64 shows what this looks like for Windows Server 2012. Verify for the **Lock pages in memory** policy that the SQL Service Account is listed under the Security Setting column. For more information on this setting, refer to Chapter 5 and Chapter 7, as these chapters both discuss this setting.

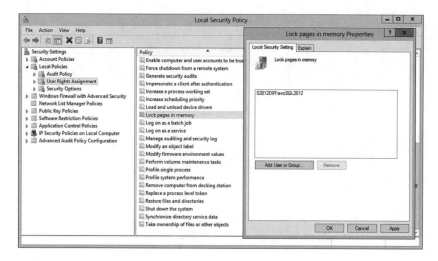

Figure 11.64 Enabling the Lock pages in memory setting.

> **NOTE**
>
> More information on the User Rights Assignment setting, refer to http://msdn.microsoft.com/en-us/library/ms178067.aspx.

Without closing the Local Security Policy Management Console, find **Perform volume maintenance tasks**. Right-click **Perform volume maintenance tasks** and select **Properties**. Add the SQL Service account (svcSQL2012, in our case) and click **OK** to commit the change. Figure 11.65 displays what this looks like on a Windows Server 2012 operating system. Verify the SQL Service account appears in the Security Setting column to the right of **Perform volume maintenance tasks** in addition to the Administrators account. For more information on this setting, review Chapter 6.

> **NOTE**
>
> More information on the Instant File Initialization setting, refer to http://msdn.microsoft.com/en-us/library/ms175935.aspx.

Repeat the enabling of AlwaysOn Availability Groups, Large Pages (if necessary), Lock Pages in Memory, and Perform Volume Maintenance steps on all SQL Servers participating in the AlwaysOn Availability Group.

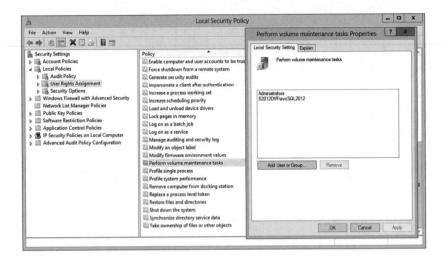

Figure 11.65   Enabling the Perform volume maintenance tasks setting.

Configuring the Min/Max Setting for SQL Server

As was discussed in Chapter 7, we are going to create a SQL Memory buffer pool, ensuring that the OS and non-SQL applications (backup programs, antivirus, and so on) have enough resources to run as expected. To do this, open Microsoft SQL Server Management Studio and right-click **SERVER NAME** and select **Properties**. On the **Server Properties - <Server Name>** page, click **Memory**. For purposes of our configuration, we left **Minimum server memory (in MB)** at the default setting of 0 and we configured **Maximum server memory (in MB)** at the default setting of 2,147,483,647 MB to see how SQL Server handles dynamically managing memory; this is shown in Figure 11.66. We left the default settings in to see what SQL 2012 can do "out of the box." This provides us a baseline to measure against as well as adheres to our "keep it simple" mantra. In additional testing, we would adjust these settings based on information and recommendations provided in Chapter 5 and Chapter 7 to determine the configuration that has the best net positive impact to our stack and weight these changes against the cost of implementing and managing these changes.

> **TIP**
>
> If you're using Hot Add Memory capabilities and memory is added dynamically, ensure that the max memory setting is adjusted to the new value.

Repeat this step for all SQL Server virtual machines.

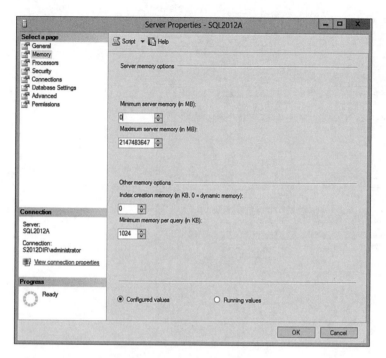

Figure 11.66   Configuring max/min memory.

Enabling Jumbo Frames

As discussed in Chapter 8, "Architecting for Performance: Network," if the network supports larger packet sizes, increasing SQL from the default packet size of 4,096 to a larger value can improve performance. The optimal value of the packet size for the packet is 8192, and this is only if your network can support jumbo frames of this size, end to end.

In the Microsoft SQL Server Management Studio, right-click **<SERVER>** and select **Properties**. On **Server Properties - <SERVER Name>**, click **Advanced** and under **Network** locate **Network Packet Size** and change this to the appropriate value, as shown in Figure 11.67.

> **NOTE**
>
> Make sure your network supports the larger packet sizes. Improper configuration can cause performance problems. DBAs and VMware admins should work with the Network team to understand the appropriate configuration based on their input and information provided in Chapter 8.

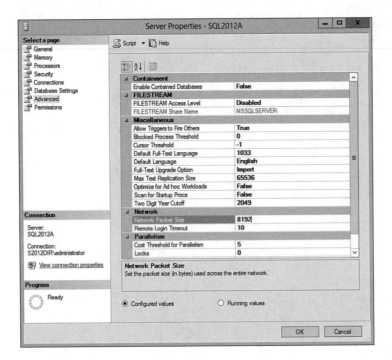

Figure 11.67   Configuring jumbo frames.

Repeat this step for all SQL Server virtual machines.

Creating Multiple tempdb Files

A recommendation Microsoft makes around the tempdb database is to create one data file per CPU. This is a setting you will want to work with the DBA team on because some systems may benefit from this setting and other systems will not. In addition, test for diminishing returns, meaning that after "x" number of additional tempdb data files, there is no benefit to performance. See Chapter 6 for more information.

> **NOTE**
>
> More information on the Instant File Initialization setting can be found at http://technet.microsoft.com/en-us/library/ms175527(v=sql.105).aspx.

On the SQL Server virtual machines, open the **SQL Server Management Studio**, expand **Databases**, expand **System Databases**, and click **tempdb**. Right-click **tempdb** and select **Properties**. Once the **Database Properties - tempdb** dialog box opens, click **Files** (located on the left). Then click **Add** and enter the proper number of additional tempdb data files. Figure 11.68 displays the tempdb configuration we used in our lab. When you are done configuring your tempdb files, click **OK** to build the files and close the dialog box.

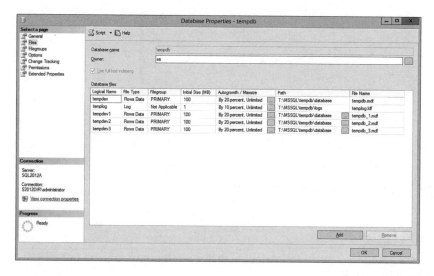

Figure 11.68 Adding tempdb data files.

Repeat this step on all SQL Servers participating in the AlwaysOn Availability Group.

To determine whether the files were created successfully, browse to the path entered for the additional tempdb data files to validate they were created. Figure 11.69 shows successful creation of our tempdb data files.

At this point, we rebooted each SQL Server virtual machine to ensure the settings we just configured are applied. We reboot them individually, making sure the first server was up and all services started before initiating the second reboot.

> **NOTE**
>
> If the SQL Service is not restarted, AlwaysOn Availability Groups will not work and some of the configuration settings are only applied at boot time, which is why we are waiting until now for a reboot.

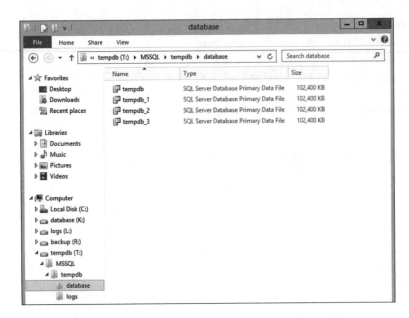

Figure 11.69   Verifying successful creation of tempdb data files.

Creating a Test Database

In this section we are going to create a test database that we will use to validate our AlwaysOn configuration is working as expected.

Open the Microsoft SQL Server Management Studio and connect into the database engine of one of the SQL Servers (SQL2012A). Once connected, expand the database engine for the SQL Server. Right-click **Databases** and select **New Database**. On the **New Database** page, enter a name for the database and click **OK**. Figure 11.70 shows us creating a test database named test01db.

Now that we have our database created, we need to back up the database. Now would be a good time to validate our database files and our log files were created in the proper locations (K:\MSSQL\database\test01db.mdf and L:\MSSQL\logs\test01db_log.ldf). Figure 11.71 confirms our database and log files were created in the proper location.

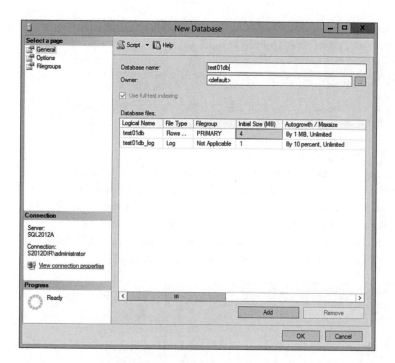

Figure 11.70   Creating a test database.

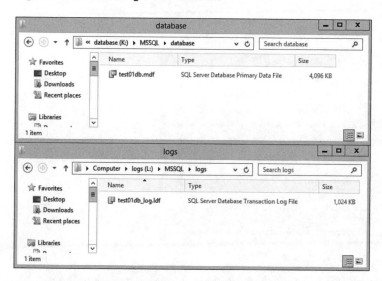

Figure 11.71   Validating database and log file creation.

Any database that is going to be placed into an AlwaysOn Availability Group requires a backup prior to joining the AlwaysOn Availability Group.

> **NOTE**
> Always back up your SQL Server database before it is joined to an AlwaysOn Availability Group.

To back up the test database that was just created, return to Microsoft SQL Server Management Studio, locate the newly created database (test01db), right-click this database, and select **Tasks, Backup...** to open the Back Up Database interface. Verify the information and click **OK** to begin the backup. This should only take a second or two; then click **OK** on the successfully backed-up message to close out the Back Up Database window. Figure 11.72 shows a successful backup of our test database, test01db.

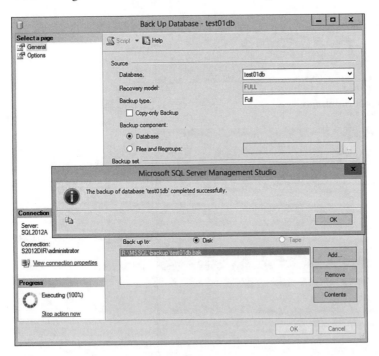

Figure 11.72 Backing up the test database.

This completes configuration of the test database. In the next section, we are going to create the Availability Group, add this database to the Availability Group, and verify we have the Availability Group functioning properly.

Creating the AlwaysOn Availability Group

In this section, we are going to create the AlwaysOn Availability Group for our SQL Servers. If Microsoft SQL Server Management Studio is not open, open it at this time. Expand the database engine (**SQL2012A**), expand **AlwaysOn High Availability**, right-click **Availability Groups**, and click **New Availability Group Wizard**. On the **Introduction**, click **Next**. On the **Specify Availability Group Name** page, enter a unique name for the Availability Group and click **Next**. Figure 11.73 shows us providing a name for our Availability Group.

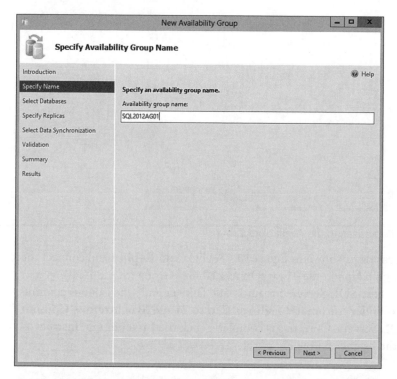

Figure 11.73 Naming the Availability Group.

On the **Select Databases** page, shown in Figure 11.74, place a check next to the test database created in the previous section. Under the Status column, it indicates whether the database is meeting the prerequisites; if the database does not, take corrective action and return to the wizard once the issues are remediated. Click **Next** to proceed.

Figure 11.74   Adding databases to the Availability Group.

On the **Specify Replicas** page, shown in Figure 11.75, click **Add Replica** and connect the other SQL Servers participating in the AlwaysOn Availability Group (SQL2012B). We are going to configure these SQL Servers for automatic failover and synchronous commits by putting check marks under **Automatic Failover (Up to 2)** and **Synchronous Commit (Up to 3)** for both SQL Servers. Once this is complete, click the **Listener** tab. Instructions for configuring the listener follow Figure 11.75.

> **NOTE**
>
> For more information on SQL Server 2012 AlwaysOn availability modes and failover types, review this article: http://technet.microsoft.com/en-us/library/ff877884.aspx.

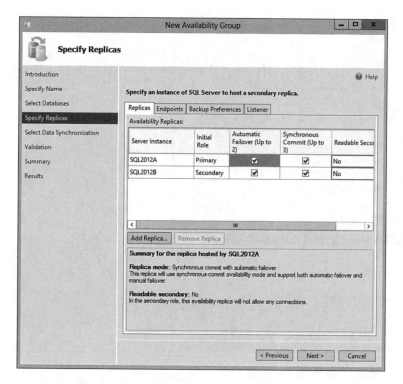

Figure 11.75   Configuring failover and commit.

On the **Listener** tab, shown in Figure 11.76, select the radio button next to **Create an availability group listener**. Fill in a **Listener DNS Name** (sql2012agl01), **Port** (1433), and ensure **Static IP** is selected for **Network Mode**. Under Network Mode, click **Add...** and enter the IP information for the listener. Once this is complete, click **OK** to close the Add IP Address dialog box. Once the listener has been configured correctly, click **Next** to continue with the wizard.

On the **Select Initial Data Synchronization** page, shown in Figure 11.77, ensure **Full** is selected and then enter a path to the Windows 8.1 share we created in a previous step (\\ LOADGEN\aobackup) and click **Next** to continue.

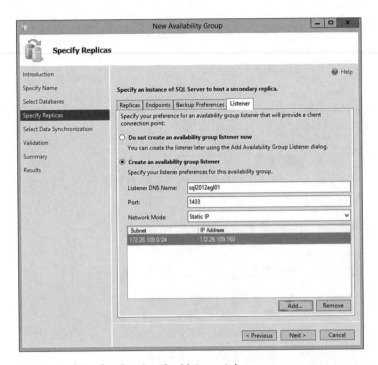

Figure 11.76 Configuring the Listener tab.

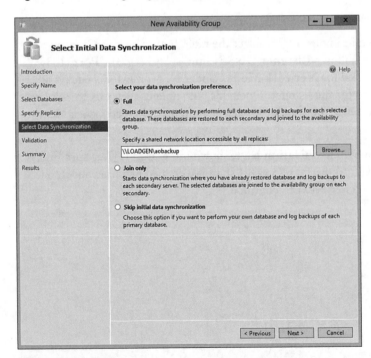

Figure 11.77 Configuring synchronization preference.

On the **Validation** page, shown in Figure 11.78, the wizard will run through preflight checks. If there are any issues identified at this time, remediate the issues and then rerun the wizard. When ready, click **Next** to continue.

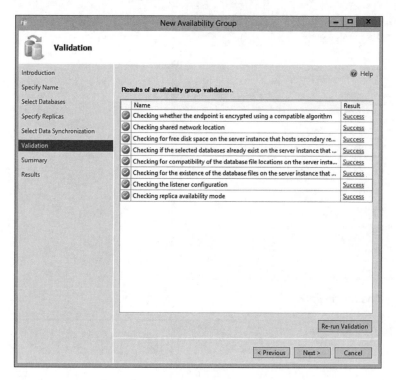

Figure 11.78   Validation of settings.

On the **Summary** page, shown in Figure 11.79, review the setting are correct and click **Finish** to create the AlwaysOn Availability Group and add the test database to it.

On the **Results** page, shown in Figure 11.80, verify all tasks have completed successfully and click **Close** to finish and exit the wizard.

Figure 11.79   Reviewing the configuration.

Figure 11.80   Successful completion of the New Availability Group Wizard.

On the Microsoft SQL Server Management Studio, expand **AlwaysOn High Availability**, **Availability Groups**, and **SQL2012AG01** (the Availability Group that was just
created). Right-click **SQL2012AG01** (or the Availability Group created) and select **Show
Dashboard**. This will show the status of the AlwaysOn Availability Group, as depicted in
Figure 11.81.

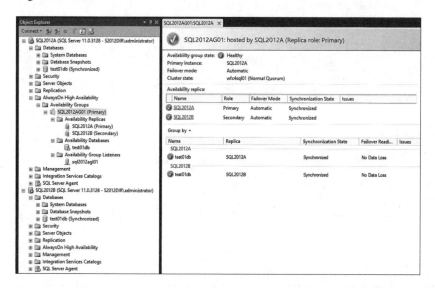

Figure 11.81   Viewing the SQL Server AlwaysOn Availability Group dashboard.

In Active Directory and DNS, we are able to view entries for the AlwaysOn Availability
Group listener (sql2012agl01 with an IP of 172.26.109.160) created via the wizard. Figure
11.82 validates this has been configured correctly as we can see the Failover listener name
listed in ADUC and the corresponding information listed in DNS.

This completes the configuration of the SQL Server AlwaysOn Availability Group. At this
point, we have successfully configured SQL Server 2012 AlwaysOn Availability Groups
between two SQL Server 2012 virtual machines and have a test database synchronizing
between the two SQL Servers. In the next section, we are going to configure the Dell
DVD Store scripts for a custom database size.

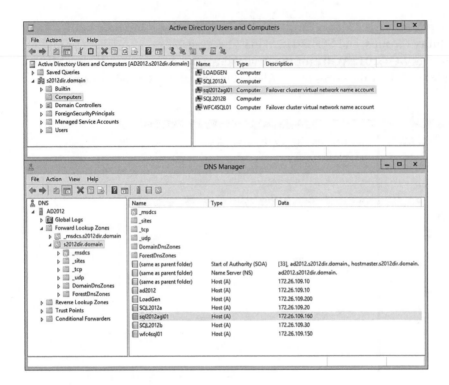

Figure 11.82   Entries created in AD and DNS.

Installing and Configuring Dell DVD Store

In this section, we are going to install and configure the Dell DVD Store for a custom database size. The Dell DVD Store comes preloaded with three sizes: small (10MB), medium (1GB), and large (100GB). If these sizes work, great. You can use the default prebuilt scripts. However, often customers require different database sizes for their performance tests. In this section, we demonstrate how to configure a custom database size, so substitute the size you require for the one we built.

We begin by downloading and installing open source binaries to allow us to run through the Perl scripts that build our custom database size. The first step is to obtain the current stable release of Strawberry Perl and install it on your Windows 8.1 system, which as of the writing of this chapter was 5.18.1.1 and was available at http://strawberryperl.com/. Strawberry Perl is 100% open source.

After Strawberry Perl (or ActivePerl) has been installed, download and extract the Dell DVD Store binaries. The Dell DVD Store binaries are available from https://github.com/ dvdstore. Download the two following files from the directory:

- ds21.tar.gz

- ds21_sqlserver.tar.gz

For reasons of space, we are downloading these files to the VMDK file we added. Depending on the size of the custom test, there may or may not be enough room on the c:\ drive for this to complete. After downloading the files, extract ds21 to the appropriate location (R:\) and extract ds21_sqlserver inside the \ds2\ folder (R:\ds2\). It is very important that this structure is maintained. See Figure 11.83 for more information.

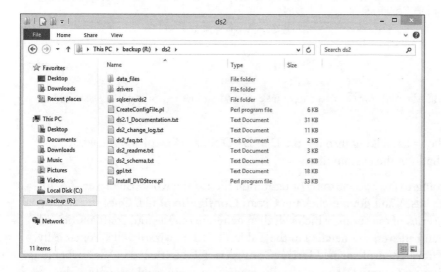

Figure 11.83 The Dell DVD Store folder hierarchy.

With Strawberry Perl installed and Dell DVD Store files downloaded and extracted, it is time to create our custom install file. To do this, browse to \ds2\ directory and double-click the **Install_DVDStore.pl** file. Table 11.5 contains the questions and answers (for our configuration) for this wizard. After each entry, press **Enter** to move on to the next question until the wizard finishes. For this configuration on the equipment we used, the build time of this script took approximately 20 minutes, and you can watch the progress by viewing the \ds2\data_files\cust, \ds2\data_files\orders, and \ds2\data_files\prod directories for file creation. The wizard will automatically close once it is finished.

> **NOTE**
>
> Don't worry about making a mistake because the output of this wizard is a text file that can be manually edited later. If DNS is not rock solid, use IP addresses instead of hostnames.

Table 11.5   Dell DVD Store Custom Install Wizard

Question	Answer
Database size	20
Database size is in	GB
Database type is	MSSQL
System type for DB Server is	WIN
File paths	K:\MSSQL\database\

> **NOTE**
>
> When entering the path for the database, make sure to enter the trailing backslash (\).

Figure 11.84 shows us walking through the Dell DVD Store Wizard and the wizard beginning the build of the custom files.

Next, we are going to create a custom configuration file for the workload driver. To do this, navigate to \ds2\ and double-click the **CreateConfigFile.pl** file. Once this opens, we will be asked a series of questions, which will then generate our custom configuration file. The questions and answers are detailed in the Table 11.6. The wizard will automatically complete once finished. A file named **DriverConfig.txt** will be created in \ds2 containing the configuration data entered. If a mistake was made or you are troubleshooting the installation, you can edit this file manually.

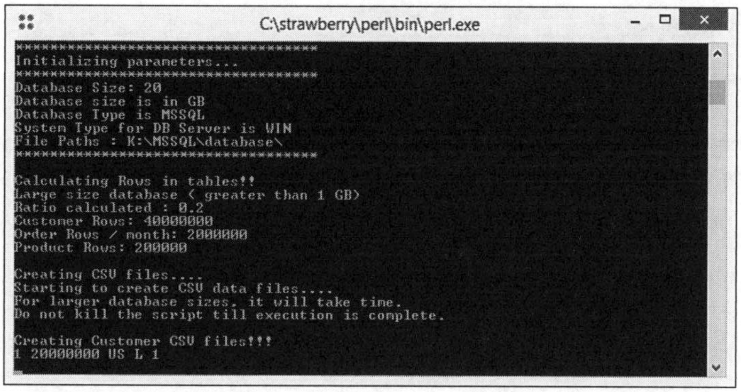

Figure 11.84   Creating the Custom Dell DVD Store install.

NOTE

We are using the Availability Group listener for the target hostname.

Table 11.6   Dell DVD Store Custom Wizard for Workload Driver

Question	Answer
Target hostname	sql2012agl01.s2012dir.domain
Database size	20GB
Target hostname for perfrmon	SQL2012a.s2012.dir.domain
Linux machine CPU display	Leave this blank
Detailed view of statistics	Y

Figure 11.85 shows us walking through the Workload Driver Configuration Wizard.

A known issue that we must address is the way the .csv and .txt files are created and their failure to import into SQL Server 2012 (SQL Server 2008 too). The reason for this is when the configuration files are created, an extra carriage return is present in the file and this causes the import into SQL to fail. By running the files through a conversion utility to remove these returns, we fix the issue. This is what the next section addresses.

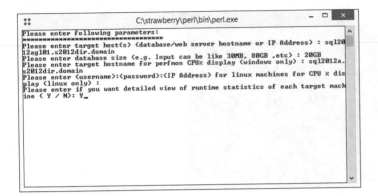

Figure 11.85   Configuring the custom workload driver.

To fix this issue, we need to run .txt and .csv files through a Unix-to-DOS conversion utility. The utility we used was a free-to-use tool located at http://www.efgh.com/software/unix2dos.htm. As of the writing of this chapter, the author has placed no restrictions on its use. Download and run unix2dos.exe by dragging and dropping .txt and .csv files onto it. This must be done starting at the ds2 folder level and all files in this hierarchy. Missing a file could result in the SQL load failing.

TIP

Copy the executable into each directory and leave it there; that way, you know which directories you have completed. In addition, sort files by **Type**, highlight all the .csv and .txt files, and then drag and drop them onto the executable. Use the **Date Modified** column to verify all files have been converted.

NOTE

Not all .txt files need to be run through the conversion utility (for example, Read Me documentation), but we just have to be on the safe side.

Once all the .csv and .txt files have been updated, copy the entire ds2 directory and its subfolders to one of the SQL Servers. For this lab, we copied ds2 to the root of the R:\ sql2012a virtual machine (backup drive). Keep in mind the free space on the drive you are copying the contents to; if there is not enough free space, find another location. If you are following along with us in terms of size of VMDKs and the size of Dell DVD Store test, you will not see an issue. If you have followed our VMDK size but then went with a larger Dell DVD Store test database size, this is where you will want to pay attention to available drive space.

Next, we will need to install the SQL Server Management Tools on the Windows 8.1 virtual machine. To do this, mount the SQL Server 2012 installation CD and select **Installation** and then **New SQL Server stand-alone installation or add feature to an existing installation**. This brings up **Setup Support Rules**, and the wizard will perform a preflight check, as shown in Figure 11.86. If any issues are identified, remediate them and rerun the preflight check. When everything passes, click **OK** to continue.

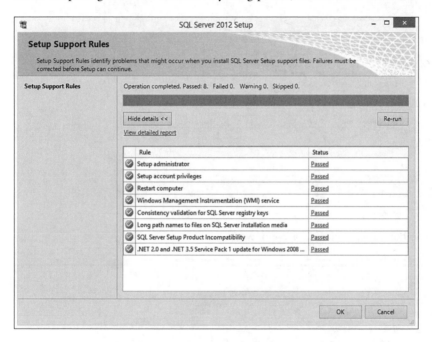

Figure 11.86   Preflight check on Windows 8.

On the **Product Key** page, choose either the free edition or enter a product key and click **Next** to continue. On the **License Terms** page, click **I accept the license terms** and click **Next** to continue. On the **Product Updates** page, click **Next** to continue. The SQL Server installation files are being prepared.

On the **Setup Support Rules** page, shown in Figure 11.87, another preflight check is executed. If any issues are identified, remediate them at this time. When ready, click **Next** to continue.

On the **Setup Role** page, shown in Figure 11.88, select **SQL Server Feature Installation** and click **Next**.

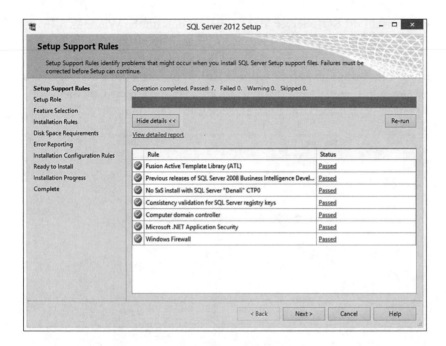

Figure 11.87   Another preflight check for Windows 8.

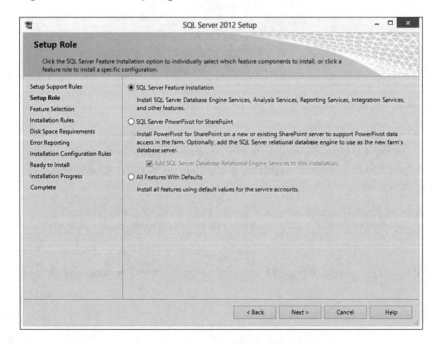

Figure 11.88   The SQL Server Feature Installation section.

On the **Feature Selection** page, select the following features (see Figure 11.89 for what this should resemble):

- Management Tools – Basic

- Management Tools – Complete

After making these selections, click **Next** to continue.

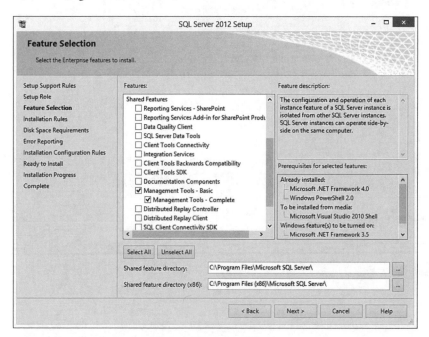

Figure 11.89   Selecting the Management Tools.

On the **Installation Rules** page, shown in Figure 11.90, a preflight check is performed based on the selections made in the previous step. If any issues are identified, remediate them and rerun the check. When ready, click **Next** to continue.

On the **Disk Space Requirements** page, validate there is enough free space available and then click **Next** to continue.

On the **Error Reporting** page, click **Next** to continue.

On the **Installation Configuration Rules** page, shown in Figure 11.91, another preflight check is performed. If any issues are identified, remediate them at this time. When ready, click **Next** to continue.

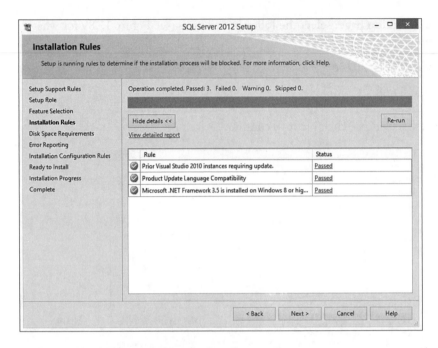

Figure 11.90   Preflight check, take 3.

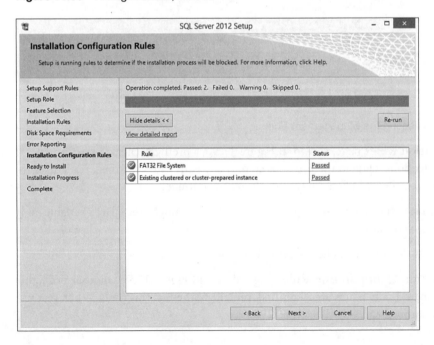

Figure 11.91   Preflight check, take 4.

On the **Ready to Install** page, shown in Figure 11.92, validate the configuration parameters and click **Install** to continue.

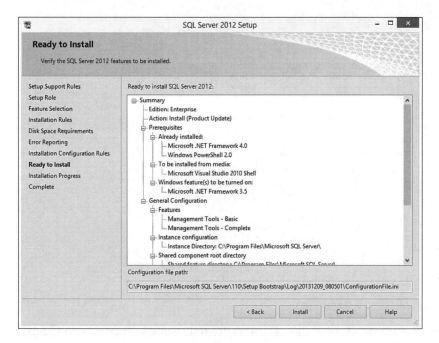

Figure 11.92   Validating the installation.

Once the installation is complete, click **Close** to complete the installation. Figure 11.93 shows a successful completion of the wizard.

To verify the client connectivity tools were installed correctly, we are going to open PowerShell and issue the following command to connect to the AlwaysOn Availability Group listener from the Windows 8.1 virtual machine:

```
osql -Usa -PVMware1! -Ssql2012agl01
```

The breakdown of the command is as follows:

- **–U** is username.

- **–P** is password (yes, that is the SA password for our lab, please don't tell anyone).

- **–S** is the remote server.

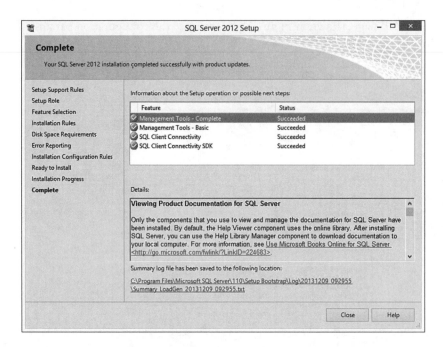

Figure 11.93   Completing the installation.

We know we have a successful connection when we are returned a **1>**, as shown in Figure 11.94. Type **exit** to close the connection; we will use PowerShell later, so you can leave it open.

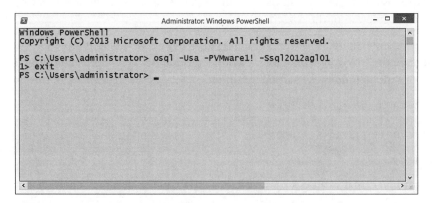

Figure 11.94   Validating connectivity.

For a quick summary of where we are at this point, we have installed and configured the Dell DVD Store on our Windows 8.1 virtual machine and copied the files over to our SQL Server virtual machine. We have installed the client connectivity for SQL Server on the Windows 8.1 virtual machine. In the next step, we will prepare the Dell DVD scripts and create the Dell DVD Store databases.

On the SQL Server 2012 virtual machine, navigate to the **\ds2\sqlserverds2** directory, as shown in Figure 11.95, and locate the **sqlserverds2_create_all_20GB.sql** file. Double-click this file to open it in Microsoft SQL Server Management Studio.

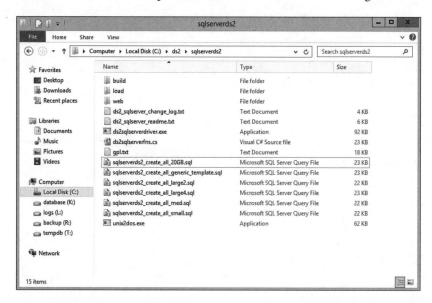

Figure 11.95   Locating the sqlserverds2_create_all_20GB.sql file.

Inside Microsoft SQL Server Management Studio, validate the paths are correct for all the .mdf and .ndf files. For our configuration, this path should be K:\MSSQL\database*.*. The one path we modified was the path to our log file. We modified this to L:\MSSQL\ logs\ds_log.ldf. After making the required changes, save the updates. Figure 11.96 shows the updated file path for our logs.

NOTE

This file can be modified at any time prior to database creation, or if you delete the d2 database, this script can be used to rebuild the database.

```
sqlserverds2_create...\administrator (69))*  ×
              FILENAME = 'K:\MSSQL\database\ds_misc.ndf',
              SIZE = 200MB
              ),
        FILEGROUP DS_CUST_FG
          (
          NAME = 'cust1',
          FILENAME = 'K:\MSSQL\database\cust1.ndf',
          SIZE = 600MB
          ),
          (
          NAME = 'cust2',
          FILENAME = 'K:\MSSQL\database\cust2.ndf',
          SIZE = 600MB
          ),
        FILEGROUP DS_ORDERS_FG
          (
          NAME = 'orders1',
          FILENAME = 'K:\MSSQL\database\orders1.ndf',
          SIZE = 300MB
          ),
          (
          NAME = 'orders2',
          FILENAME = 'K:\MSSQL\database\orders2.ndf',
          SIZE = 300MB
          ),
        FILEGROUP DS_IND_FG
          (
          NAME = 'ind1',
          FILENAME = 'K:\MSSQL\database\ind1.ndf',
          SIZE = 150MB
          ),
          (
          NAME = 'ind2',
          FILENAME = 'K:\MSSQL\database\ind2.ndf',
          SIZE = 150MB
          )
      LOG ON
          (
          NAME = 'ds_log',
          FILENAME = 'L:\MSSQL\logs\ds_log.ldf',
          SIZE = 1000MB
          )
      GO
```

Figure 11.96   Modifying the sqlserverds2_create_all_20GB.sql file.

Open PowerShell on the SQL Server virtual machine and navigate to the \ds2\
sqlserverds2 directory and issue the following command (see Figure 11.97):

```
osql -Usa -PVMware1! -i sqlserverds2_create_all_20GB.sql
```

The time it takes to create the databases will depend on the custom size you created.
To validate the script is building the databases, navigate to the database directory (K:\
MSSQL\database\) and log directory (L:\MSSQL\logs\) to validate the files have been
created and are growing in size as the script runs. In our environment, it took approximately 40 minutes to build the 20GB database.

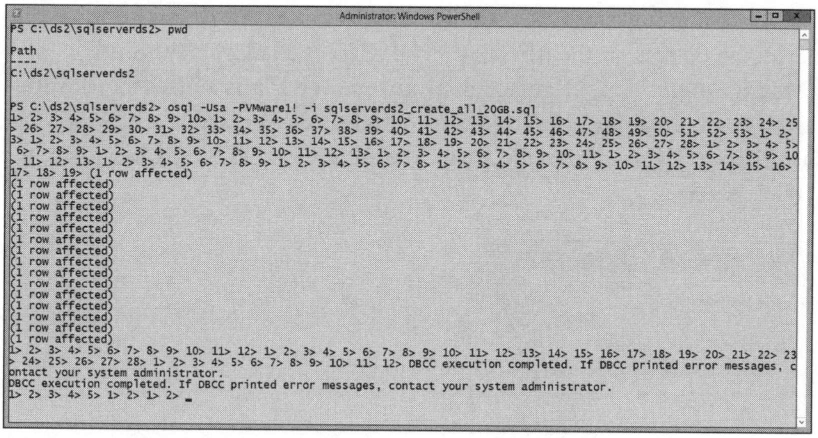

Figure 11.97 Building the databases.

To validate the databases have been properly created, you can issue the following commands, as shown in Figure 11.98:

- `osql -Usa -P<password>`
- `use ds2`
- `go`
- `select count(*) from products`
- `go`

The command will return the number of rows affected; in our configuration, the value returned was 200,000. It is alright to exit PowerShell at this time.

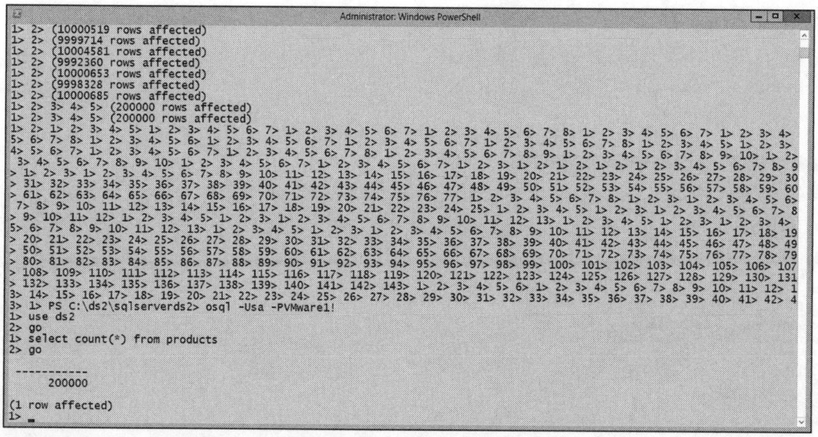

Figure 11.98 Validating the database build.

One of the first tasks we are going to run is to update the database statistics to improve database performance. To do this, in the Microsoft SQL Server Management Studio interface, expand **Management**. Then right-click **Maintenance Plans** and select **Maintenance Plan Wizard**. On the first page of the **Maintenance Plan Wizard**, click **Next**. On the **Select Plan Properties** page, provide a name for the plan (DS2 MP), as shown in Figure 11.99, and click **Next**.

Figure 11.99 Naming the maintenance plan.

On the **Select Maintenance Tasks** page, shown in Figure 11.100, select **Update Statistics** and click **Next**.

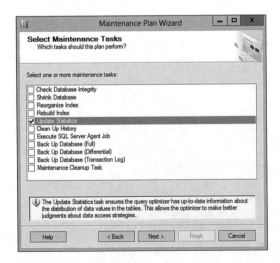

Figure 11.100 Selecting the Update Statistics option.

On the **Select Maintenance Task Order** page, shown in Figure 11.101, click **Next**.

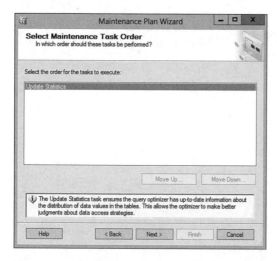

Figure 11.101   Order of operations, order of one.

On the **Define Update Statistics Task** page, shown in Figure 11.102, use the drop-down to select the **DS2** database. In the **Update:** section, verify **All existing statistics** is selected. Under **Scan type:**, select **Sample by** radio button, change the value to **18 Percent**, and then click **Next**.

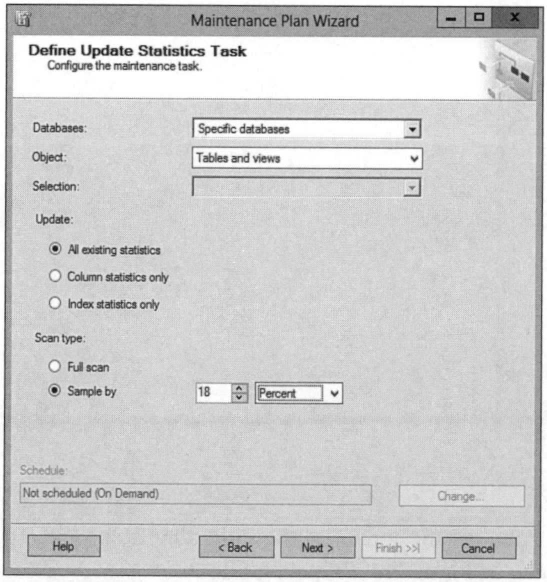

Figure 11.102   Defining the Update Statistics task.

On the **Select Report Options** page, shown in Figure 11.103, click **Next** unless other options are desired.

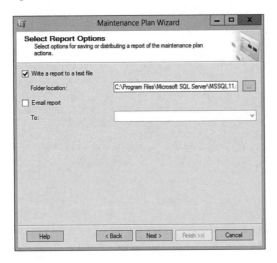

Figure 11.103   Reporting options.

On the **Complete the Wizard** page, shown in Figure 11.104, validate the settings and click **Finish** to begin the task.

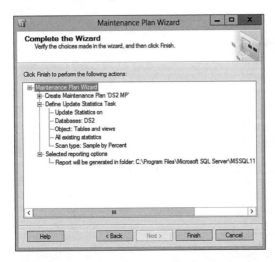

Figure 11.104   Validating the wizard configuration.

The maintenance plan will now execute, providing an update as the individual steps are executed. Once the wizard finishes, as shown in Figure 11.105, click **Close**.

Figure 11.105 Completing the Maintenance Plan Wizard.

Now that we have created the task, we need to run it. To run the task, expand **Maintenance Plans**, right-click the plan that was just created (DS2 MP), and select **Execute**. Figure 11.106 shows how to execute the maintenance plan you just created.

Figure 11.106 Running the maintenance plan.

When the maintenance task is finished running (in our environment, it took approximately 10 minutes), click **Close**. You should see a success message like the one shown in Figure 11.107 when the task is done.

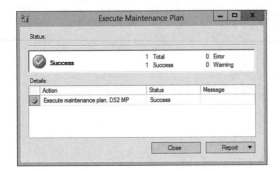

Figure 11.107   Task completion.

Now that we have optimized the DS2 database, we need to perform a database backup. There will be two database backup operations that need to occur. The first is a full backup and the second is a backup of the transaction logs. To begin, in the Microsoft SQL Server Management Studio, expand **Databases** and right-click **DS2, Tasks, Back Up…**. On the **Back Up Database – DS2** page, click **OK**. Once the backup operation completes, click **OK**. Figure 11.108 provides a screenshot of what this looks like.

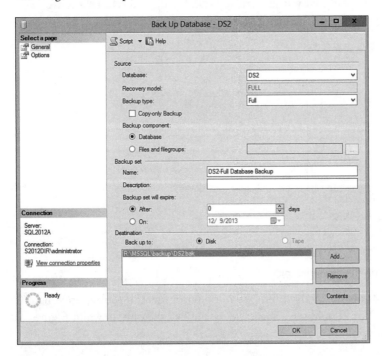

Figure 11.108   Full backup of DS2 database.

After the full backup job completes, once again right-click **DS2 > Tasks > Back Up....**
On the **Back Up Database – DS2** page, change **Backup type** to **Transaction Log** and
click **OK**. When the transaction log backup is complete, click **OK**. Figure 11.109 demonstrates a transaction log backup for our DS2 database.

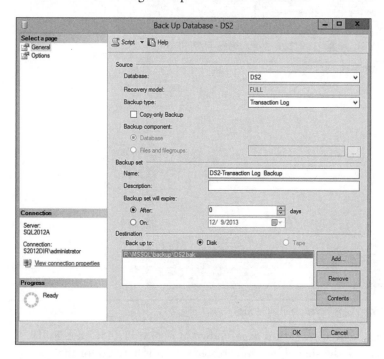

Figure 11.109   Transaction log backup.

> **NOTE**
>
> The transaction logs must be backed up prior to adding the DS2 database to the
> AlwaysOn Availability Group.

Now we are going to add the DS2 database to our AlwaysOn Availability Group. To do
this, open the Microsoft SQL Server Management Studio and expand **AlwaysOn High
Availability, Availability Groups**. Right-click the previously created Availability Group
(SQL2012AG01) and select **Add Database....** On the **Introduction** page, shown in
Figure 11.110, click **Next**. On the **Select Databases** page, select **DS2** and click **Next**.

Figure 11.110   Adding DS2 to the Availability Group.

On the **Select Initial Data Synchronization** page, shown in Figure 11.111, leave **Full** selected and ensure the path to the shared location created earlier is entered for the location (\\LOADGEN\aobackup). Click **Next** to continue.

On the **Connect to Existing Secondary Replicas** page, click **Connect…** and connect to the secondary instance. Click **Next** to continue. Figure 11.112 shows how we configured SQL2012A to connect with SQL2012B.

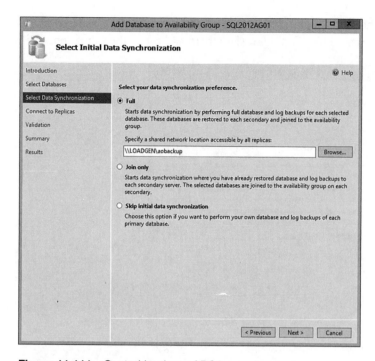

Figure 11.111   Central backup of DS2.

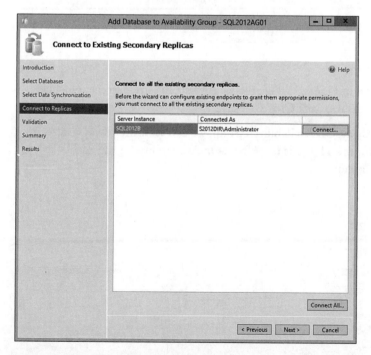

Figure 11.112   Connecting to the secondary.

On the **Validation** page, shown in Figure 11.113, ensure all validation checks return a successful result. If any issues are identified, remediate them and rerun the validation.

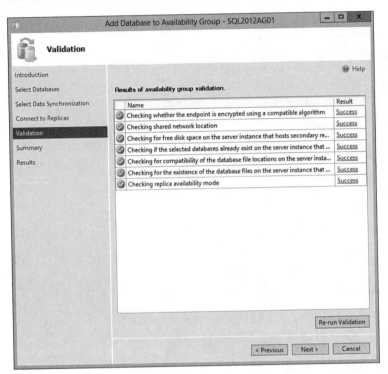

Figure 11.113   Validation check.

On the **Results** page, shown in Figure 11.114, review the settings are correct and click **Finish**. When the wizard finishes, click **Close**.

To view the status of the AlwaysOn Availability Group, we can view the AlwaysOn Availability Group dashboard. Figure 11.115 is the AlwaysOn Availability Group dashboard showing the configuration is running.

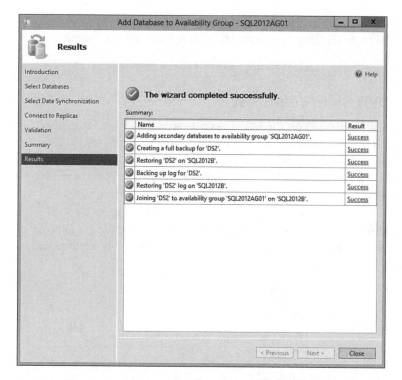

Figure 11.114   Successful addition of DS2 to the AlwaysOn Availability Group.

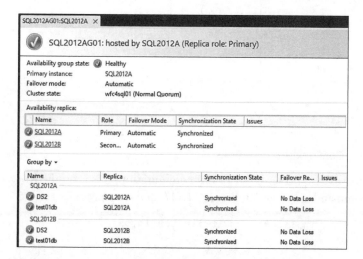

Figure 11.115   AlwaysOn Availability Group dashboard with the DS2 database.

This completes the installation and configuration of the Dell DVD Store database into a SQL Server 2012 AlwaysOn Availability Group. In the next section, we will execute the load test.

Running the Dell DVD Store Load Test

To execute the test, we will need to be on the Windows 8.1 virtual machine. The first thing to do is modify the **DriverConfig.txt** file for our test. By default, the test will run indefinitely; therefore, we'll change the test to run for 120 minutes. The reason for this change is so the test does not run forever. To stress your system further, you can change several of the variables included in the DriverConfig.txt file. We are starting with the defaults so that we have a baseline for how our system performs. This way, as we make changes, we understand their impact. For more information on what each setting entails, review the **ds2driver_doc.txt** file located in the \ds2\drivers directory. The change we made is shown in Figure 11.116: run_time=120.

Figure 11.116   Modifying DriverConfig.txt.

From PowerShell, navigate to \ds2\sqlserverds2\ (for our configuration, this is on the R: drive). Type the following command, as shown in Figure 11.117, and then press **Enter**:

```
ds2sqlsserverdriver.exe --config_file=r:\ds2\DriverConfig.txt
```

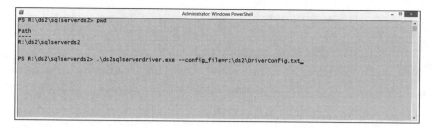

Figure 11.117   Kicking off the Dell DVD Store load test.

Taking a quick peek at vCenter Infrastructure Navigator, shown in Figure 11.118, we can see that the relationships have automatically updated to represent the AlwayOn Availability Group configuration as well as the initiation of the Dell DVD Store test. We can see that the SQL Servers have established a relationship between themselves and that the LoadGen virtual machine has established a connection to the SQL Listener currently resident on SQL 2012 a.

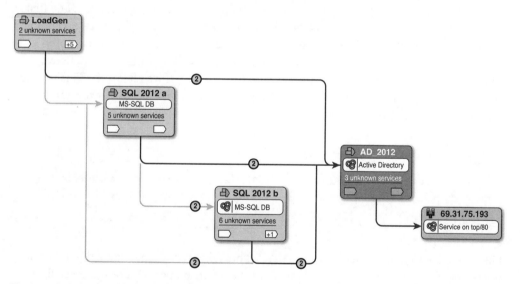

Figure 11.118   Updated screenshot from VIN.

When the run is complete, Dell DVD Store will present the final results and end the test, as shown in Figure 11.119.

```
User name newuser38262564 already exists
et= 7297.5 n_overall=460747 opm=3788 rt_tot_lastn_max_msec=41 rt_tot_avg_msec=15 rt_tot_sampled=17 rollbacks: n=9334 %=  2.0
host sql2012a.s2012dir.domain CPU%=   8.5
et= 7307.7 n_overall=461323 opm=3787 rt_tot_lastn_max_msec=78 rt_tot_avg_msec=15 rt_tot_sampled=17 rollbacks: n=9347 %=  2.0
host sql2012a.s2012dir.domain CPU%=   8.5
et= 7317.8 n_overall=461871 opm=3786 rt_tot_lastn_max_msec=268 rt_tot_avg_msec=15 rt_tot_sampled=18 rollbacks: n=9361 %=  2.0
host sql2012a.s2012dir.domain CPU%=   8.5

Final (3/29/2014 1:05:42 PM): et= 7317.8 n_overall=461871 opm=3786 rt_tot_lastn_max=268 rt_tot_avg=15 n_login_overall=369343 n_newcust_overall=92528 n_b
rowse_overall=1385324 n_purchase_overall=461871 rt_login_avg_msec=4 rt_newcust_avg_msec=2 rt_browse_avg_msec=0 rt_purchase_avg_msec=8 rt_tot_sampled=18
n_rollbacks_overall=9361 rollback_rate =   2.0%
host sql2012a.s2012dir.domain CPU%=   8.5
Thread 0: exiting
Controller (3/29/2014 1:05:42 PM): all threads stopped, exiting
n_purchase_from_start= 464940 n_rollbacks_from_start= 9422
Run over
PS R:\ds2\sqlserverds2> _
```

Figure 11.119 The Dell DVD Store run completed.

> **NOTE**
>
> If you see **User name newuserXXXXXXXX already exists,** as shown in the first line in Figure 11.119, where X is an integer, this represents a user signing in and that user name is already taken. This is based on the `pct_newcustomers` setting in the DriverConfig.txt file. Changing this to 0 eliminates this message from appearing.

Now that our run is complete, let's review the data presented in Figure 11.119. The first value we see is `et`. The `et` value specifies the amount of time the test has been executing. The value will specify the amount of time either since the test began (warm-up time, which by default is 1 minute) or since warm-up time ended. You will see this updated approximately every 10 seconds during the run. For our test, if we review the Final results, we see `et = 7317.8`. This value is presented in seconds, so that means our test ran for 121.963 minutes after the stats were reset.

> **NOTE**
>
> Stats are reset after the warm-up time has been achieved. If your system requires longer ramp-up time, this is a configurable value, `warmup_time=X`, and is located in the Driver-Config.txt file.

The next value we come across is `n_overall`. This value represents the total number of orders processed after the stats were reset after the warm-up period. For the preceding test, we have a value of `n_overall=461871`, so we know that a total of 461,871 orders were processed during this test period.

Moving on, the next value is `opm`. The `opm` value indicates the orders per minute. For the preceding test, we have a value of 3786, meaning we handled 3,786 orders per minute. This value will change, as you will see in the test, and is a rolling update of the last minute.

The next value is `rt_tot_lastn_max`. This value represents the experience of the last 100 users, in milliseconds, for their ordering experience. For our test, we have a value of `rt_tot_lastn_max=268`, which means the last 100 users experienced 268 milliseconds of delay across the steps of their purchasing experience.

The next value we see is `rt_tot_avg`. This value represents the total response time experienced by a user during their ordering cycle. This includes logging in, creating a new user account, browsing inventory, and purchasing product. For our test, we had a value of `rt_tot_avg=15`, which means the user experienced an average of 15-millisecond response time.

The `n_login_overall` value represents the total number of logins. For our run, the result returned was `n_login_overall=369343`, meaning we had 369,343 logins for the entire test. Unlike the previous results, which provide a snapshot of performance at that current moment, this value represent the total number of logins for the duration of the test.

The next cumulative value we are presented with is the `n_newcust_overall` value. This value represents how many new customers registered during the test period. For our test, the value we achieved was `n_newcust_overall=92528`, meaning we had 92,528 new customers.

Next, we have the `n_browse_overall` value presented. This value represents the total number of browses experienced during a run. For our run, the value returned was `n_browse_overall=1385324`, meaning we had 1,385,324 browses.

The next value in our results chain is `n_purchase_overall`. This value represents, as you might guess, the total number of purchases during a given run. For our run, the value returned was `n_purchase_overall=461871`, meaning we has 461,871 purchases go through our system.

How about login experience? The next value, `rt_login_avg_msec`, provides us with the average login time in milliseconds for a user. For our run, we received a `rt_login_avg_msec=4`, meaning our users' login time for the system, on average, was 4 milliseconds.

What about new user experience? The `rt_newcust_avg_msec` metric tells us how long it takes for a new user to register themselves with our service. For our test, the value we received was `rt_newcust_avg_msec=2`, meaning a new user registration took 2 milliseconds.

How about the browse time? Metric `rt_browse_avg_msec` represents browse time. For our run, the value returned was `rt_browse_avg_msec=0`.

The average purchase time is represented in the `rt_purchase_avg_msec` value. For our run, we received a result of `rt_purchase_avg_msec=8`, meaning it took an average of 8 milliseconds for a purchase to complete.

What happens if a customer is trying to order something but there is not enough of that product in stock and the order needs to roll back? This is represented as a total number experienced during the entire run in the `n_rollbacks_overall` value. For our run, we received a value of `n_rollbacks_overall=9361`, meaning we had 9,361 orders rolled back due to a lack of product.

The value `rollback_rate` represents the percentage of rollbacks and is derived by the following formula, as described in ds2driver_doc.txt:

```
n_rollback_overall / n_overall * 100%
```

For our test, we received a value of `rollback_rate = 2.0%`, meaning we had 2.0% of our orders rolled back. The math is 9361/461871*100%.

How stressed was the vCPU of our host? The `host <servername> CPU%` will provide this information. The result we received for our run was `host sql2012a.s2012dir.domain CPU%= 8.5`, which states our sql2012a virtual machine ran at about 8.5% CPU utilization, so we barely touched the system from a CPU perspective.

The final two values are `n_purchase_from_start` and `n_rollbacks_from_start`, which represent the total number of purchases and rollbacks from the start of the test, including warm-up time, through exiting of the thread(s). For our test, these values are represented as `n_purchase_from_start= 464940` and `n_rollbacks_from_start= 9422`, respectively.

What does this all mean? It means we have a baseline. For an out-of-the-box test, running for 120 minutes (2 hours), with 1 minute of warm-up time, our configuration was able to process 464,940 orders, averaging 3,786 orders per minutes, with 369,343 logins into the system, and customers experienced an average latency of 15 milliseconds while progressing through their order. The average login time was 4 milliseconds, it took us 2 milliseconds to sign up a new user, we had a 2.0% rollback rate due to insufficient product, and our host SQL Server displayed a CPU utilization of 8.5%. Figure 11.120 shows a graphical representation based on 10-minute intervals for the number of logins and orders per minute. Based on this data, we can see that we have near linear scalability for our logins and our operations per minute took about 20 minutes to reach a steady state for our configuration.

Now that we have the results from our initial test, it is time to determine which variables we are going to manipulate and determine the impact of these settings base on our test. A suggestion here is to also rerun the test with all the defaults in place, but test vSphere and SQL Server–related functionality and the impact these have on performance. For example, test vMotion, vSphere HA, and your affinity rules work (these were previously configured). Also test shutting down the active SQL Server, disconnecting the network from the virtual machines, and so on.

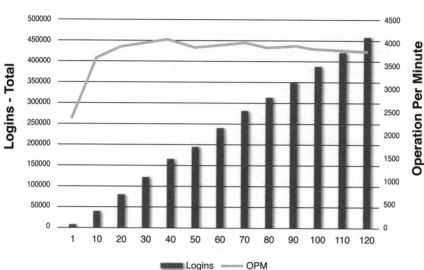

Figure 11.120   Graphical results of OPM and logins from the Dell DVD Store test.

Once you are ready to get started with additional testing, you will need to reset the Dell DVD Store database. The first step in this process is to remove the DS2 database from the AlwaysOn Availability Group. The reason for removal is the script we use to reset the database will fail if you attempt to run it while DS2 is part of an AlwaysOn Availability Group. Once the DS2 database is removed, open the **sqlserverds2_cleanup_20GB.sql** file located in the **\ds2\sqlserverds2\build** directory.

We will run the script from the SQL Server on which we built the database via the Microsoft SQL Server Management Studio, as shown in Figure 11.121. Once the script is loaded, click the **Execute** button to begin.

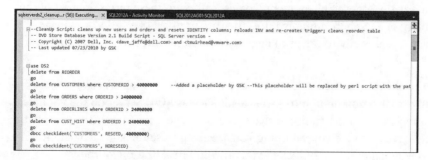

Figure 11.121   Resetting the Dell DVD Store test.

This concludes the section on running the Dell DVD Store test with SQL Server 2012 running on Windows 2012.

Now that you have successfully run the test, we encourage you to reset the configuration and rerun the test several times, testing various features native to the vSphere platform and SQL Server itself. For example, test vMotion while the system is running to see the effect on an active node or a passive node. Test the anti-affinity rule to see how it works. Test vSphere HA by powering down an ESXi host. Test SQL Server resiliency by simulating failovers. Test your backup/recovery procedures to determine the best way to recover from a failure. You now have a test environment that can be leveraged for repeated testing, so use it!

Summary

In this chapter, we walked through a complete, end-to-end configuration of a SQL Server performance test on vSphere 5.5 with SQL 2012 as our database engine and Windows Server 2012 as our guest operating system. This chapter builds on all the previous chapters in this book; however, it does not include all the possible variations and tweaks. We set up a "base" installation from which you are able to manipulate various levers within vSphere, Windows, and SQL to find the optimal configuration for your environment.

We discussed the importance of baselining these tests. It is important to baseline not only the initial test but also all subsequent tests to understand the impact of the configuration change made and to determine if the change provides enough value to be rolled into production.

In addition to changing the levels of vSphere, Windows, or SQL, use this as an opportunity to validate (or in some cases, demonstrate to others in the organization) features within vSphere. For example, many DBAs are not familiar with vMotion, Storage vMotion, HA, and many other vSphere technologies. Although these terms are part of the everyday vocabulary of a vSphere administrator, they are not part of a DBA or management's vernacular. Use this environment to demonstrate these features and how they work under load.

Finally, we want to thank you, the reader, for your interest in our book. We are all very passionate about virtualization of high I/O workloads such as SQL Server on the vSphere platform and appreciate the opportunity to share what we have learned over the years with you. We hope we have provided you value and you are able to use the knowledge in this book in your professional life. Best of luck to you on your virtualization journey.

—Michael Corey, Jeff Szastak, and Michael Webster

Additional Resources

With this book, we have attempted to create the most comprehensive guide to virtualizing your most demanding databases. The key to success in virtualizing your databases is knowledge. This appendix is loaded with additional resources available to you.

Additional Documentation Sources

VMware has some excellent additional documentation and white papers on how to virtualize a SQL Server database. The trick is to know where to find this documentation.

Before we give you a URL to these white papers, let's look at how to find them from the VMware home page in case the URL we give you becomes invalid. To help make our directions a little easier to follow, refer to Figures A.1 and A.2.

Figure A.1   Navigating to key SQL Server documentation from the home page.

Starting with Figure A.1, you can see that step 1 instructs you to go to the VMware home page. The trick then is to find the link **Virtualizing Enterprise Applications** (shown in step 2) at the bottom of the home page and click it. This will take you to the web page shown in step 3. VMware considers the SQL Server database a business-critical application, just like it does Microsoft Exchange, Oracle, and SAP. Therefore, if you were to perform a web search, you should use the terms "SQL Server Business Critical Application" to locate the page holding the white papers.

At the bottom of the web page shown in Figure A.2, in step 4 you will see a section named Microsoft SQL Server. In this section, click the link **Learn More About SQL Server Virtualization** (this is indicated by the arrow in Figure A.2). Clicking this link will take you to step 5. This section of the website is dedicated to virtualizing a SQL Server database on vSphere.

TIP

The URL to some useful white papers on how to virtualize SQL Server is http://www.vmware.com/business-critical-apps/sql-virtualization.

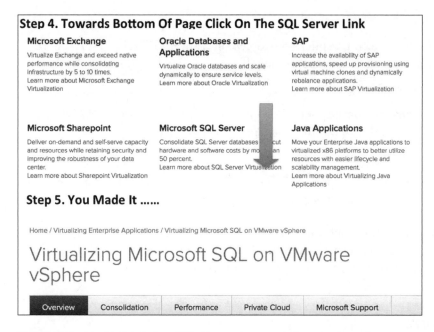

Figure A.2 Navigating to key SQL Server documentation, continued.

At the bottom of this page, you will see a section titled Related Resources. You have finally arrived at the mother lode of additional white papers. VMware has done an excellent job on many of these white papers, and it is well worth your time to read them. Here are a few of my favorites from the VMware site:

- DBA Guide to Databases on VMware—White Paper

  http://www.vmware.com/files/pdf/solutions/DBA_Guide_to_Databases_on_VMware-WP.pdf

- SQL Server on VMware—Availability and Recovery Options

  http://www.vmware.com/files/pdf/solutions/SQL_Server_on_VMware-Availability_and_Recovery_Options.pdf

- SQL Server on VMware—Best Practices Guide

  http://www.vmware.com/files/pdf/solutions/SQL_Server_on_VMware-Best_Practices_Guide.pdf

- Setup for Failover Clustering and Microsoft Cluster Service

  http://pubs.vmware.com/vsphere-55/topic/com.vmware.ICbase/PDF/vsphere-esxi-vcenter-server-551-setup-mscs.pdf

- vSphere Storage

  http://pubs.vmware.com/vsphere-55/topic/com.vmware.ICbase/PDF/vsphere-esxi-vcenter-server-551-storage-guide.pdf

- vSphere Resource Management

  http://pubs.vmware.com/vsphere-55/topic/com.vmware.ICbase/PDF/vsphere-esxi-vcenter-server-551-resource-management-guide.pdf

- vSphere Monitoring & Performance

  http://pubs.vmware.com/vsphere-55/topic/com.vmware.ICbase/PDF/vsphere-esxi-vcenter-server-551-monitoring-performance-guide.pdf

Now that SQL Server 2014 is out, we are sure some excellent additions will be made to this list soon. Therefore, we recommend you take the time to check back to this web page from time to time and look for an updated version of our book.

User Groups

Industry user groups are one of the most important resources you have available to you in support of technology. The best part is, no matter where you are in the world, odds are there is a technology group near you. Here are a few technology user groups focused on SQL Server and virtualization that you should take the time to learn about.

VMUG: The VMware Users Group

The following is from the VMUG home page:

> The VMware User Group (VMUG) is an independent, global, customer-led organization, created to maximize members' use of VMware and partner solutions through knowledge sharing, training, collaboration, and events. With over 90,000 members worldwide, we are the largest organization for virtualization users.
>
> Our standing partnership with VMware has allowed us to create an ever-growing network of customers and partners who continue to strategically impact VMware products and services.

VMUG runs excellent high-quality technical events all over the globe. Participating in the events VMUG hosts are free. The organization is dedicated to helping you successfully deploy VMware's technology. VMUG is such a good resource, you will see it mentioned several times in this book.

To learn more about VMUG, go to http://www.vmug.com/.

PASS: Professional Association of SQL Server

The following is from the PASS home page:

> *PASS is an independent, not-for-profit organization run by and for the community. With a growing membership of more than 100K, PASS supports data professionals throughout the world who use the Microsoft data platform.*
>
> *PASS strives to fulfill its mission by:*
>
> - *Facilitating member networking and the exchange of information through our local and virtual chapters, online events, local and regional events, and international conferences*
>
> - *Delivering high-quality, timely, technical content for in-depth learning and professional development*

Anyone serious about SQL Server should take the time to learn more about PASS. The PASS community is loaded with people who want to help. To learn more about PASS, go to http://www.sqlpass.org/. The Professional Association of SQL Server runs numerous events all year long, all over the globe. The granddaddy of all events for PASS is the PASS Summit, which is held each year. To learn more about the PASS Summit, go to http://www.sqlpass.org/summit/2014/Home.aspx.

PASS—Virtualization Virtual Chapter

The PASS—Virtualization Virtual Chapter's mission statement is as follows:

> *The Virtualization Virtual Chapter is dedicated to better management of SQL Servers in virtual environments such as Microsoft Hyper-V and vSphere.*

The Virtual Chapter does an excellent job of running virtual events all throughout the year. The many events the group runs are virtual, so no matter where you are located, there is no excuse for not attending. As long as you have access to the Internet, you have access to a number of free, high-quality events all throughout the year, 100% focused on virtualization of SQL Server.

To learn more about the Virtual Chapter, go to http://virtualization.sqlpass.org/.

PASS SQLSaturday

During the past few VMworld events at which we have presented on database virtualization, we always take the time to ask the audience the question, "How many people in the audience have heard of or have attended a SQLSaturday event?" It never ceases to amaze us at a presentation on SQL Server database virtualization what a low percentage of the audience raises their hands. Usually the response is under 20%.

For those of you who have no idea what a SQLSaturday event is, it's the best thing an industry user group has done in years. This comes from a person who has been actively involved in user groups for over 30 years. My hat is off to the leadership of the Professional Association of SQL Server who have lived up to their mission by embracing the concept of SQLSaturday and nurturing their growth, almost since their inception.

The best way to describe SQL Saturday is to quote the main SQLSaturday website, which is located at http://www.sqlsaturday.com/:

> *PASS SQLSaturday's are free 1-day training events for SQL Server professionals that focus on local speakers, providing a variety of high-quality technical sessions, and making it all happen through the efforts of volunteers. Whether you're attending a SQLSaturday or thinking about hosting your own, we think you'll find it's a great way to spend a Saturday—or any day.*

Even though the website talks about "local speakers," many SQLSaturdays I have attended in the U.S. have drawn high-quality speakers from all across the country. It's a great place to see a Microsoft MVP speak. The best part about the event besides the high-quality education is the SQL Server community, which is awesome. People are committed to the community and want to help. You should take the time to volunteer for a local SQLSaturday and become part of the event itself.

A little bit of trivia: Where and when was the first SQL Saturday held?

The answer is Orlando, Florida in 2007. The last time I checked, there have been well over 250 SQLSaturday events held all over the world. SQLSaturdays are high-quality events that should not be missed if you are serious about becoming a better technologist.

VMware Community

Another great source of information on database virtualization is the VMware Community site. This resource can be reached at https://communities.vmware.com. Membership in the VMware Community is free. Figure A.3 shows two sections of the VMware Community home page to give you a sense of what's available on the site. Well over 100 forums are available—or if you like, you can start a new one.

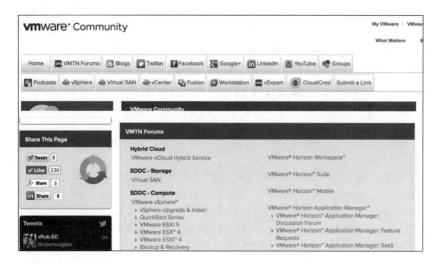

Figure A.3   The VMware Community home page.

Facebook Groups

As of October 2013, over 500 million people use Facebook and over 70 different languages are supported. Within the Facebook site are a number of Facebook Groups focused on VMware. If you are not familiar with Facebook Groups, here's a description from the Facebook site:

> *Facebook Groups are the place for small group communication and for people to share their common interests and express their opinion. Groups allow people to come together around a common cause, issue or activity to organize, express objectives, discuss issues, post photos, and share related content.*

With over 500 million people on Facebook, it's no wonder a number of groups have emerged focused on VMware. One group I would like to point out is the VMware vExpert group. This used to be a closed group, but on April 17, 2014 it was opened up to the public. To access the VMware vExpert Facebook Group, go to https://www.facebook.com/groups/57751806694/.

Note that you must first be logged in to your Facebook account. This is just one of many Facebook Groups devoted to VMware.

Blogs

Twenty years ago, if you wanted to get timely high-quality technical information, your options were limited:

- Big industry tradeshows (such as VMworld and the PASS Summit)
- The latest books on the topic
- The vendor's newest class on the topic

Today, high-quality information is coming out near real time in blogs. A word of caution, though: Information over time can become outdated, and authors of blogs are not always good about going back and deleting or updating their information as it becomes outdated. Therefore, always take the time to use a little common sense when obtaining information from the Internet. You should look at the credentials of the blog's author and when the last time the information was updated.

An example of an excellent blog that contains useful information on virtualization is Long White Virtual Clouds: All Things VMware, Cloud, and Virtualizing Business Critical Applications, located at http://longwhiteclouds.com/. The author of this blog is Michael Webster, one of the authors of this book. A sample of Michael Webster's blog is shown in Figure A.4.

Figure A.4   Long White Virtual Clouds: a high-quality blog on virtualization.

vLaunchPad

A useful site to know about is vLaunchPad: Your Gateway to the VMware Universe, which is located at http://thevpad.com/. This website asks people each year to vote for their favorite blogs on virtualization. Michael's Long White Virtual Cloud blog came in #13 out of over 300 blogs. Looking at the many blogs on the vLaunchPad site can be an excellent source of information on virtualization.

For example, here are the top five sites:

1. Yellow-Bricks, by Duncan Epping (http://www.yellow-bricks.com/)
2. virtuallyGhetto, by William Lam (http://www.virtuallyghetto.com/)
3. Frank Denneman Blog (http://frankdenneman.nl/)

4. Cormac Hogan (http://cormachogan.com/)

5. Scott Lowe Blog (http://blog.scottlowe.org/)

SQL Rock Star Thomas LaRock

A very useful blog with a Microsoft SQL Server focus is Thomas LaRock's blog located at http://thomaslarock.com/. Here's Tom's bio, from the Professional Association of SQL Server website:

> *Thomas LaRock is a seasoned IT professional with over a decade of technical and management experience. Currently serving as a Head Geek at Solarwinds, he has progressed through several roles in his career including programmer, analyst, and DBA.*
>
> *A PASS member for 10 years, Thomas has been on the PASS Board of Directors since 2009, serving as VP, Marketing, before becoming PASS President in 2014. Thomas holds a MS degree in Mathematics from Washington State University and is a SQL Server MCM, a SQL Server MVP, a Microsoft Certified Trainer, and a VMware vExpert.*

Tom knows a lot about Microsoft SQL Server and is also very wired into the SQL Server community. This makes Tom uniquely qualified to create a list of people whose SQL Server blogs are worth reading. Tom's blog list is one that I trust. You can find this list at http://thomaslarock.com/rankings/.

The newest category in Tom's list is Virtualization. At the time this book was written, Tom has two names listed in this category:

- Allan Hirt (http://www.sqlha.com/blog/)
- David Klee (http://www.davidklee.net/)

Both Allan and David have excellent blogs that are worth a read. They both come at the topic of virtualization from a SQL Server perspective first and foremost. They are also frequent speakers at SQLSaturday events all over the country.

Twitter: 140 Characters of Real-Time Action

For years, a lot of people have questioned the value of Twitter: How could a 140-character text message possibly have value? Yet, on January 15, 2009, when Captain Chesley B. "Sully" Sullenberger and the crew of US Airways Flight 1549 landed that plane on the Hudson River in New York without a single loss of life, we all heard about it from Twitter first. Yes, this information was on Twitter first—not CNN, not the local news, but on Twitter. Twitter is about real-time access to information.

A shout-out on Twitter can get you an immediate timely answer or a suggestion on where to find the right answer. Taking the time to follow people such as @Sqlrockstar, @SqlHa, @vcdxnz001, @szastak, @michael_corey, and @Kleegeek can provide you with an excellent support system of help. A great place to start is to follow the many SQL Server MVPs out there.

Index

Numbers

I

J

N

U

X-Y-Z

vmware PRESS

Virtualizing SQL Server with VMware®

Doing IT Right

Michael Corey
Jeff Szastak
Michael Webster

Foreword by Duncan Epping

FREE
Online Edition

Your purchase of *Virtualizing SQL Server with VMware* includes access to a free online edition for 45 days through the **Safari Books Online** subscription service. Nearly every VMware Press book is available online through **Safari Books Online**, along with thousands of books and videos from publishers such as Addison-Wesley Professional, Cisco Press, Exam Cram, IBM Press, O'Reilly Media, Prentice Hall, Que, and Sams.

Safari Books Online is a digital library providing searchable, on-demand access to thousands of technology, digital media, and professional development books and videos from leading publishers. With one monthly or yearly subscription price, you get unlimited access to learning tools and information on topics including mobile app and software development, tips and tricks on using your favorite gadgets, networking, project management, graphic design, and much more.

Activate your FREE Online Edition at
informit.com/safarifree

STEP 1: Enter the coupon code: WXGWNCB.

STEP 2: New Safari users, complete the brief registration form.
Safari subscribers, just log in.

If you have difficulty registering on Safari or accessing the online edition,
please e-mail customer-service@safaribooksonline.com